Shugo Chara!

11

PEACH-PIT

Translated by
Satsuki Yamashita

Lettered by
North Market Street Graphics

KC
KODANSHA
COMICS

Shugo Chara! volume 11 is a work of fiction. Names, characters, places, and incidents are the products of the author's imagination or are used fictitiously. Any resemblance to actual events, locales, or persons, living or dead, is entirely coincidental.

A Kodansha Comics Trade Paperback Original.

Published in the United States by Kodansha Comics, an imprint of Kodansha USA Publishing, LLC, New York.

Publication rights for this English edition arranged through Kodansha Ltd., Tokyo.

First published in Japan in 2010 by Kodansha Ltd., Tokyo.

ISBN 978-1-935-42983-8

Original cover design by Akiko Omo.

Printed in the United States of America.

www.kodanshacomics.com

9 8 7 6 5 4 3 2 1

Translator: Satsuki Yamashita
Lettering: North Market Street Graphics

Contents

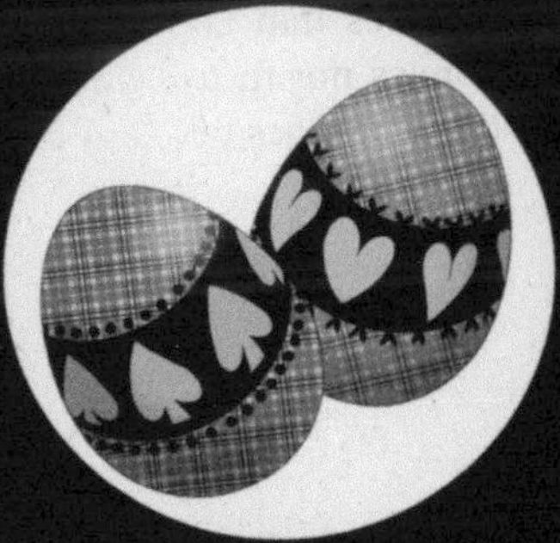
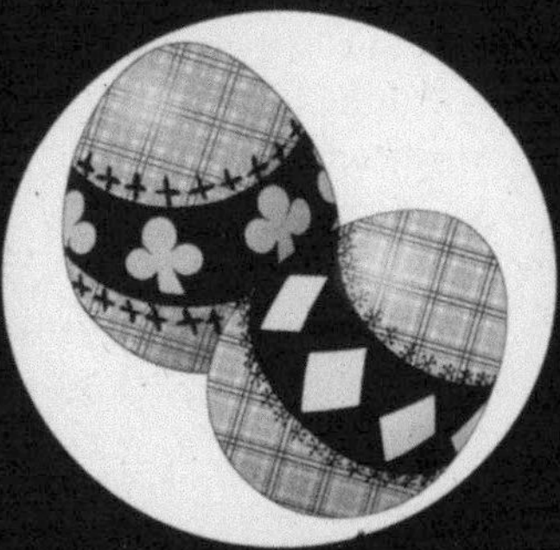

Honorifics Explained

Throughout the Kodansha Comics books, you will find Japanese honorifics left intact in the translations. For those not familiar with how the Japanese use honorifics and, more important, how they differ from American honorifics, we present this brief overview.

Politeness has always been a critical facet of Japanese culture. Ever since the feudal era, when Japan was a highly stratified society, use of honorifics—which can be defined as polite speech that indicates relationship or status—has played an essential role in the Japanese language. When addressing someone in Japanese, an honorific usually takes the form of a suffix attached to one's name (example: "Asuna-san"), is used as a title at the end of one's name, or appears in place of the name itself (example: "Negi-sensei," or simply "Sensei!").

Honorifics can be expressions of respect or endearment. In the context of manga and anime, honorifics give insight into the nature of the relationship between characters. Many English translations leave out these important honorifics and therefore distort the feel of the original Japanese. Because Japanese honorifics contain nuances that English honorifics lack, it is our policy at Kodansha Comics not to translate them. Here, instead, is a guide to some of the honorifics you may encounter in Kodansha Comics books.

-san: This is the most common honorific and is equivalent to Mr., Miss, Ms., or Mrs. It is the all-purpose honorific and can be used in any situation where politeness is required.

-sama: This is one level higher than "-san" and is used to confer great respect.

-dono: This comes from the word "tono," which means "lord." It is an even higher level than "-sama" and confers utmost respect.

-kun: This suffix is used at the end of boys' names to express familiarity or endearment. It is also sometimes used by men among friends, or when addressing someone younger or of a lower station.

-chan:	This is used to express endearment, mostly toward girls. It is also used for little boys, pets, and even among lovers. It gives a sense of childish cuteness.
Bozu:	This is an informal way to refer to a boy, similar to the English terms "kid" and "squirt."
Sempai/ Senpai:	This title suggests that the addressee is one's senior in a group or organization. It is most often used in a school setting, where underclassmen refer to their upperclassmen as "sempai." It can also be used in the workplace, such as when a newer employee addresses an employee who has seniority in the company.
Kohai:	This is the opposite of "sempai" and is used toward underclassmen in school or newcomers in the workplace. It connotes that the addressee is of a lower station.
Sensei:	Literally meaning "one who has come before," this title is used for teachers, doctors, or masters of any profession or art.
-[blank]:	This is usually forgotten in these lists, but it is perhaps the most significant difference between Japanese and English. The lack of honorific means that the speaker has permission to address the person in a very intimate way. Usually, only family, spouses, or very close friends have this kind of permission. Known as *yobisute,* it can be gratifying when someone who has earned the intimacy starts to call one by one's name without an honorific. But when that intimacy hasn't been earned, it can be very insulting.

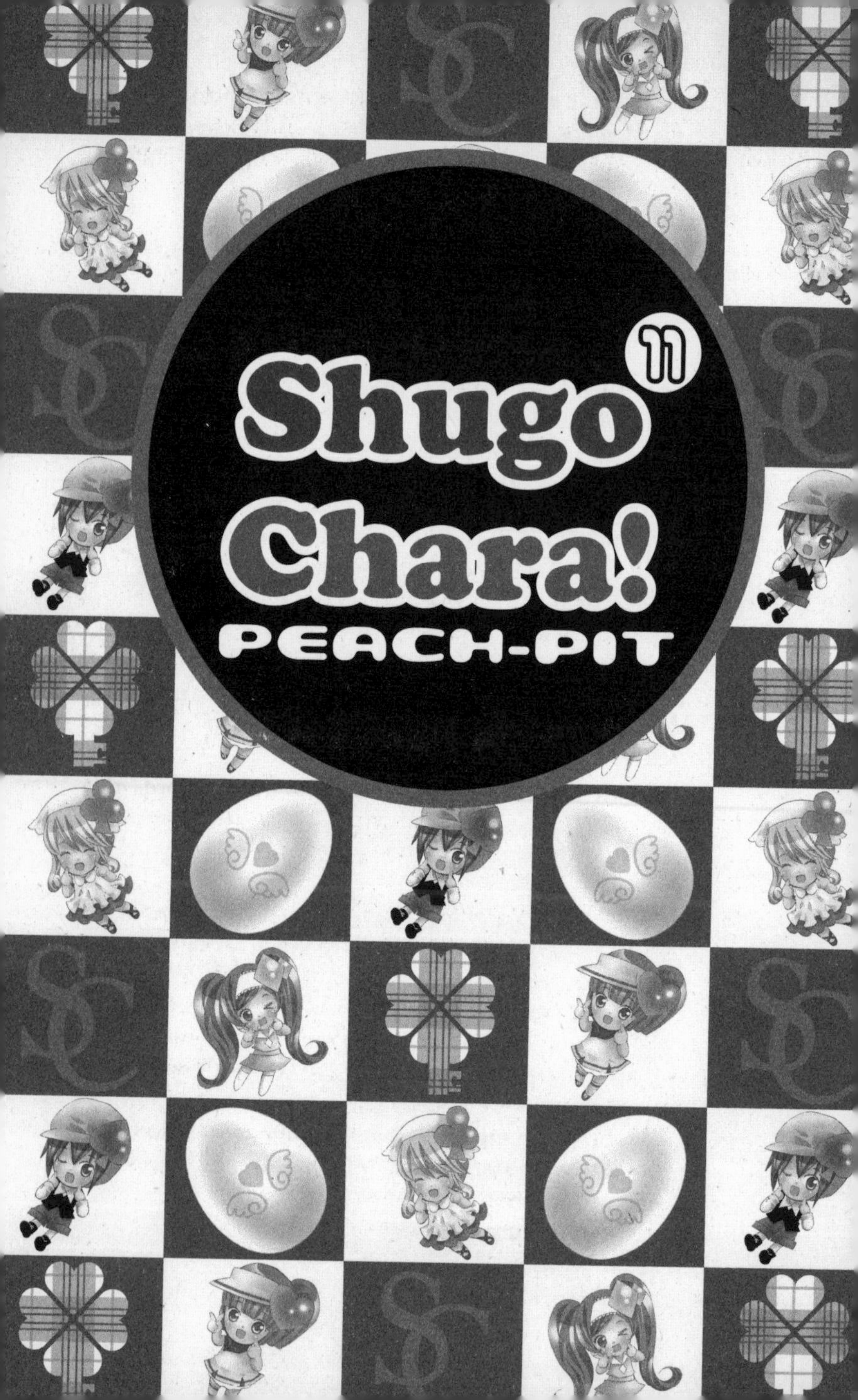
Shugo Chara! 11
PEACH-PIT

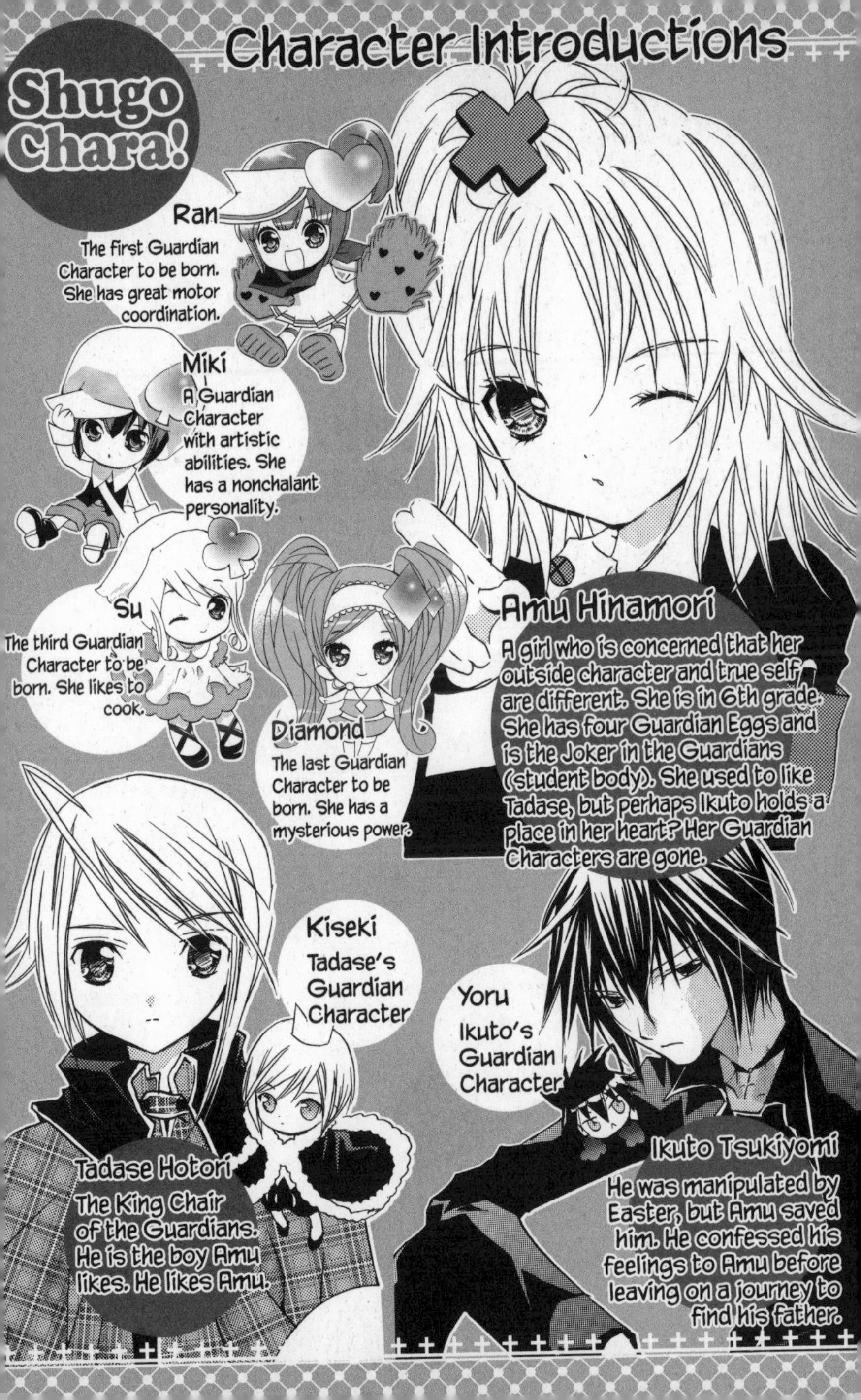
Character Introductions
Shugo Chara!
Ran
The first Guardian Character to be born. She has great motor coordination.
Miki
A Guardian Character with artistic abilities. She has a nonchalant personality.
Su
The third Guardian Character to be born. She likes to cook.
Diamond
The last Guardian Character to be born. She has a mysterious power.
Amu Hinamori
A girl who is concerned that her outside character and true self are different. She is in 6th grade. She has four Guardian Eggs and is the Joker in the Guardians (student body). She used to like Tadase, but perhaps Ikuto holds a place in her heart? Her Guardian Characters are gone.
Kiseki
Tadase's Guardian Character
Yoru
Ikuto's Guardian Character
Tadase Hotori
The King Chair of the Guardians. He is the boy Amu likes. He likes Amu.
Ikuto Tsukiyomi
He was manipulated by Easter, but Amu saved him. He confessed his feelings to Amu before leaving on a journey to find his father.

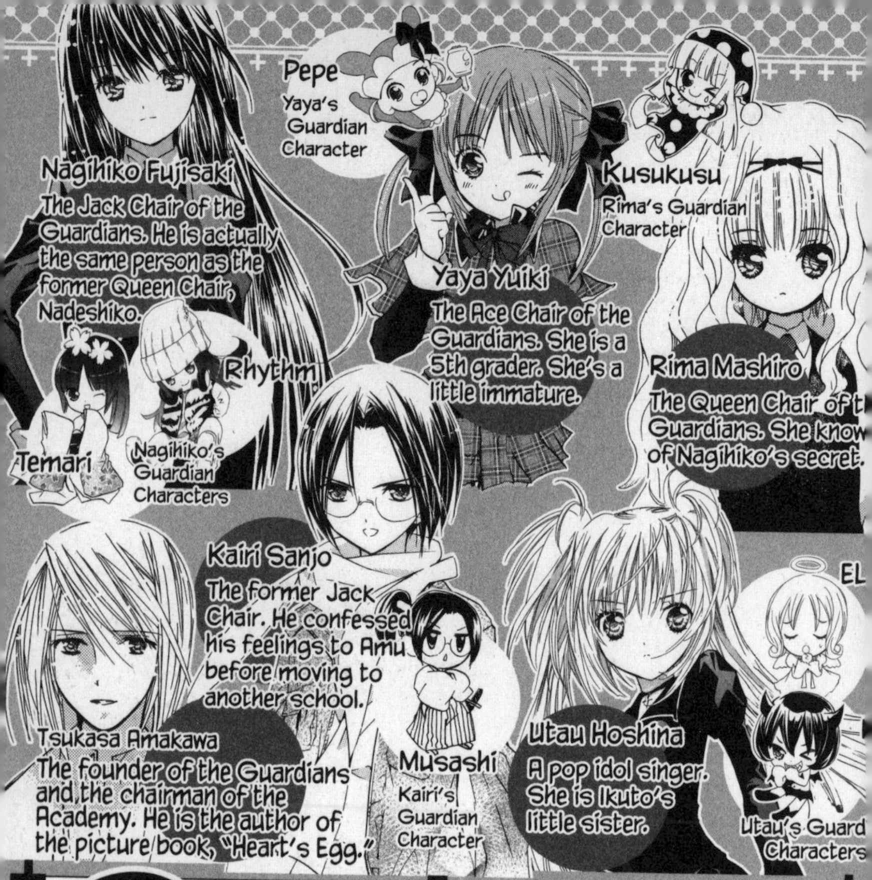
Pepe
Yaya's Guardian Character
Kusukusu
Rima's Guardian Character
Nagihiko Fujisaki
The Jack Chair of the Guardians. He is actually the same person as the former Queen Chair, Nadeshiko.
Yaya Yuiki
The Ace Chair of the Guardians. She is a 5th grader. She's a little immature.
Rima Mashiro
The Queen Chair of t
Guardians. She know
of Nagihiko's secret.
Rhythm
Temari
Nagihiko's Guardian Characters
Kairi Sanjo
The former Jack Chair. He confessed his feelings to Amu before moving to another school.
EL
Tsukasa Amakawa
The founder of the Guardians and the chairman of the Academy. He is the author of the picture book, "Heart's Egg."
Musashi
Kairi's Guardian Character
Utau Hoshina
A pop idol singer. She is Ikuto's little sister.
Utau's Guard
Characters

The Story So Far

- Amu is a cool and awesome girl. However, the truth is, that is a fake personality, and inside she is shy and a little cynical. One day, she wished that she could be more true to herself, and the next day she found three eggs in her bed! Amu was recruited to become the Joker of the Guardians at Seiyo Academy, and ever since, she's become good friends with other Guardian Character holders.
- There was a bad company known as Easter that was stealing countless Heart's Eggs from children. Amu and the rest of the Guardians fought against Easter and returned the Eggs to their rightful owners.
- After the battle, Ikuto decided to go on a journey. Although Ikuto was becoming more significant to Amu, she said goodbye and wished him luck.
- One day, as she was approaching graduation, Ran, Miki, and Su disappeared. She decided to go find them with Diamond, who claims to be the navigator to the future.

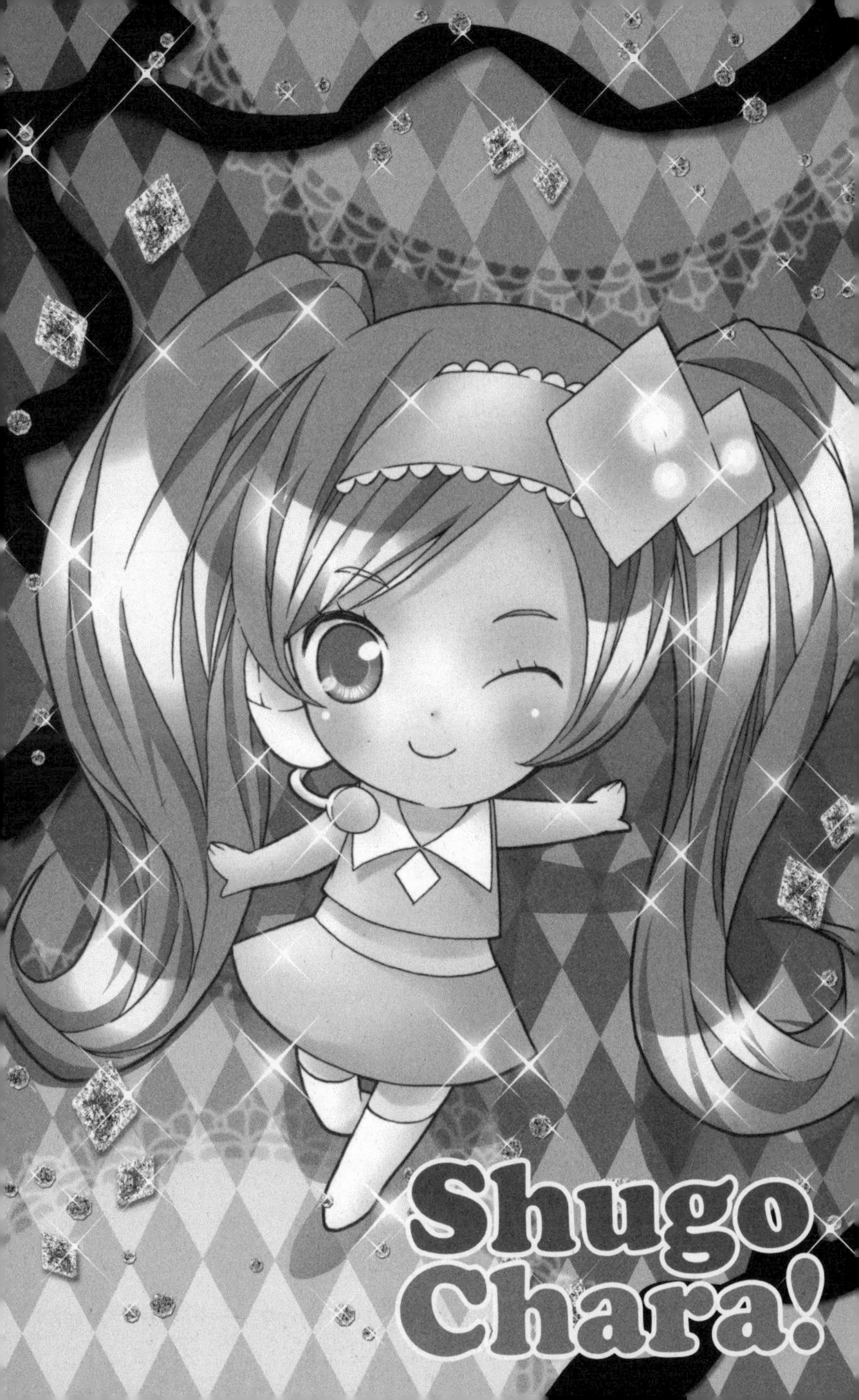
Shugo
Chara!

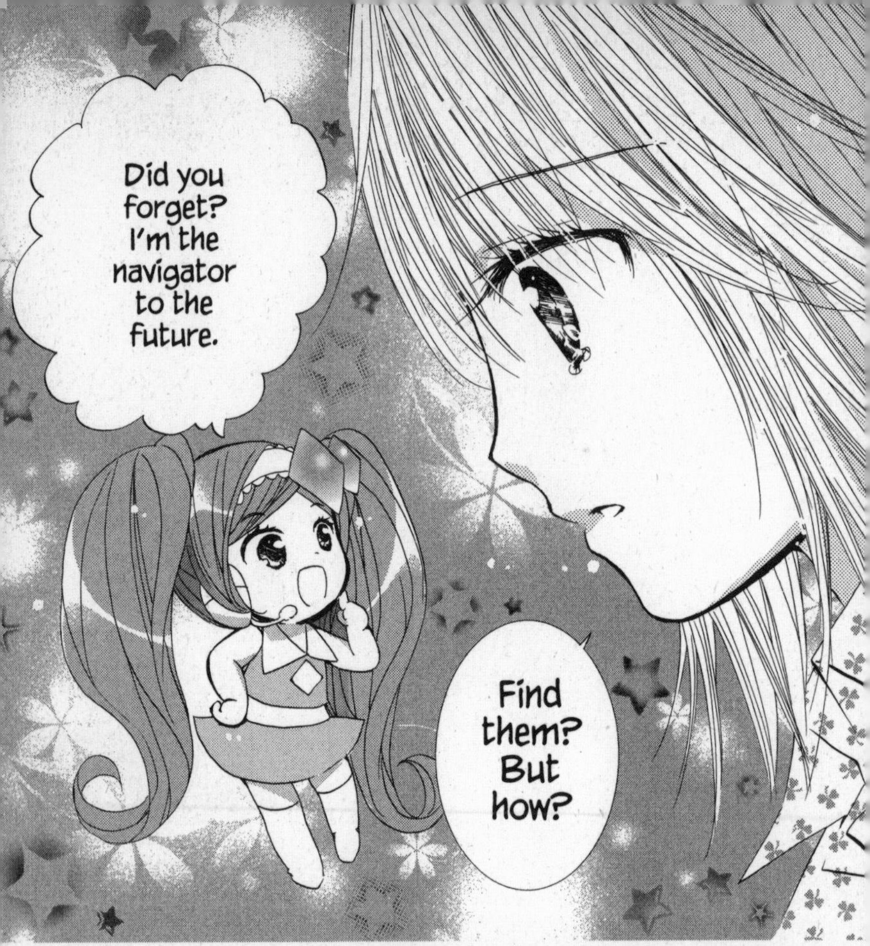
Find them? But how?
Did you forget? I'm the navigator to the future.

Hello-peach!

wow

(This is a new way to say hello). This is PEACH-PIT! "Shugo Chara!" finally reached volume 11 ♥

Amu-chan ran out of fingers for the cover, so we had her Guardian Characters help out ♥

Oh! By the way, this is Shibuko Ebara. (That was slow of me...)

Anyway, on to the Q&A ♥ The first question...

Q1. Did you decide on a name for this peach?

Hee hee...actually... to be continued.

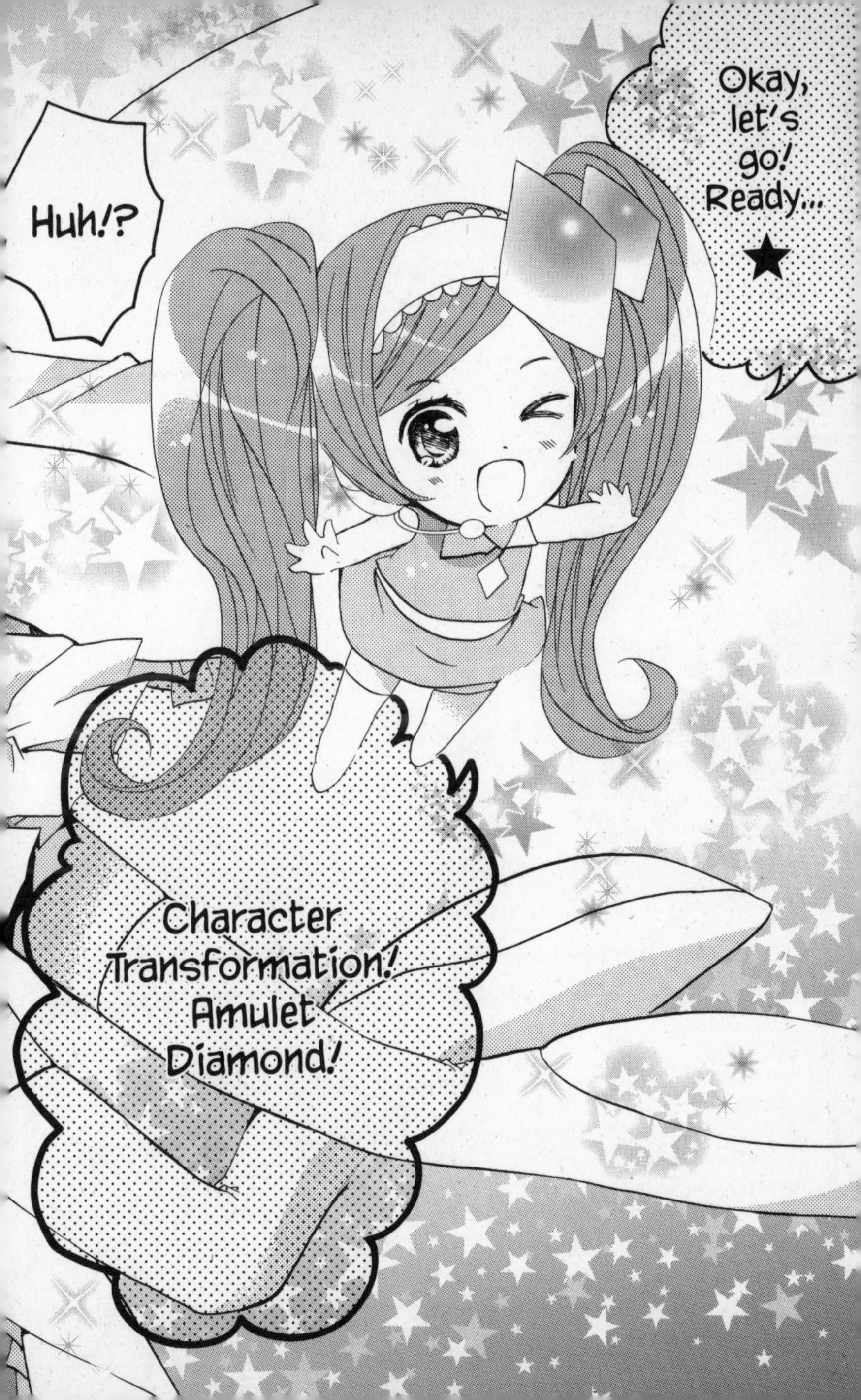
Okay, let's go! Ready... ★
Huh!?
Character Transformation! Amulet Diamond!

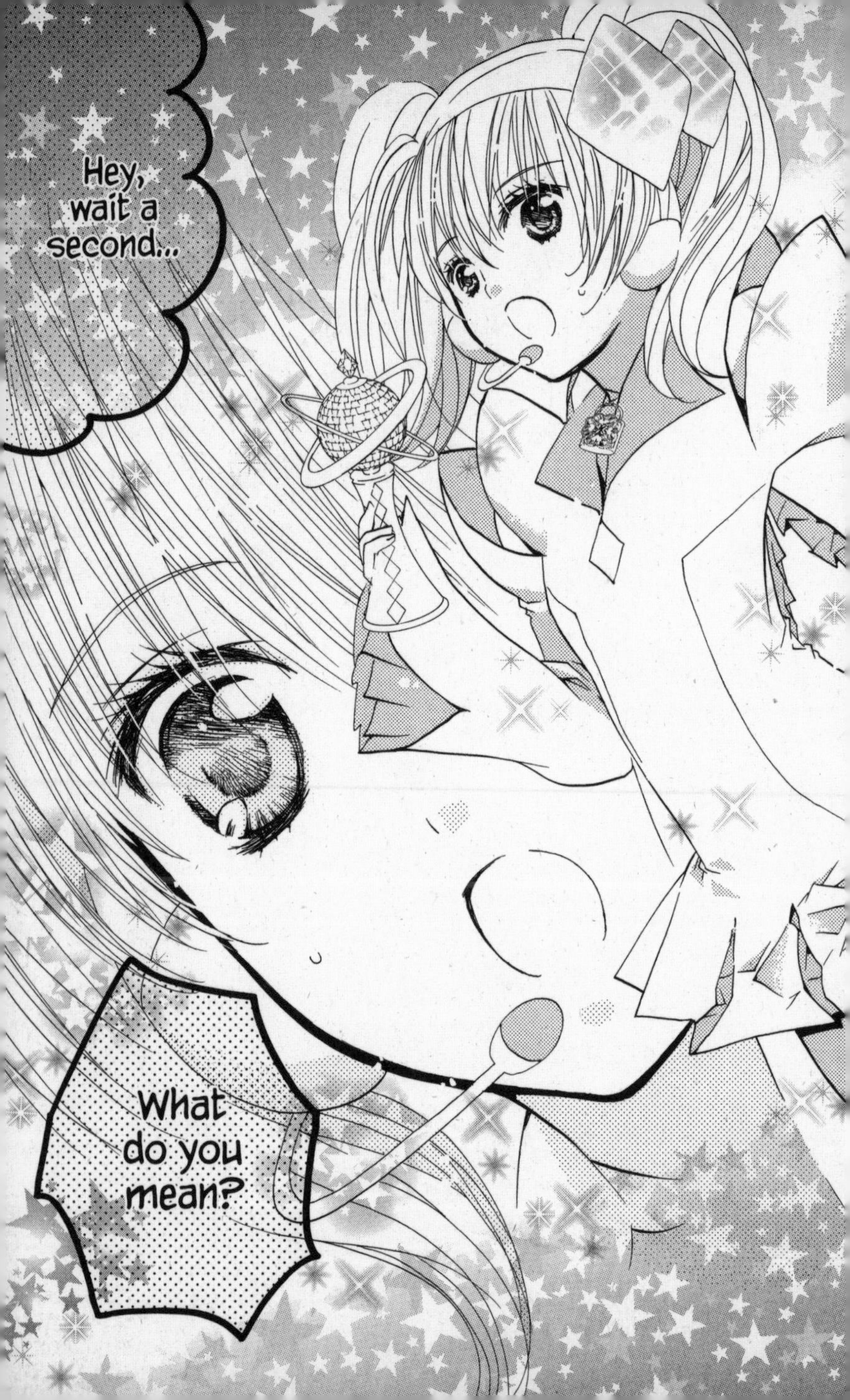
Hey, wait a second...
What do you mean?

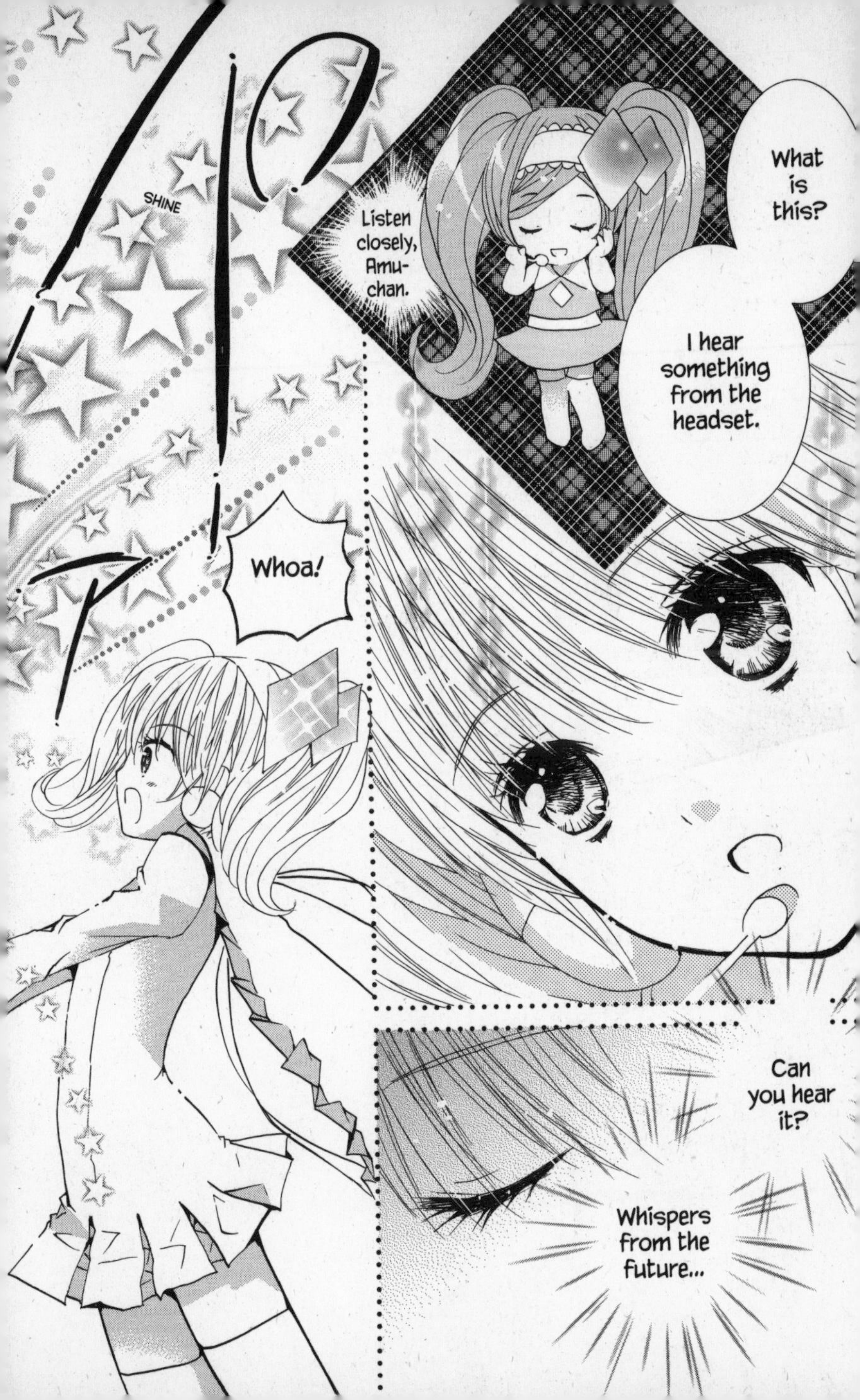
What is this?
I hear something from the headset.
Listen closely, Amu-chan.
Can you hear it?
Whispers from the future...
SHINE
Whoa!

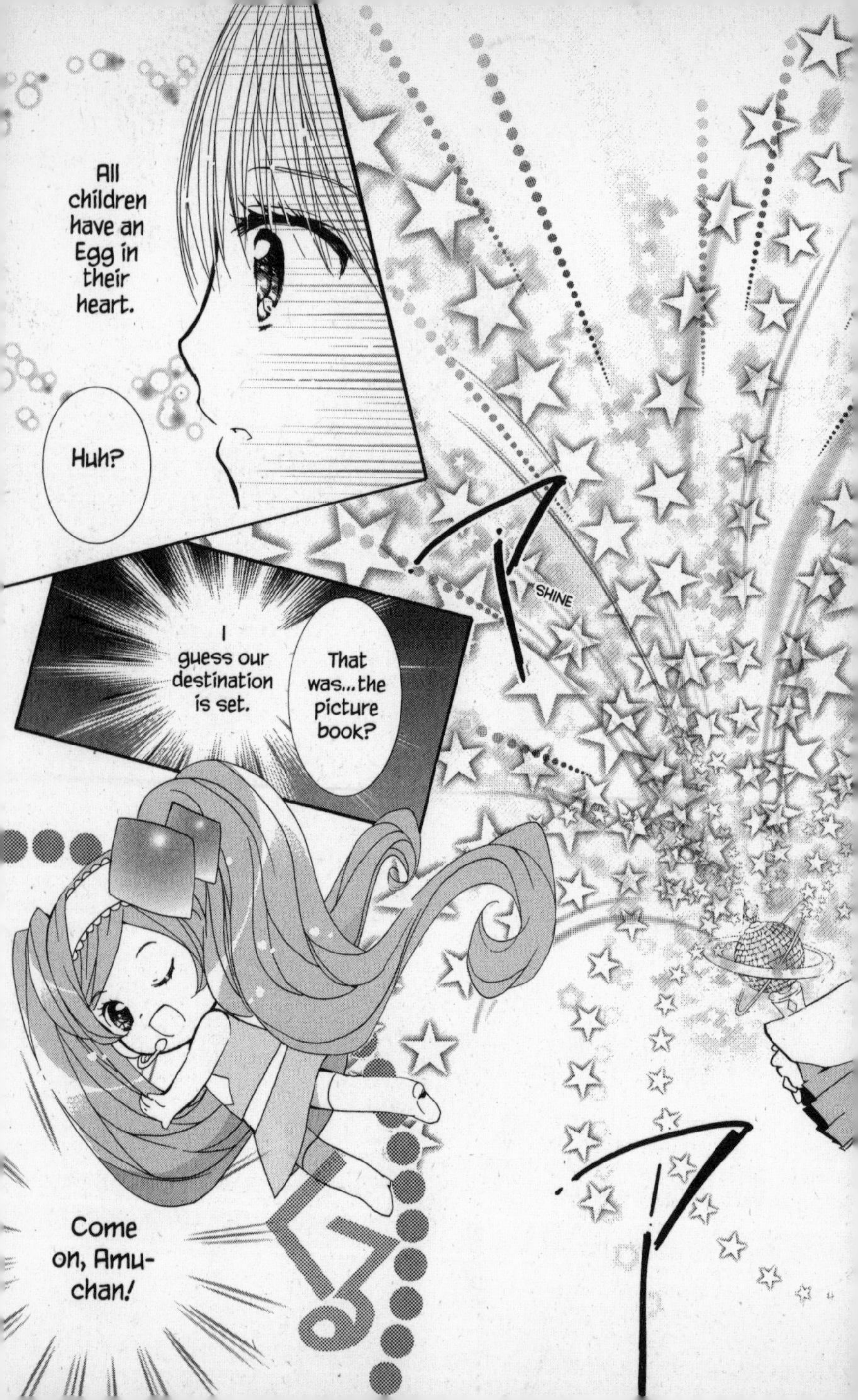
All children have an Egg in their heart.
Huh?
SHINE
That was...the picture book?
I guess our destination is set.
Come on, Amu-chan!

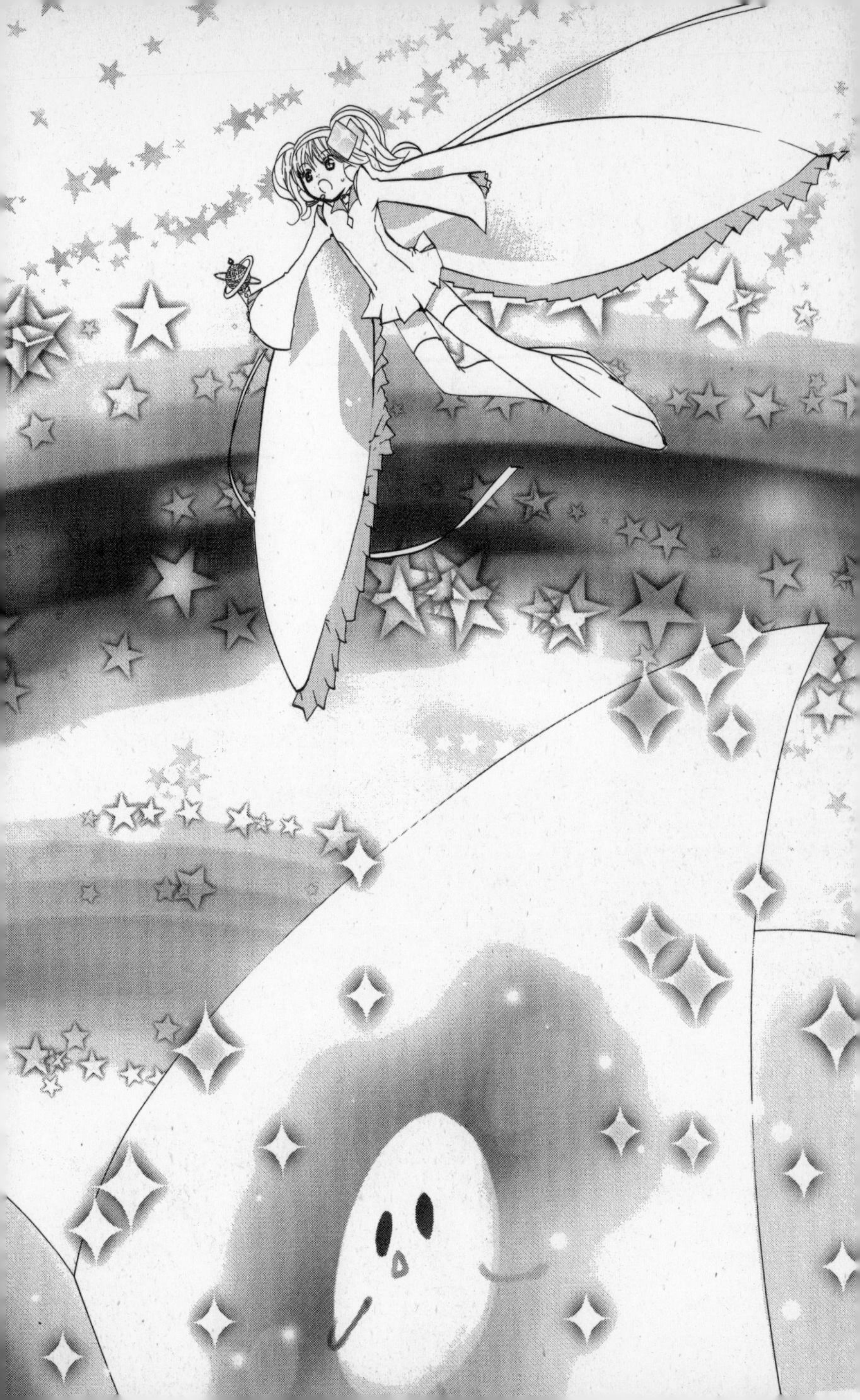

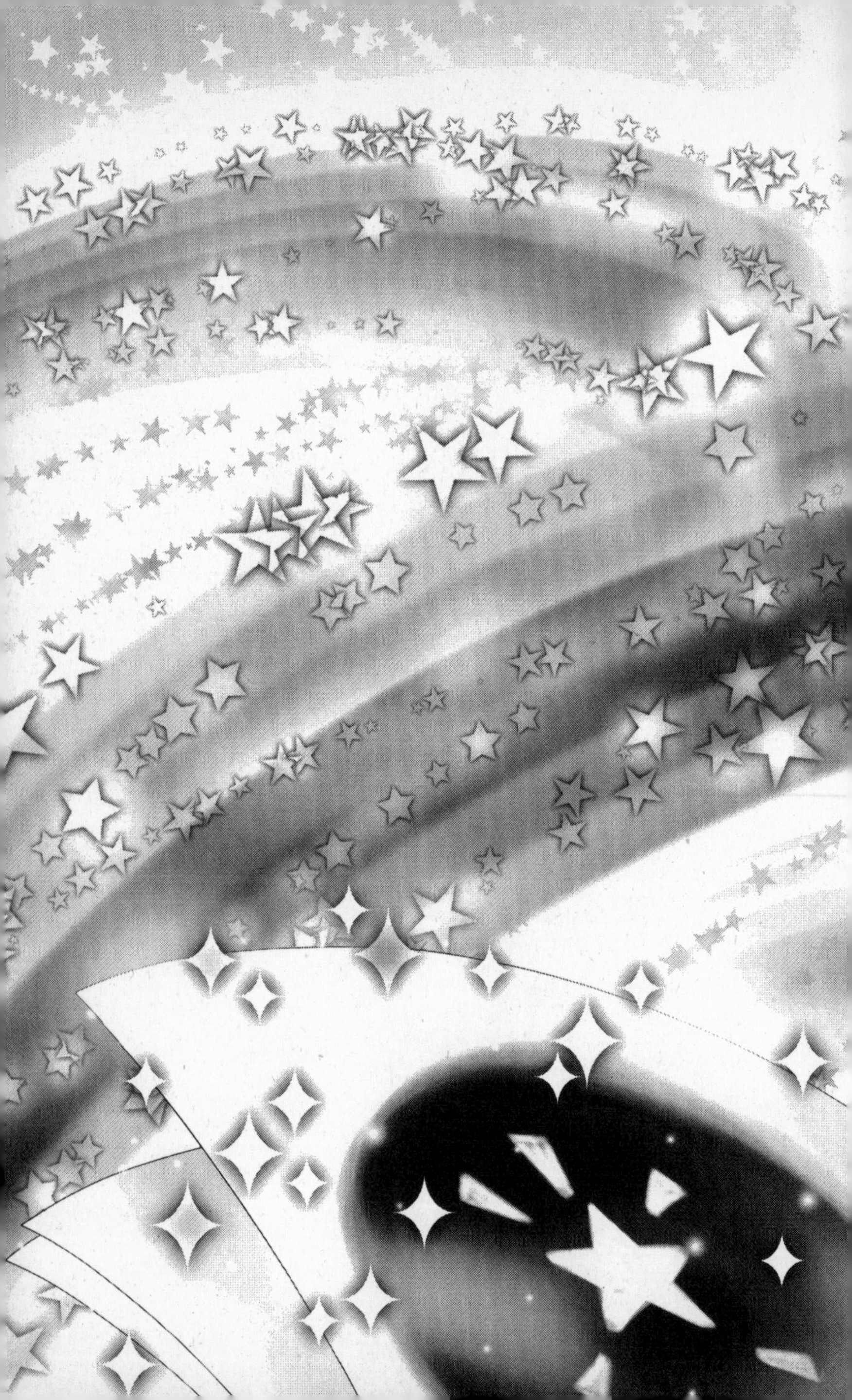

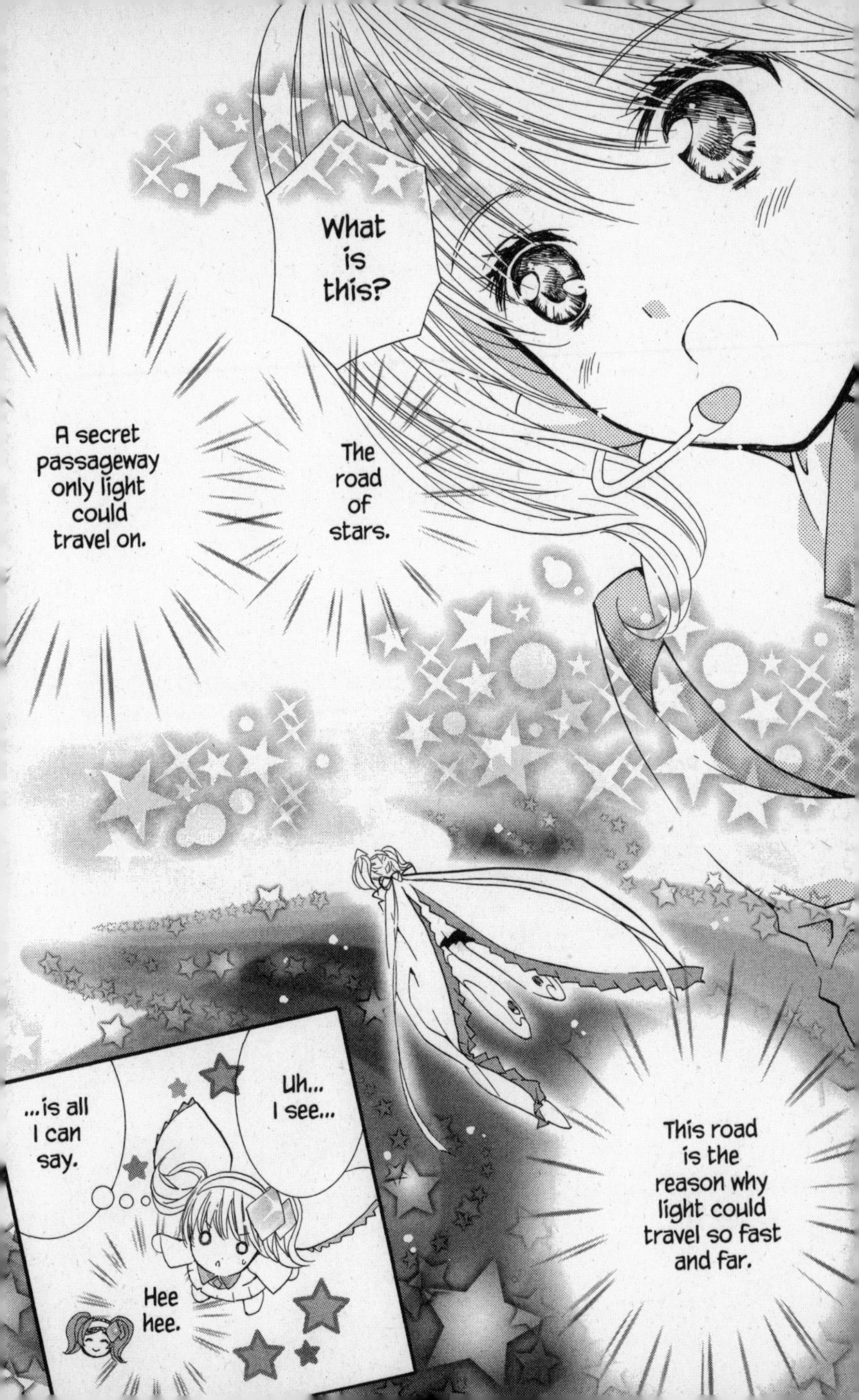
What is this?
The road of stars.
A secret passageway only light could travel on.
This road is the reason why light could travel so fast and far.
Uh... I see...
...is all I can say.
Hee hee.

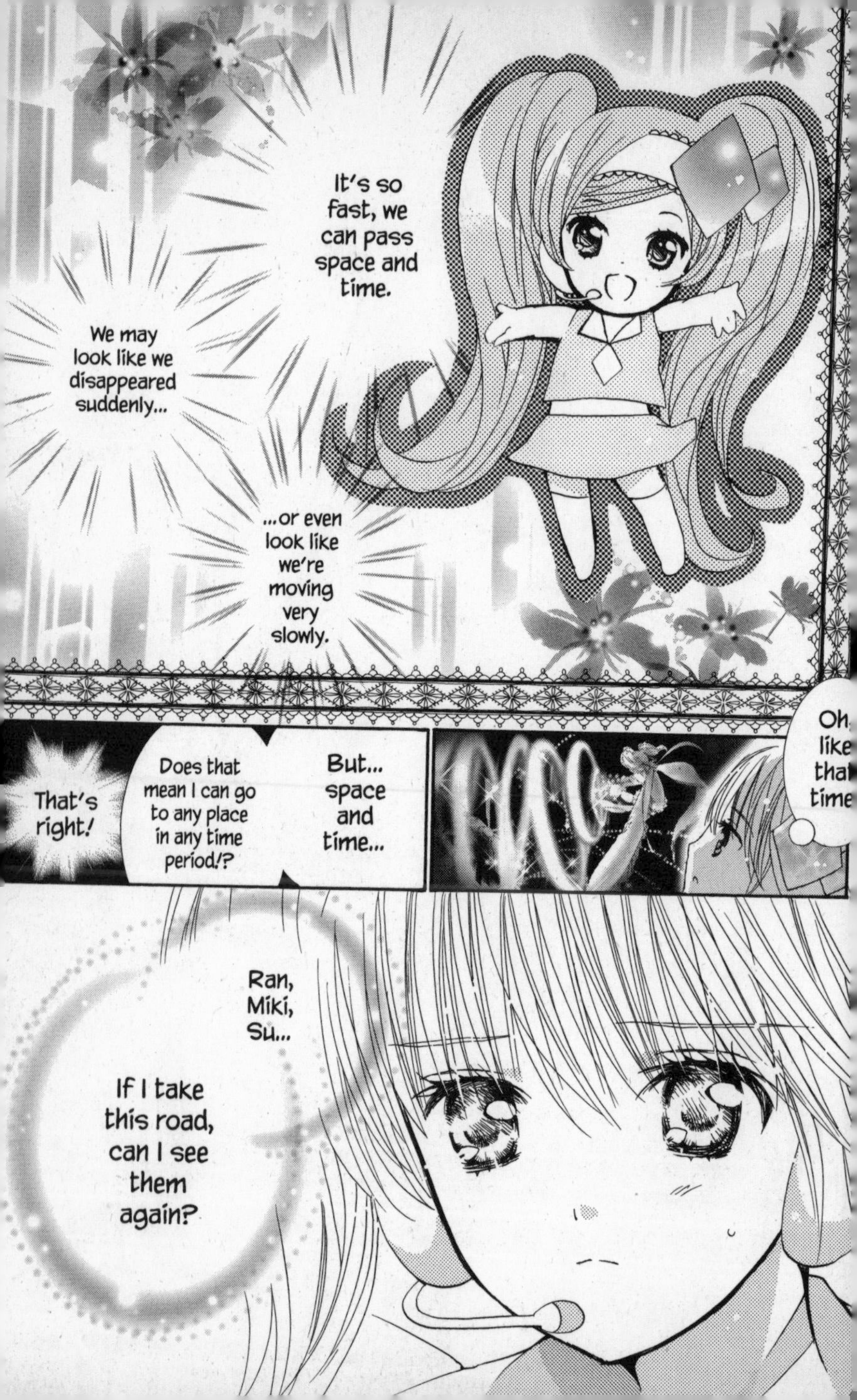
It's so fast, we can pass space and time.
We may look like we disappeared suddenly...
...or even look like we're moving very slowly.
Oh, like tha time
But... space and time...
Does that mean I can go to any place in any time period!?
That's right!
Ran, Miki, Su...
If I take this road, can I see them again?

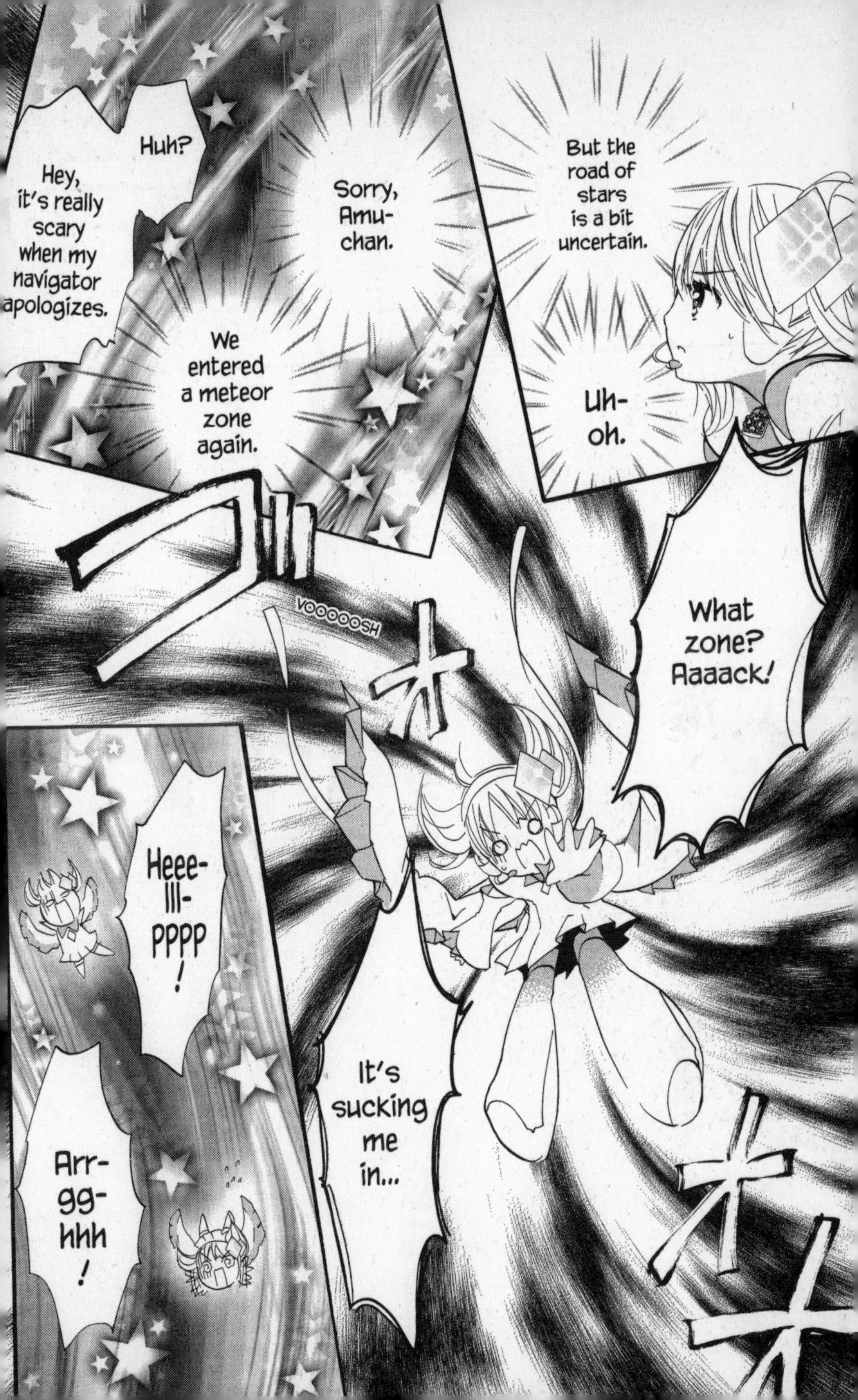
But the road of stars is a bit uncertain.
Uh-oh.
Sorry, Amu-chan.
We entered a meteor zone again.
Huh?
Hey, it's really scary when my navigator apologizes.
What zone? Aaaack!
VOOOOOSH
It's sucking me in...
Heee-lll-pppp!
Arr-gg-hhh!

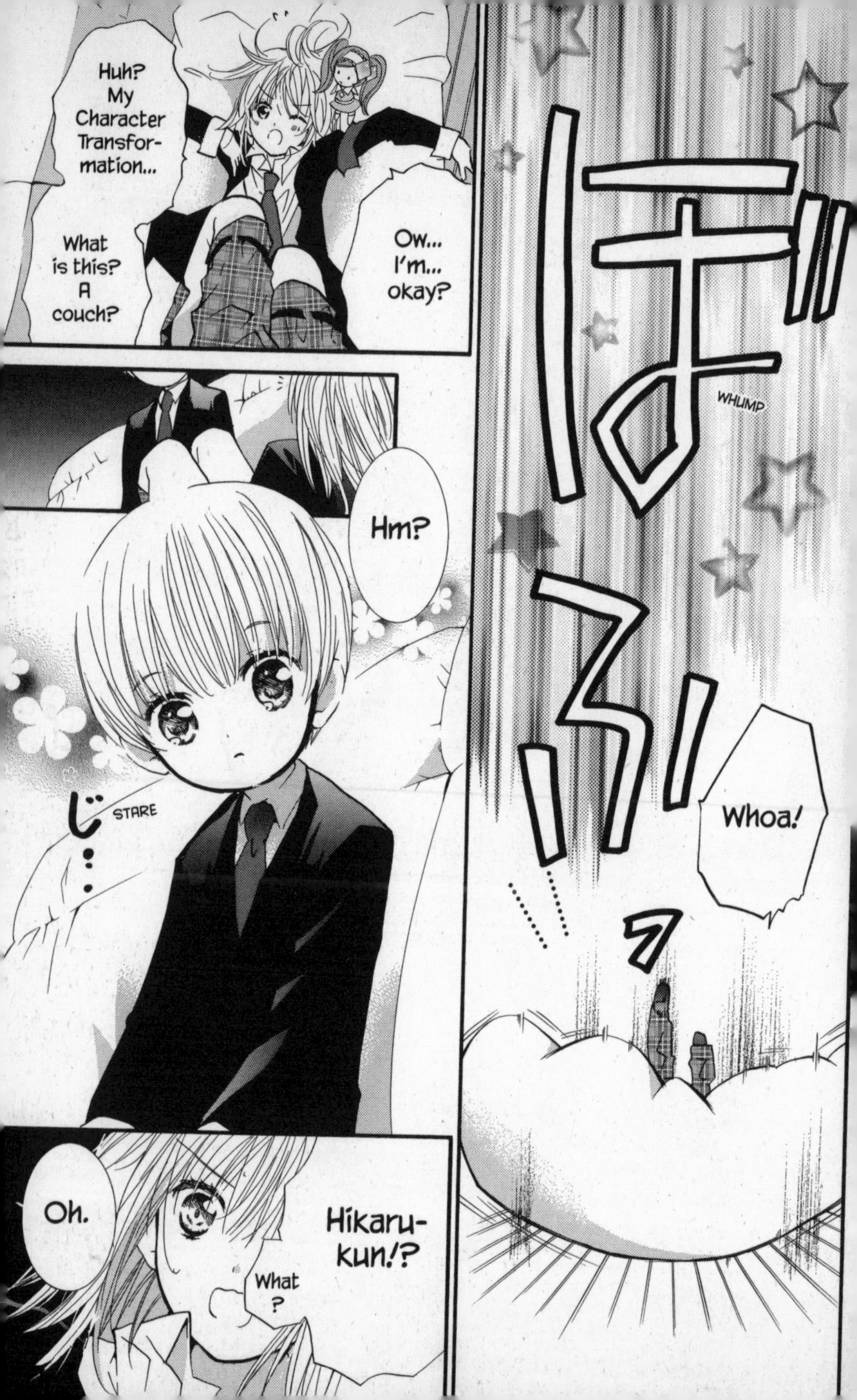
ぼふっ
WHUMP
Whoa!
Ow... I'm... okay?
Huh? My Character Transformation...
What is this? A couch?
Hm?
じ…
STARE
Hikaru-kun!?
What?
Oh.

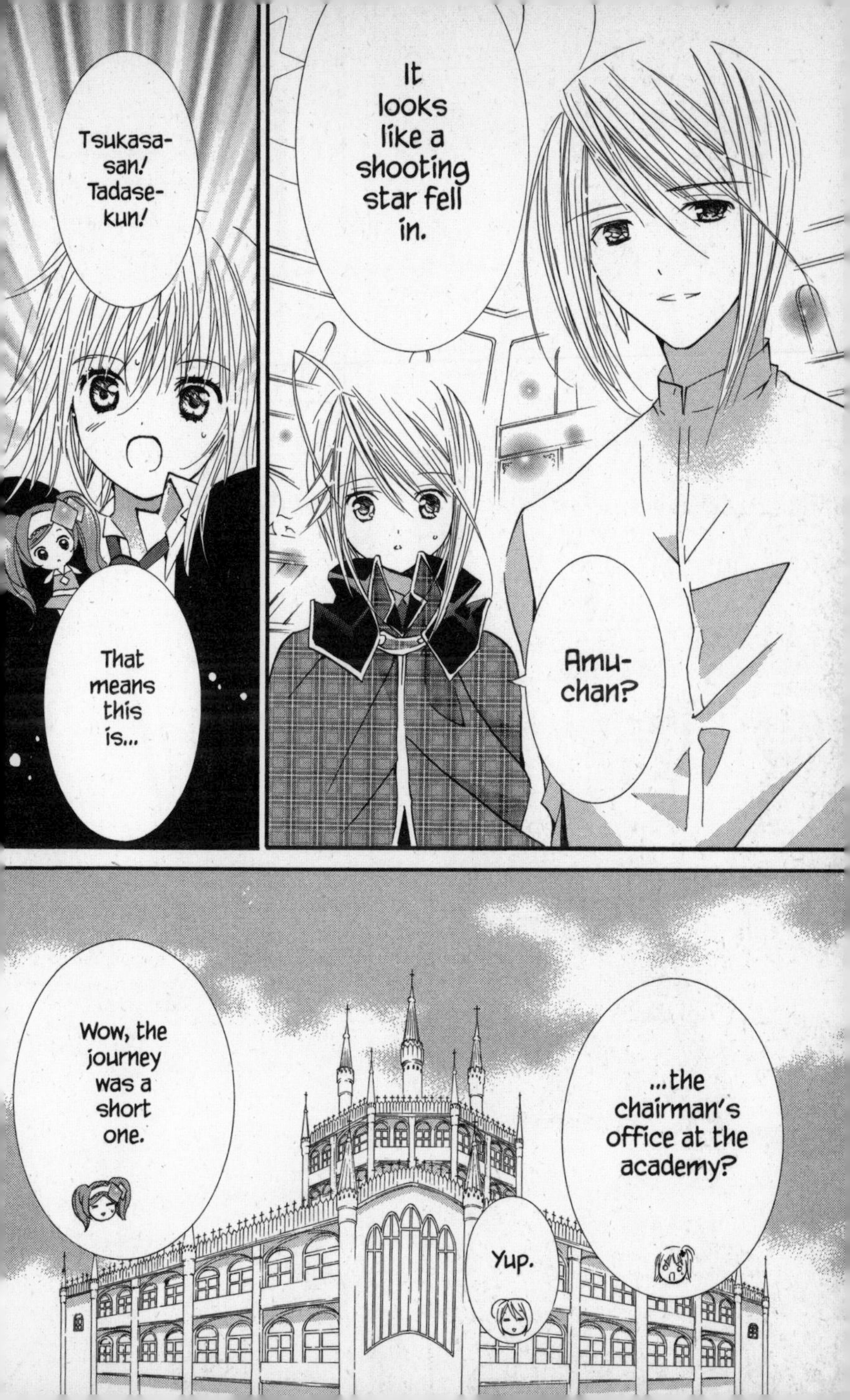

It looks like a shooting star fell in.
Amu-chan?
Tsukasa-san! Tadase-kun!
That means this is...
...the chairman's office at the academy?
Yup.
Wow, the journey was a short one.

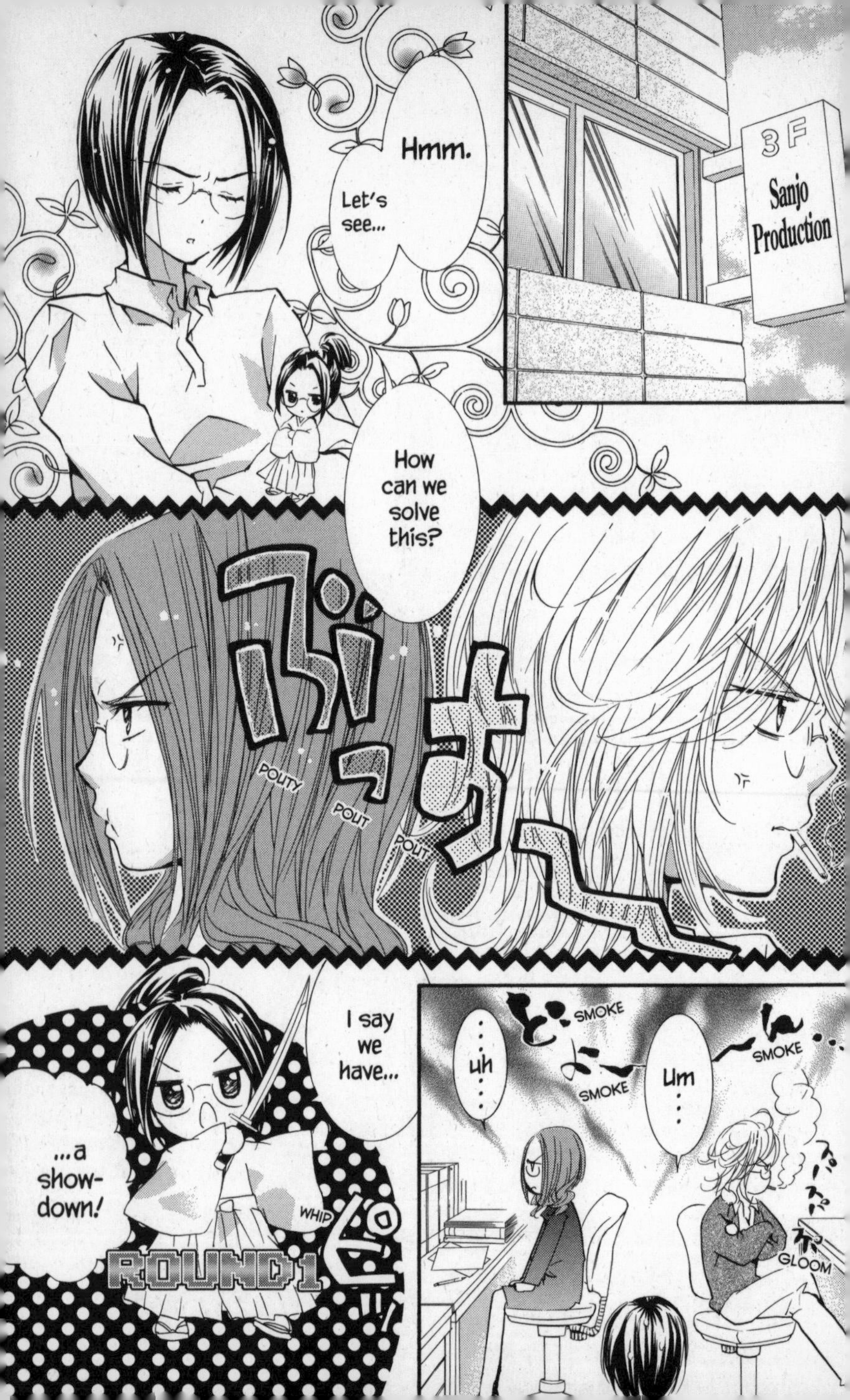
3F
Sanjo Production
Hmm.
Let's see...
How can we solve this?
POUTY
POUT
POUT
...uh...
Um...
SMOKE
SMOKE
SMOKE
GLOOM
I say we have...
...a showdown!
WHIP
ROUND1

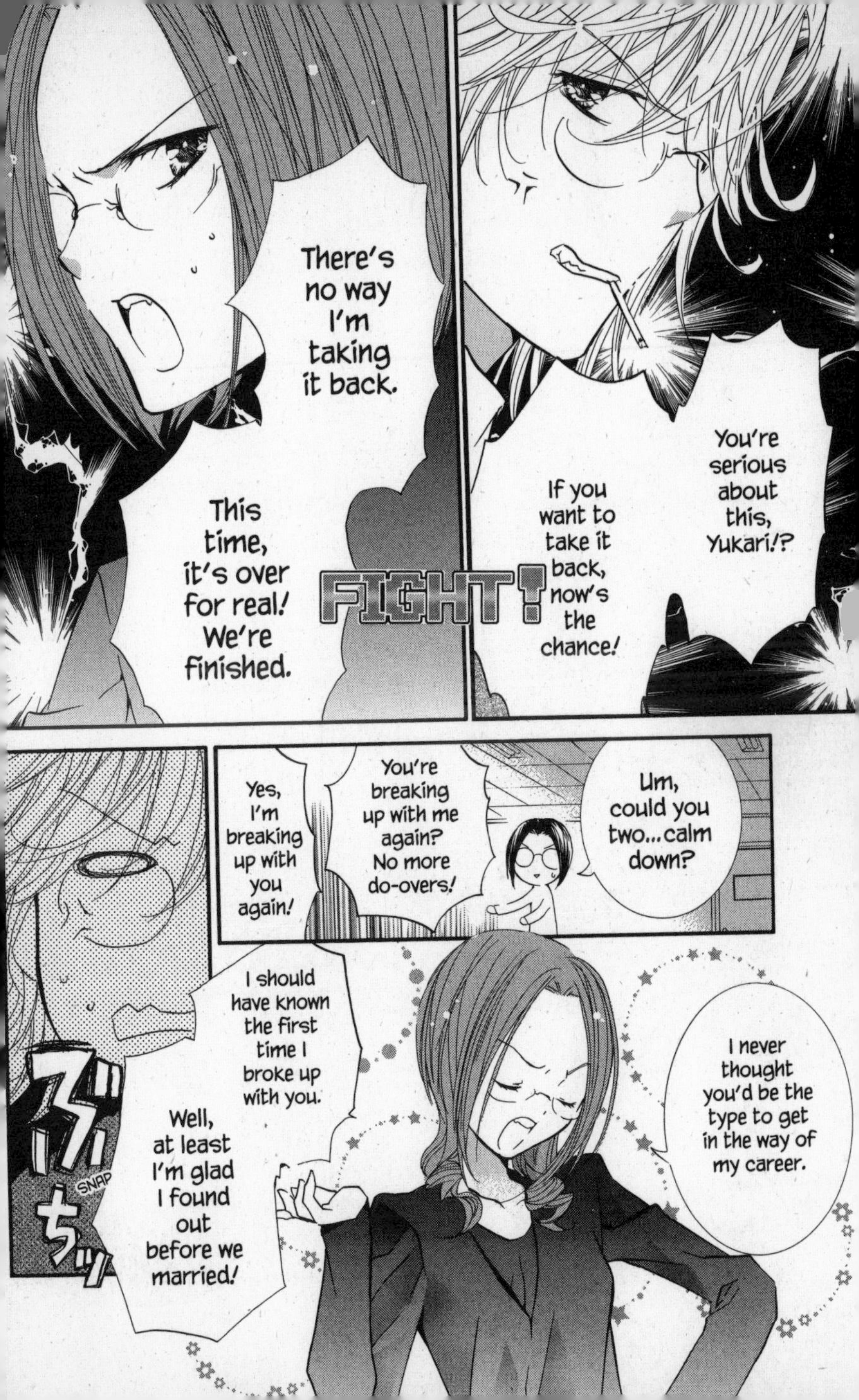
You're serious about this, Yukari!?
If you want to take it back, now's the chance!
FIGHT!
There's no way I'm taking it back.
This time, it's over for real! We're finished.
Um, could you two...calm down?
You're breaking up with me again? No more do-overs!
Yes, I'm breaking up with you again!
I never thought you'd be the type to get in the way of my career.
I should have known the first time I broke up with you.
Well, at least I'm glad I found out before we married!
SNAP

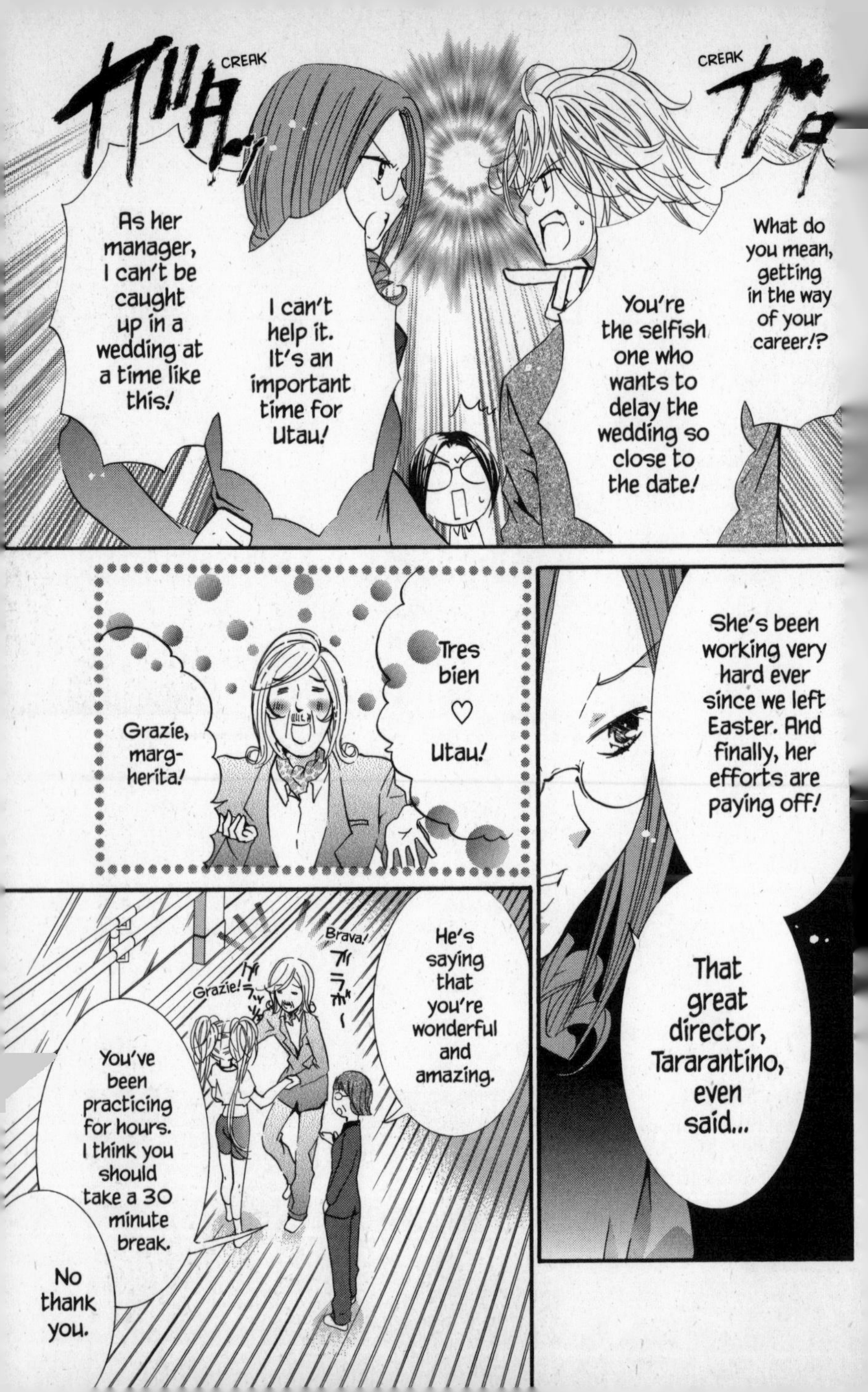
CREAK
What do you mean, getting in the way of your career!?
You're the selfish one who wants to delay the wedding so close to the date!
CREAK
I can't help it. It's an important time for Utau!
As her manager, I can't be caught up in a wedding at a time like this!
She's been working very hard ever since we left Easter. And finally, her efforts are paying off!
That great director, Tararantino, even said...
Tres bien ♡ Utau!
Grazie, margherita!
He's saying that you're wonderful and amazing.
Brava!
Grazie!
You've been practicing for hours. I think you should take a 30 minute break.
No thank you.

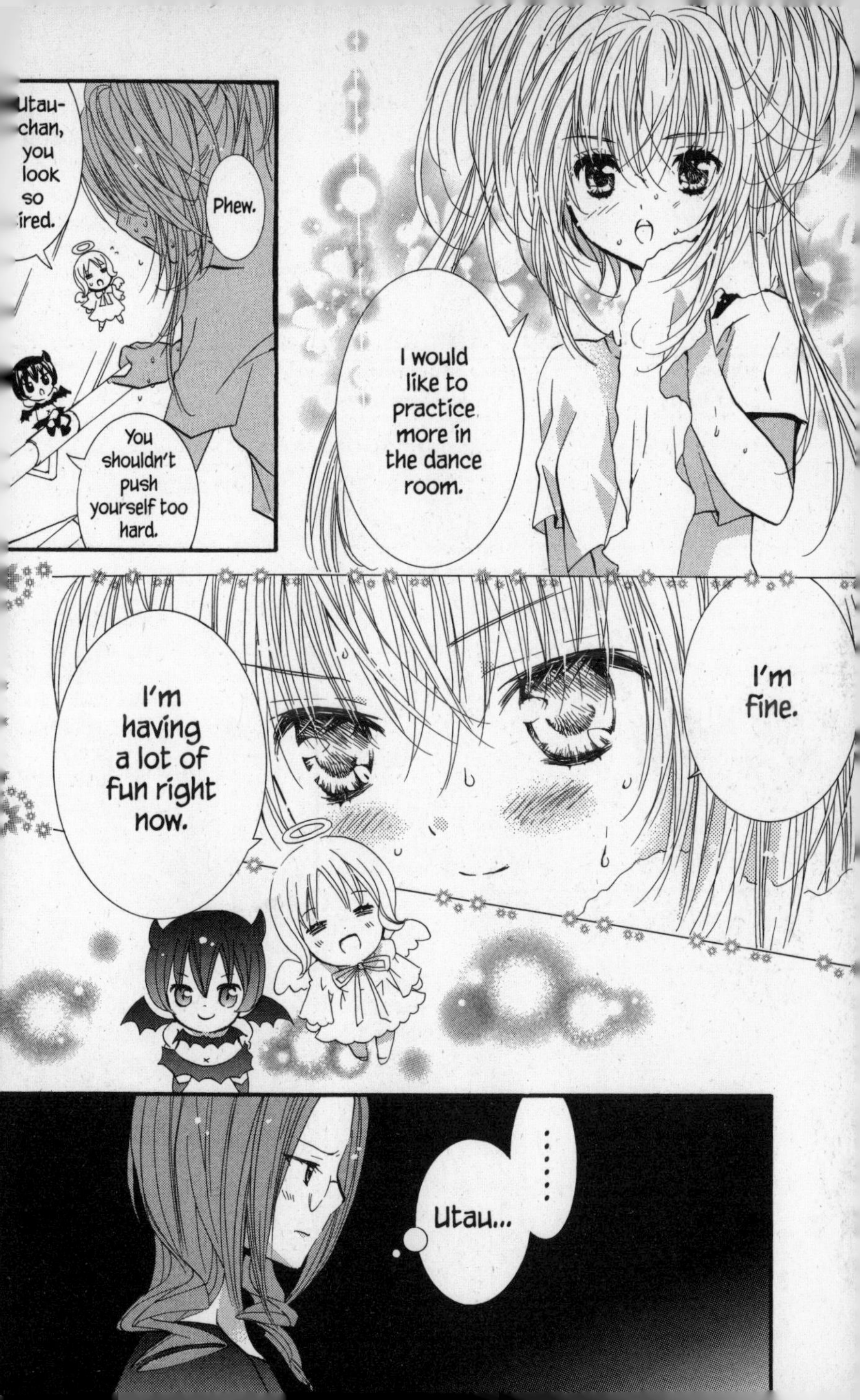

I would like to practice more in the dance room.
Phew.
Utau-chan, you look so ired.
You shouldn't push yourself too hard.
I'm fine.
I'm having a lot of fun right now.
......
Utau...

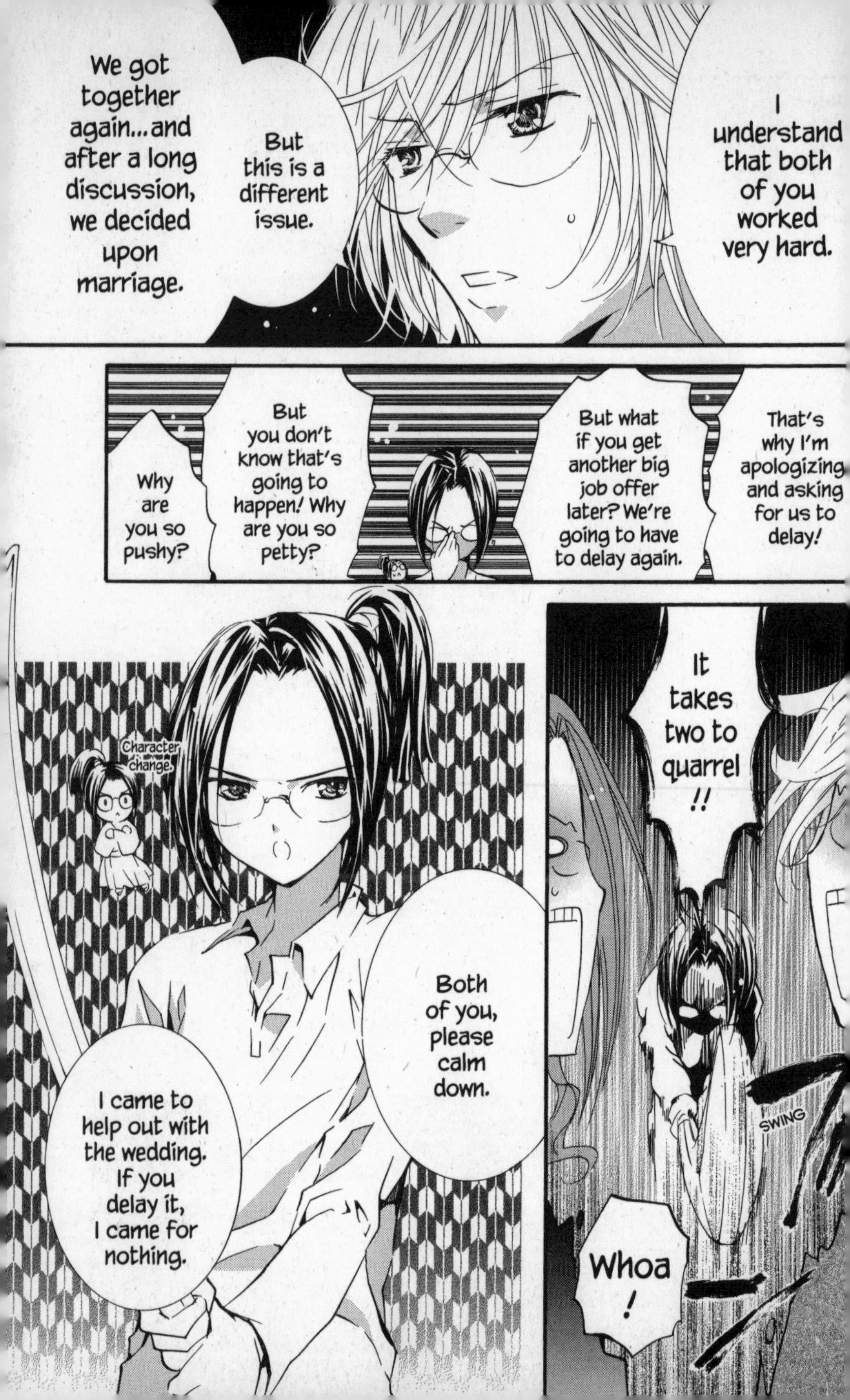

I understand that both of you worked very hard.
But this is a different issue.
We got together again...and after a long discussion, we decided upon marriage.
That's why I'm apologizing and asking for us to delay!
But what if you get another big job offer later? We're going to have to delay again.
But you don't know that's going to happen! Why are you so petty?
Why are you so pushy?
It takes two to quarrel!!
SWING
Whoa!
Character change.
Both of you, please calm down.
I came to help out with the wedding. If you delay it, I came for nothing.

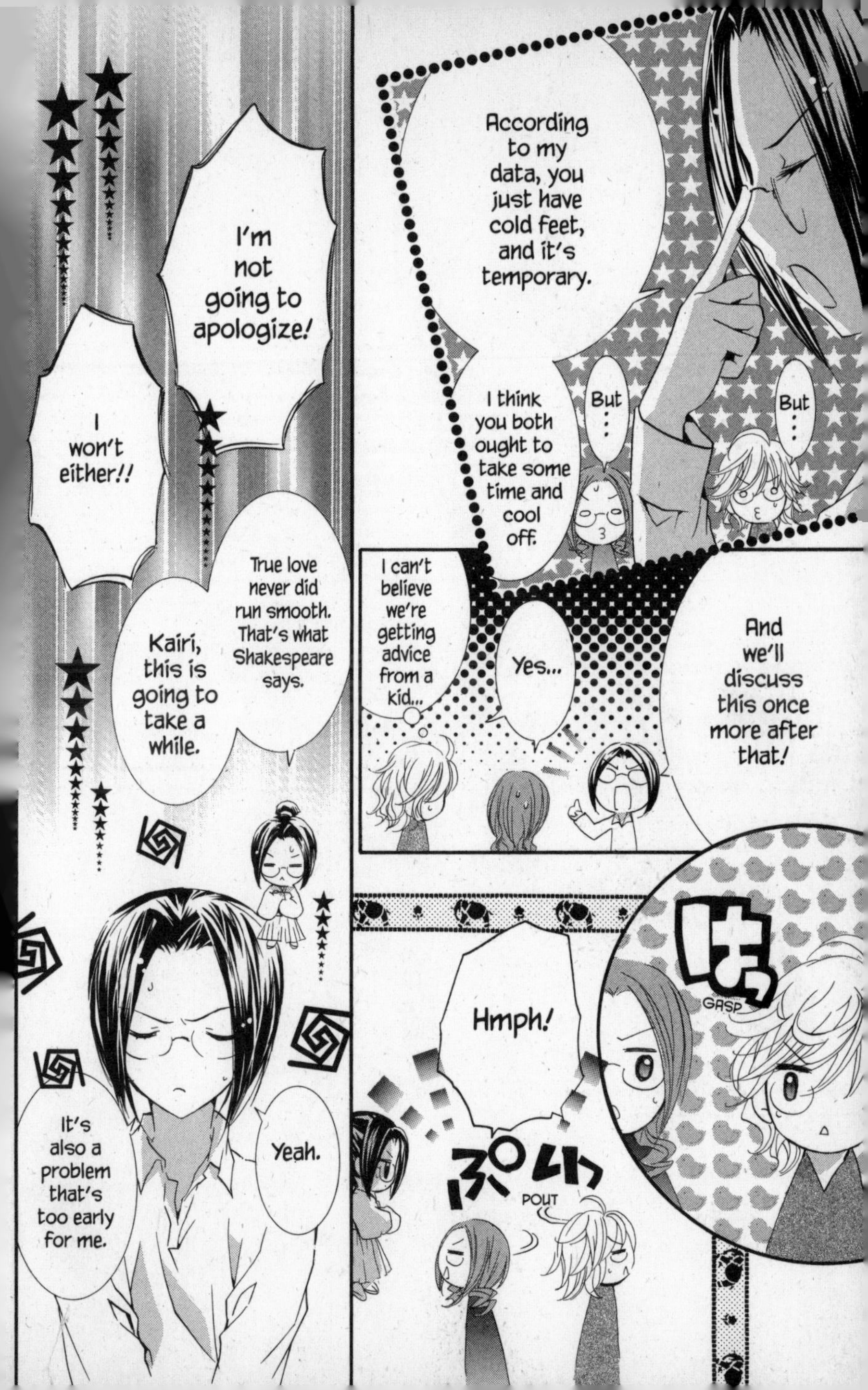
According to my data, you just have cold feet, and it's temporary.
I think you both ought to take some time and cool off.
But...
But...
And we'll discuss this once more after that!
Yes...
I can't believe we're getting advice from a kid...
はっ
GASP
Hmph!
ぷいっ
POUT
I'm not going to apologize!
I won't either!!
True love never did run smooth. That's what Shakespeare says.
Kairi, this is going to take a while.
Yeah.
It's also a problem that's too early for me.

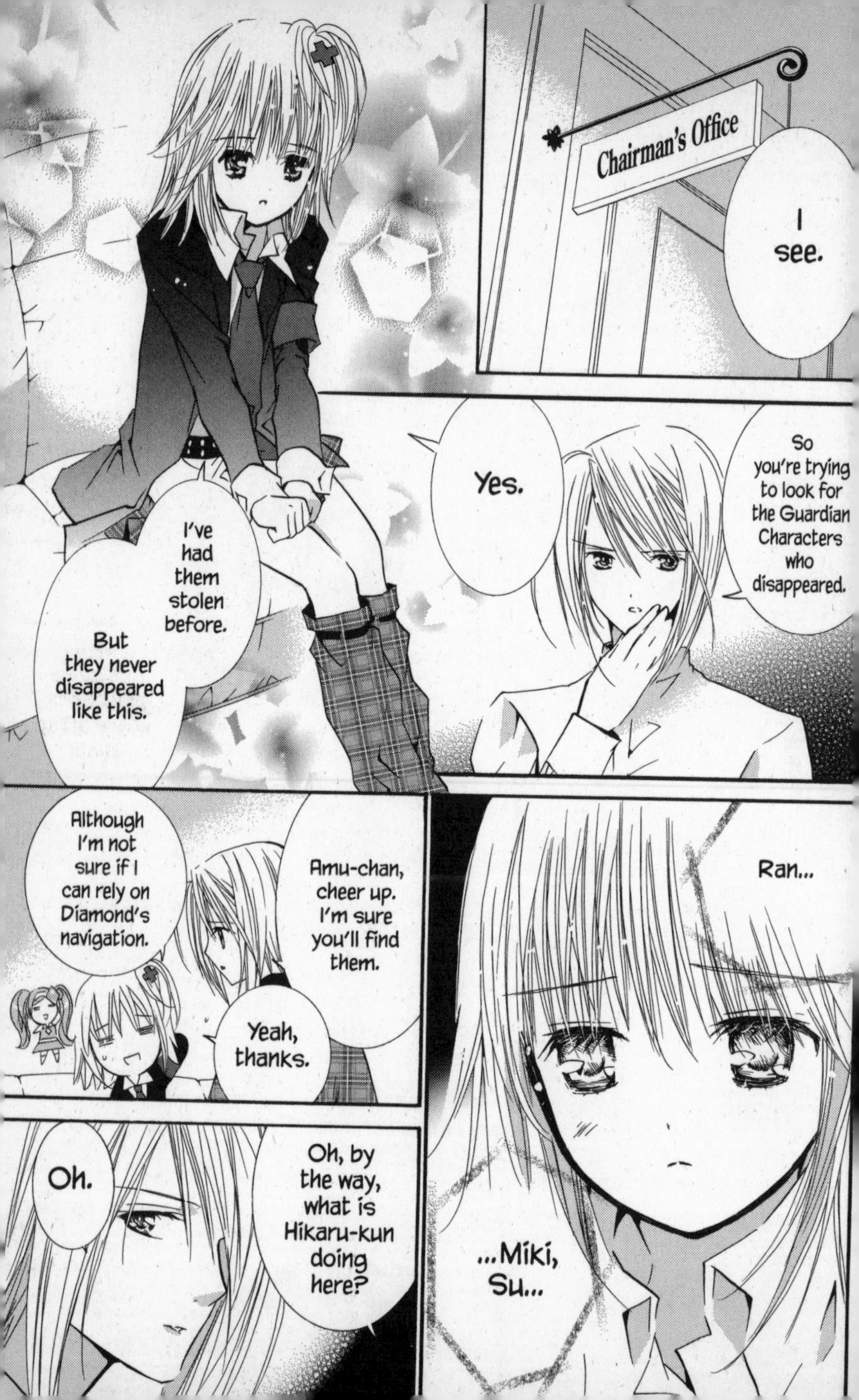
Chairman's Office
I see.
So you're trying to look for the Guardian Characters who disappeared.
Yes.
I've had them stolen before.
But they never disappeared like this.
Ran...
...Miki, Su...
Amu-chan, cheer up. I'm sure you'll find them.
Although I'm not sure if I can rely on Diamond's navigation.
Yeah, thanks.
Oh, by the way, what is Hikaru-kun doing here?
Oh.

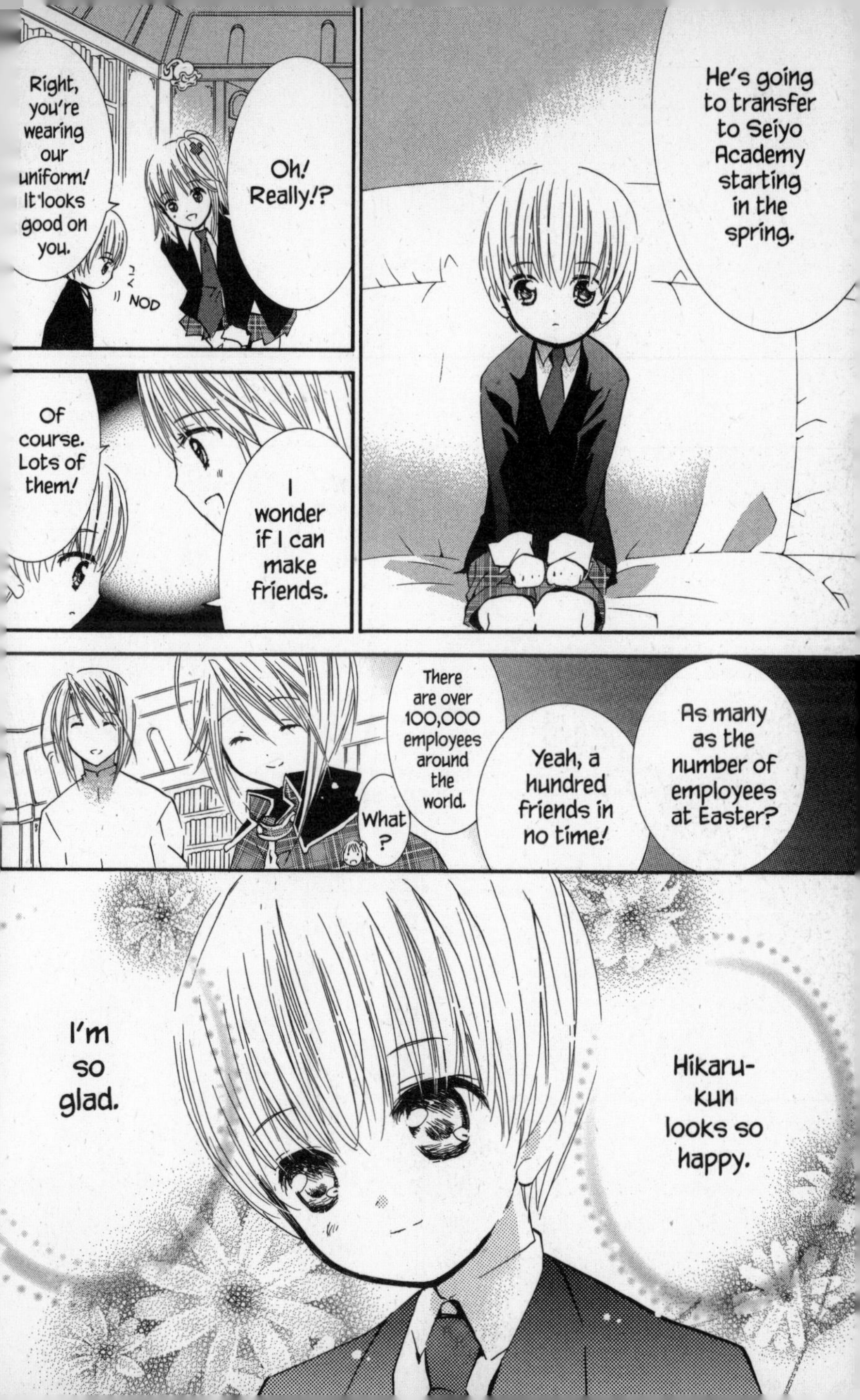
He's going to transfer to Seiyo Academy starting in the spring.
Oh! Really!?
Right, you're wearing our uniform! It looks good on you.
NOD
I wonder if I can make friends.
Of course. Lots of them!
As many as the number of employees at Easter?
Yeah, a hundred friends in no time!
There are over 100,000 employees around the world.
What?
Hikaru-kun looks so happy.
I'm so glad.

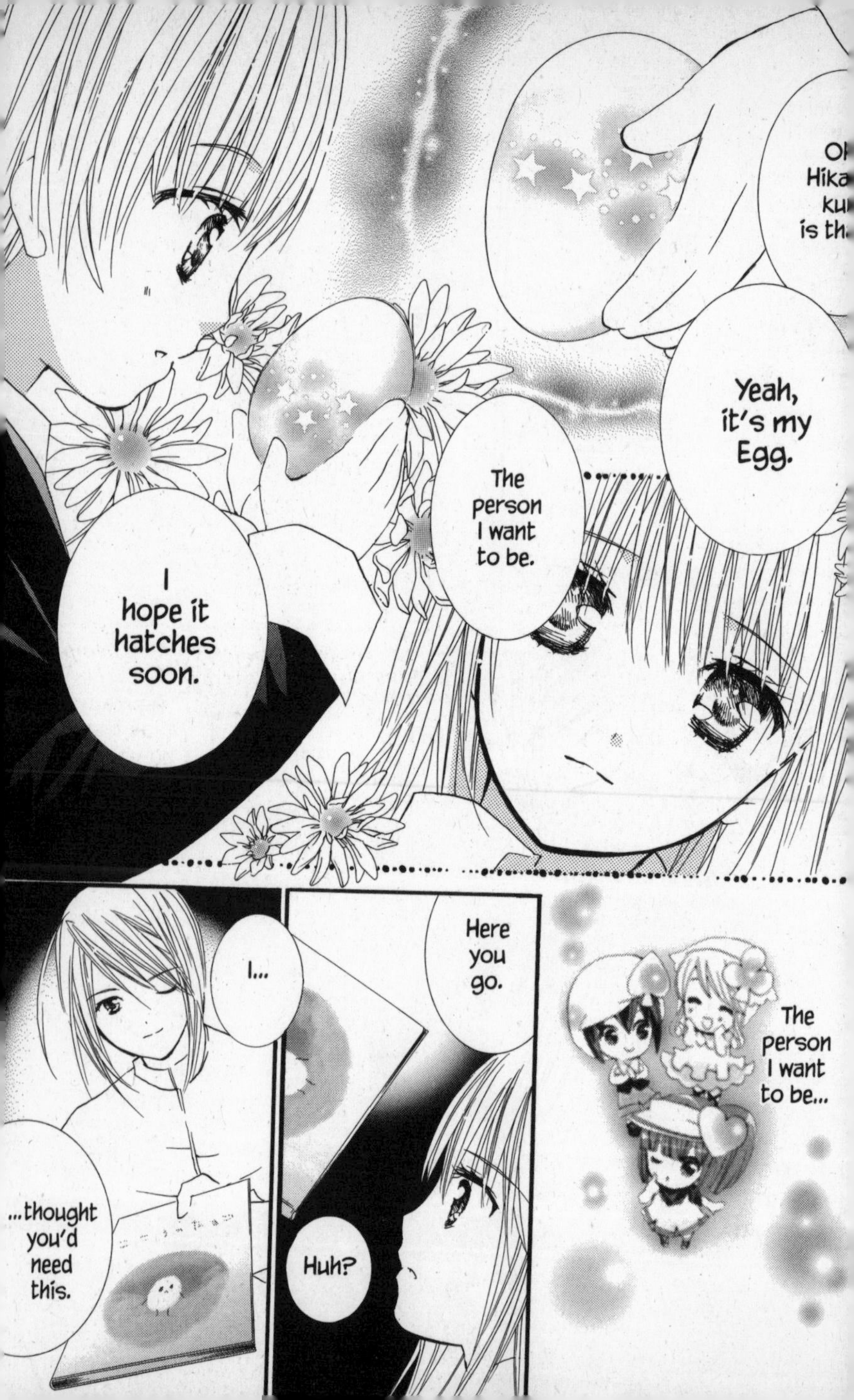

O Hika ku is th
Yeah, it's my Egg.
The person I want to be.
I hope it hatches soon.
The person I want to be...
Here you go.
Huh?
I...
...thought you'd need this.

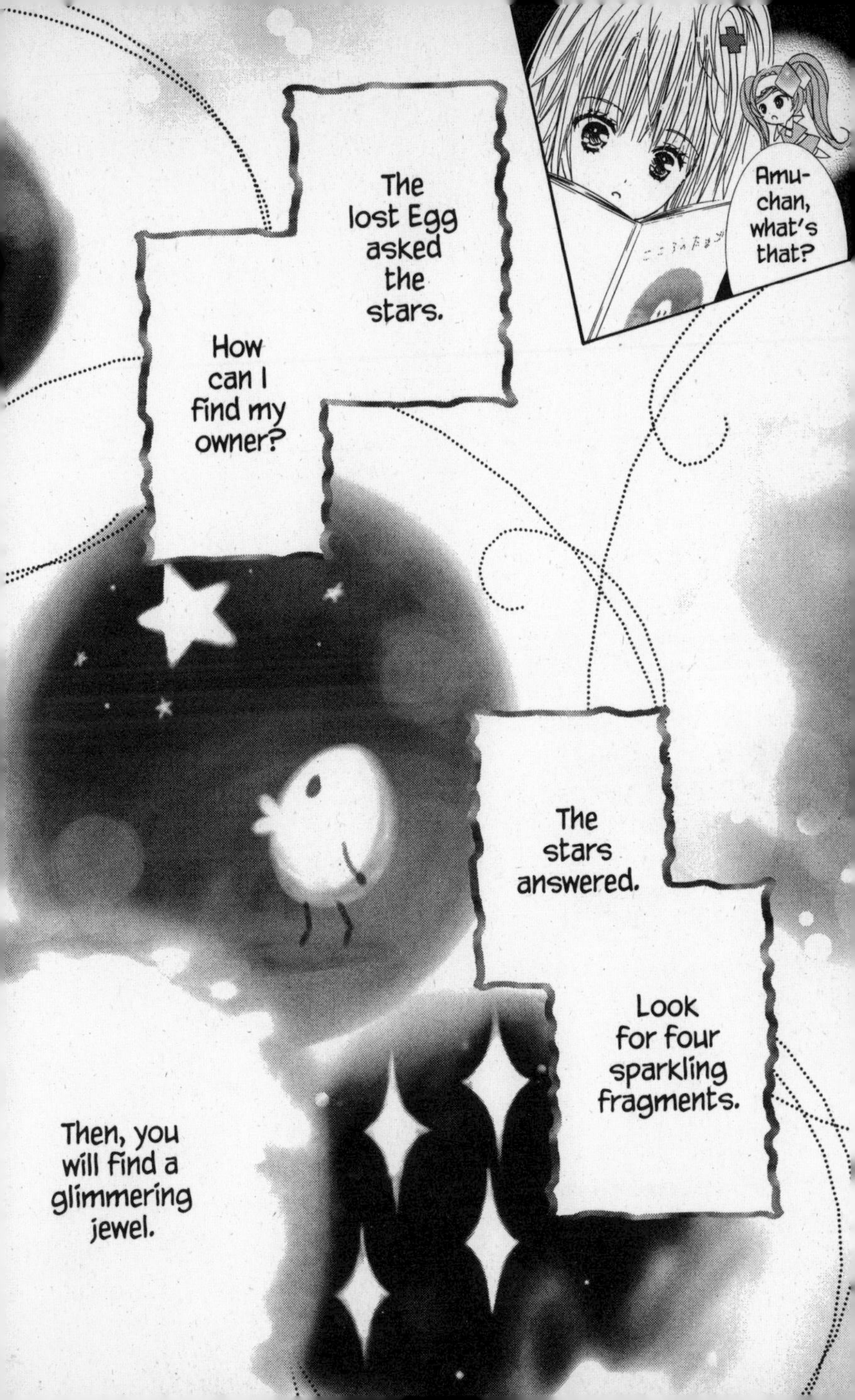
Amu-chan, what's that?
The lost Egg asked the stars.
How can I find my owner?
The stars answered.
Look for four sparkling fragments.
Then, you will find a glimmering jewel.

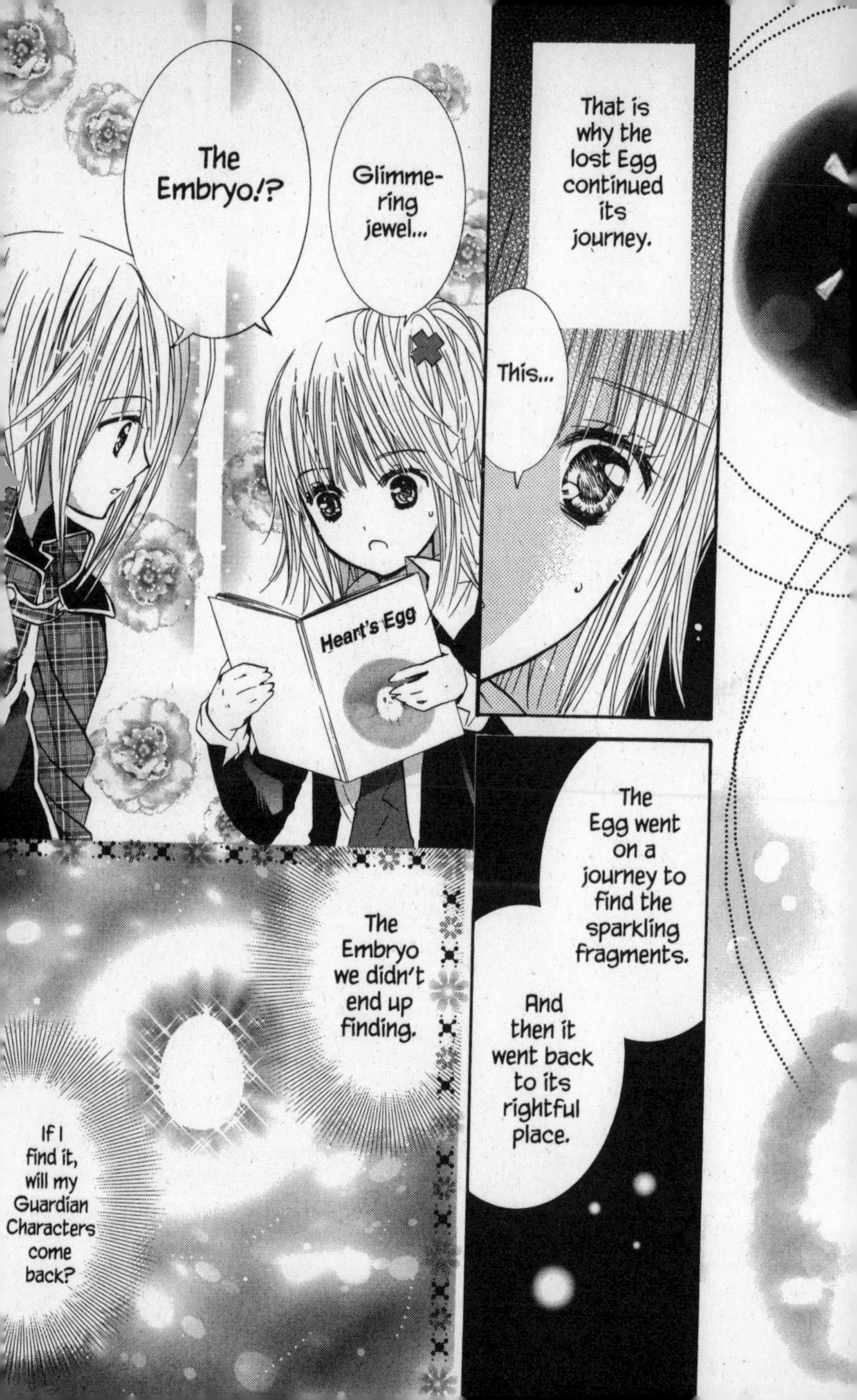
That is why the lost Egg continued its journey.
This...
Glimmering jewel...
The Embryo!?
Heart's Egg
The Egg went on a journey to find the sparkling fragments.
And then it went back to its rightful place.
The Embryo we didn't end up finding.
If I find it, will my Guardian Characters come back?

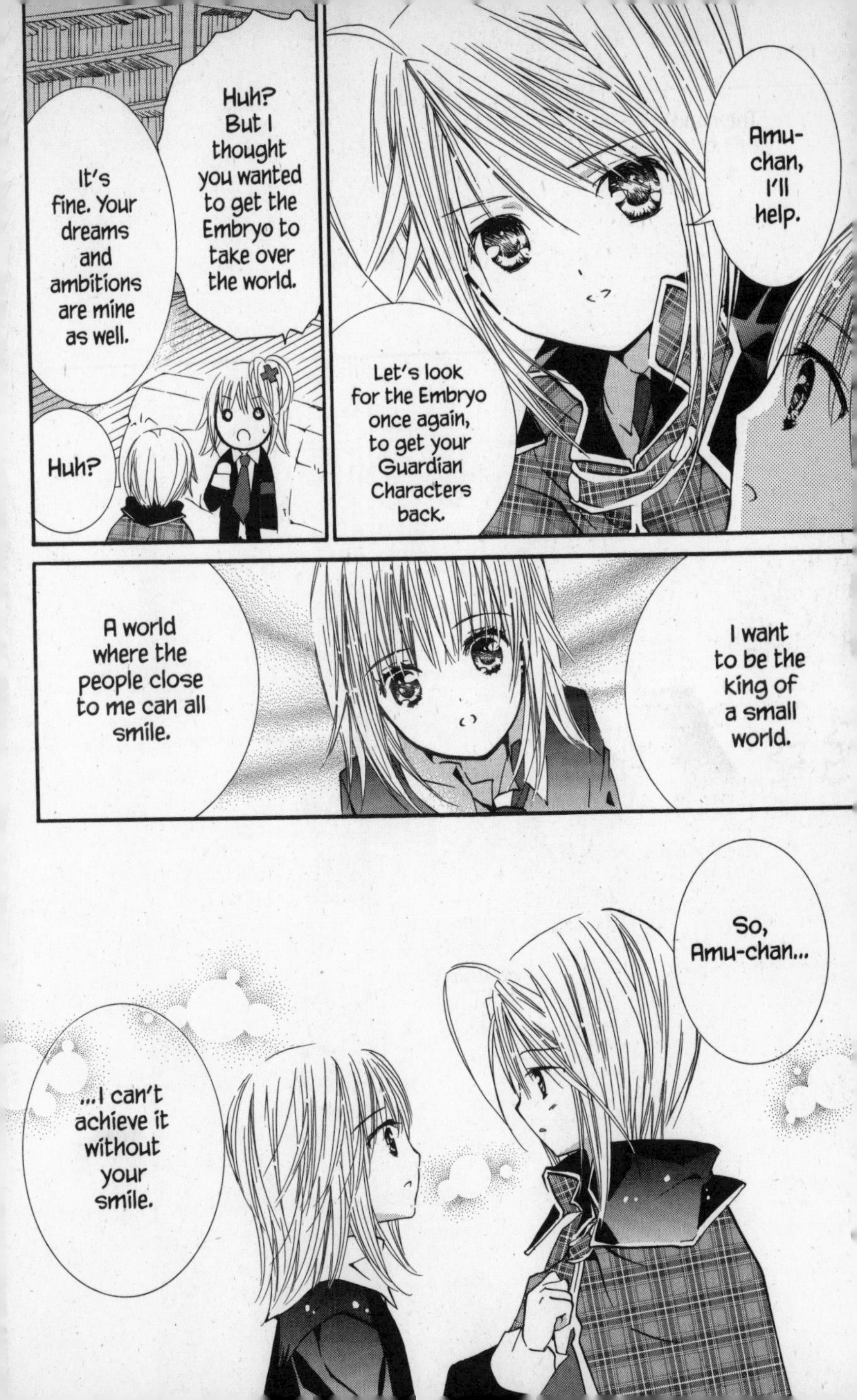

Amu-chan, I'll help.
Let's look for the Embryo once again, to get your Guardian Characters back.
Huh? But I thought you wanted to get the Embryo to take over the world.
It's fine. Your dreams and ambitions are mine as well.
Huh?
I want to be the king of a small world.
A world where the people close to me can all smile.
So, Amu-chan...
...I can't achieve it without your smile.

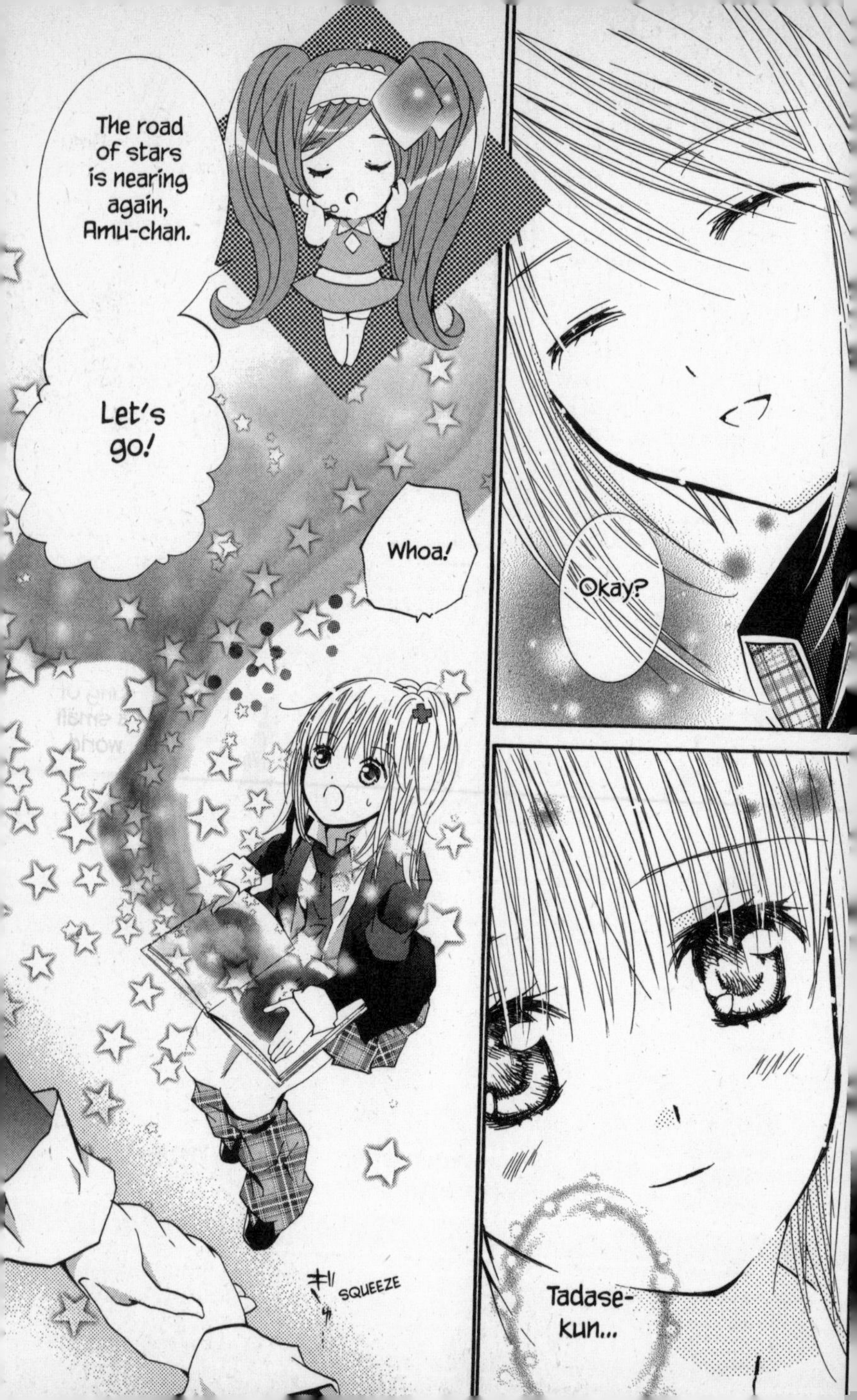
Okay?
Tadase-kun...
The road of stars is nearing again, Amu-chan.
Let's go!
Whoa!
SQUEEZE

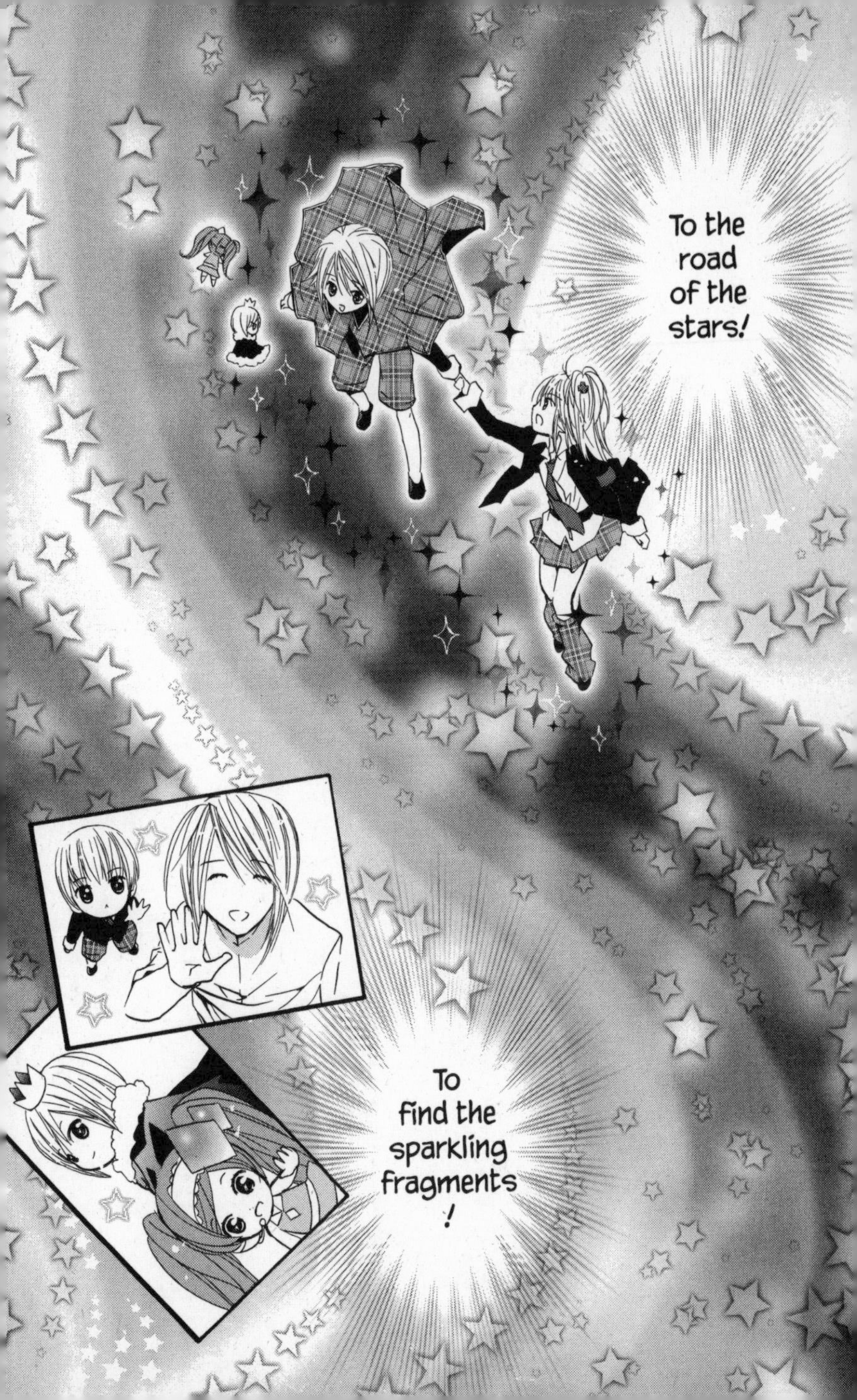
To the road of the stars!
To find the sparkling fragments!

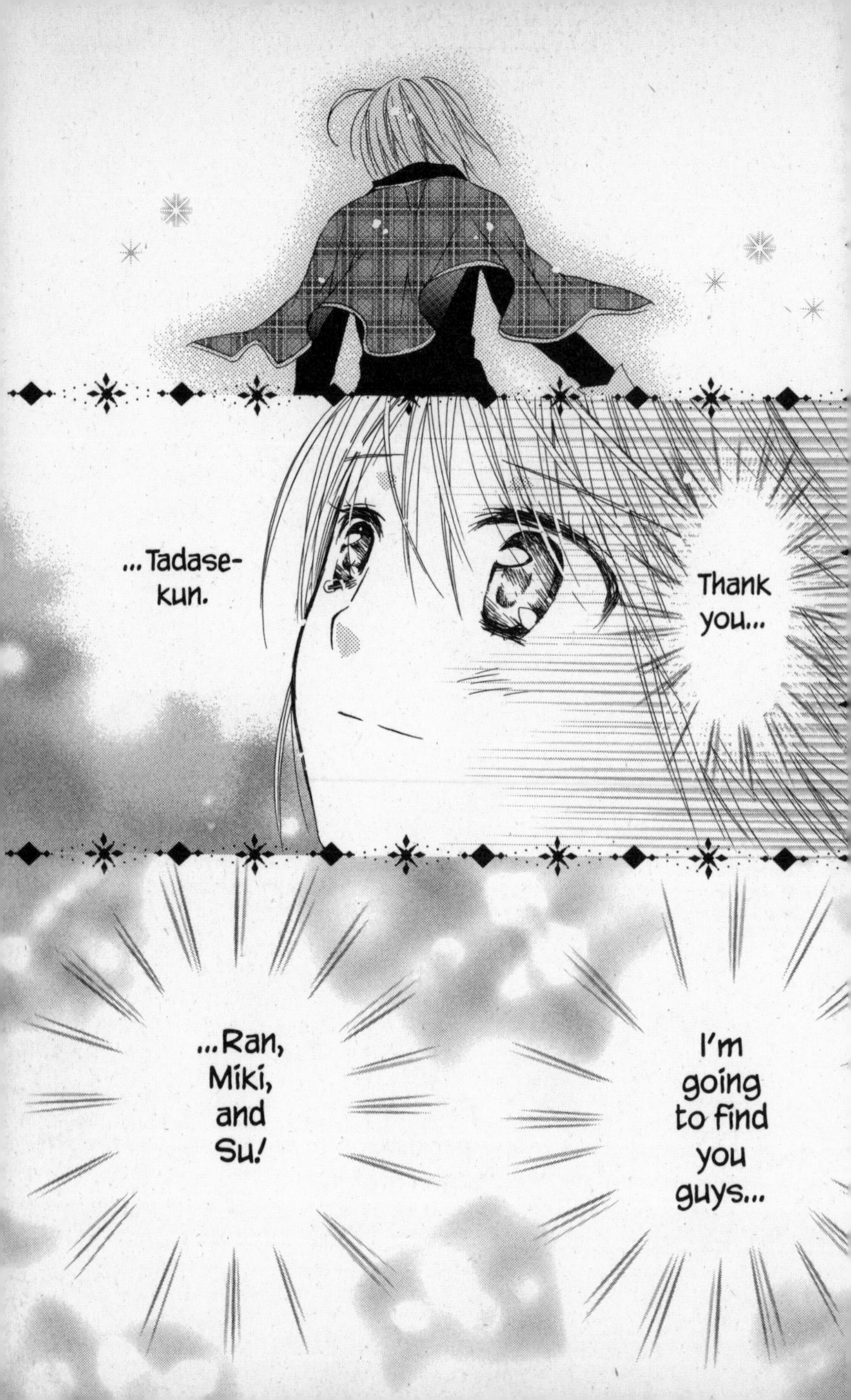
Thank you...
...Tadase-kun.
I'm going to find you guys...
...Ran, Miki, and Su!

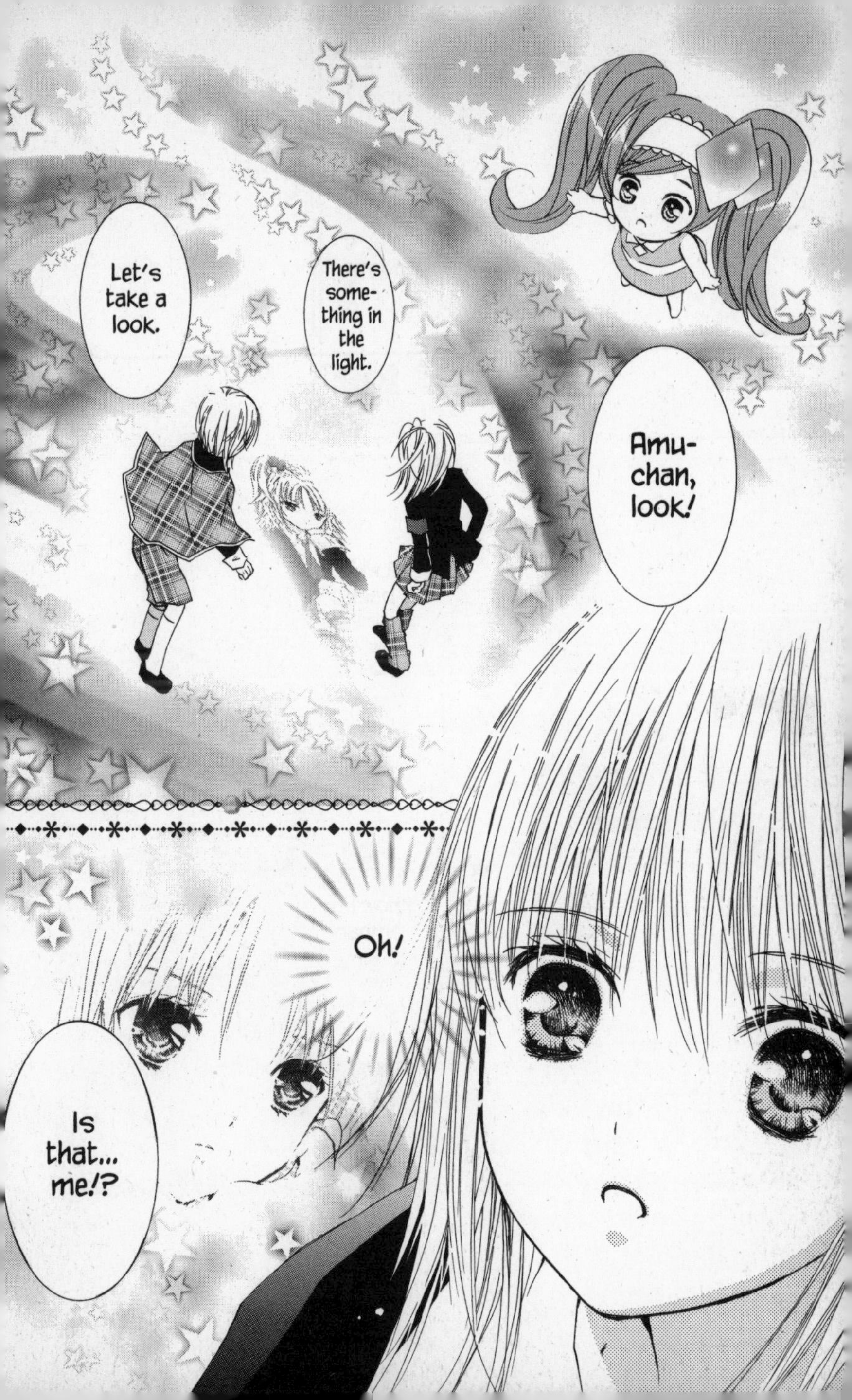
Amu-chan, look!
There's something in the light.
Let's take a look.
Oh!
Is that... me!?

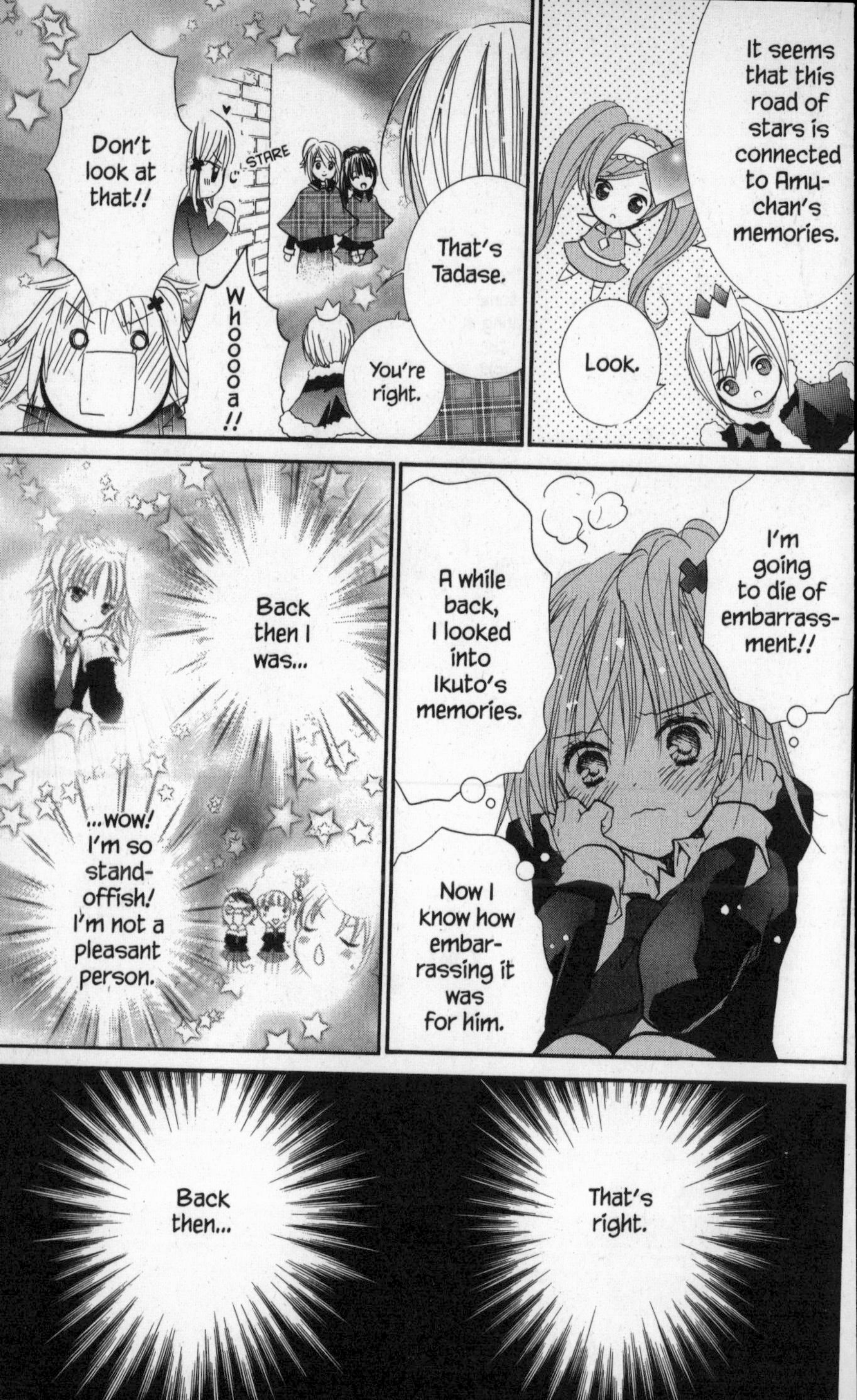
It seems that this road of stars is connected to Amu-chan's memories.
Look.
STARE
That's Tadase.
You're right.
Don't look at that!!
Whooooa!!
I'm going to die of embarrass-ment!!
A while back, I looked into Ikuto's memories.
Now I know how embar-rassing it was for him.
Back then I was...
...wow! I'm so stand-offish! I'm not a pleasant person.
That's right.
Back then...

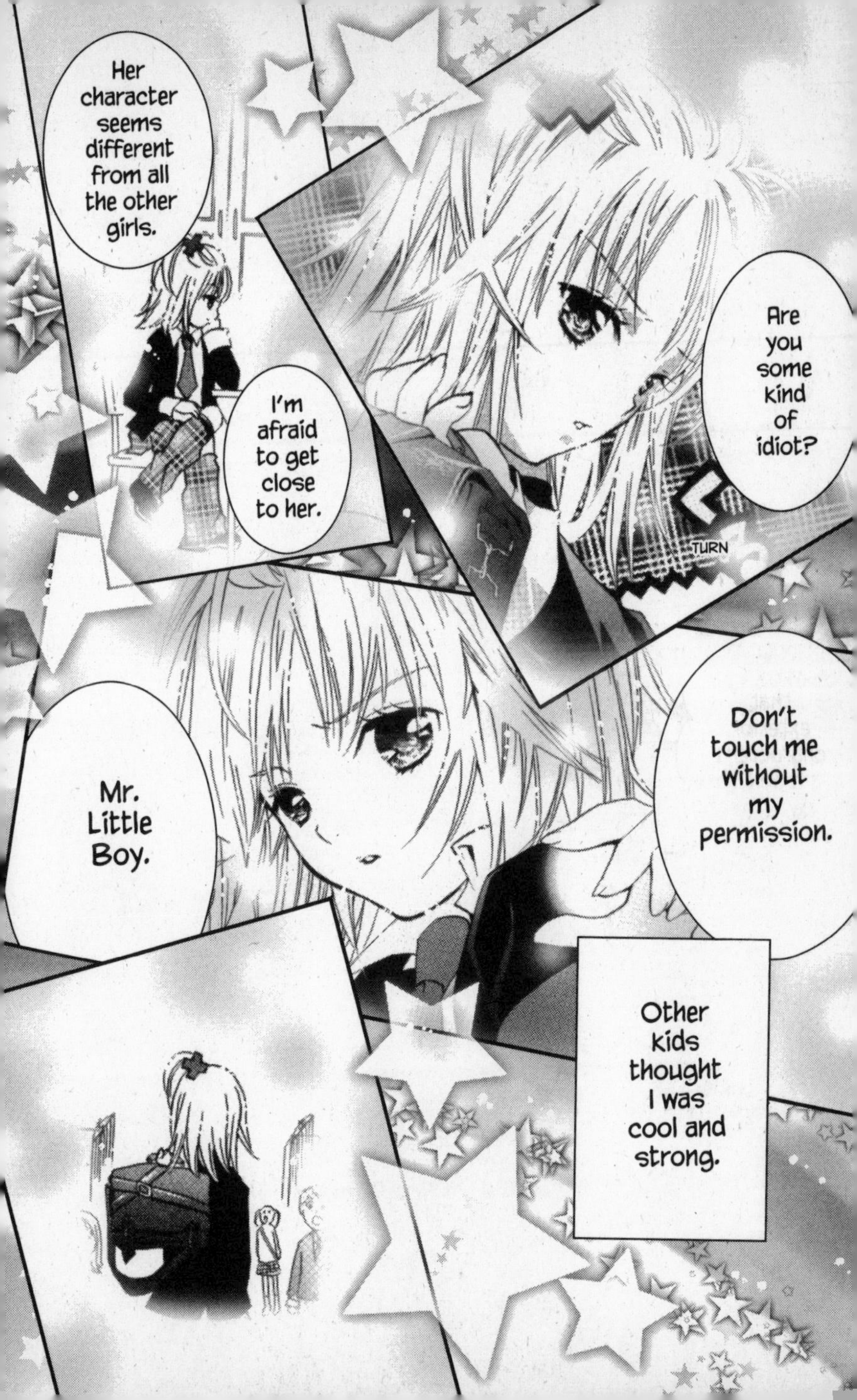
Her character seems different from all the other girls.
I'm afraid to get close to her.
Are you some kind of idiot?
TURN
Don't touch me without my permission.
Mr. Little Boy.
Other kids thought I was cool and strong.

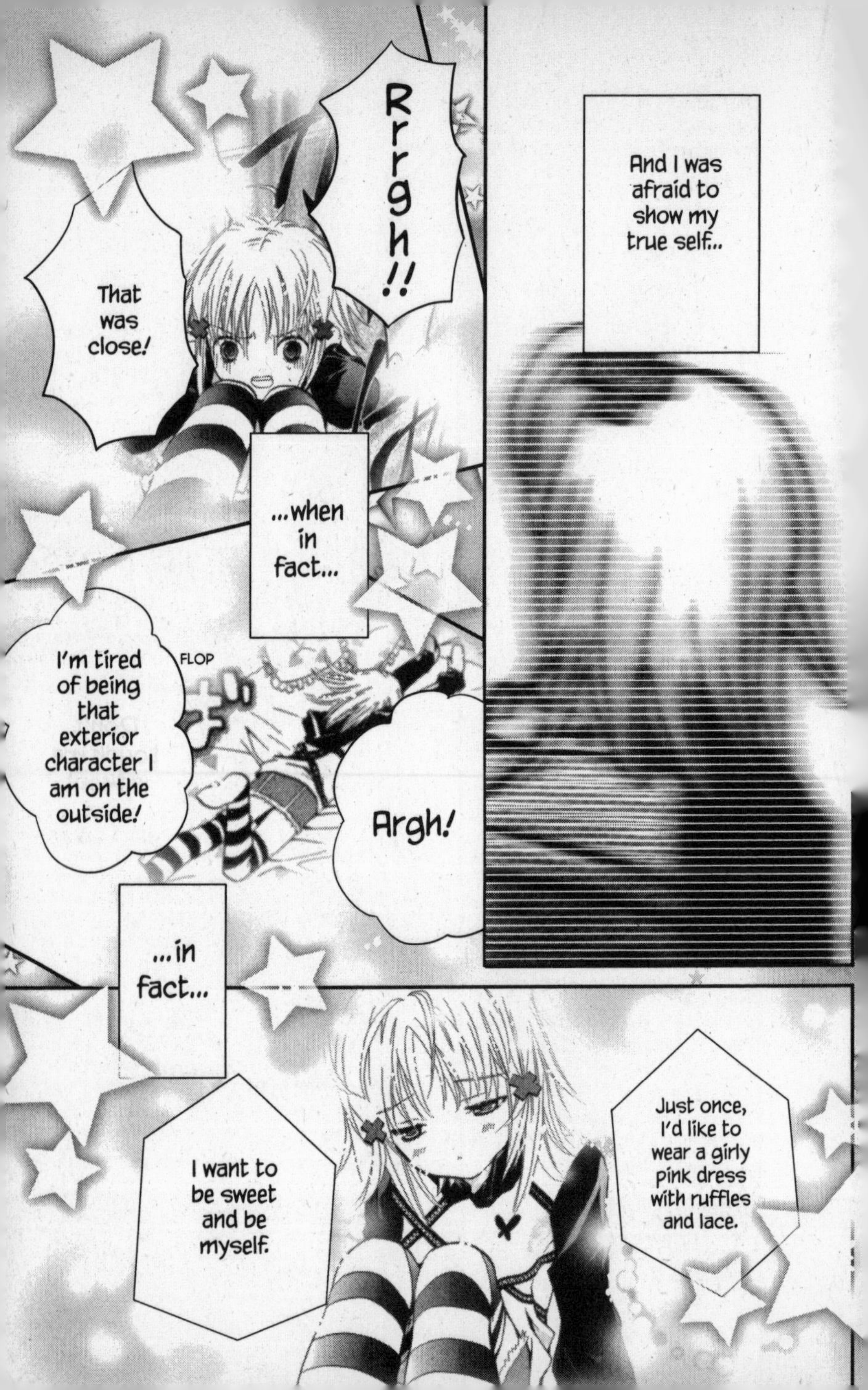
And I was afraid to show my true self...
Rrrgh!!
That was close!
...when in fact...
Argh!
FLOP
I'm tired of being that exterior character I am on the outside!
...in fact...
Just once, I'd like to wear a girly pink dress with ruffles and lace.
I want to be sweet and be myself.

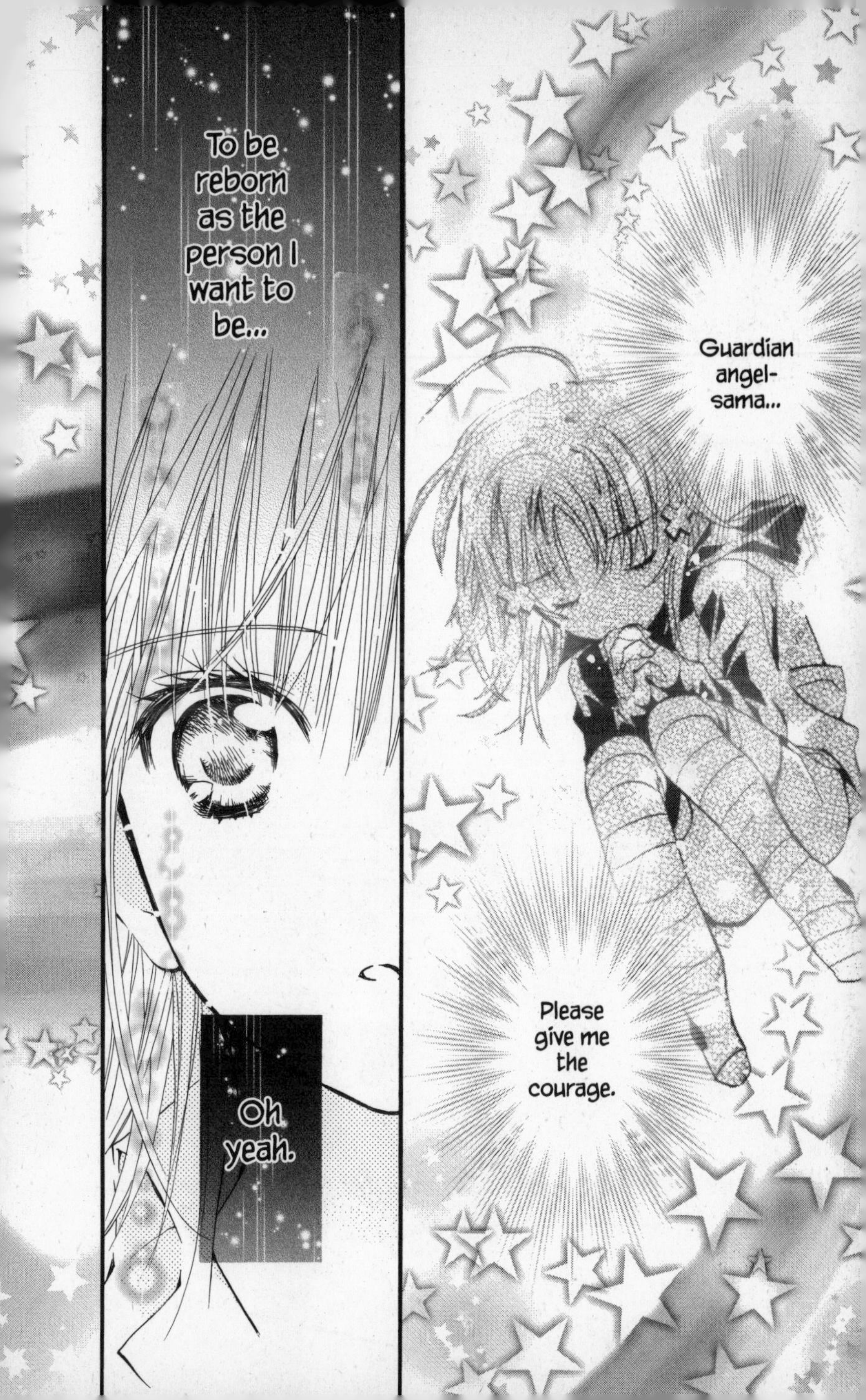
Guardian angel-sama...
Please give me the courage.
To be reborn as the person I want to be...
Oh yeah.

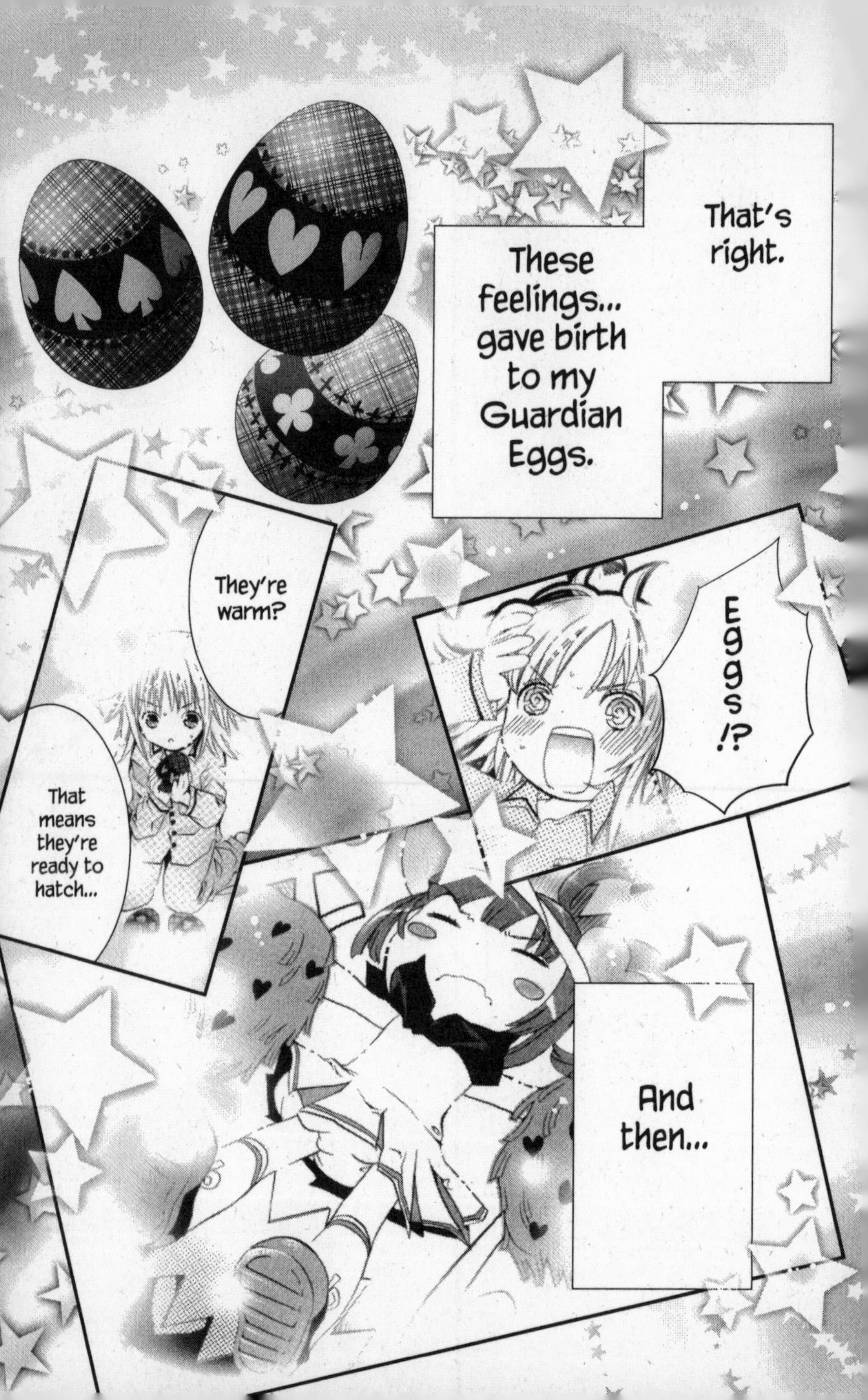
That's right.
These feelings... gave birth to my Guardian Eggs.
Eggs!?
They're warm?
That means they're ready to hatch...
And then...

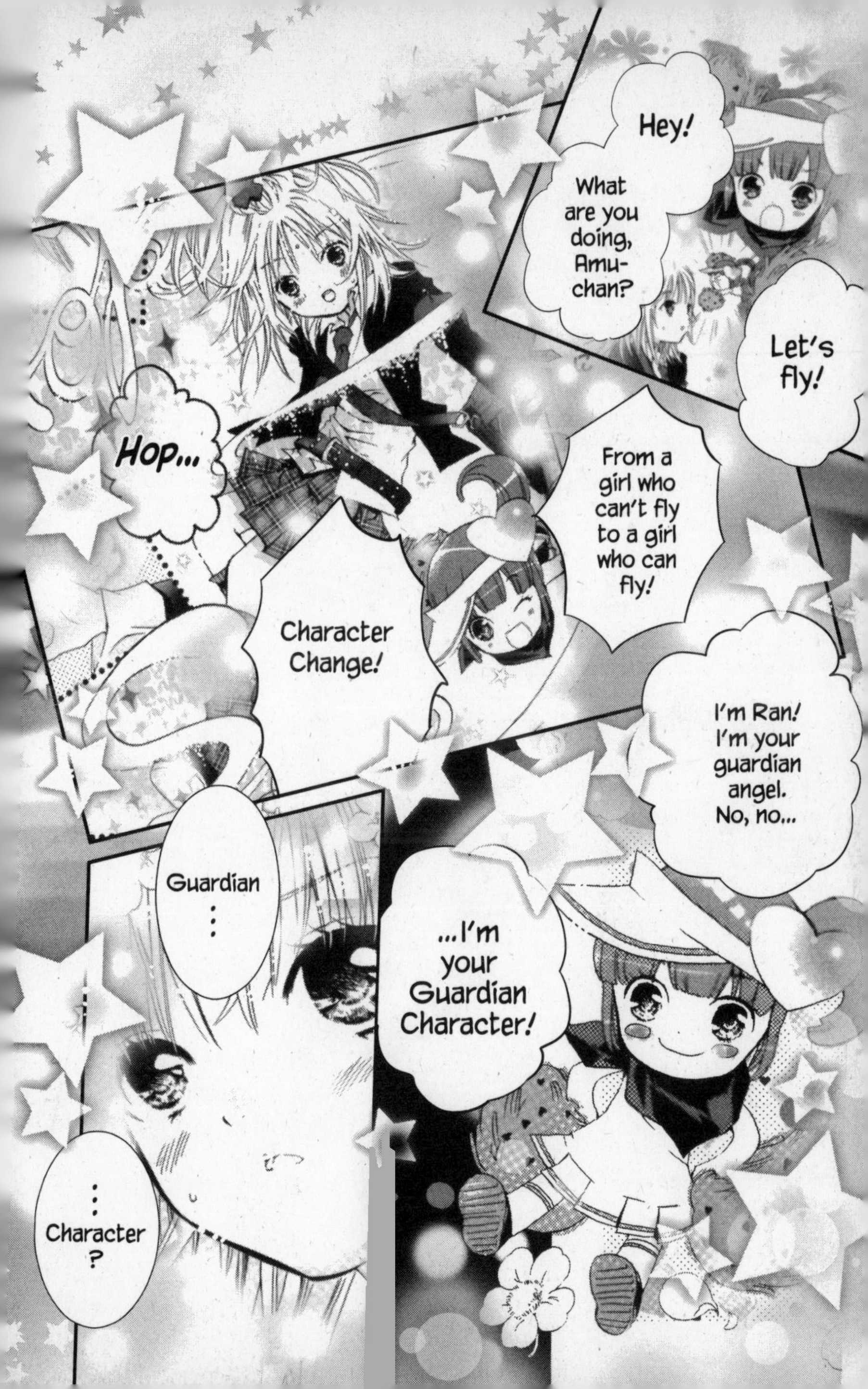
Hey!
What are you doing, Amu-chan?
Let's fly!
Hop...
From a girl who can't fly to a girl who can fly!
Character Change!
I'm Ran! I'm your guardian angel. No, no...
...I'm your Guardian Character!
Guardian...
...Character?

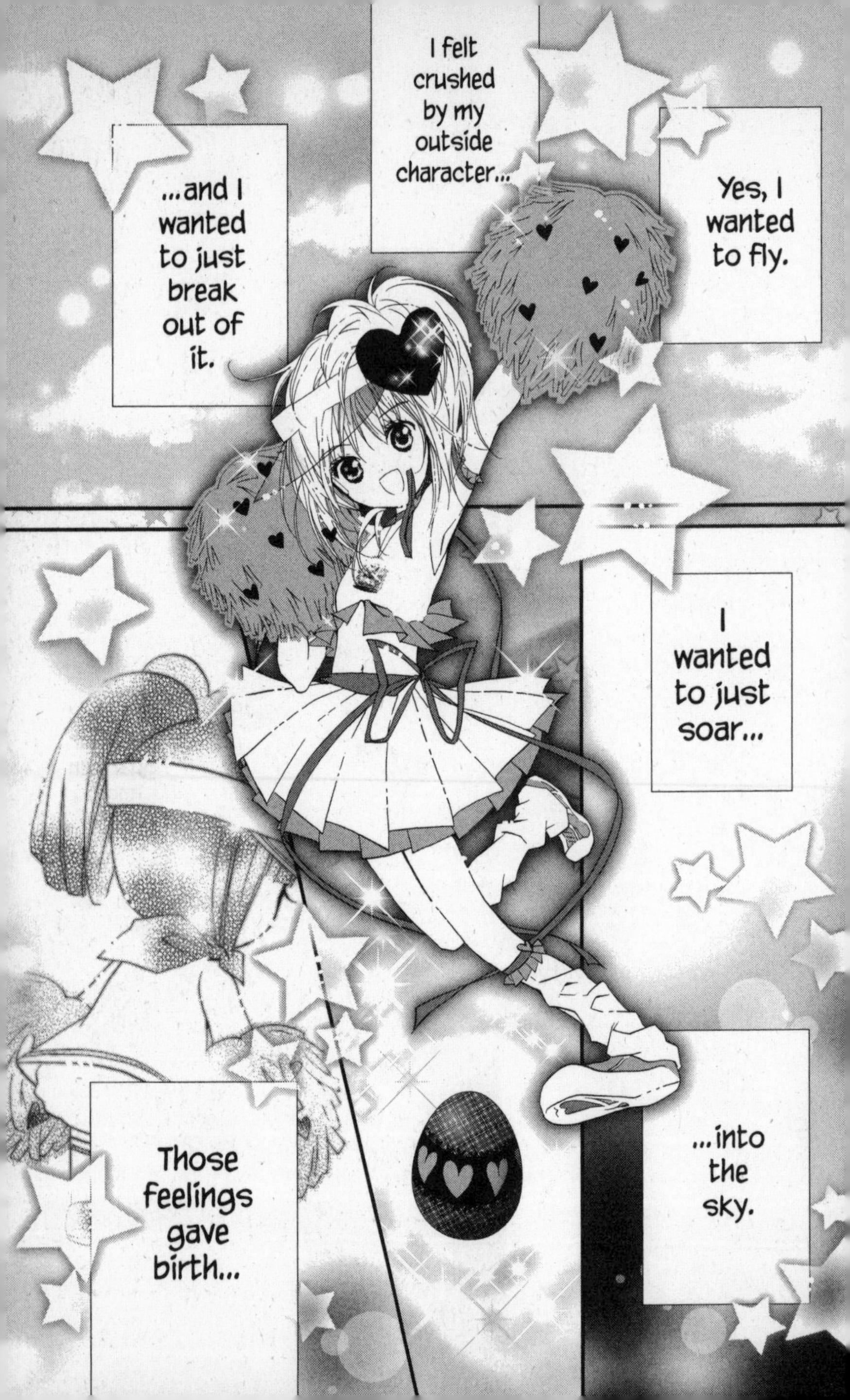
I felt crushed by my outside character...
...and I wanted to just break out of it.
Yes, I wanted to fly.
I wanted to just soar...
...into the sky.
Those feelings gave birth...

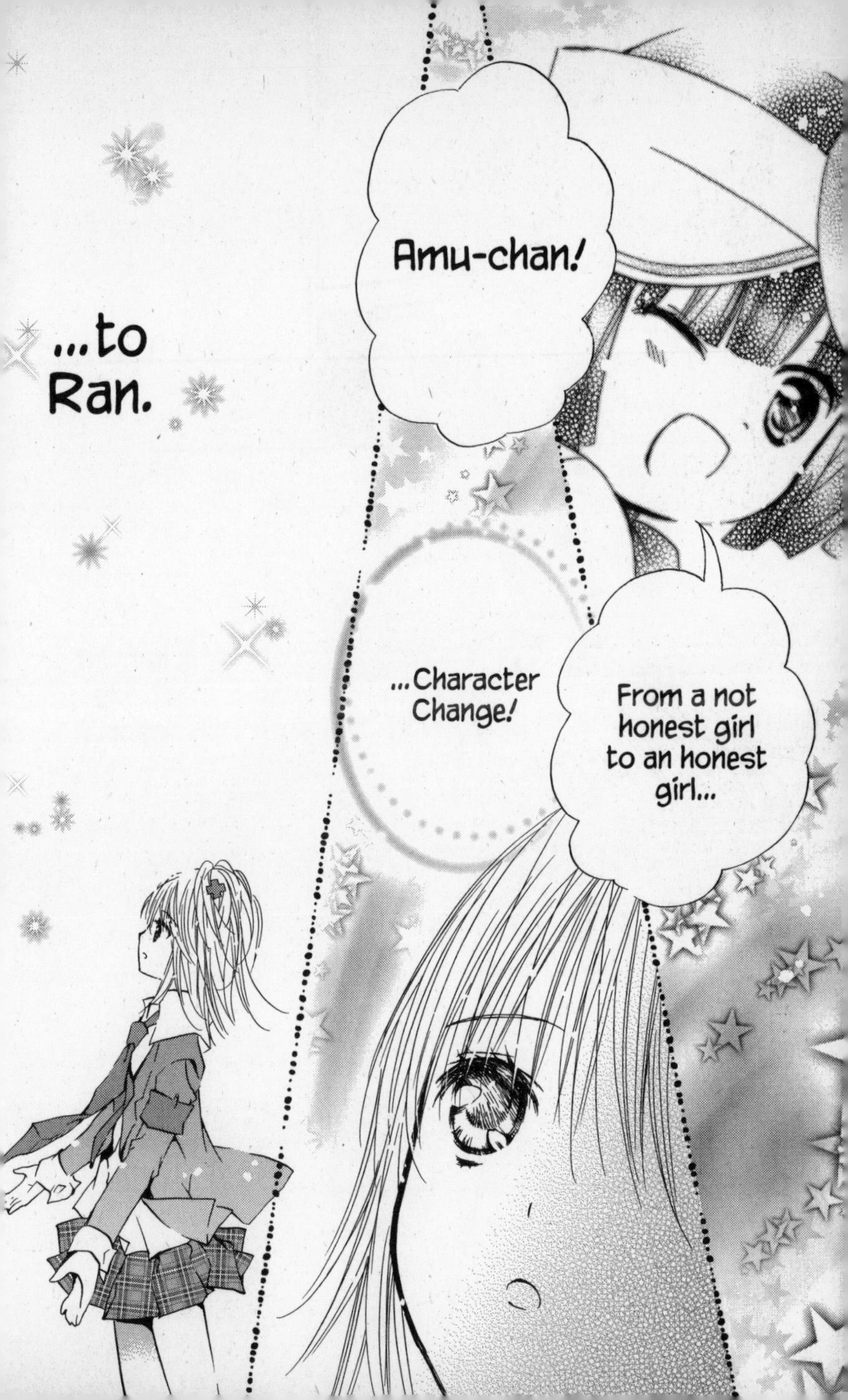
Amu-chan!
From a not honest girl to an honest girl...
...Character Change!
...to Ran.

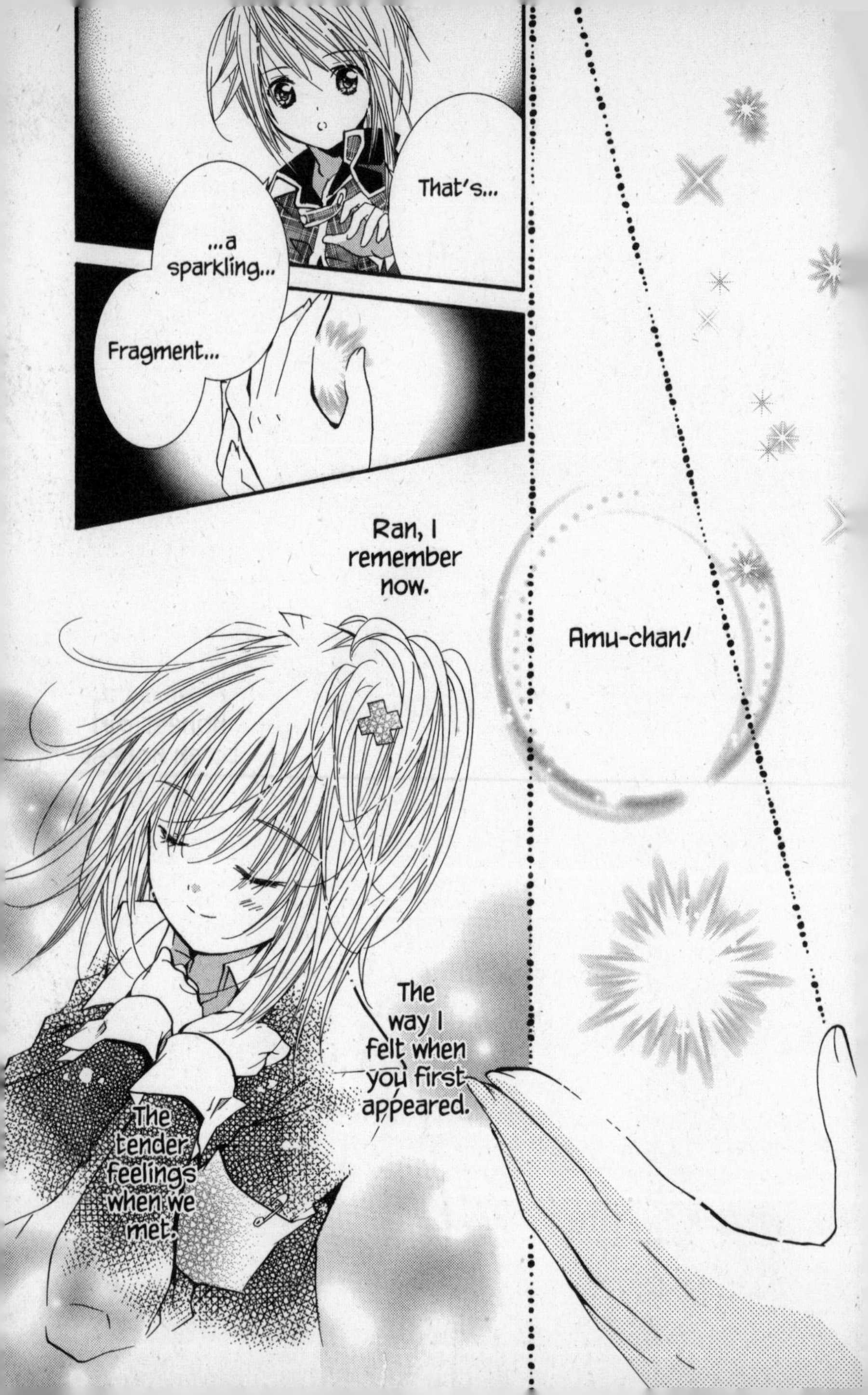
Amu-chan!
That's...
...a sparkling...
Fragment...
Ran, I remember now.
The way I felt when you first appeared.
The tender feelings when we met.

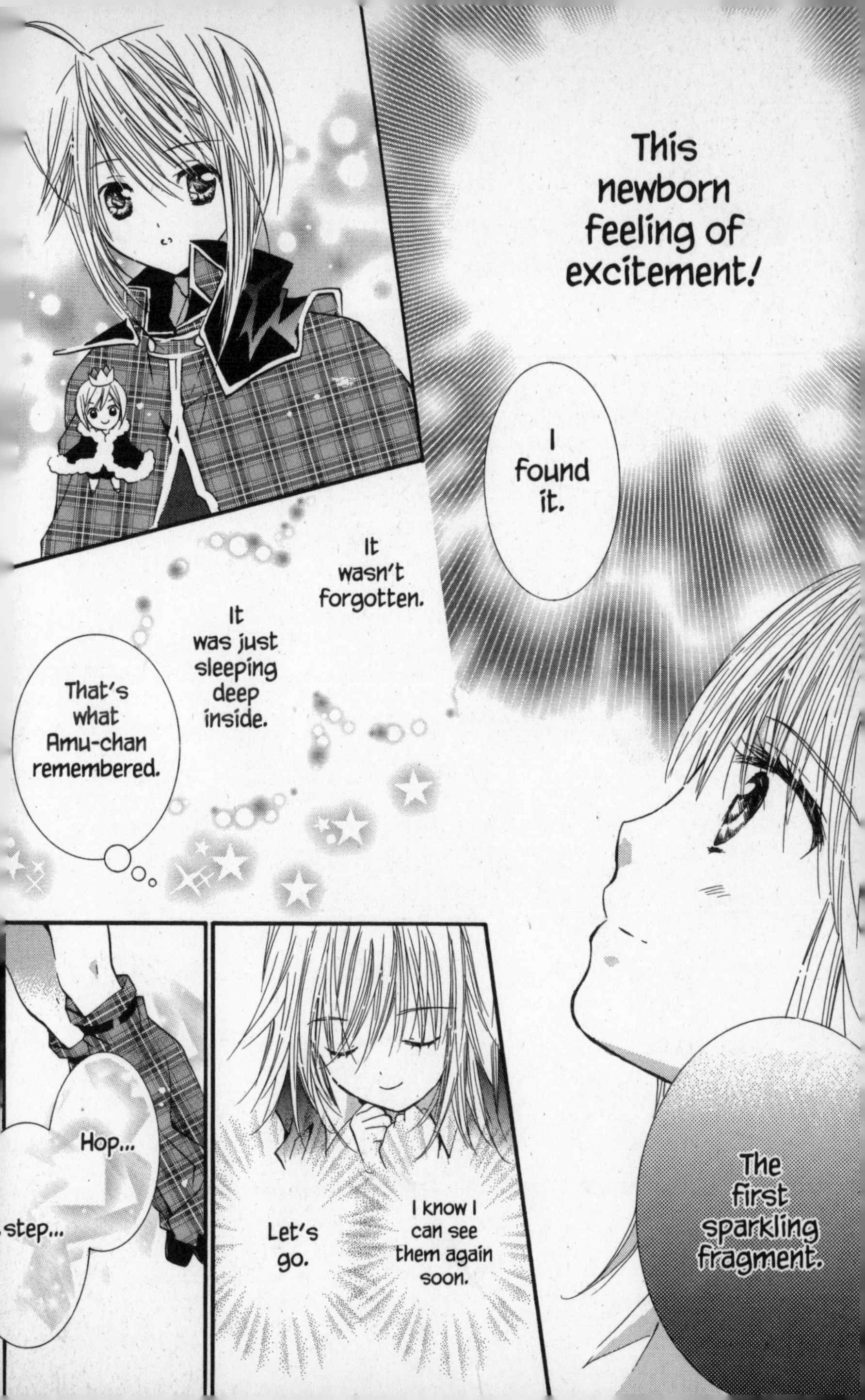
This newborn feeling of excitement!
I found it.
The first sparkling fragment.
It wasn't forgotten.
It was just sleeping deep inside.
That's what Amu-chan remembered.
I know I can see them again soon.
Let's go.
Hop...
step...

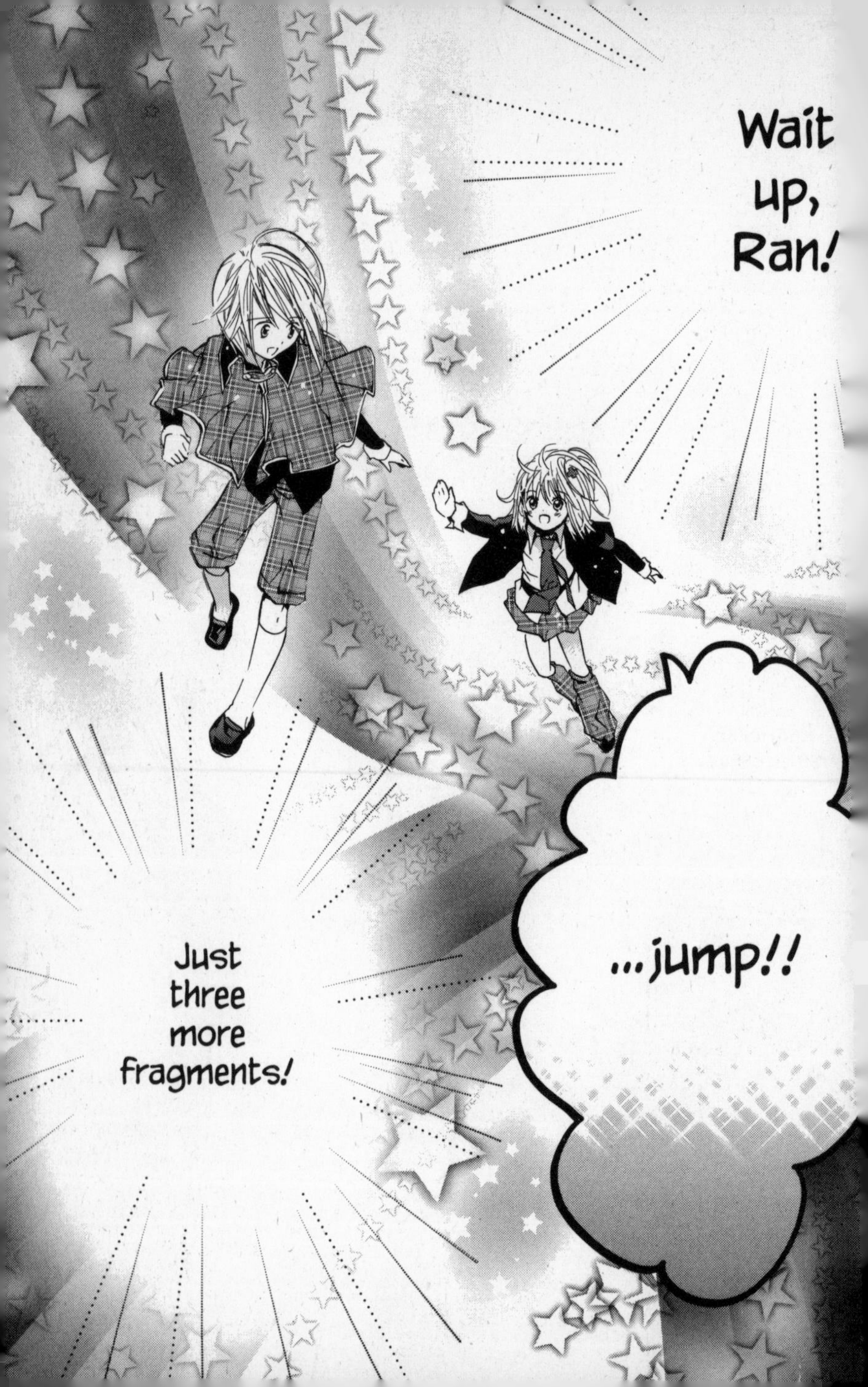
Wait up, Ran!
...jump!!
Just three more fragments!

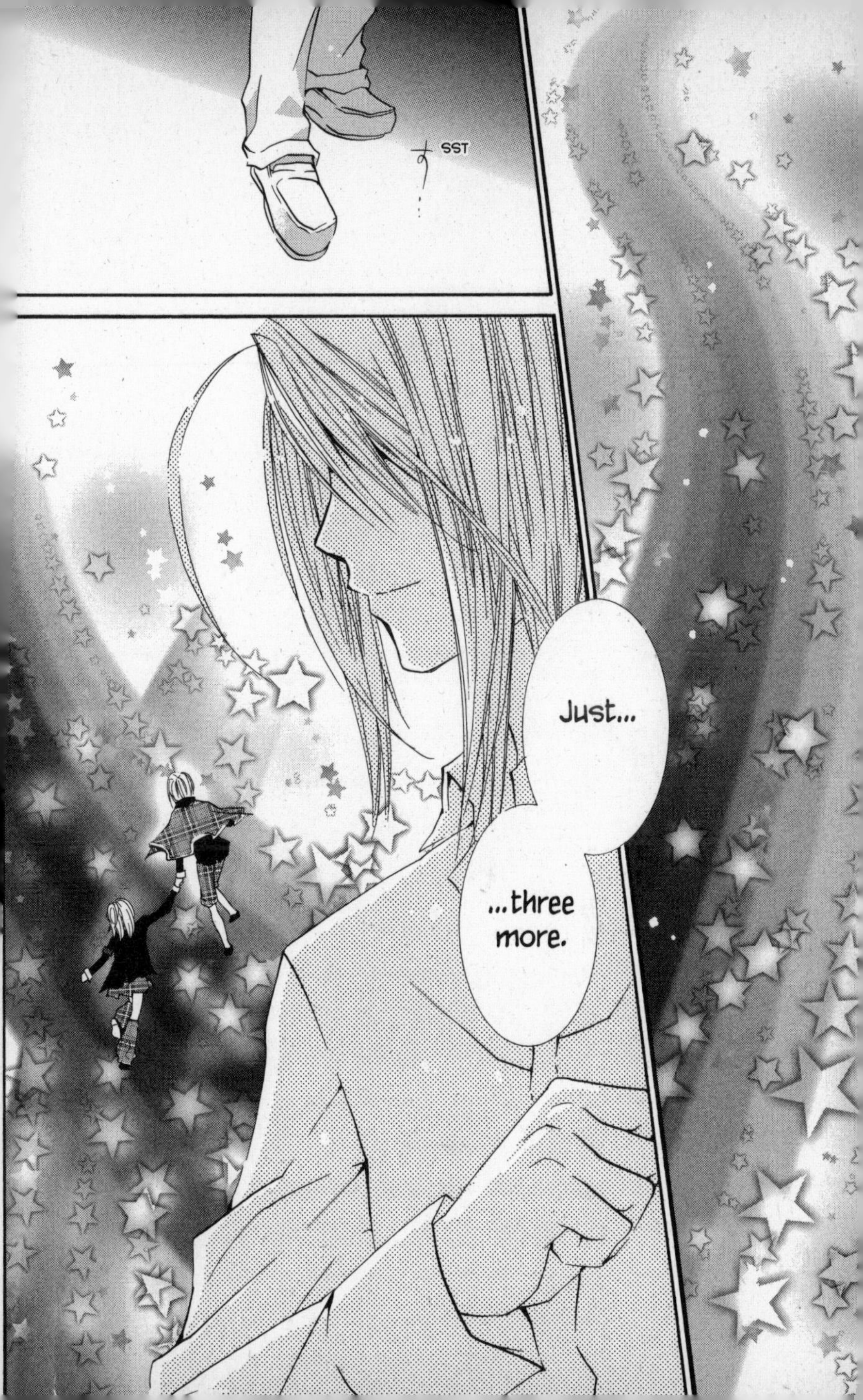
SST
Just...
...three more.

Shugo Chara!

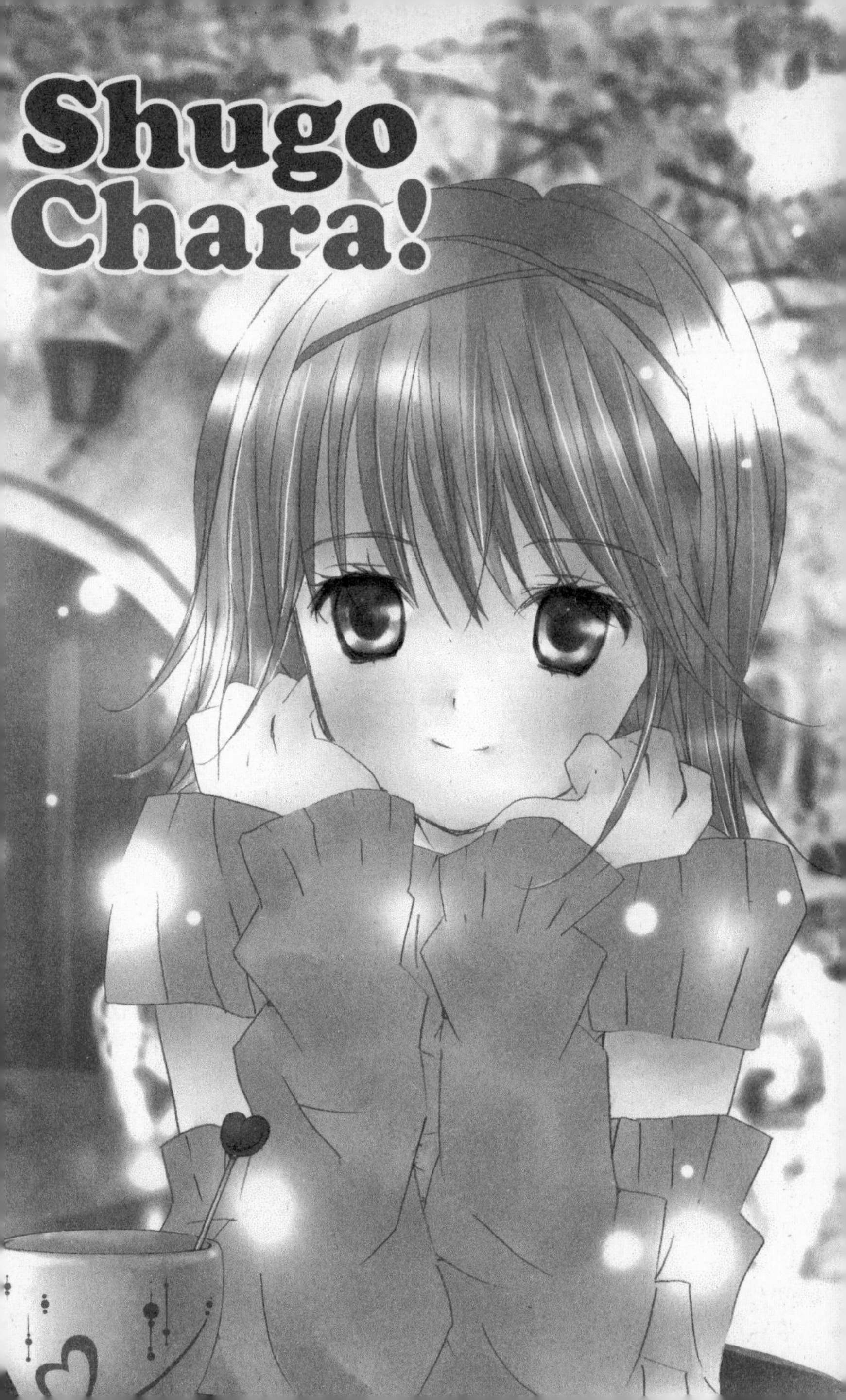
Shugo
Chara!

I followed the road of stars...

...and found the first sparkling fragment.

Now I just need three more!

A1. There were so many great ideas, so we'll announce the final name in volume 12!
Thank you everyone...

    All suggestions were good and it was hard to decide.

Some of the names include:

Picchi, Pi-chan, Momoko, Momo, MomoPi, Pi-kun, Pitton, Pittocchi, Pimo-chan,
Peach-man, Momorin, Momoccho, Moppi, Momon, Momosuke...etc.
There were many, many more ♥ I can't fit them all here!

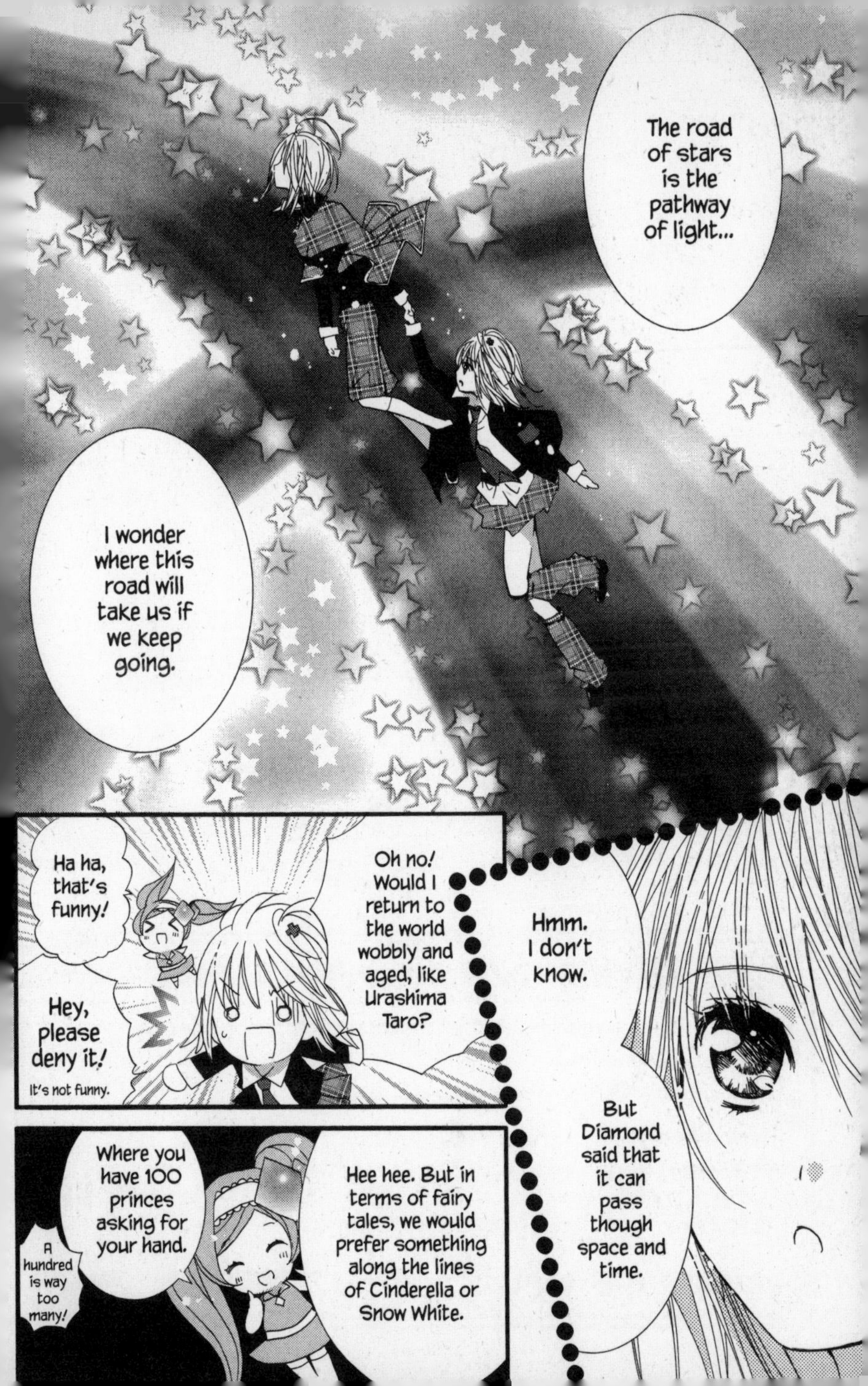
The road of stars is the pathway of light...
I wonder where this road will take us if we keep going.
Hmm. I don't know.
But Diamond said that it can pass though space and time.
Oh no! Would I return to the world wobbly and aged, like Urashima Taro?
Ha ha, that's funny!
Hey, please deny it!
It's not funny.
Hee hee. But in terms of fairy tales, we would prefer something along the lines of Cinderella or Snow White.
Where you have 100 princes asking for your hand.
A hundred is way too many!

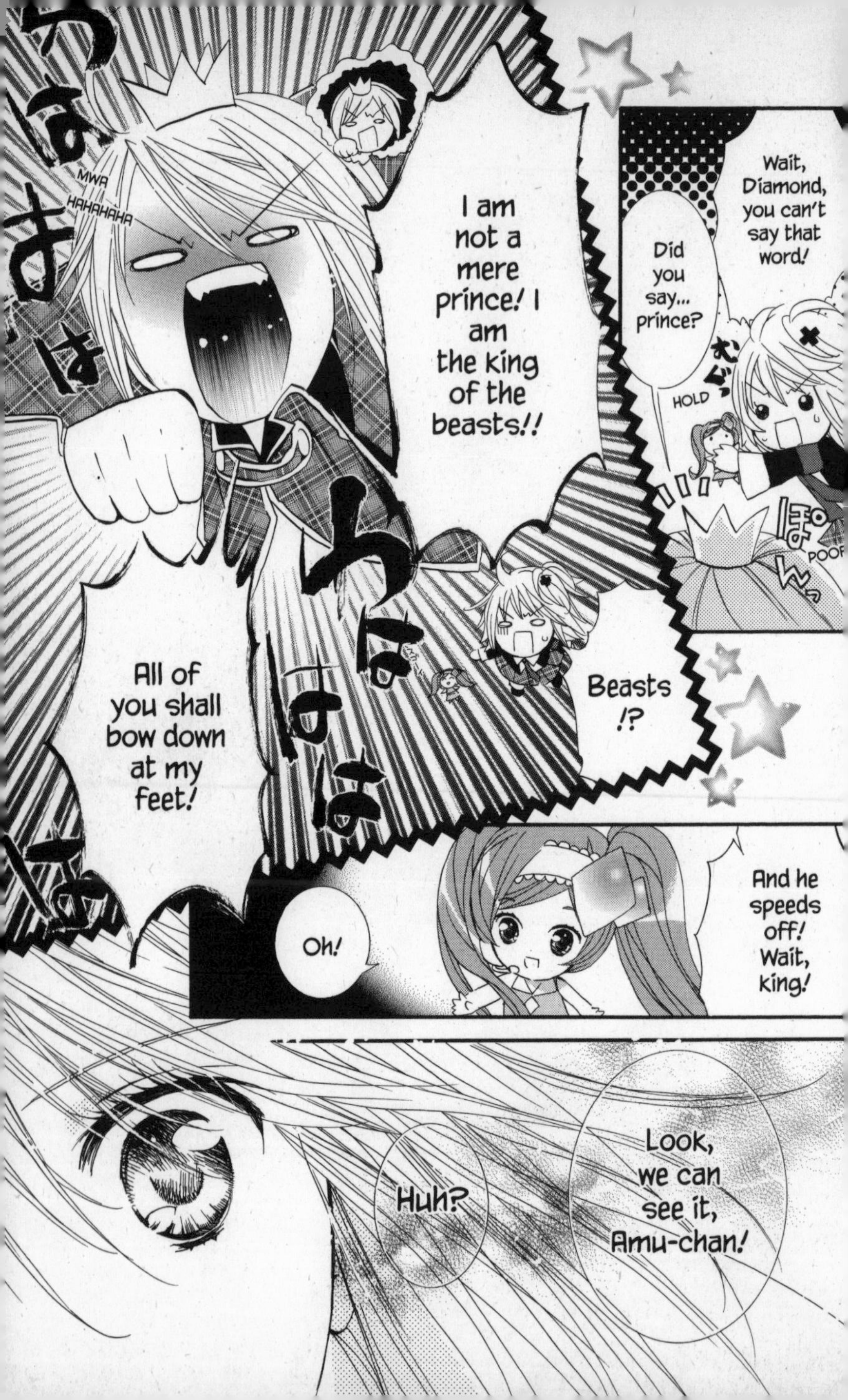
Wait, Diamond, you can't say that word!
Did you say... prince?
HOLD
POOF
I am not a mere prince! I am the king of the beasts!!
MWA HAHAHAHA
All of you shall bow down at my feet!
Beasts!?
And he speeds off! Wait, king!
Oh!
Look, we can see it, Amu-chan!
Huh?

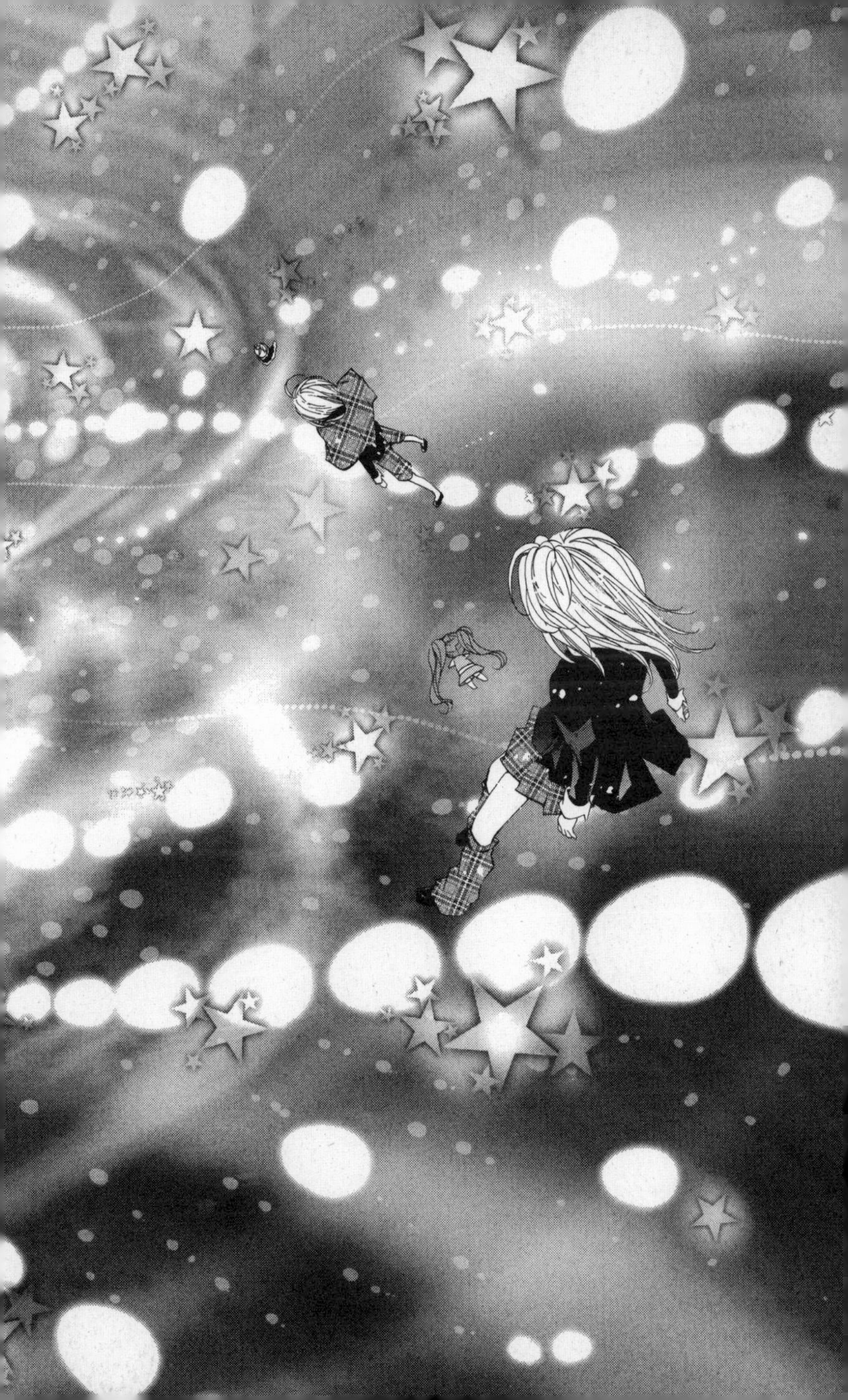

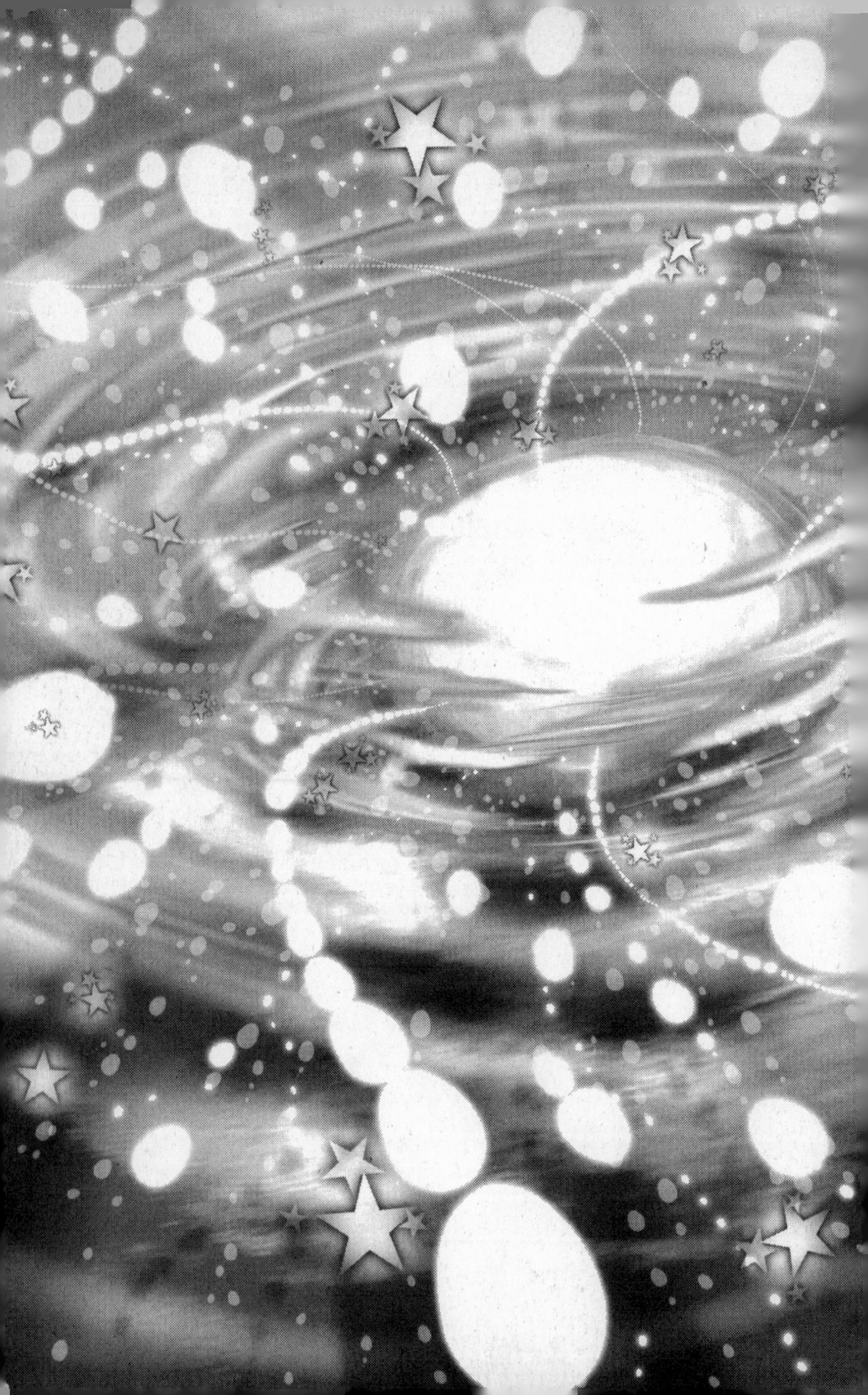

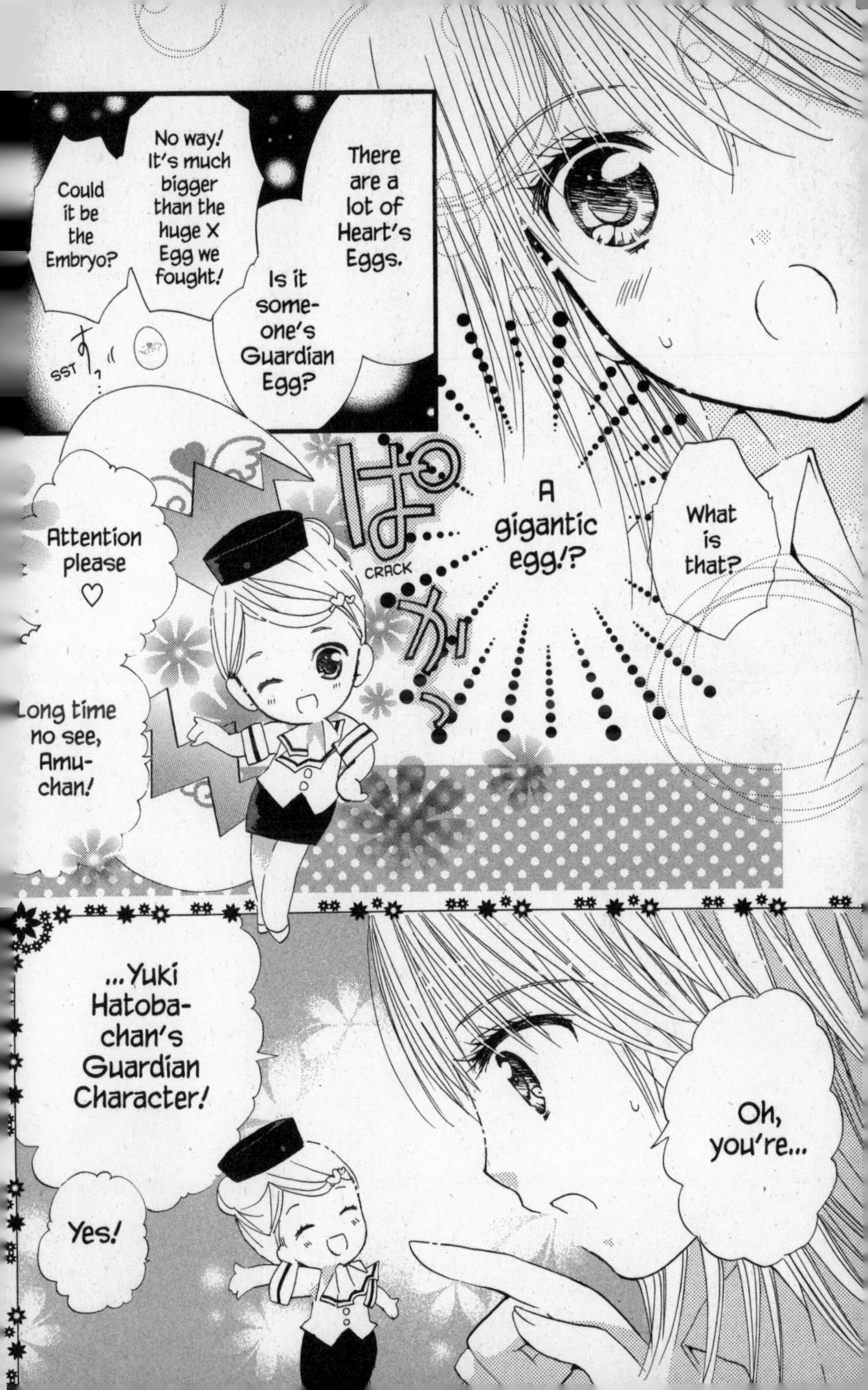

What is that?
A gigantic egg!?
There are a lot of Heart's Eggs.
Is it someone's Guardian Egg?
No way! It's much bigger than the huge X Egg we fought!
Could it be the Embryo?
SST
CRACK
Attention please ♡
Long time no see, Amu-chan!
Oh, you're...
...Yuki Hatoba-chan's Guardian Character!
Yes!

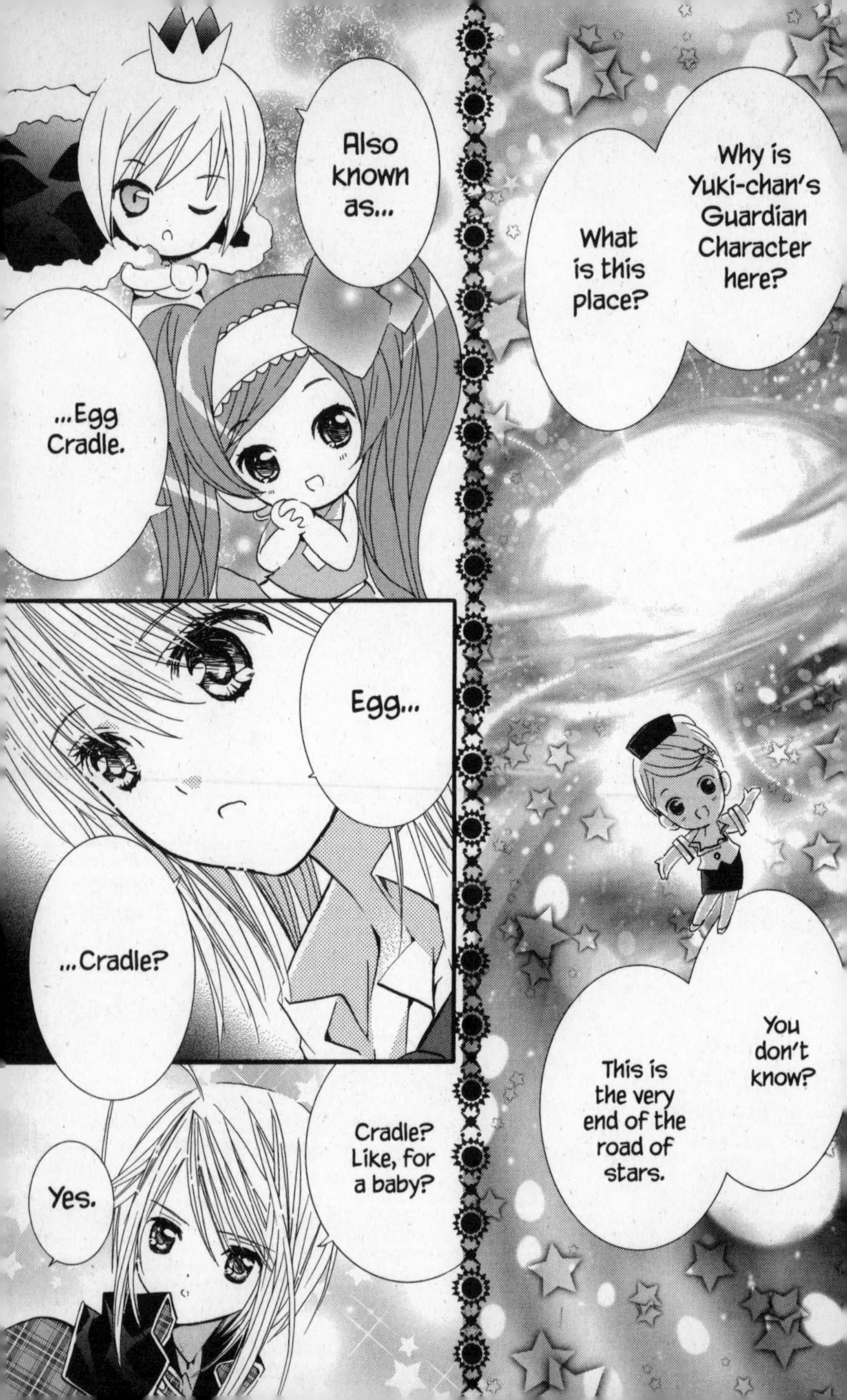
Why is Yuki-chan's Guardian Character here?
What is this place?
You don't know?
This is the very end of the road of stars.
Also known as...
...Egg Cradle.
Egg...
...Cradle?
Cradle? Like, for a baby?
Yes.

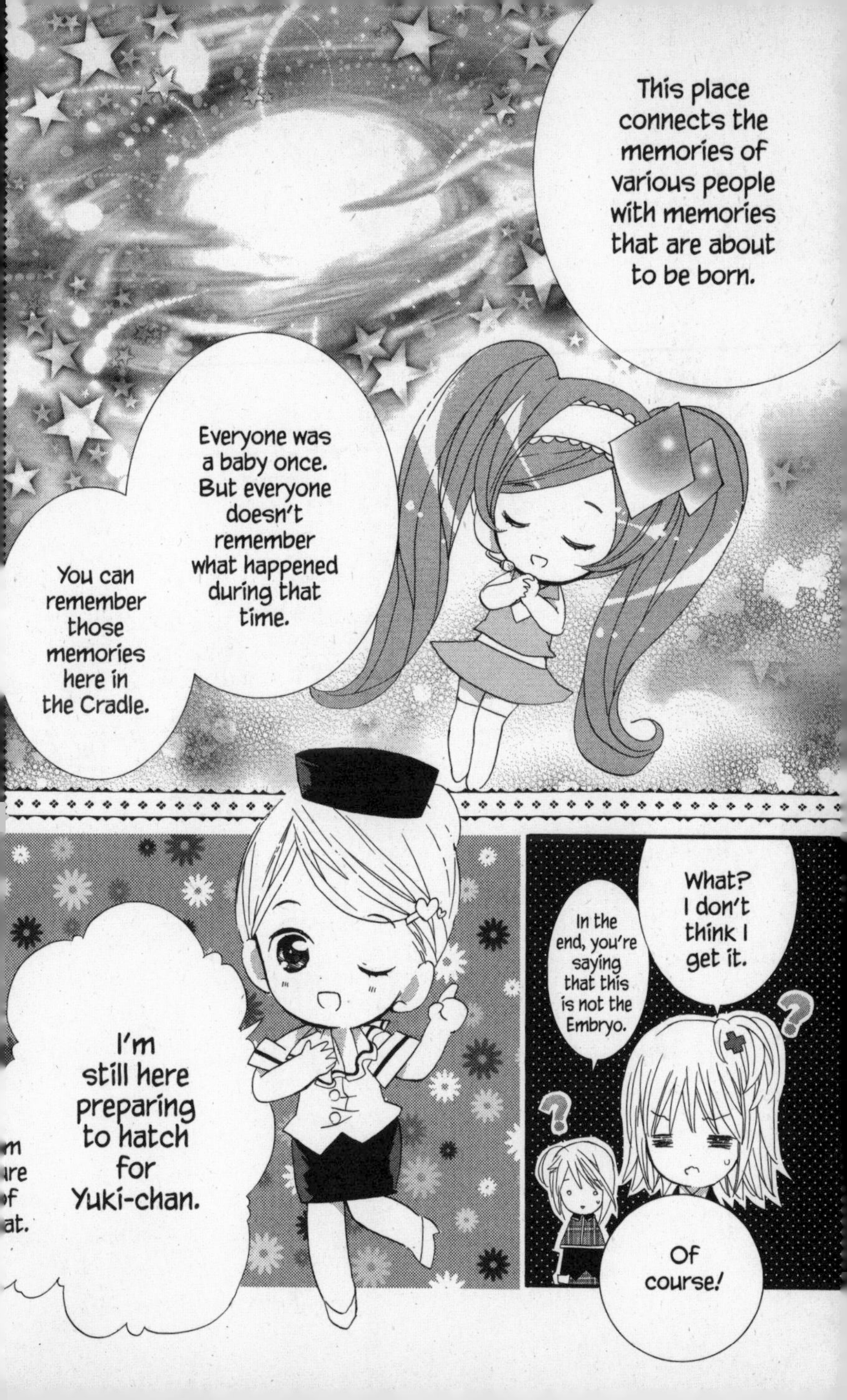
This place connects the memories of various people with memories that are about to be born.
Everyone was a baby once. But everyone doesn't remember what happened during that time.
You can remember those memories here in the Cradle.
What? I don't think I get it.
In the end, you're saying that this is not the Embryo.
Of course!
I'm still here preparing to hatch for Yuki-chan.

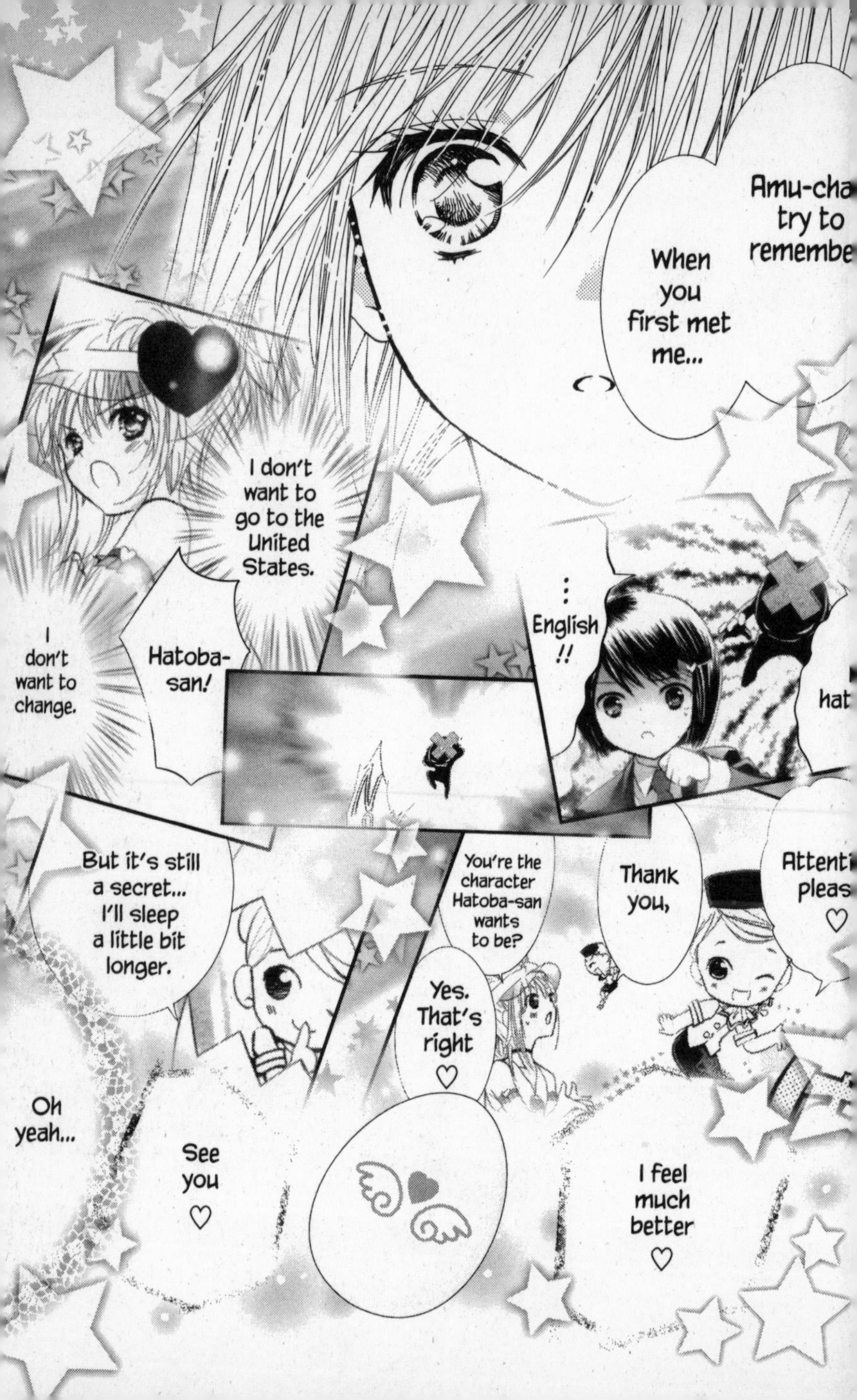
Amu-cha try to remembe
When you first met me...
hat
...English !!
I don't want to go to the United States.
Hatoba-san!
I don't want to change.
Attenti pleas ♡
Thank you,
You're the character Hatoba-san wants to be?
Yes. That's right ♡
But it's still a secret... I'll sleep a little bit longer.
I feel much better ♡
See you ♡
Oh yeah...

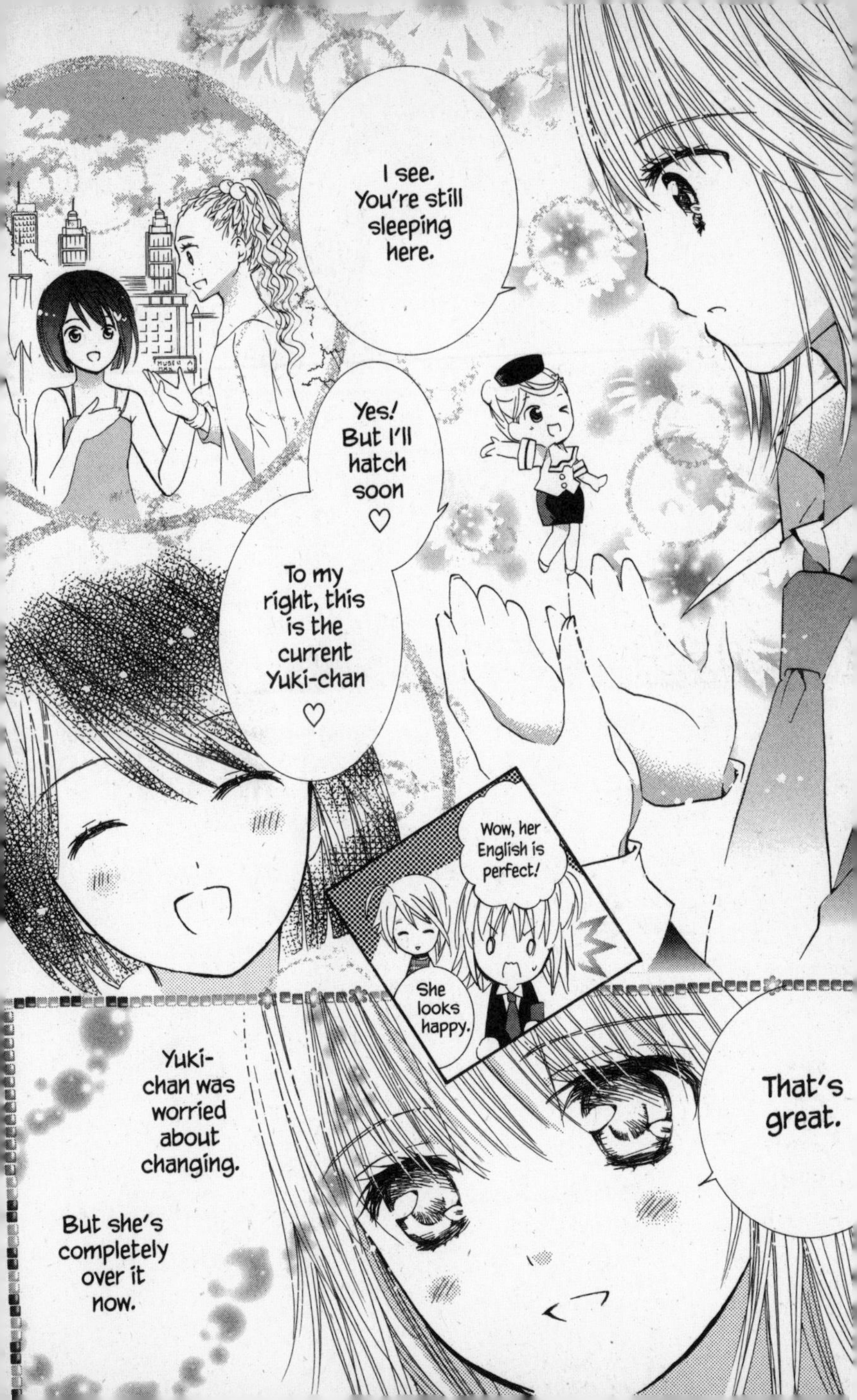
I see. You're still sleeping here.
Yes! But I'll hatch soon ♡
To my right, this is the current Yuki-chan ♡
Wow, her English is perfect!
She looks happy.
That's great.
Yuki-chan was worried about changing.
But she's completely over it now.

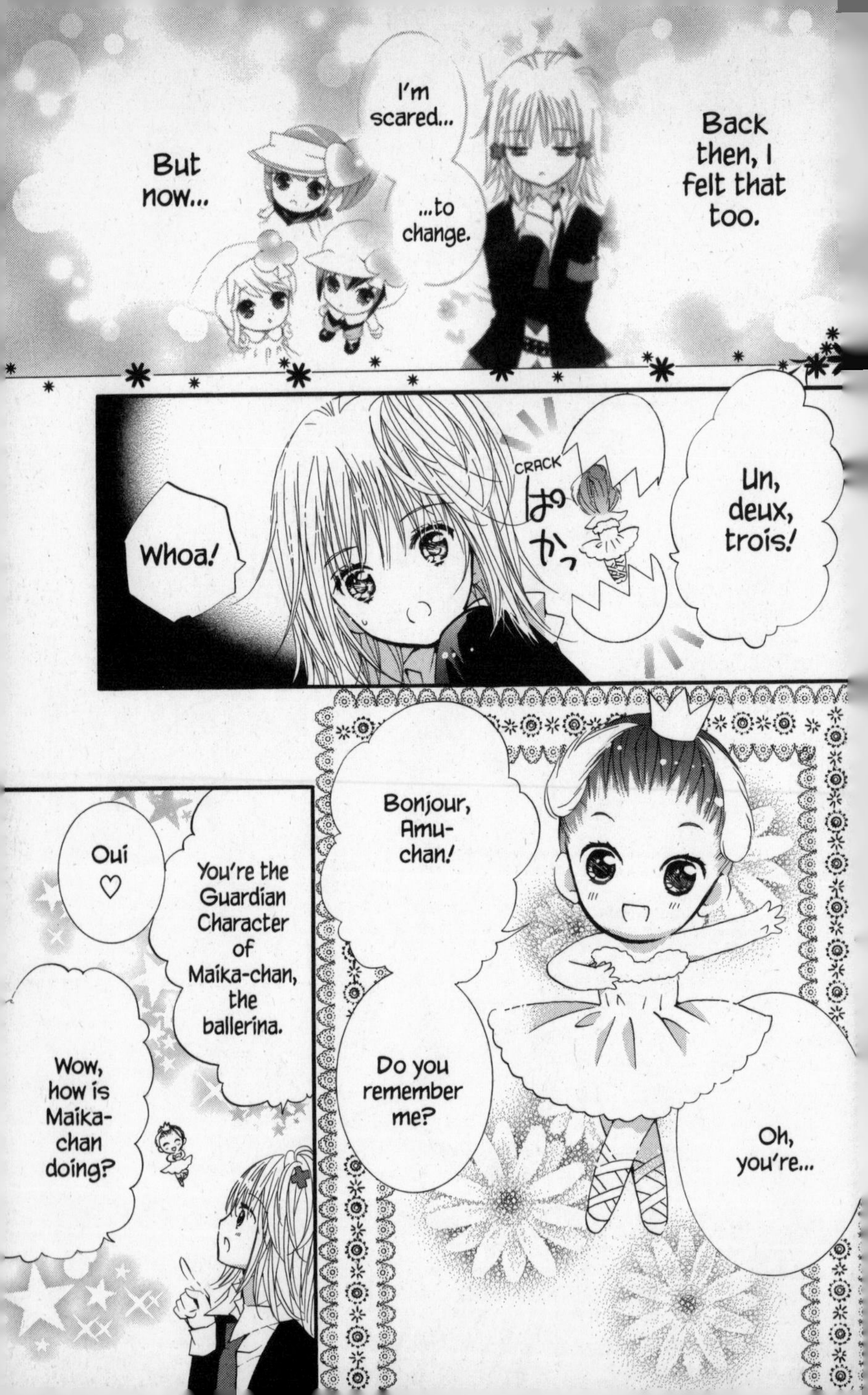

Back then, I felt that too.
I'm scared...
...to change.
But now...
Un, deux, trois!
CRACK
ぱかっ
Whoa!
Bonjour, Amu-chan!
Do you remember me?
Oh, you're...
You're the Guardian Character of Maika-chan, the ballerina.
Oui ♡
Wow, how is Maika-chan doing?

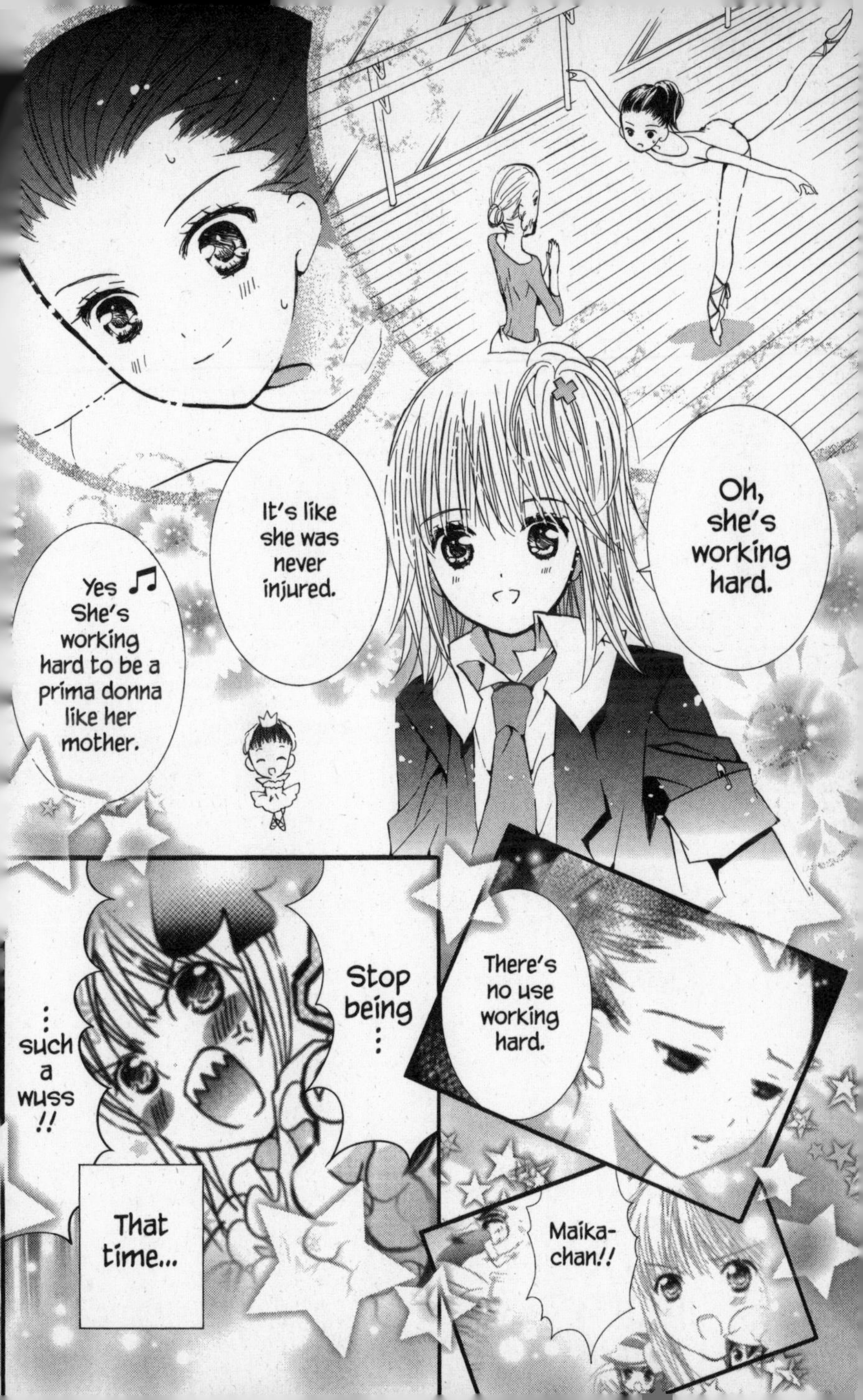
Oh, she's working hard.
It's like she was never injured.
Yes ♫ She's working hard to be a prima donna like her mother.
There's no use working hard.
Maika-chan!!
Stop being...
...such a wuss!!
That time...

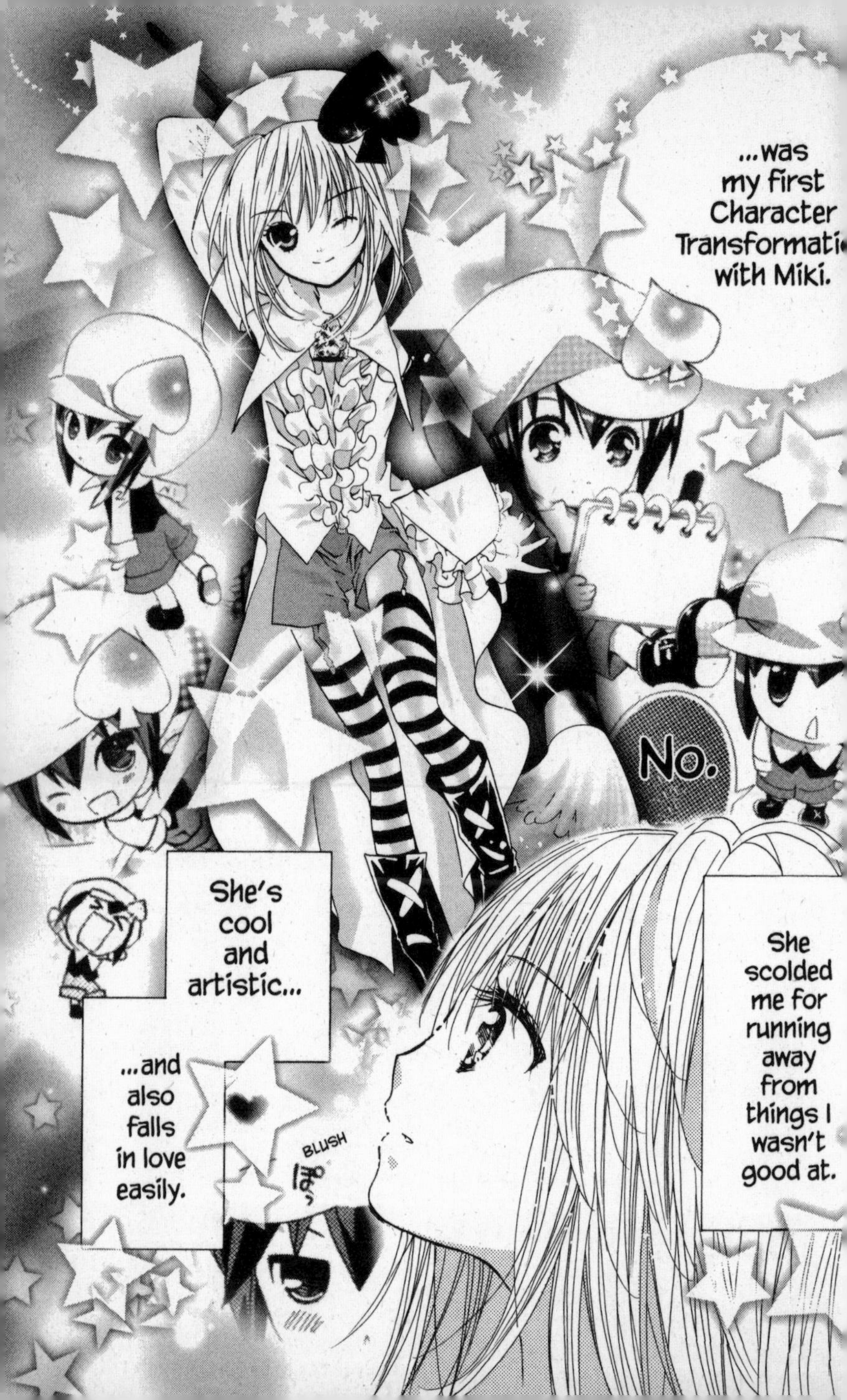
...was my first Character Transformati with Miki.
No.
She scolded me for running away from things I wasn't good at.
She's cool and artistic...
...and also falls in love easily.
BLUSH

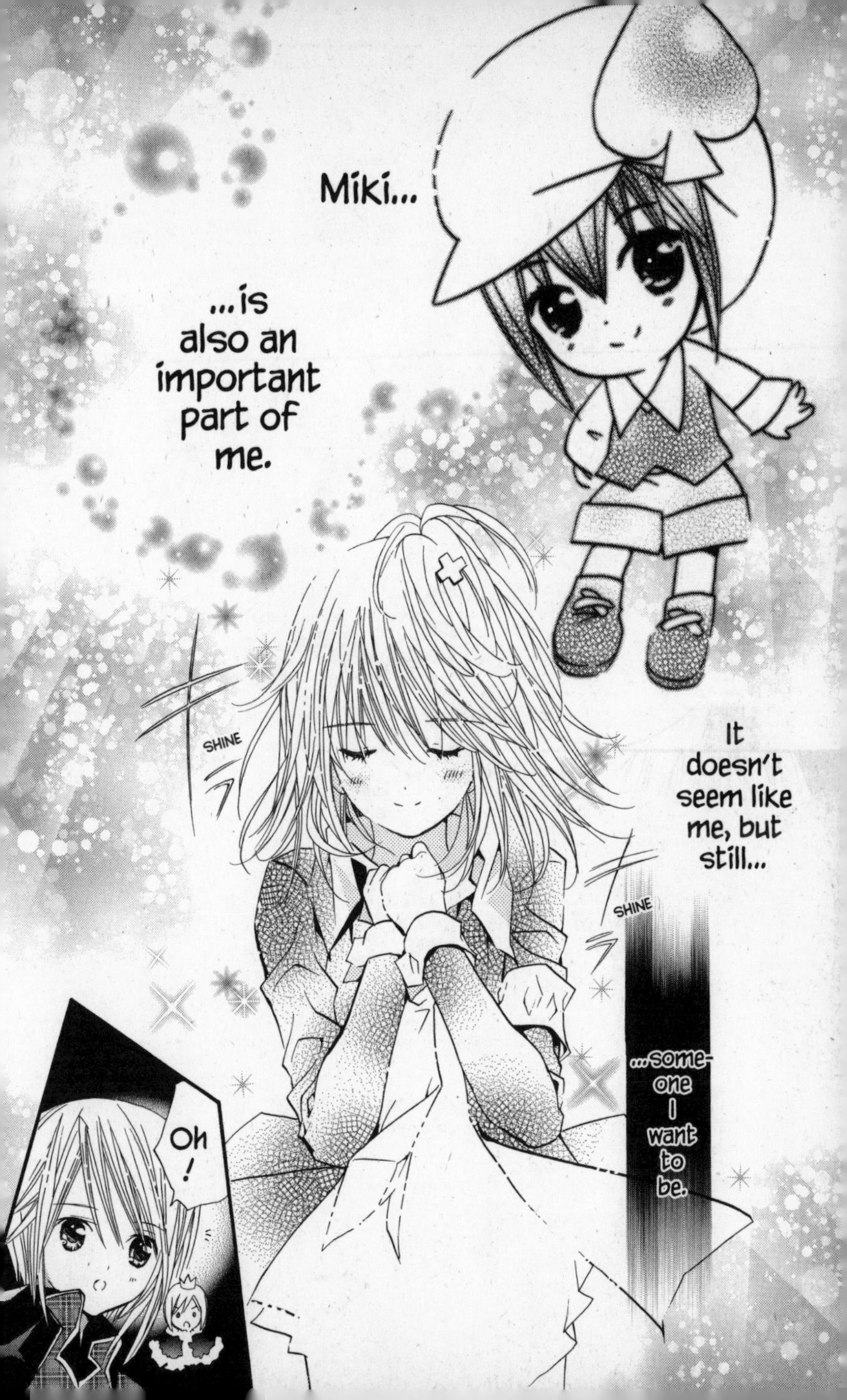
Miki...
...is also an important part of me.
It doesn't seem like me, but still...
SHINE
SHINE
...some-one I want to be.
Oh!

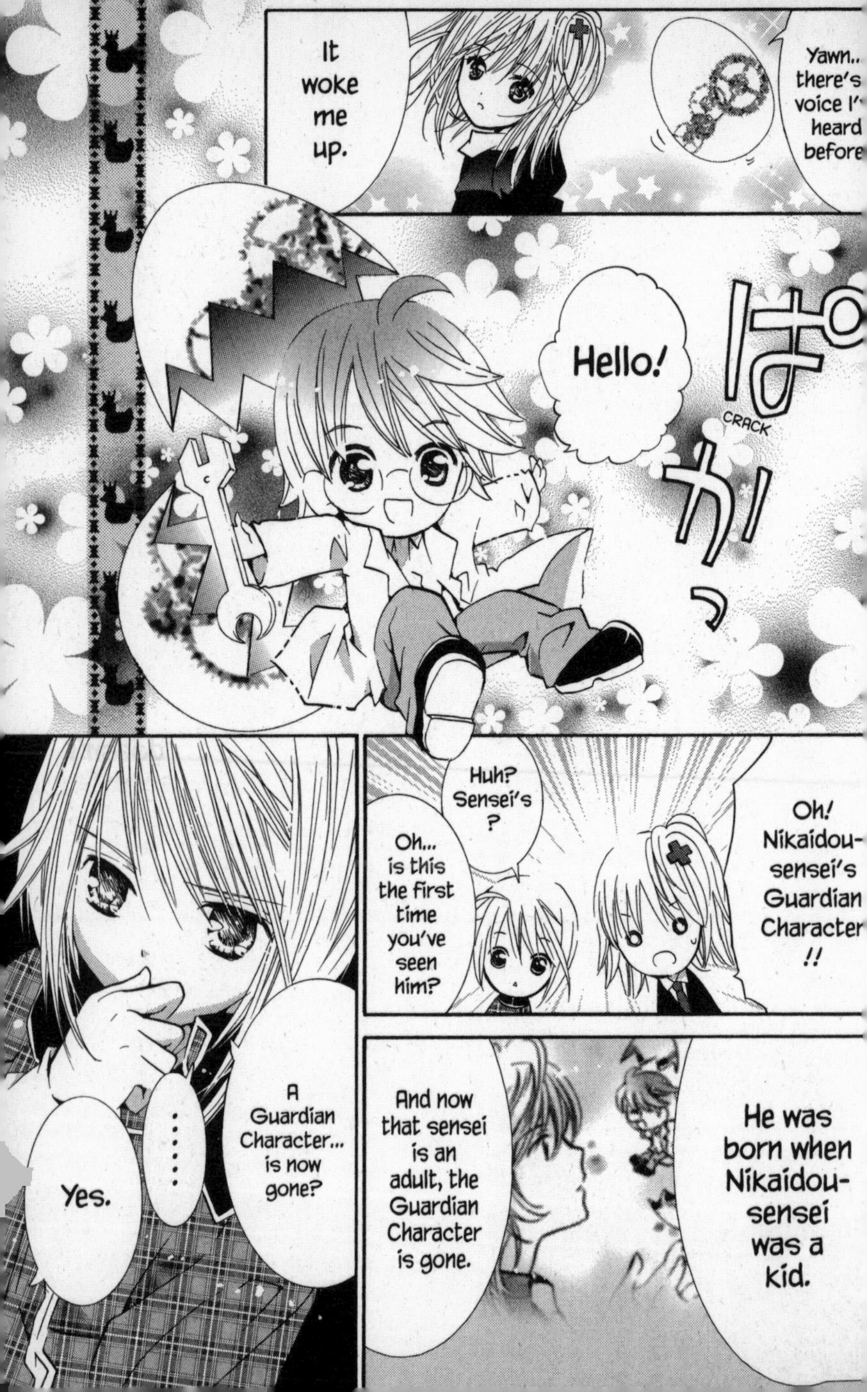

Yawn.. there's voice I' heard before
It woke me up.
ぱかっ
CRACK
Hello!
Oh! Nikaidou-sensei's Guardian Character !!
Huh? Sensei's ?
Oh... is this the first time you've seen him?
He was born when Nikaidou-sensei was a kid.
And now that sensei is an adult, the Guardian Character is gone.
A Guardian Character... is now gone?
......
Yes.

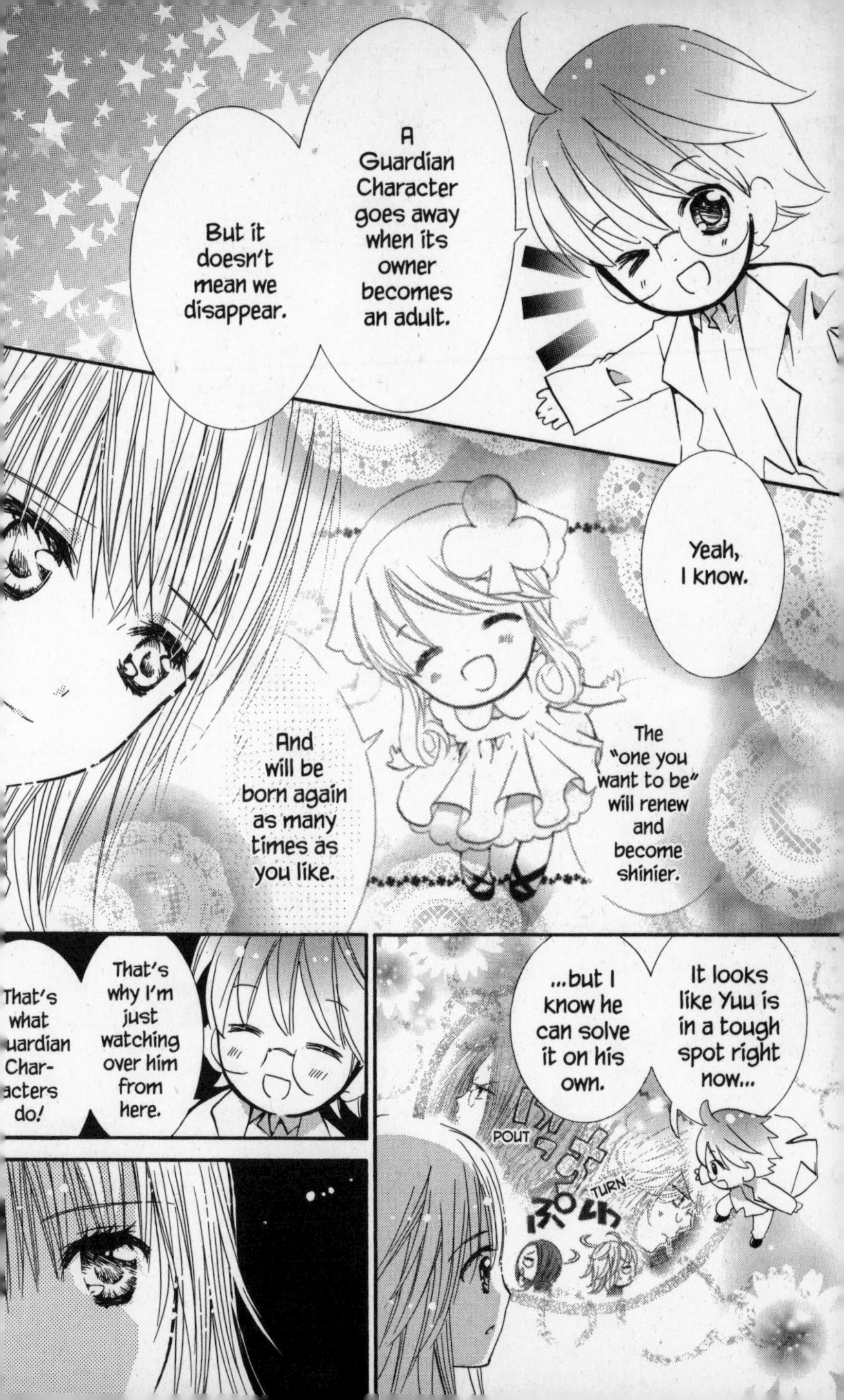
A Guardian Character goes away when its owner becomes an adult.
But it doesn't mean we disappear.
Yeah, I know.
The "one you want to be" will renew and become shinier.
And will be born again as many times as you like.
It looks like Yuu is in a tough spot right now...
...but I know he can solve it on his own.
POUT
TURN
That's why I'm just watching over him from here.
That's what uardian Char- acters do!

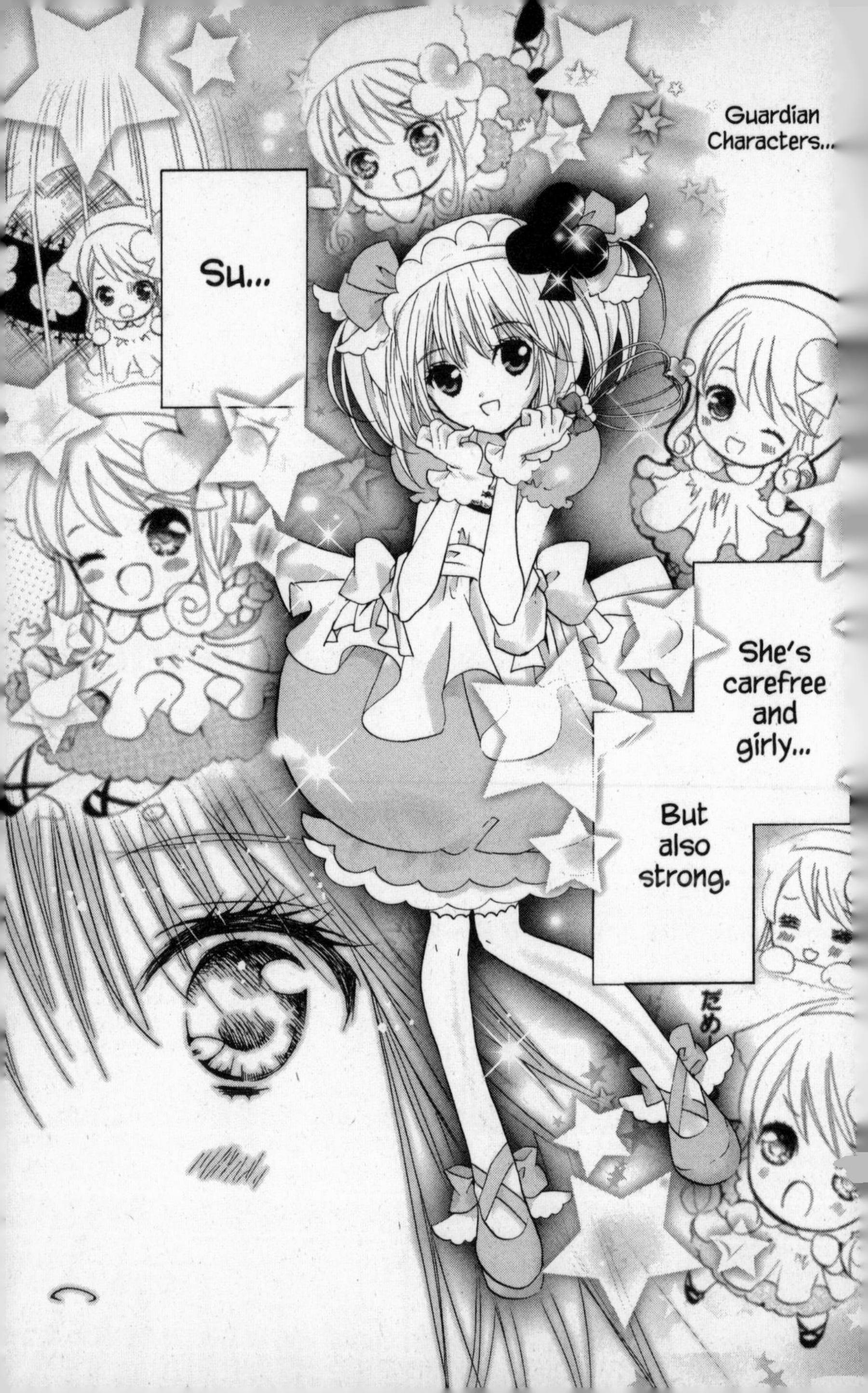
Guardian Characters...
Su...
She's carefree and girly...
But also strong.
だめー

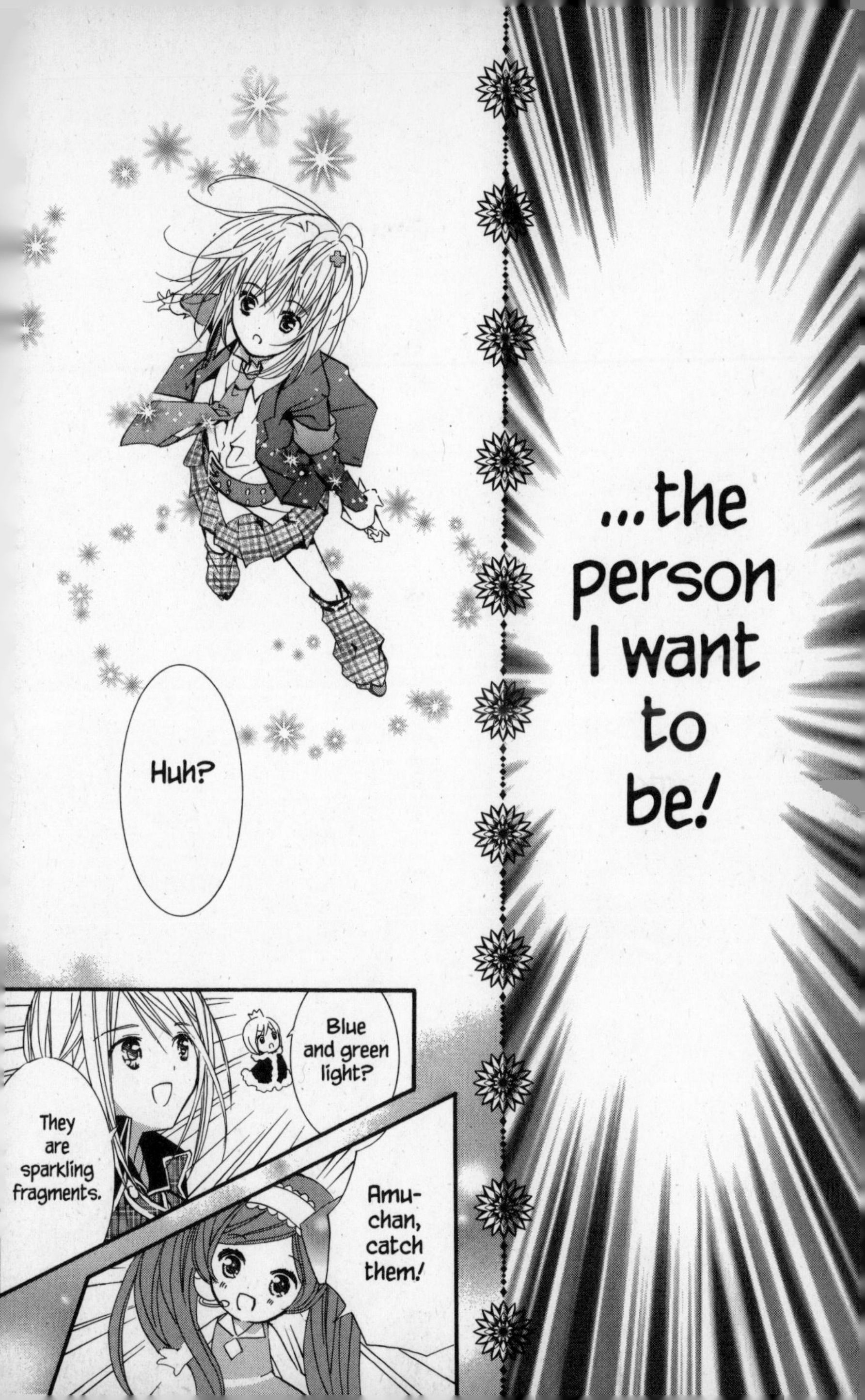
...the person I want to be!
Huh?
Blue and green light?
They are sparkling fragments.
Amu-chan, catch them!

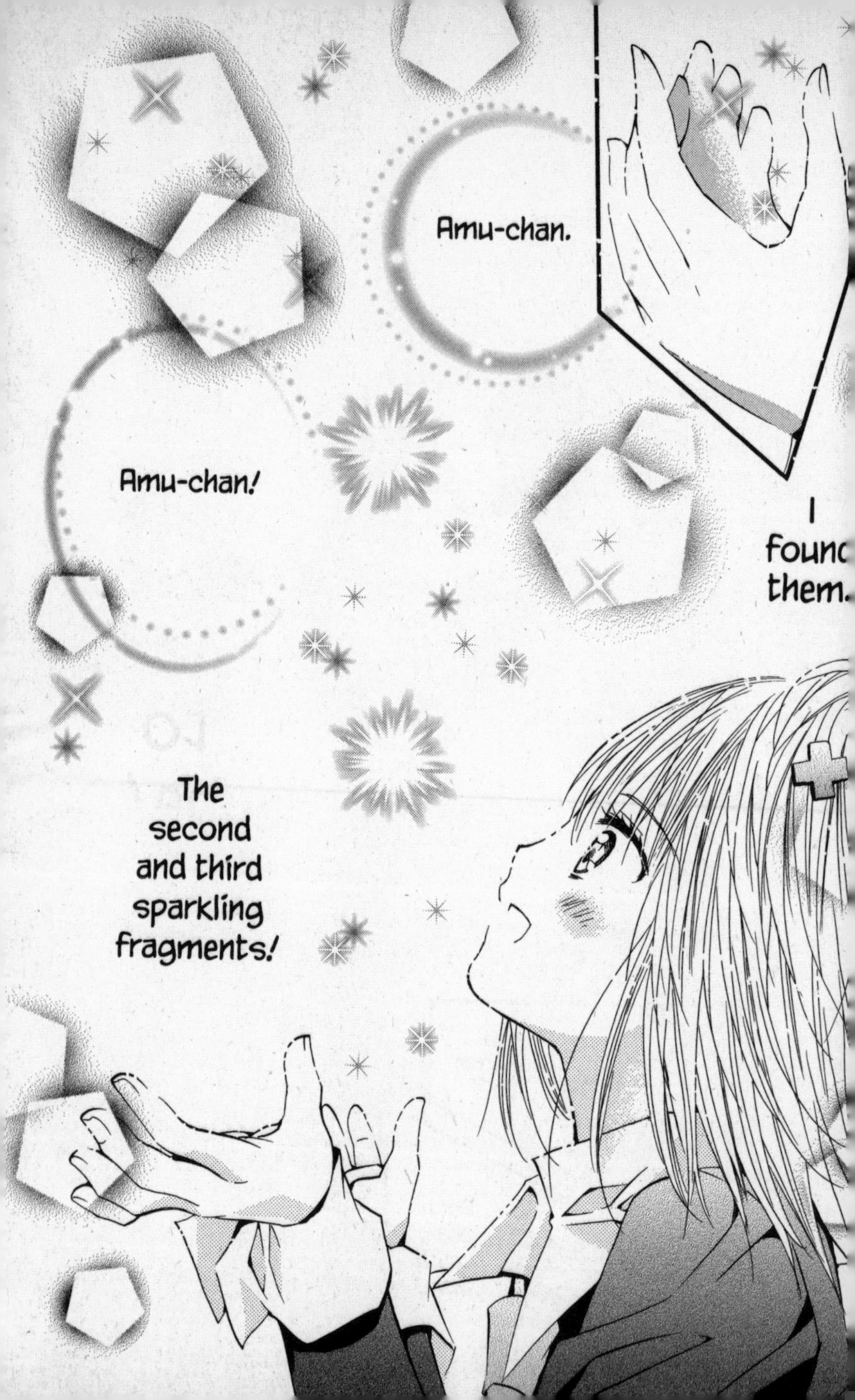
Amu-chan.
Amu-chan!
I found them.
The second and third sparkling fragments!

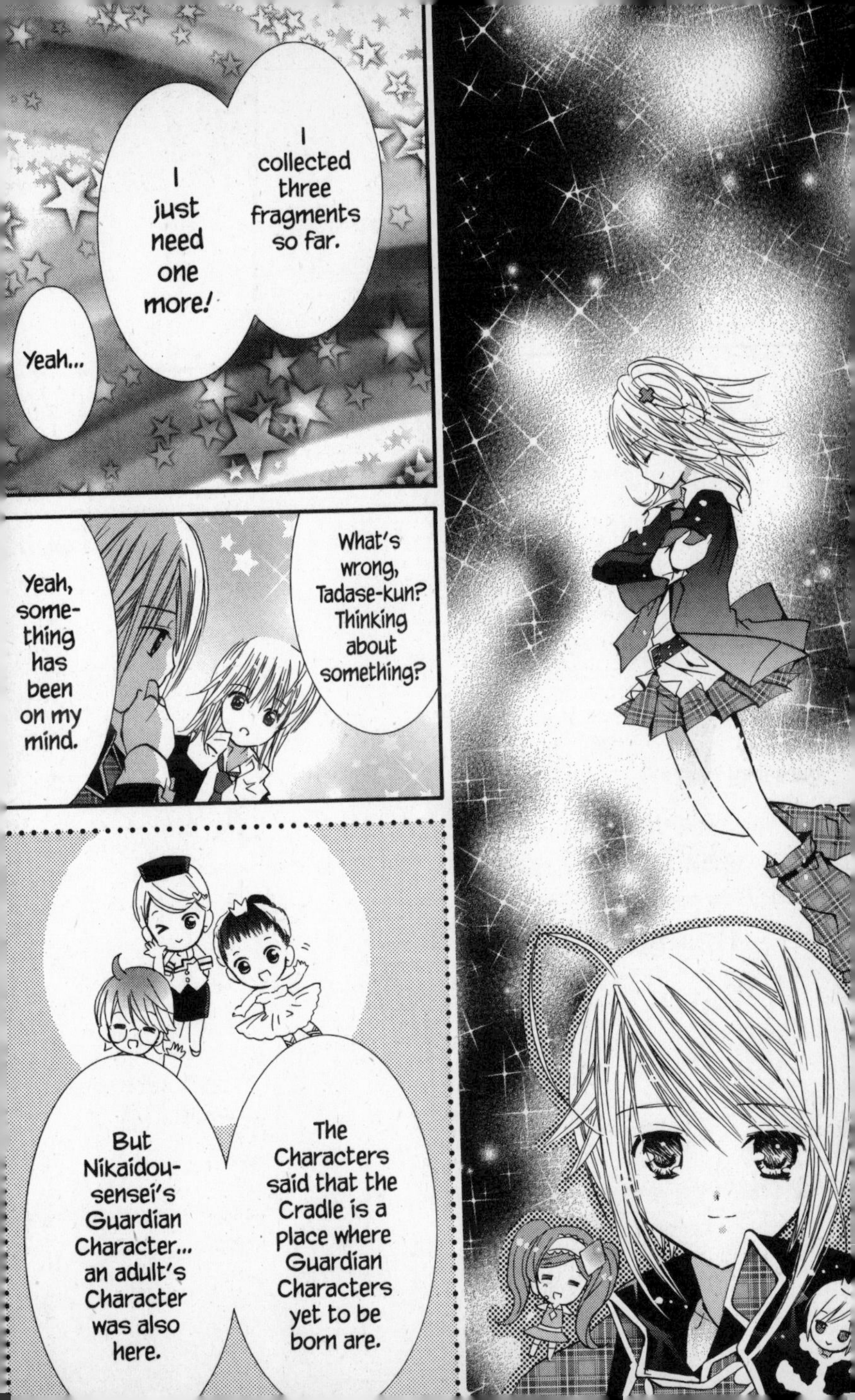
I collected three fragments so far.
I just need one more!
Yeah...
What's wrong, Tadase-kun? Thinking about something?
Yeah, something has been on my mind.
The Characters said that the Cradle is a place where Guardian Characters yet to be born are.
But Nikaidou-sensei's Guardian Character... an adult's Character was also here.

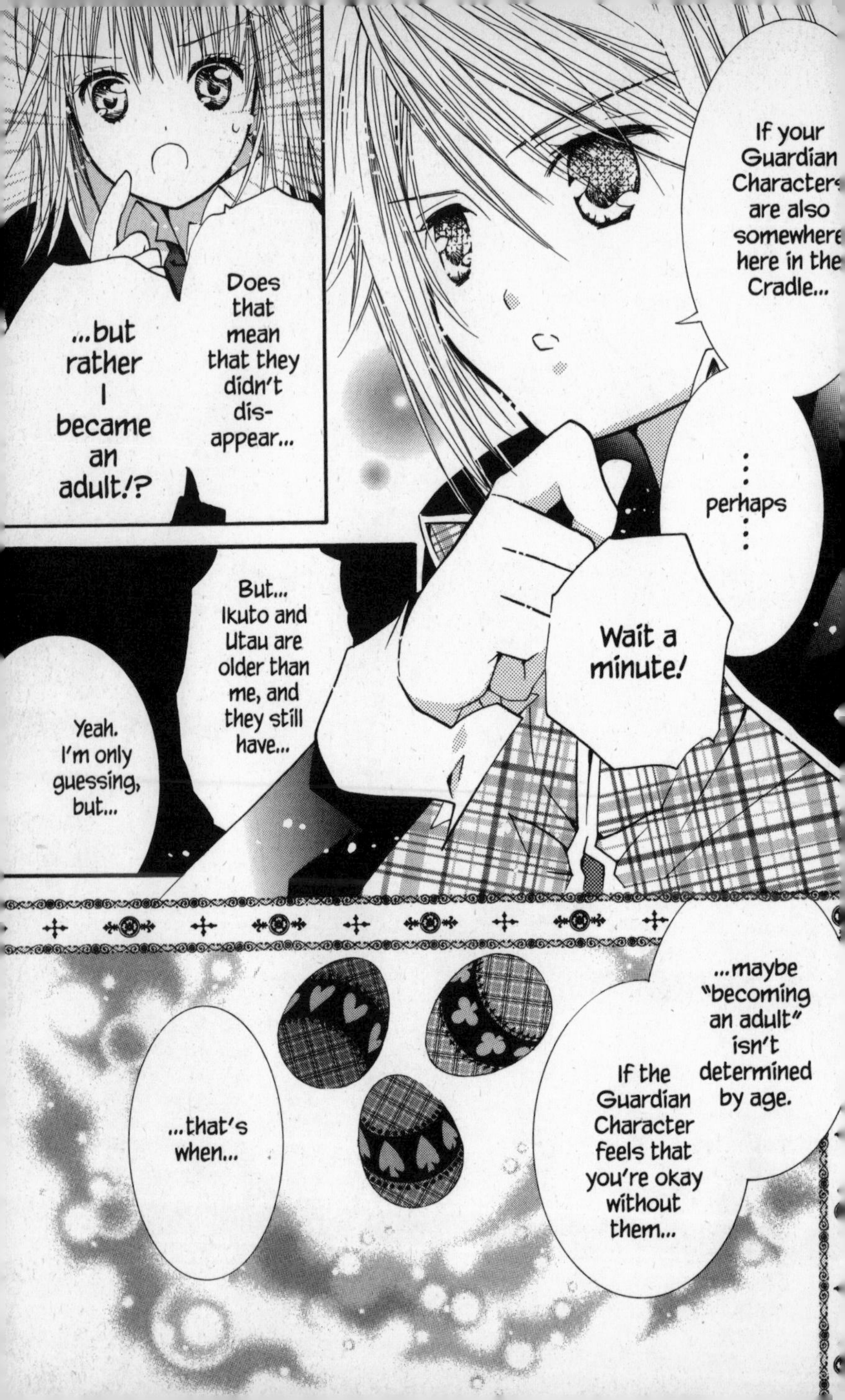
If your Guardian Characters are also somewhere here in the Cradle...
...perhaps...
Wait a minute!
Does that mean that they didn't dis-appear...
...but rather I became an adult!?
But... Ikuto and Utau are older than me, and they still have...
Yeah. I'm only guessing, but...
...maybe "becoming an adult" isn't determined by age.
If the Guardian Character feels that you're okay without them...
...that's when...

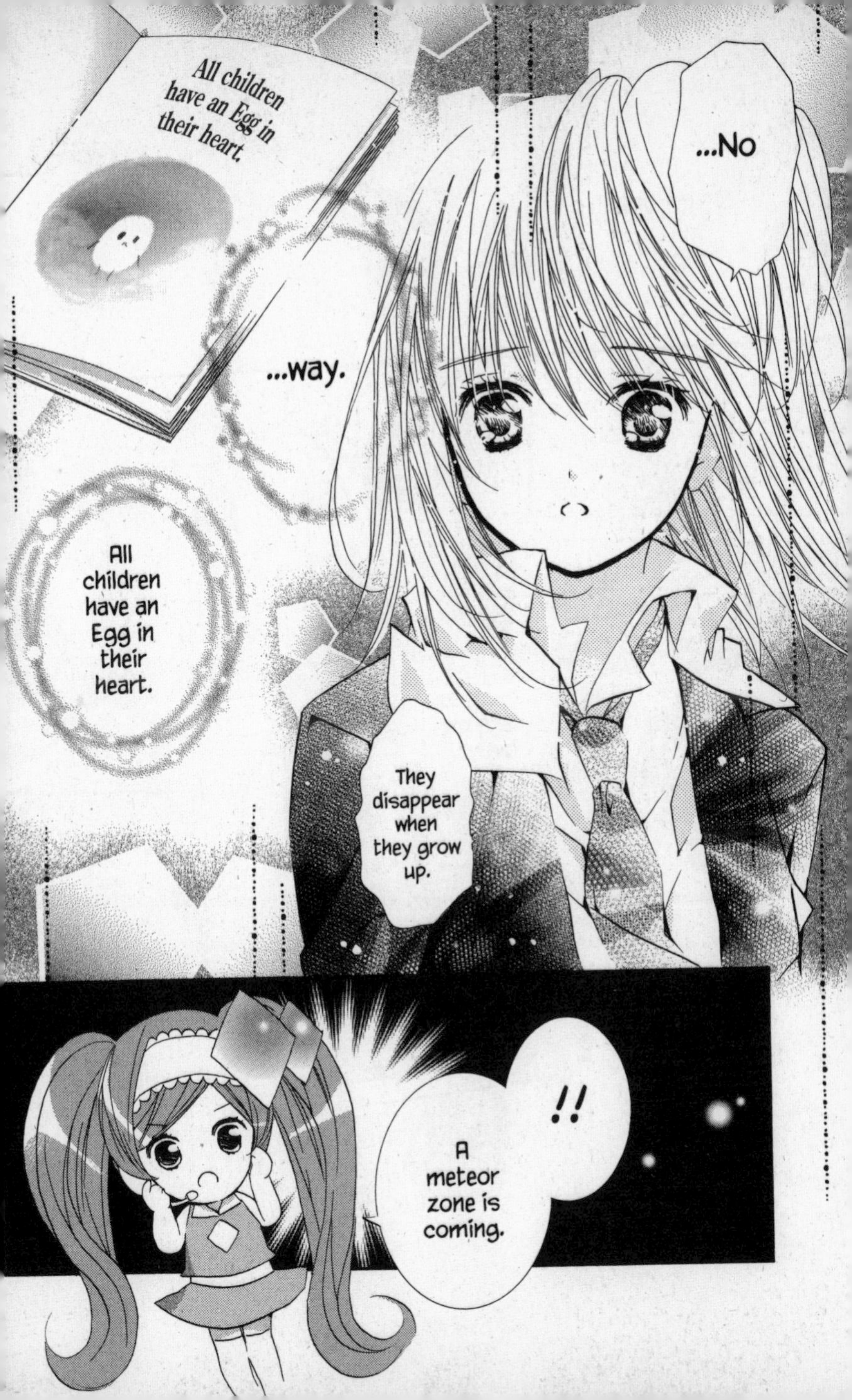
...No
...way.
All children have an Egg in their heart.
All children have an Egg in their heart.
They disappear when they grow up.
!!
A meteor zone is coming.

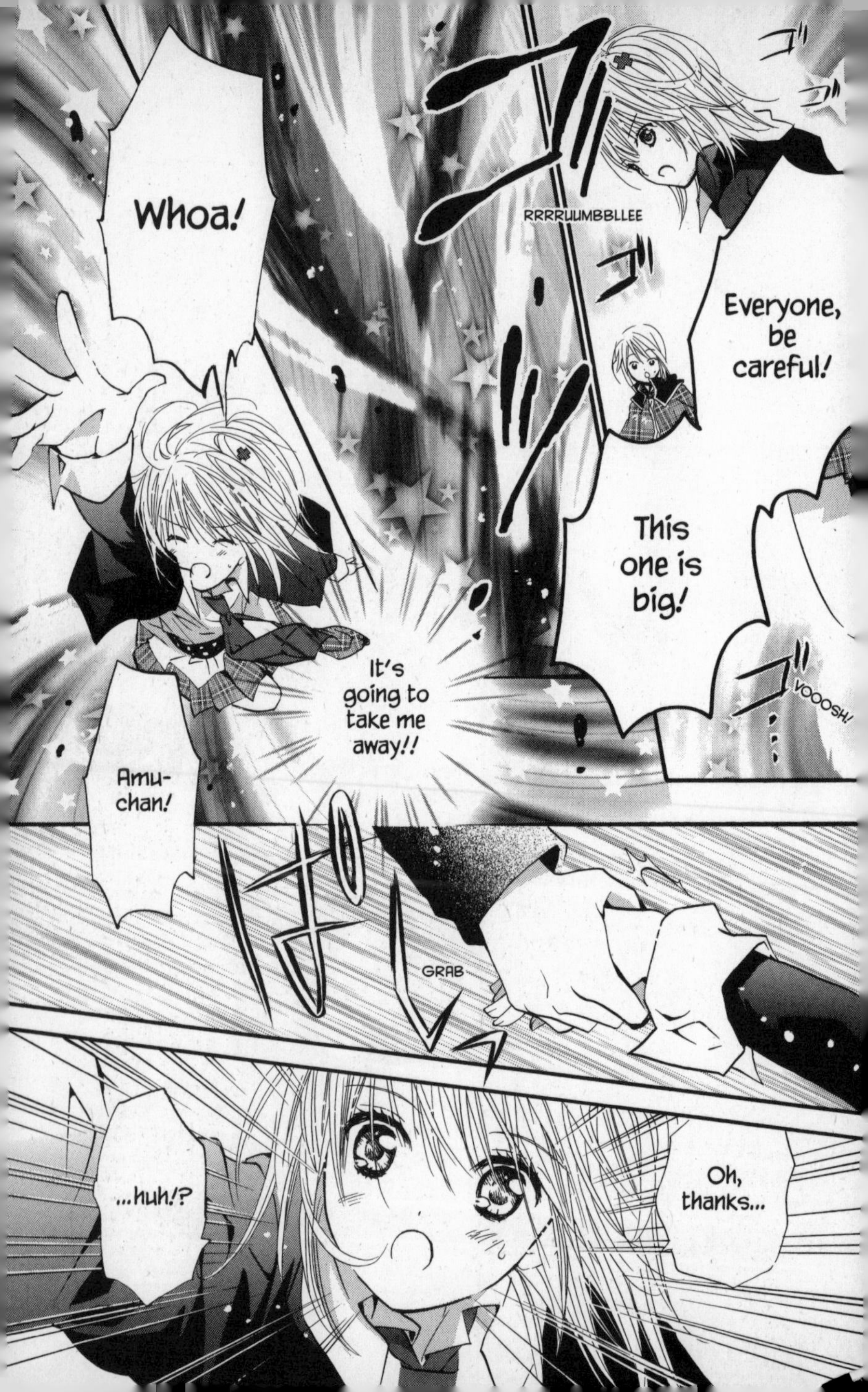
RRRRUUMBBLLEE
Everyone, be careful!
This one is big!
VOOOSH!
Whoa!
It's going to take me away!!
Amu-chan!
GRAB
Oh, thanks...
...huh!?

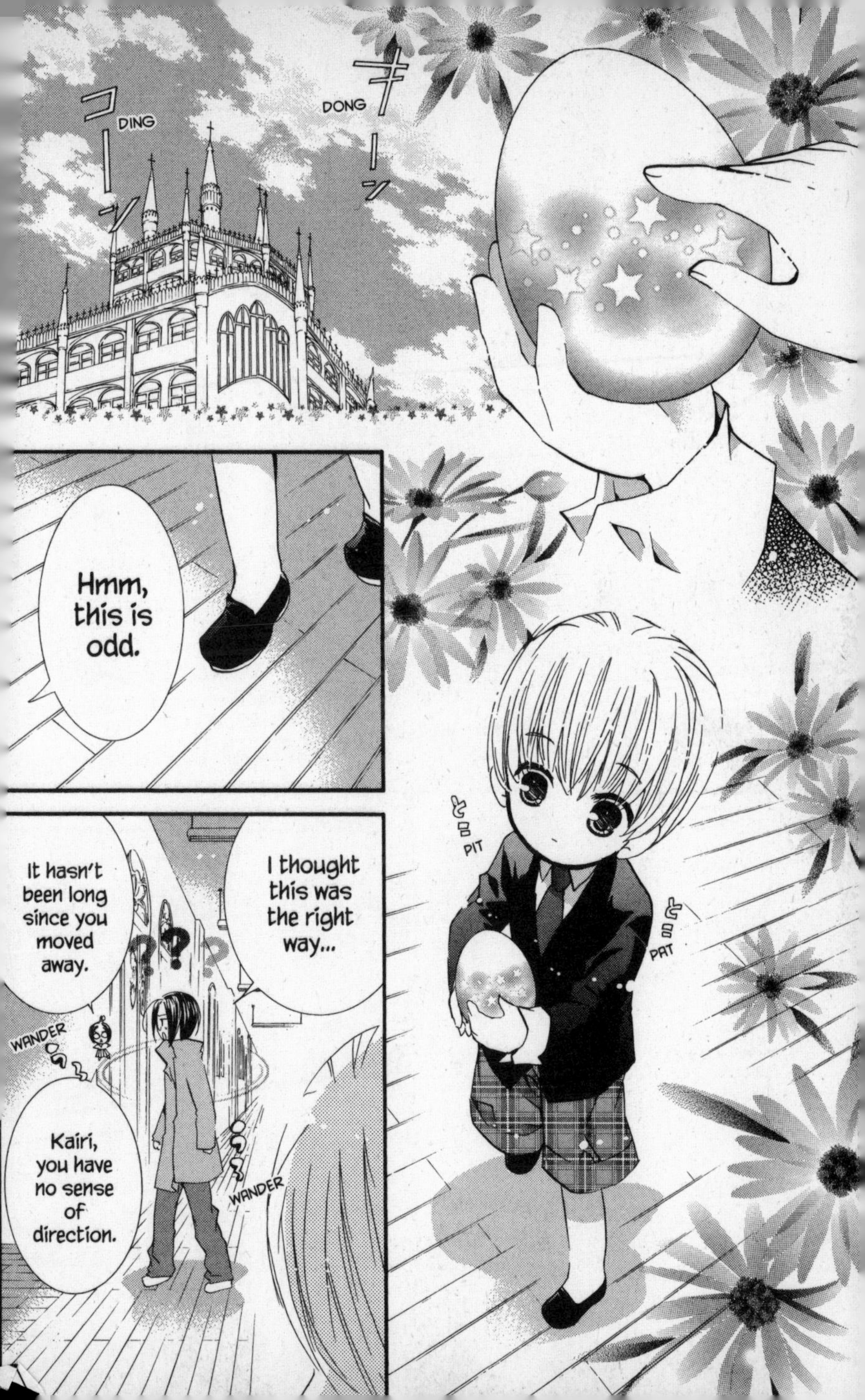

DONG
DING
PIT
PAT
Hmm, this is odd.
I thought this was the right way...
It hasn't been long since you moved away.
WANDER
Kairi, you have no sense of direction.
WANDER

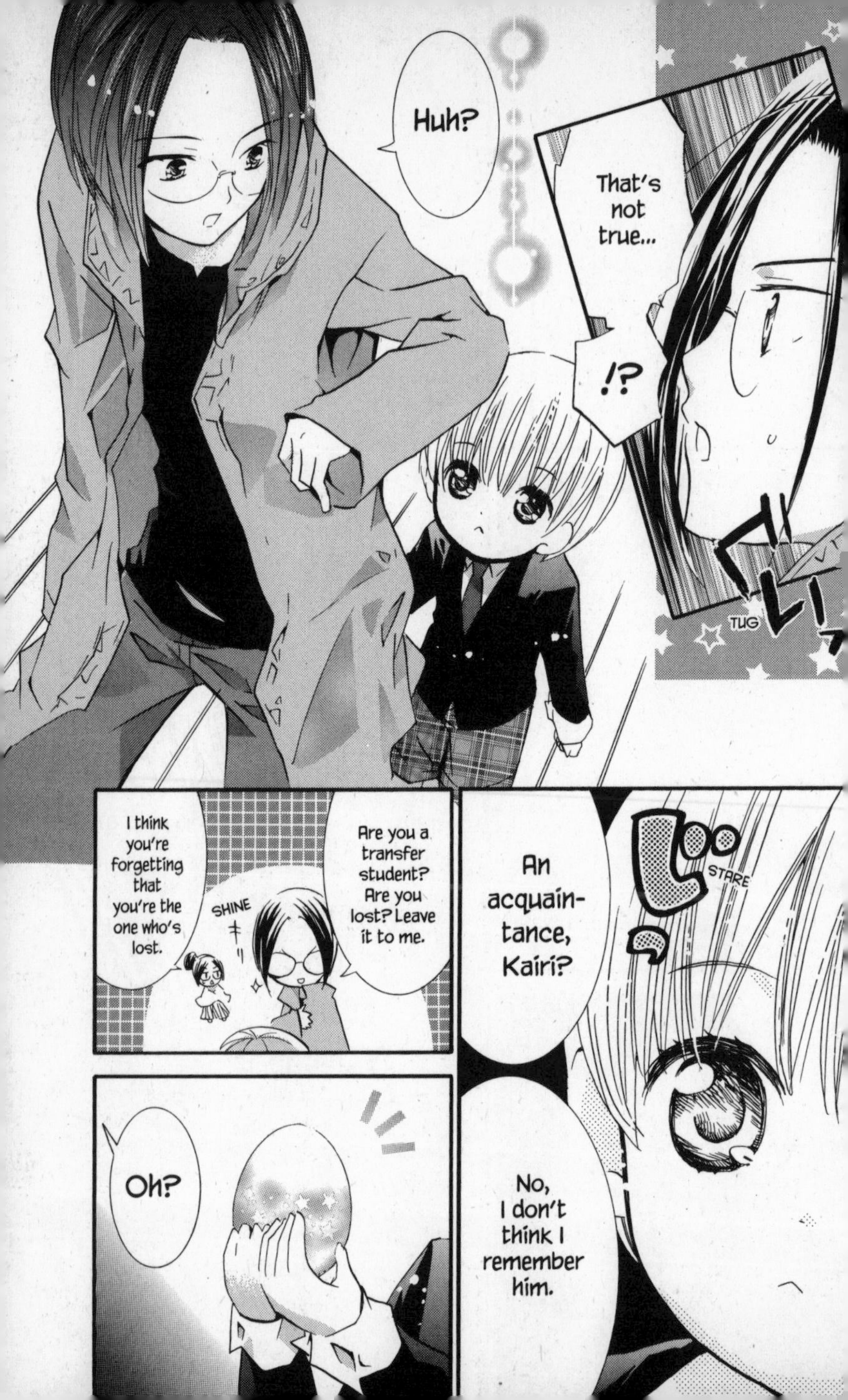

That's not true...
!?
TUG
Huh?
An acquaintance, Kairi?
STARE
No, I don't think I remember him.
Are you a transfer student? Are you lost? Leave it to me.
SHINE
I think you're forgetting that you're the one who's lost.
Oh?

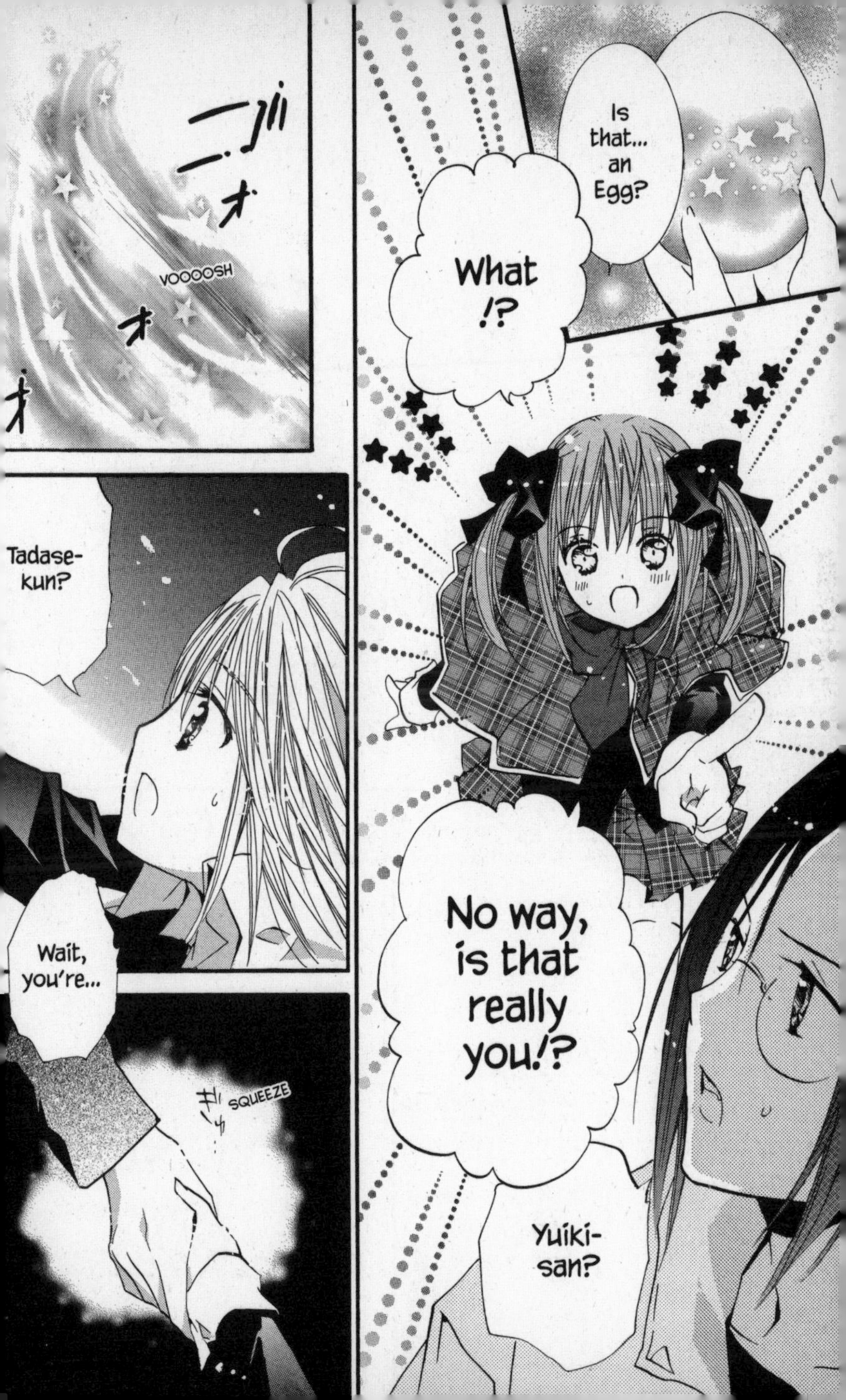
Is that... an Egg?
What!?
No way, is that really you!?
Yuiki-san?
VOOOOSH
Tadase-kun?
Wait, you're...
SQUEEZE

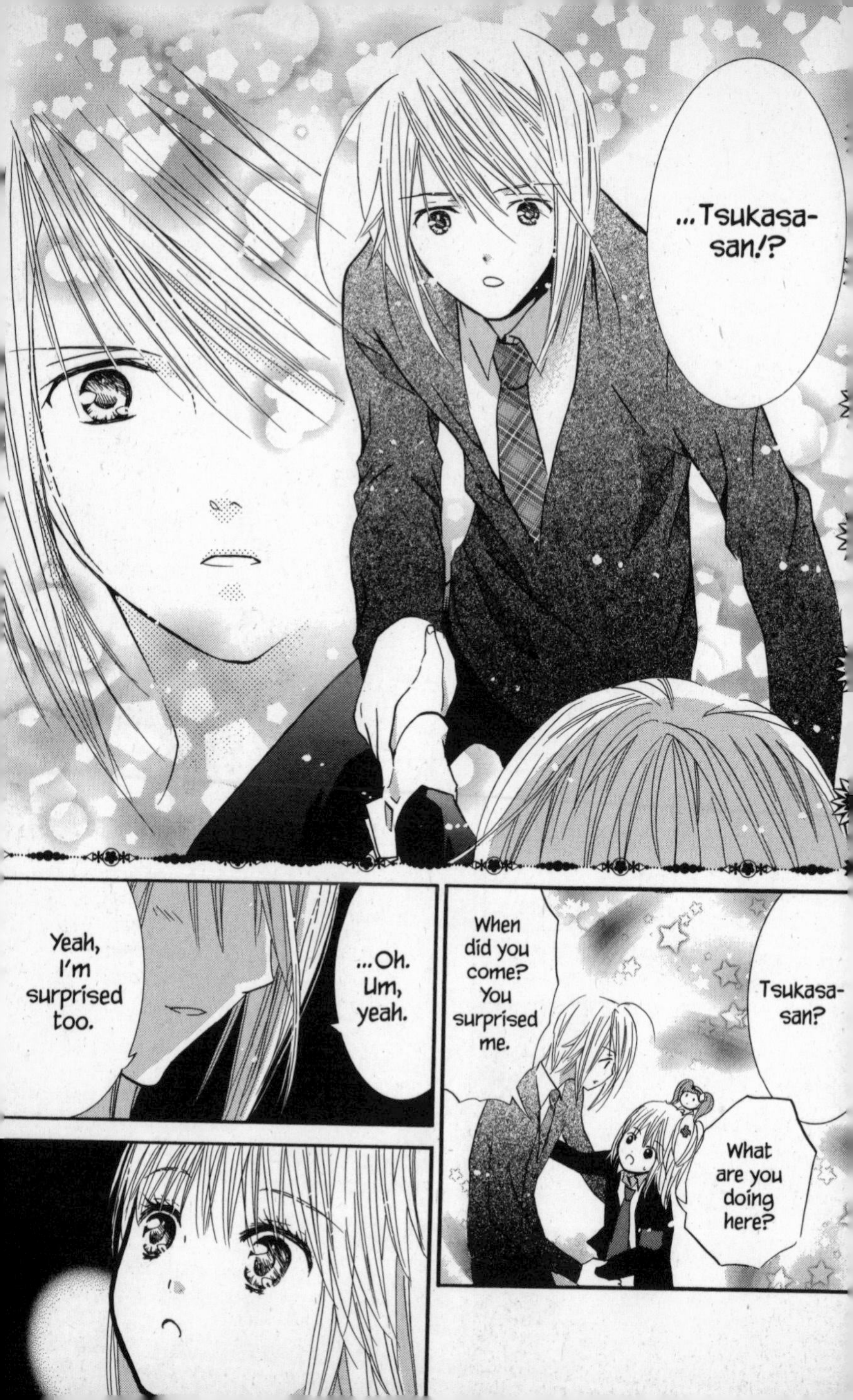
...Tsukasa-san!?
Tsukasa-san?
What are you doing here?
When did you come? You surprised me.
...Oh. Um, yeah.
Yeah, I'm surprised too.

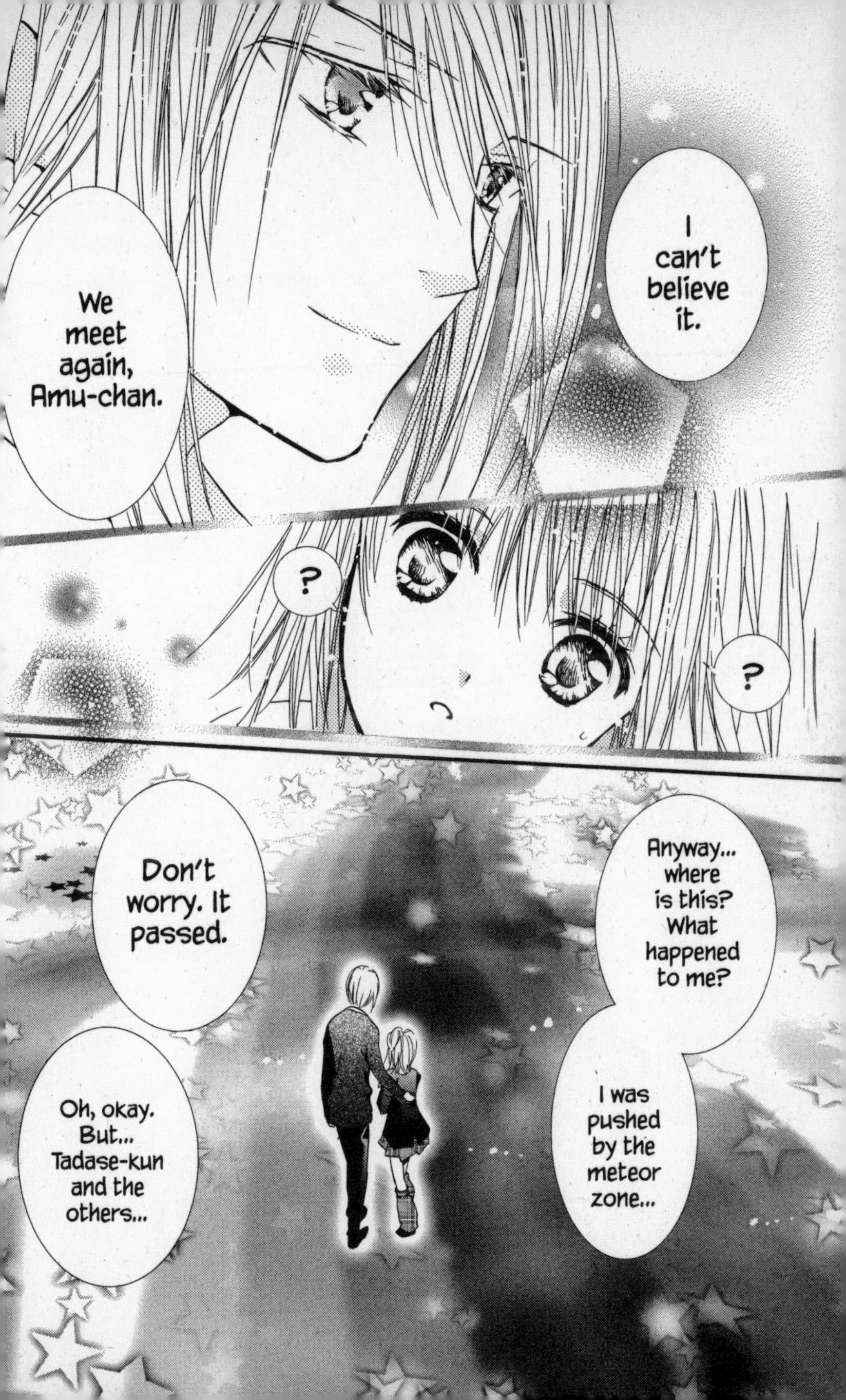
I can't believe it.
We meet again, Amu-chan.
?
?
Anyway... where is this? What happened to me?
Don't worry. It passed.
I was pushed by the meteor zone...
Oh, okay. But... Tadase-kun and the others...

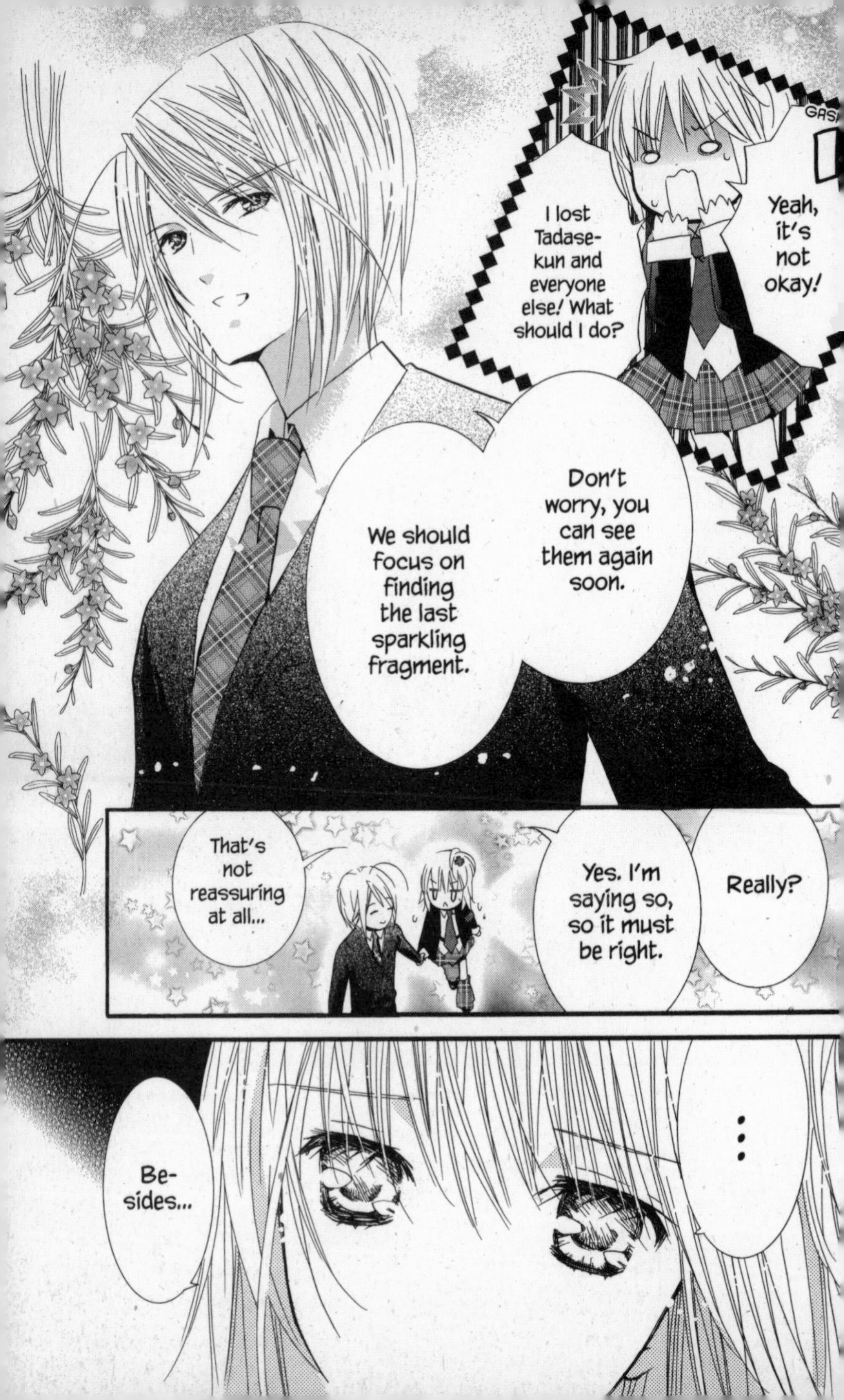
GAS
Yeah, it's not okay!
I lost Tadase-kun and everyone else! What should I do?
Don't worry, you can see them again soon.
We should focus on finding the last sparkling fragment.
Really?
Yes. I'm saying so, so it must be right.
That's not reassuring at all...
...
Besides...

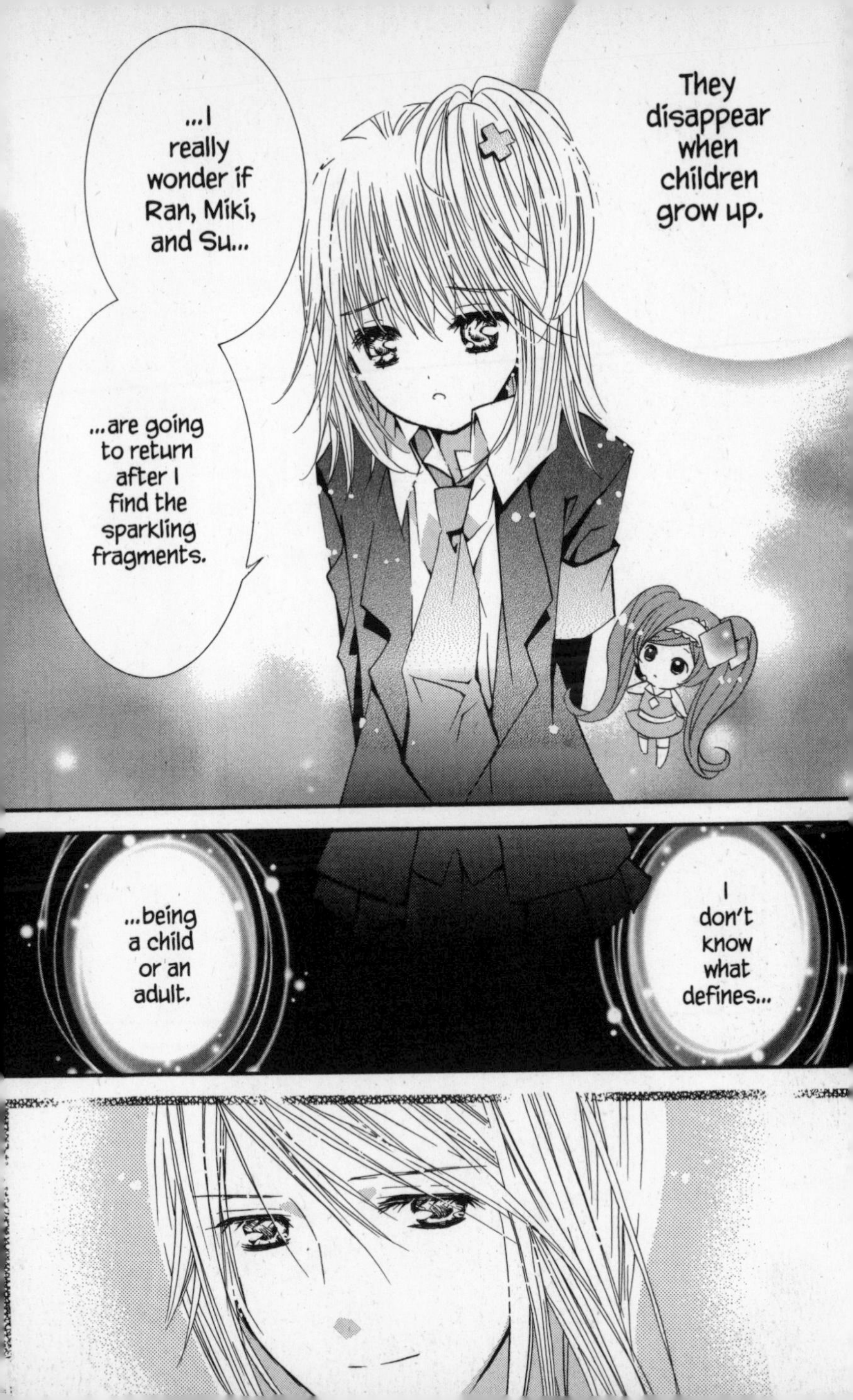

They disappear when children grow up.
...I really wonder if Ran, Miki, and Su...
...are going to return after I find the sparkling fragments.
I don't know what defines...
...being a child or an adult.

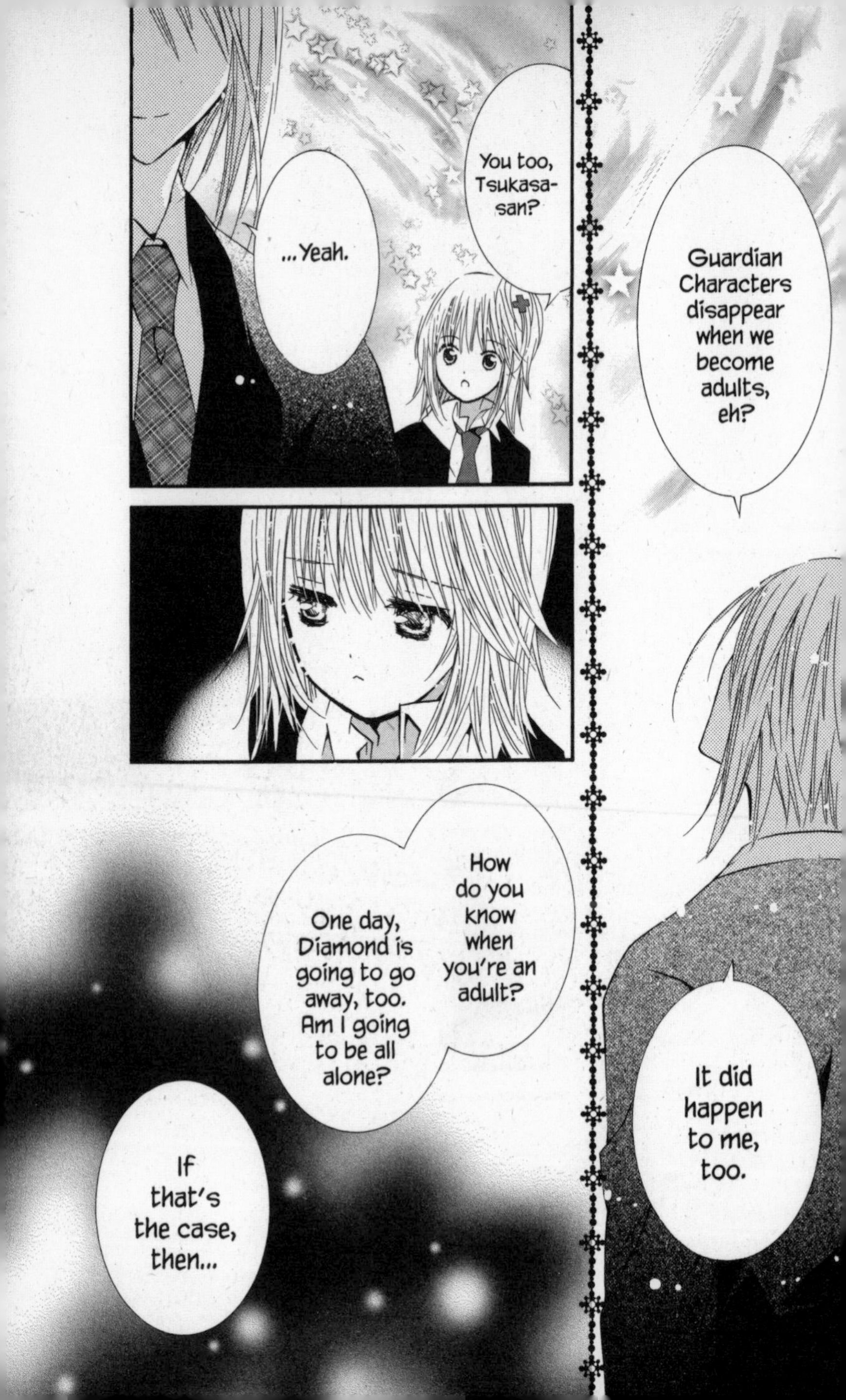
Guardian Characters disappear when we become adults, eh?
It did happen to me, too.
You too, Tsukasa-san?
...Yeah.
How do you know when you're an adult?
One day, Diamond is going to go away, too. Am I going to be all alone?
If that's the case, then...

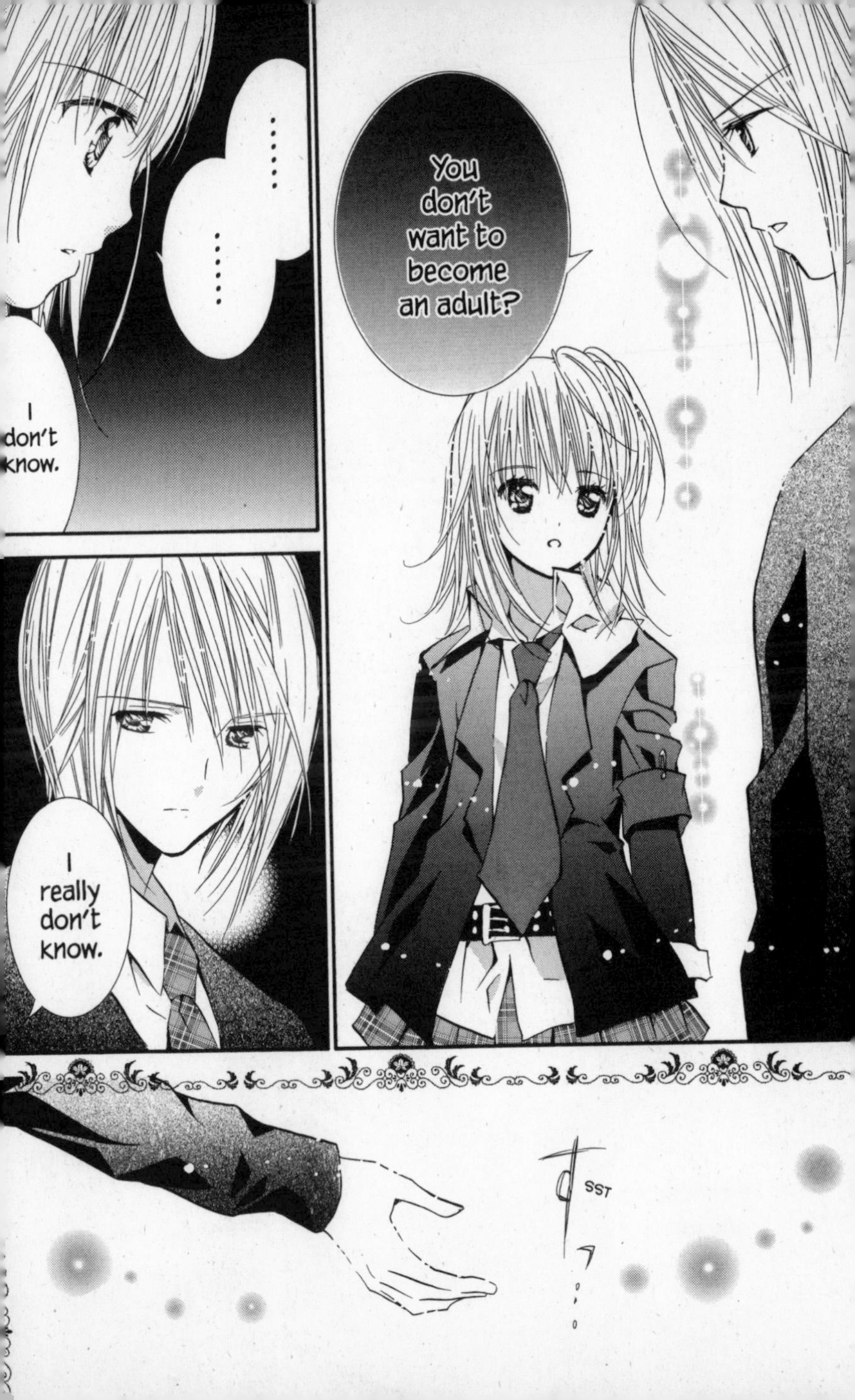
You don't want to become an adult?
......
......
I don't know.
I really don't know.
SST

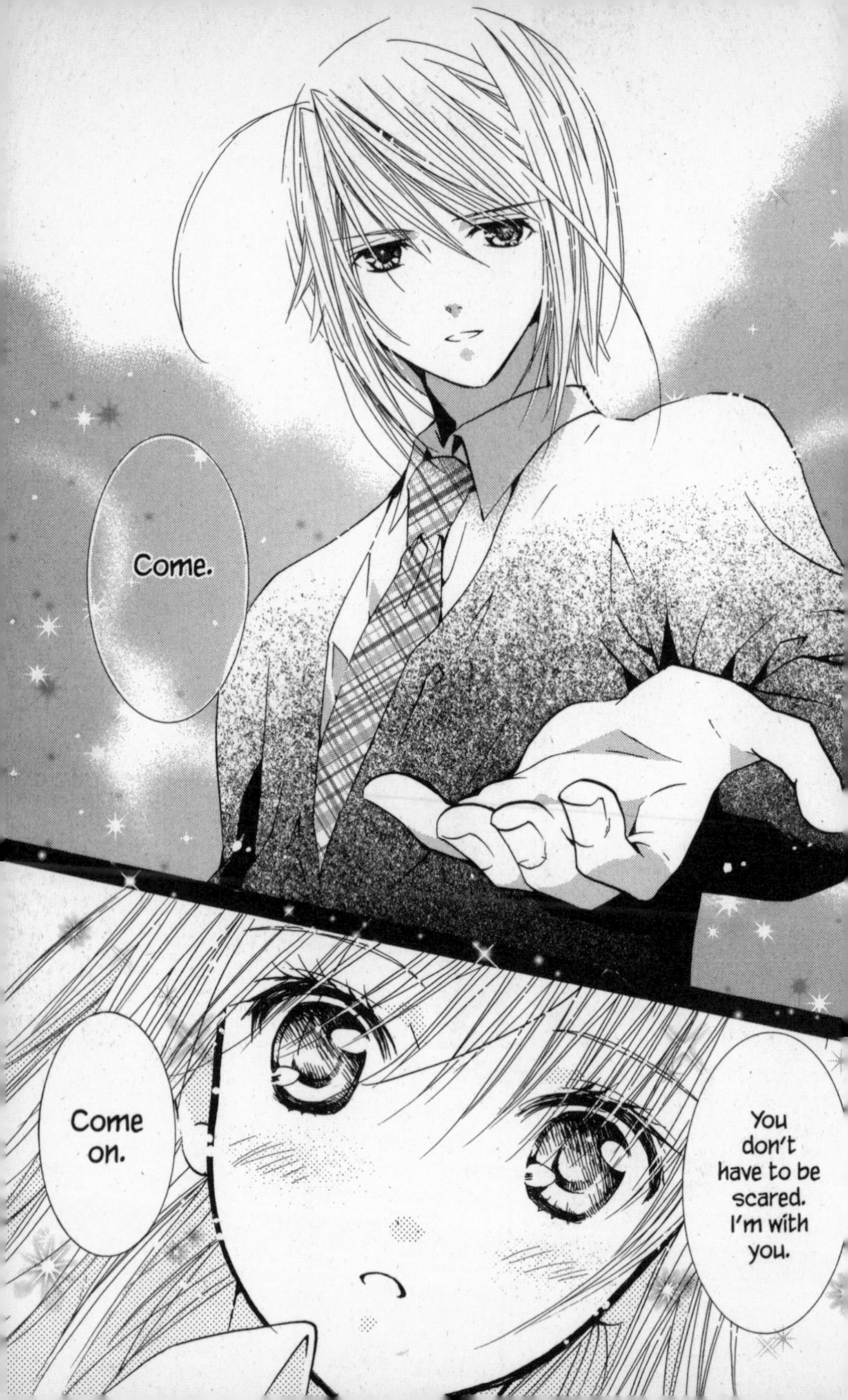
Come.
You don't have to be scared. I'm with you.
Come on.

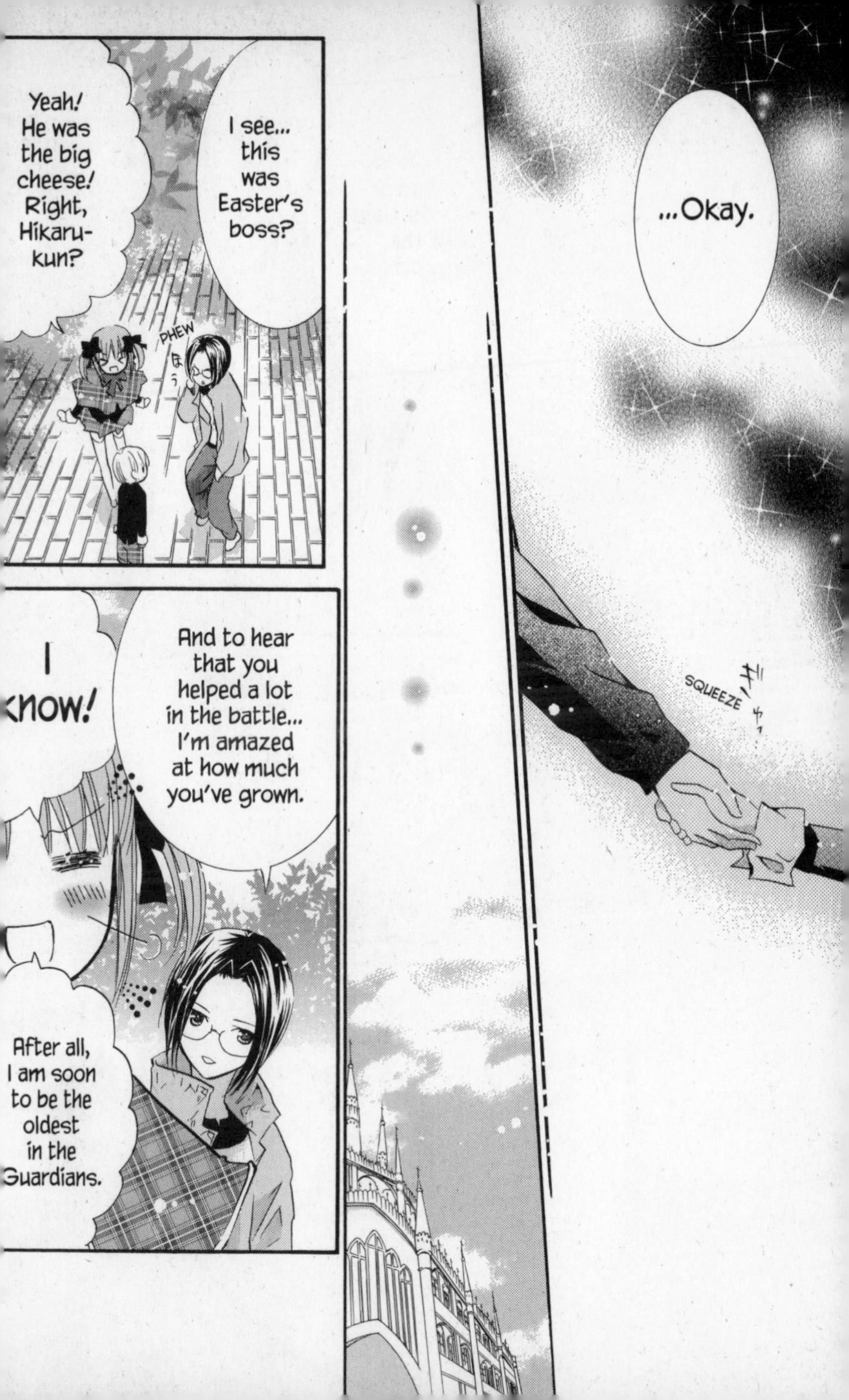
...Okay.
SQUEEZE
I see... this was Easter's boss?
Yeah! He was the big cheese! Right, Hikaru-kun?
PHEW
ほう
And to hear that you helped a lot in the battle... I'm amazed at how much you've grown.
I know!
After all, I am soon to be the oldest in the Guardians.

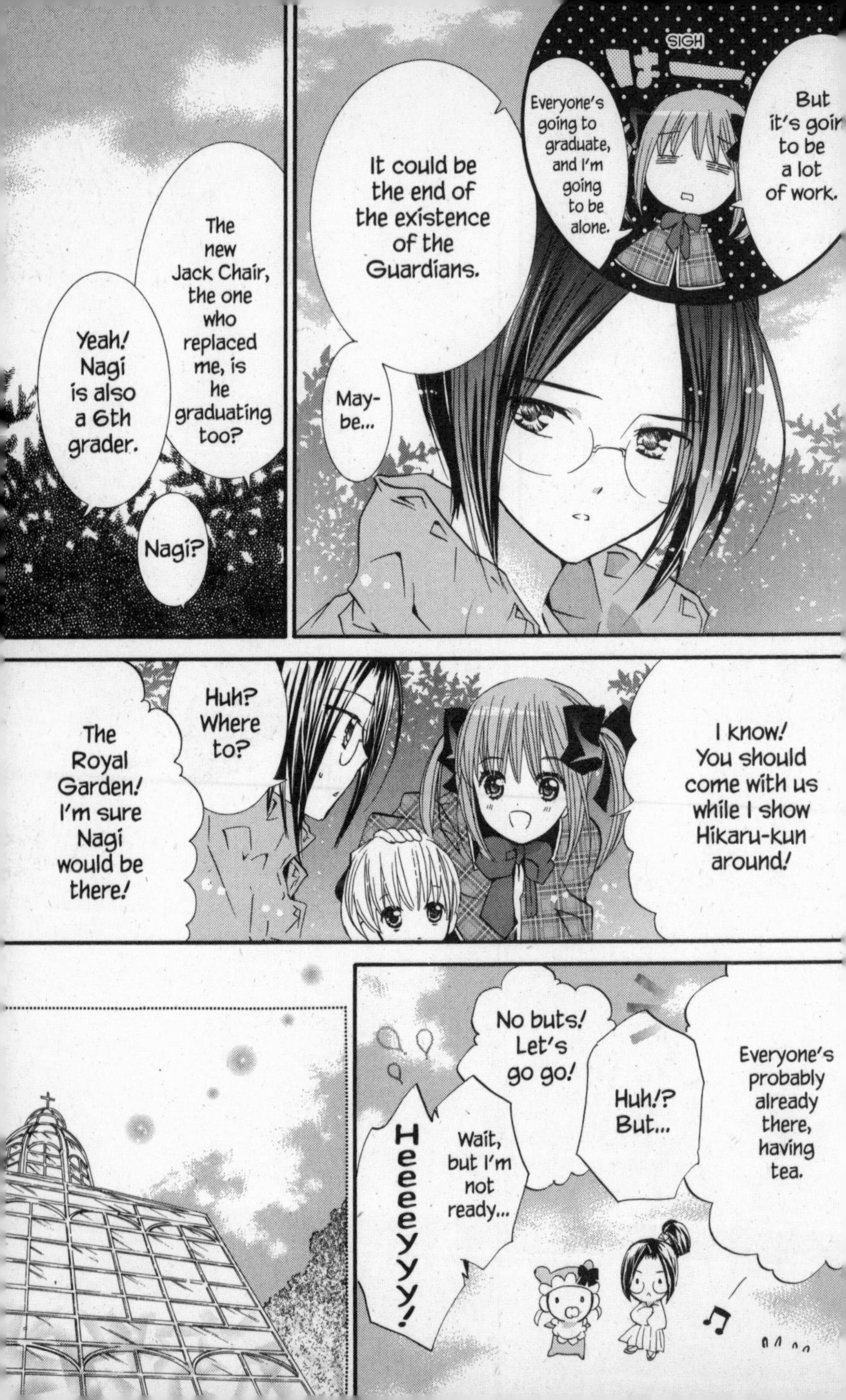
SIGH
But it's goin to be a lot of work.
Everyone's going to graduate, and I'm going to be alone.
It could be the end of the existence of the Guardians.
May-be...
The new Jack Chair, the one who replaced me, is he graduating too?
Yeah! Nagi is also a 6th grader.
Nagi?
I know! You should come with us while I show Hikaru-kun around!
Huh? Where to?
The Royal Garden! I'm sure Nagi would be there!
Everyone's probably already there, having tea.
Huh!? But...
No buts! Let's go go!
Wait, but I'm not ready...
Heeeeyyyy!

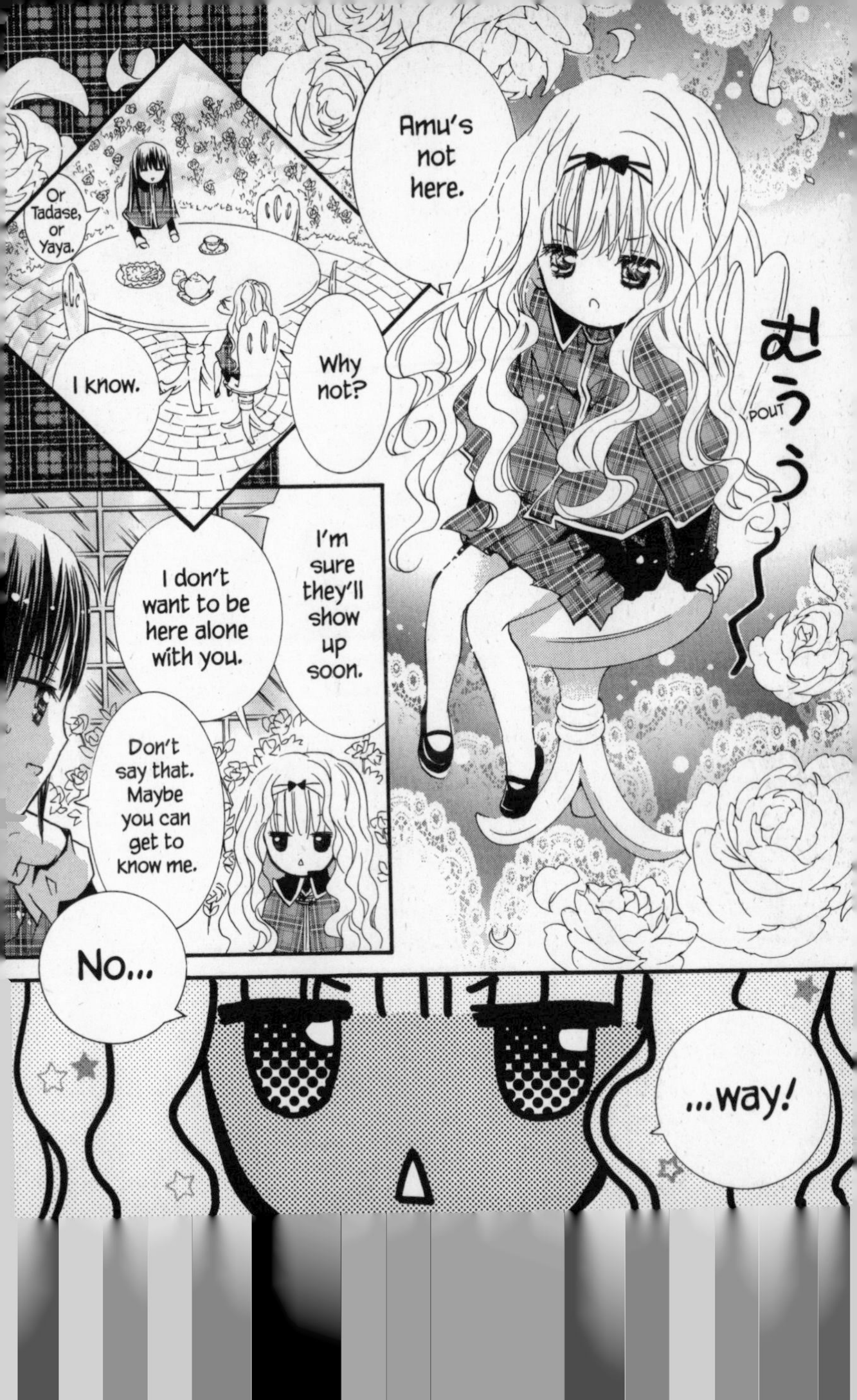
Amu's not here.
むぅぅ
POUT
Or Tadase, or Yaya.
Why not?
I know.
I'm sure they'll show up soon.
I don't want to be here alone with you.
Don't say that. Maybe you can get to know me.
No...
...way!

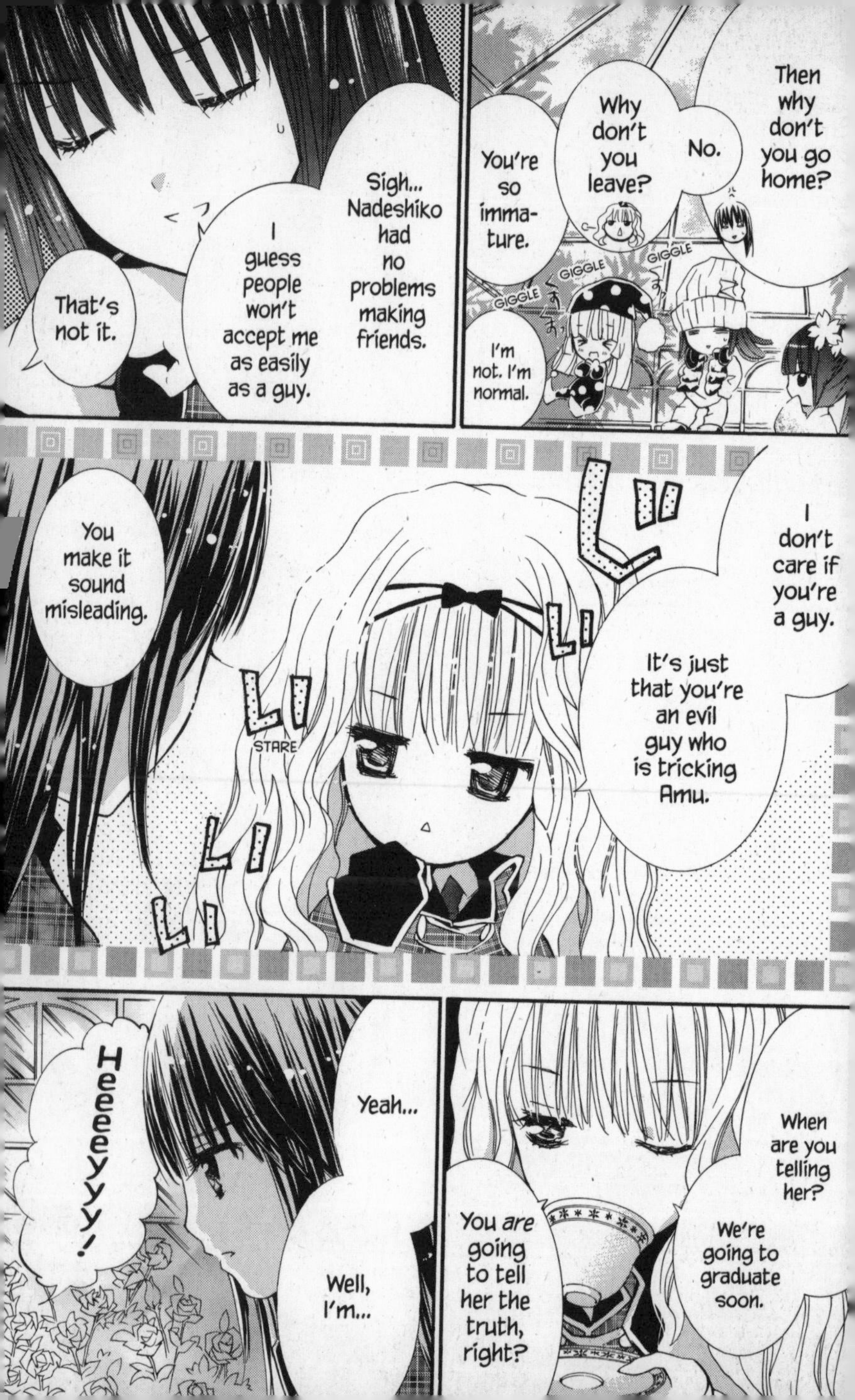

Then why don't you go home?
No.
Why don't you leave?
You're so imma-ture.
GIGGLE
GIGGLE
GIGGLE
I'm not. I'm normal.
Sigh... Nadeshiko had no problems making friends.
I guess people won't accept me as easily as a guy.
That's not it.
I don't care if you're a guy.
It's just that you're an evil guy who is tricking Amu.
STARE
You make it sound misleading.
When are you telling her?
We're going to graduate soon.
You *are* going to tell her the truth, right?
Yeah...
Well, I'm...
Heeeeyyy!

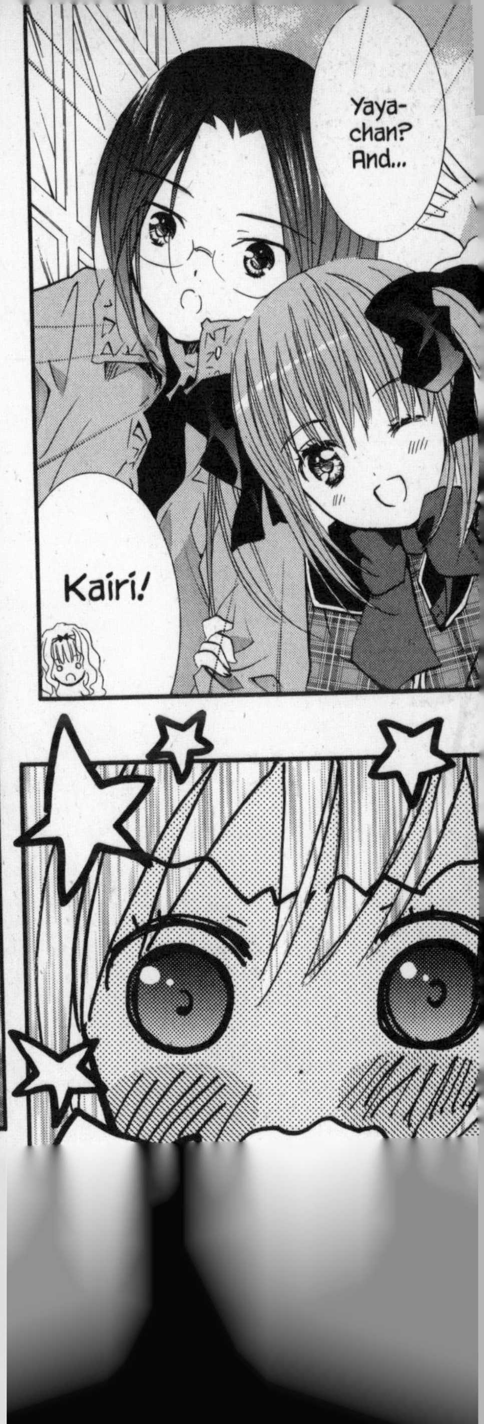
Yaya-chan? And...
Kairi!

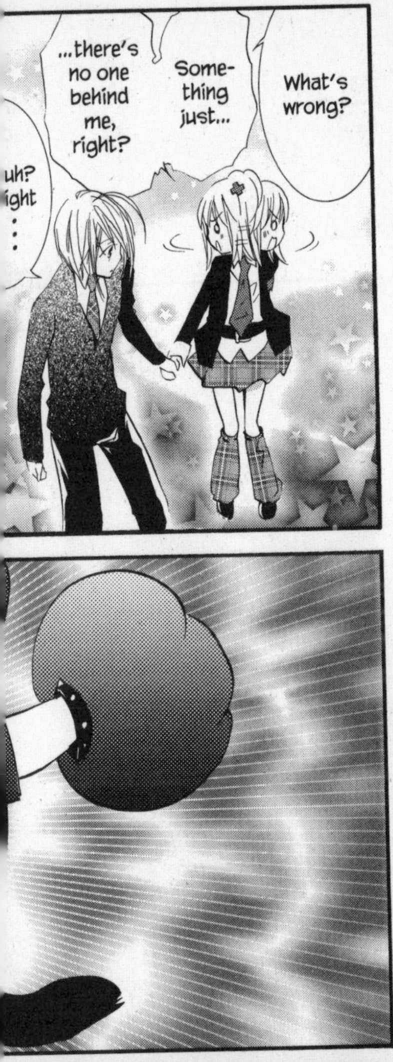
What's wrong?
Some-thing just...
...there's no one behind me, right?
uh? ight . . .

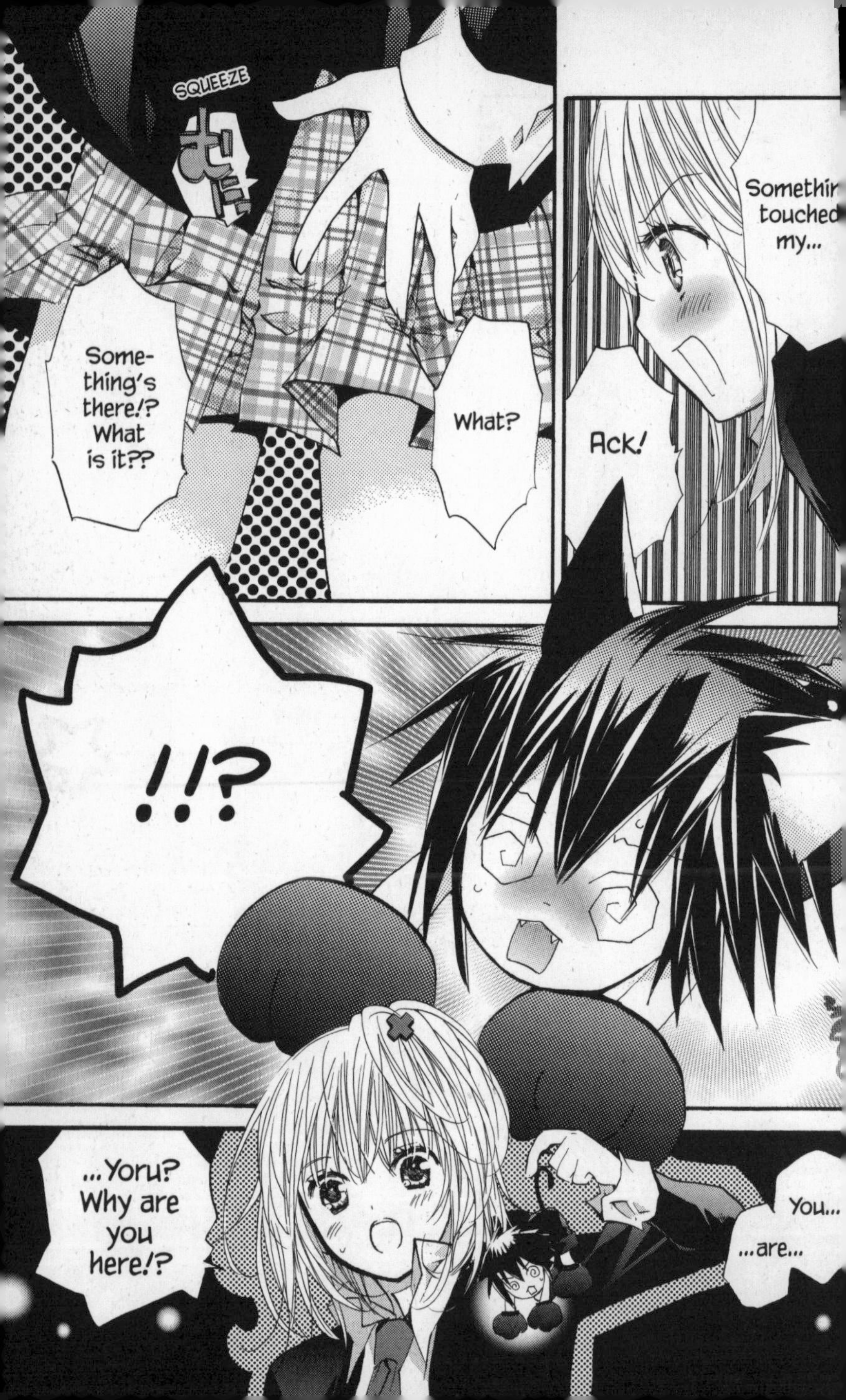
Somethin touched my...
Ack!
SQUEEZE
What?
Some-thing's there!? What is it??
!!?
You... ...are...
...Yoru? Why are you here!?

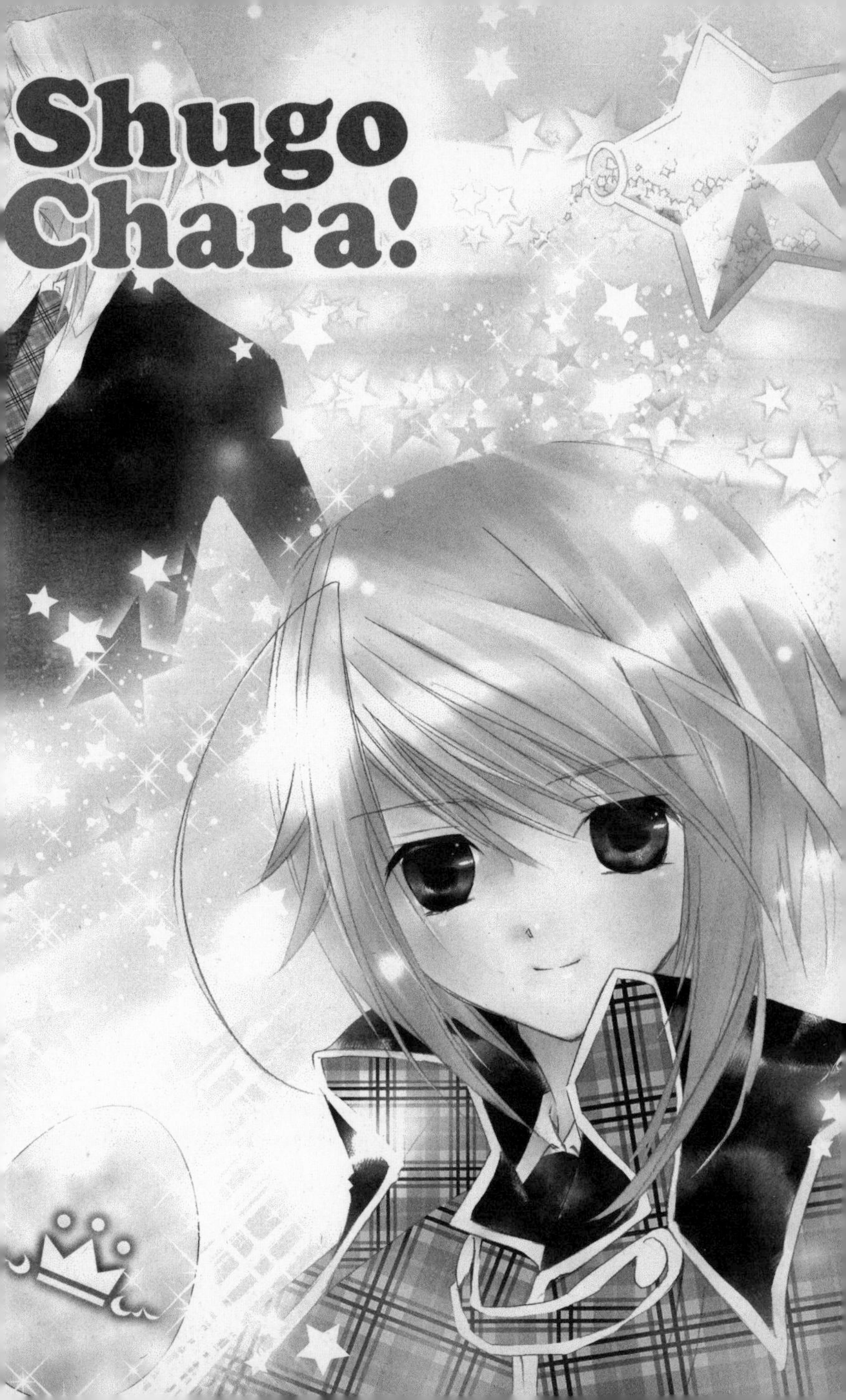
Shugo
Chara!

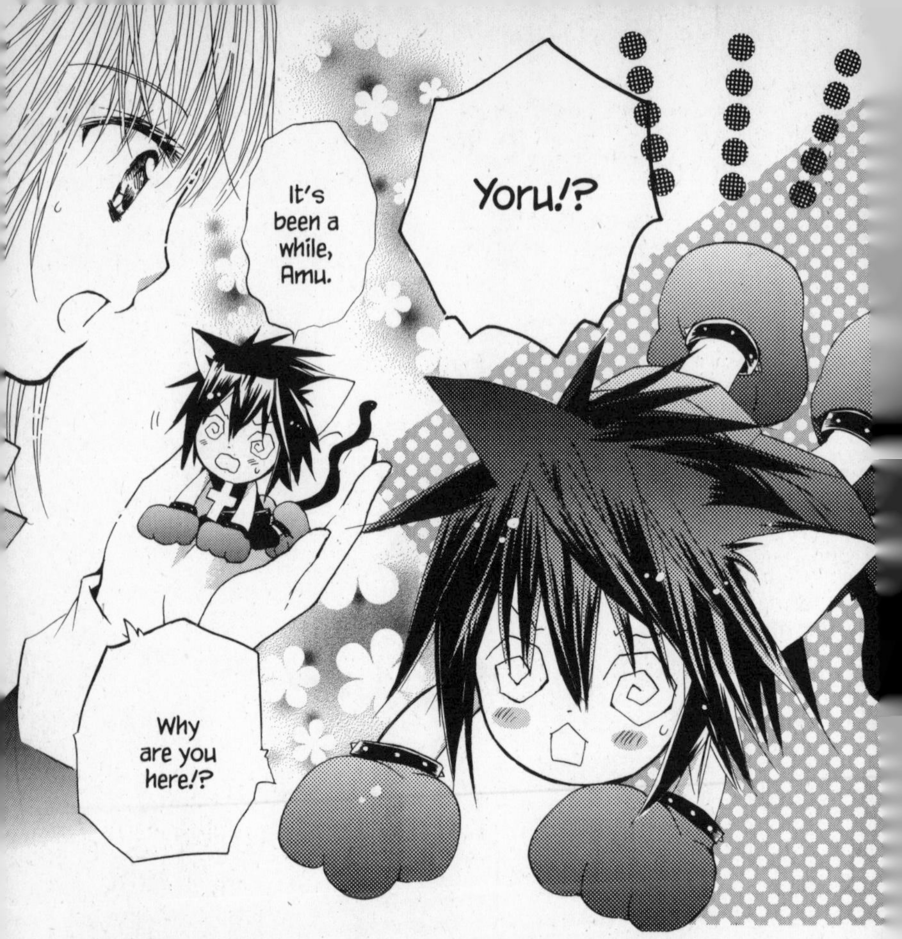
Yoru!?
It's been a while, Amu.
Why are you here!?

So the name will be chosen out of the list!

Please look forward to volume 12 ♥ ♥

Q2. Do you wear glasses?

A2. I don't! Both of us have very good vision and we don't wear contacts either! But we do like characters who wear glasses, so every manga we draw will have at least one character wearing glasses.

Q3. Could Ikuto play other instruments beside the violin?

A3. He can play the piano and the viola!

Q4. I'm thinking of getting a cat. What kind of cat do you have?

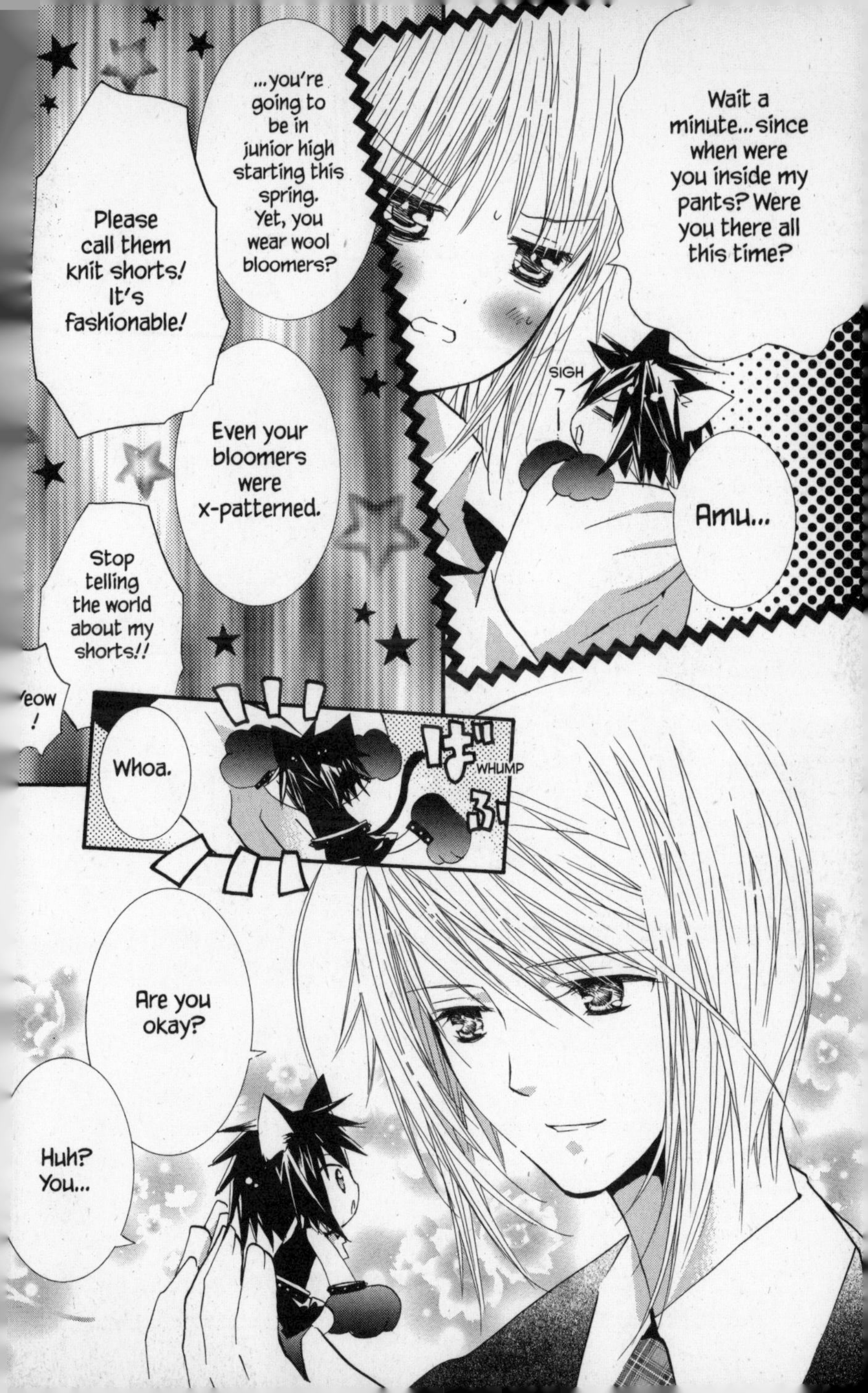
Wait a minute...since when were you inside my pants? Were you there all this time?
SIGH
Amu...
...you're going to be in junior high starting this spring. Yet, you wear wool bloomers?
Please call them knit shorts! It's fashionable!
Even your bloomers were x-patterned.
Stop telling the world about my shorts!!
eow!
ばふ
WHUMP
Whoa.
Are you okay?
Huh? You...

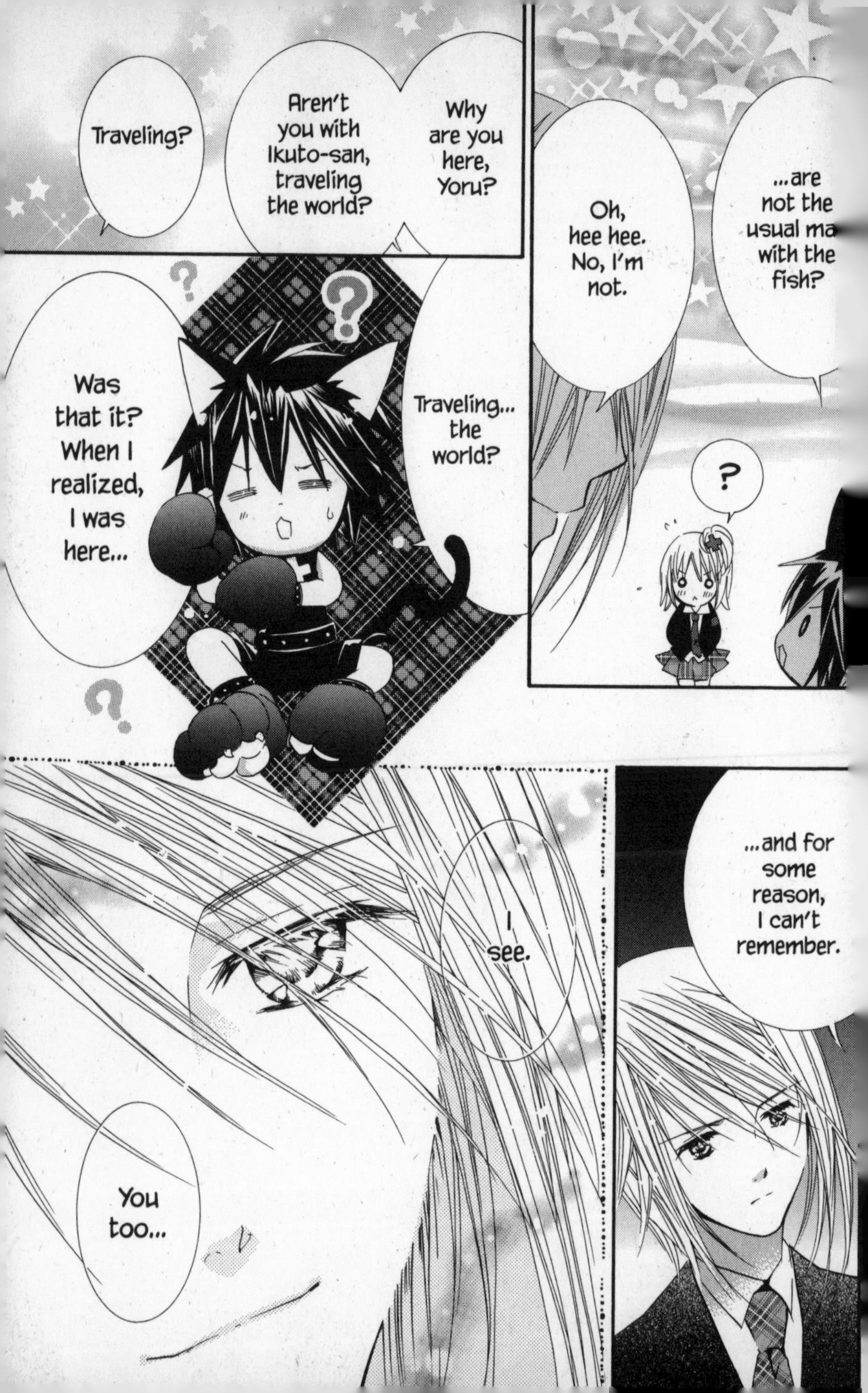

...are not the usual ma with the fish?
Oh, hee hee. No, I'm not.
?
Why are you here, Yoru?
Aren't you with Ikuto-san, traveling the world?
Traveling?
Traveling... the world?
Was that it? When I realized, I was here...
...and for some reason, I can't remember.
I see.
You too...

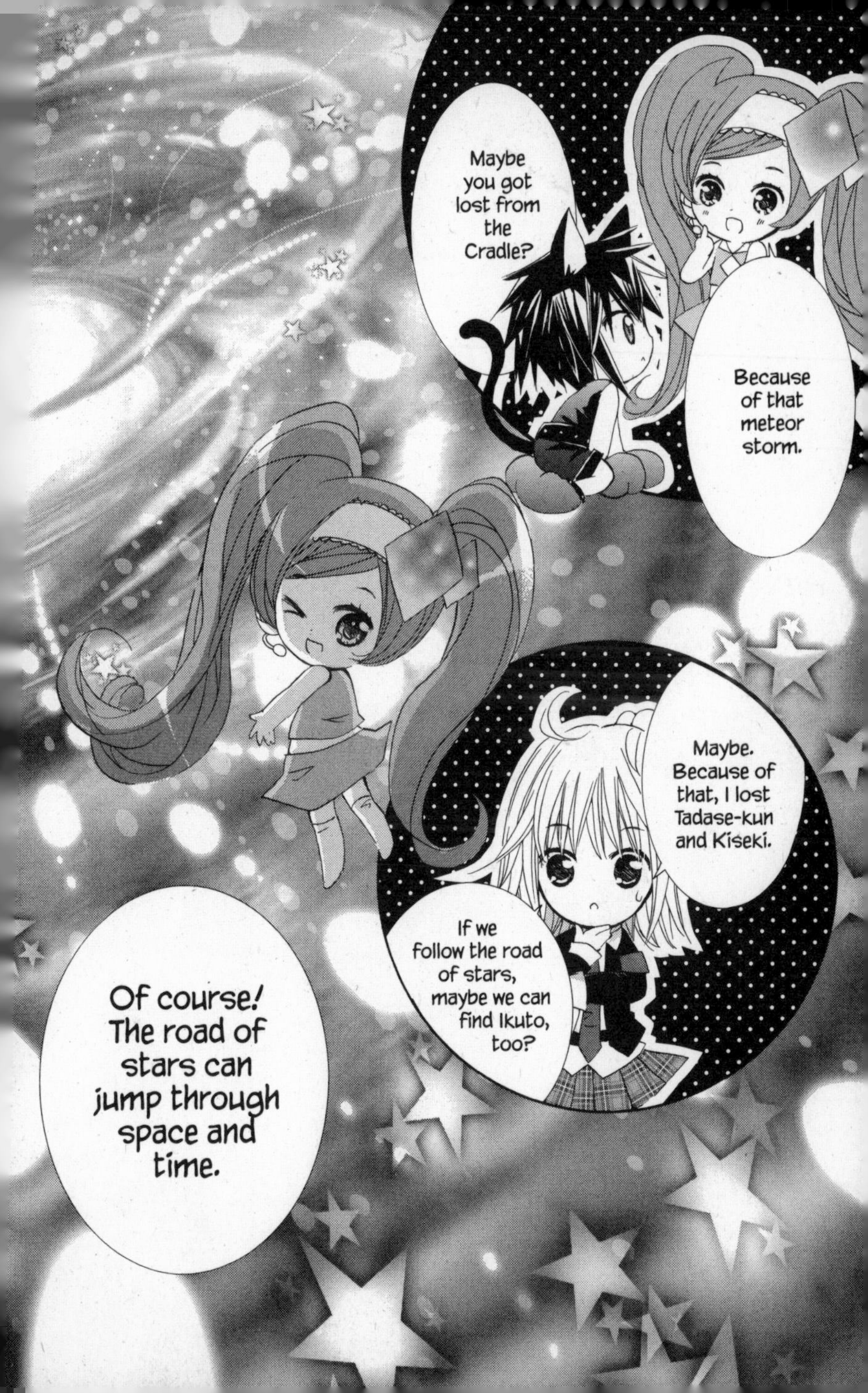
Maybe you got lost from the Cradle?
Because of that meteor storm.
Maybe. Because of that, I lost Tadase-kun and Kiseki.
If we follow the road of stars, maybe we can find Ikuto, too?
Of course! The road of stars can jump through space and time.

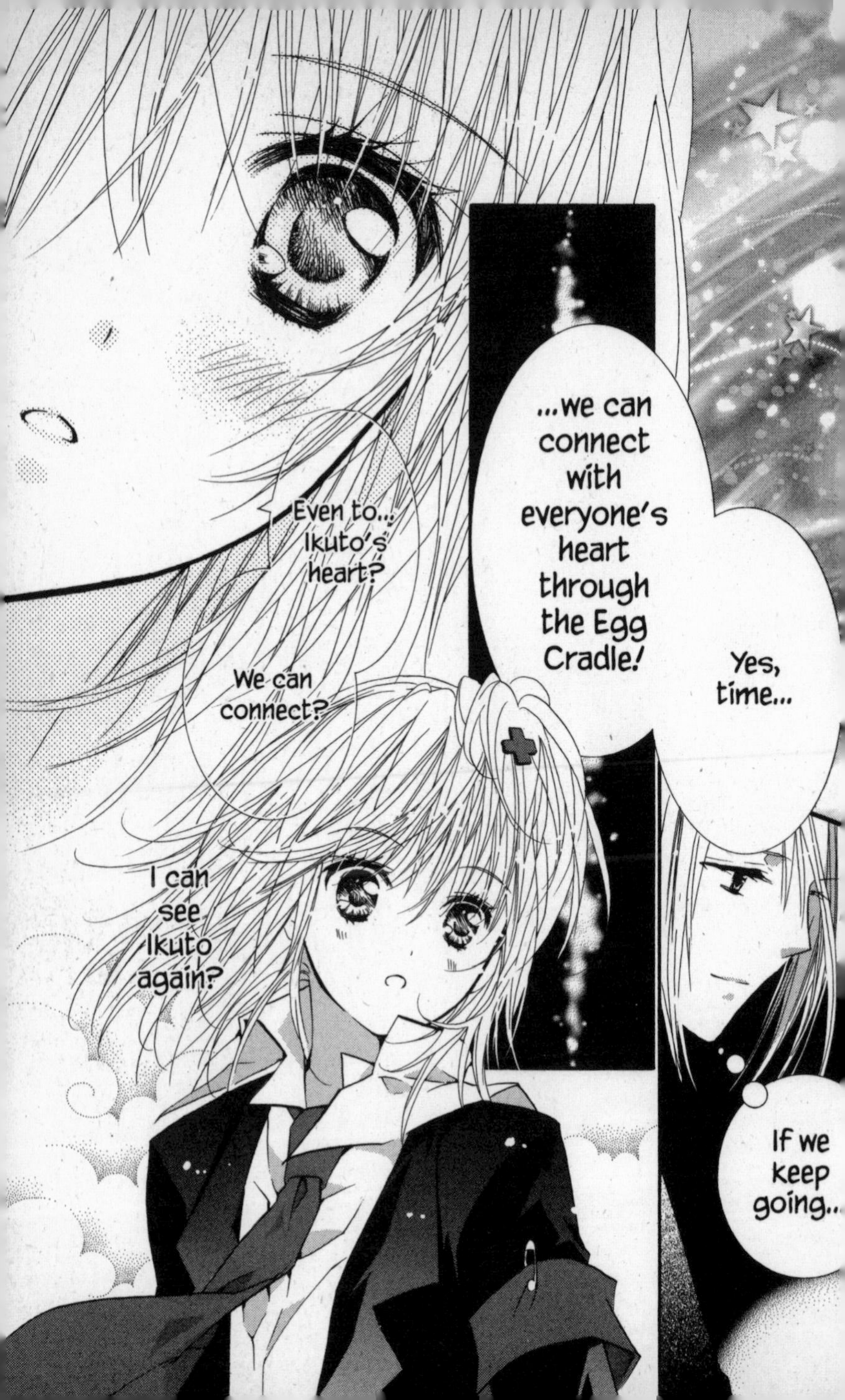
Yes, time...
If we keep going...
...we can connect with everyone's heart through the Egg Cradle!
Even to... Ikuto's heart?
We can connect?
I can see Ikuto again?

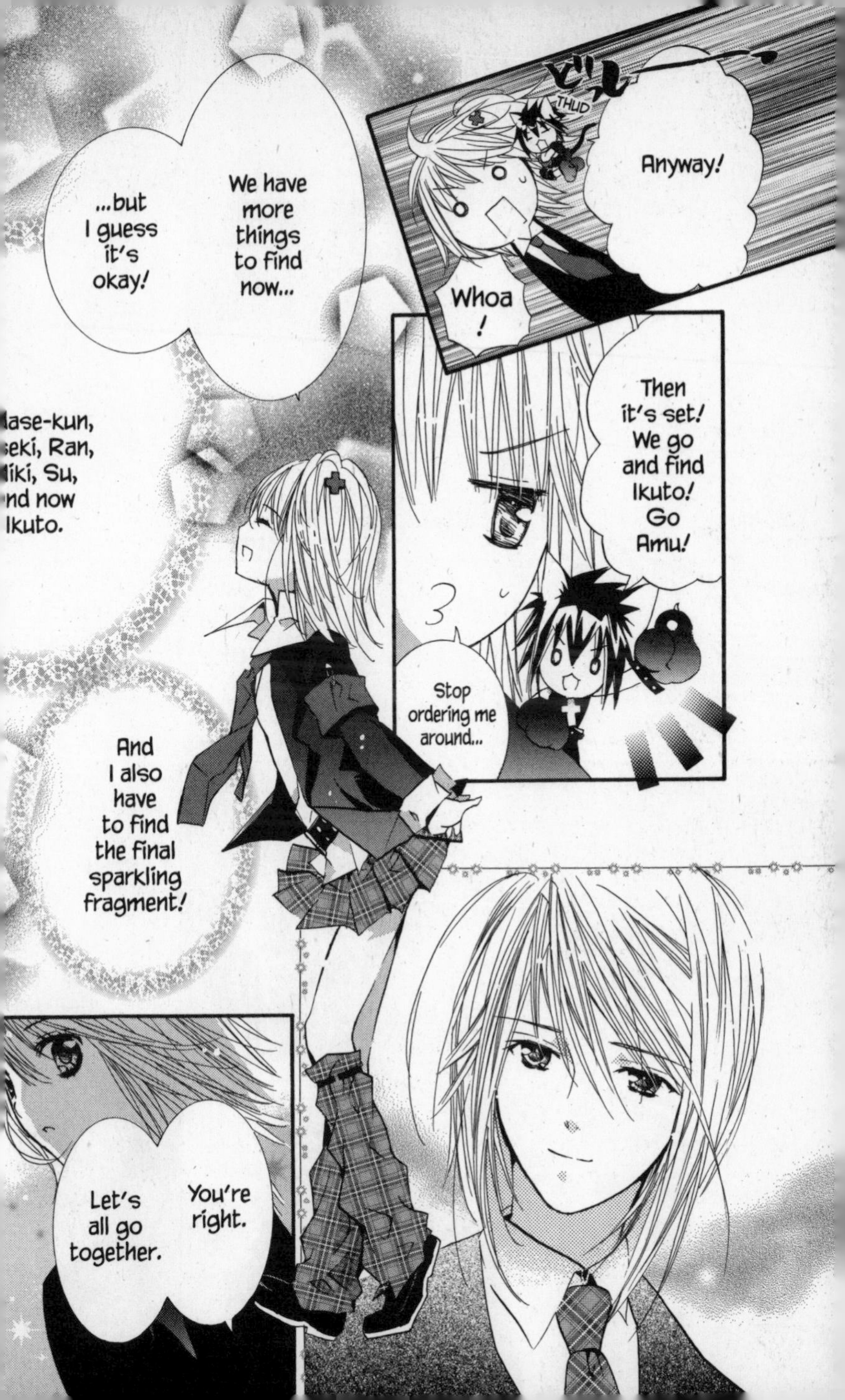

THUD
Anyway!
Whoa!
Then it's set! We go and find Ikuto! Go Amu!
Stop ordering me around...
We have more things to find now...
...but I guess it's okay!
ase-kun, eki, Ran, iki, Su, nd now Ikuto.
And I also have to find the final sparkling fragment!
You're right.
Let's all go together.

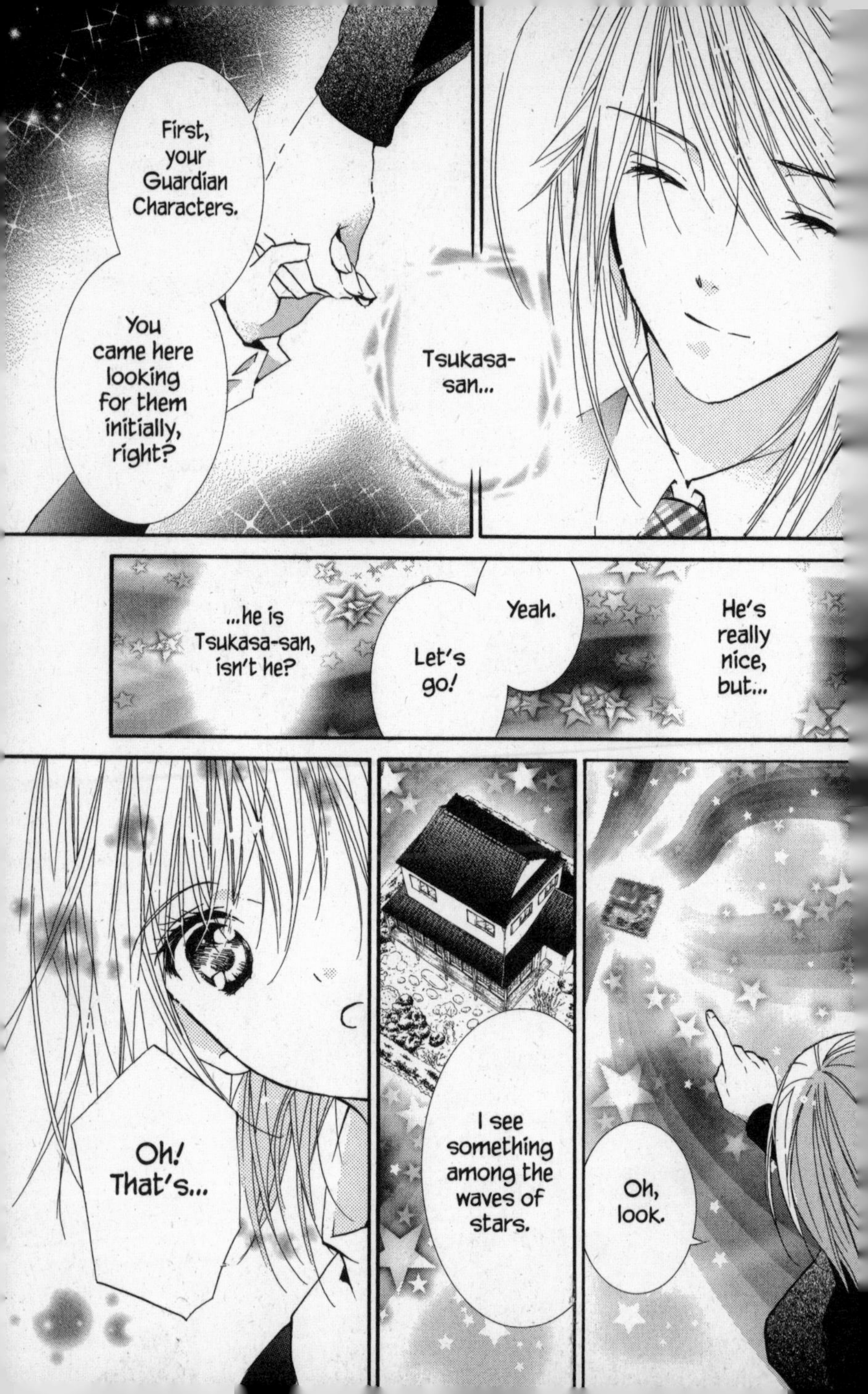
Tsukasa-san...
First, your Guardian Characters.
You came here looking for them initially, right?
He's really nice, but...
Yeah.
Let's go!
...he is Tsukasa-san, isn't he?
Oh, look.
I see something among the waves of stars.
Oh! That's...

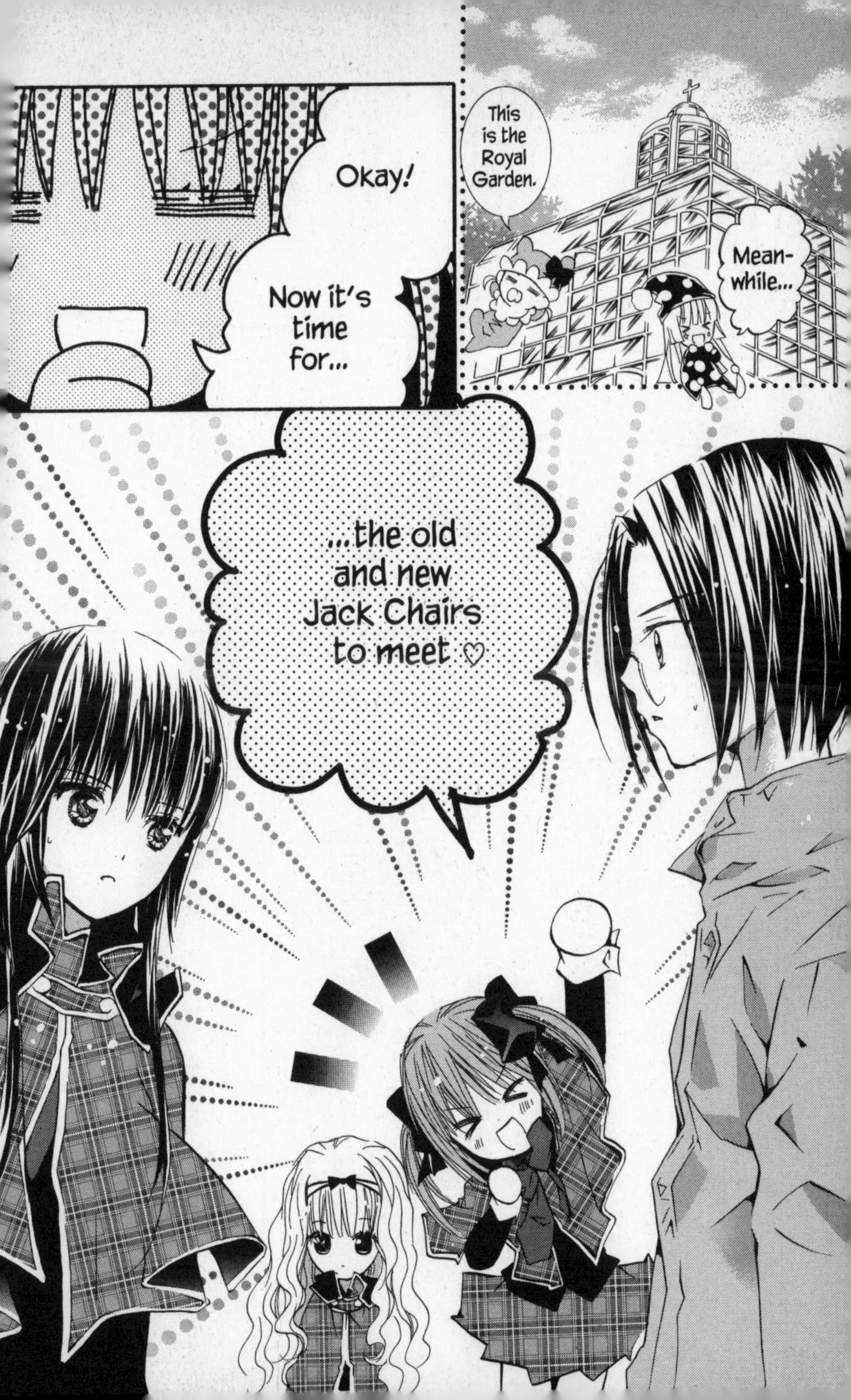
Mean-while...
This is the Royal Garden.
Okay!
Now it's time for...
...the old and new Jack Chairs to meet ♡

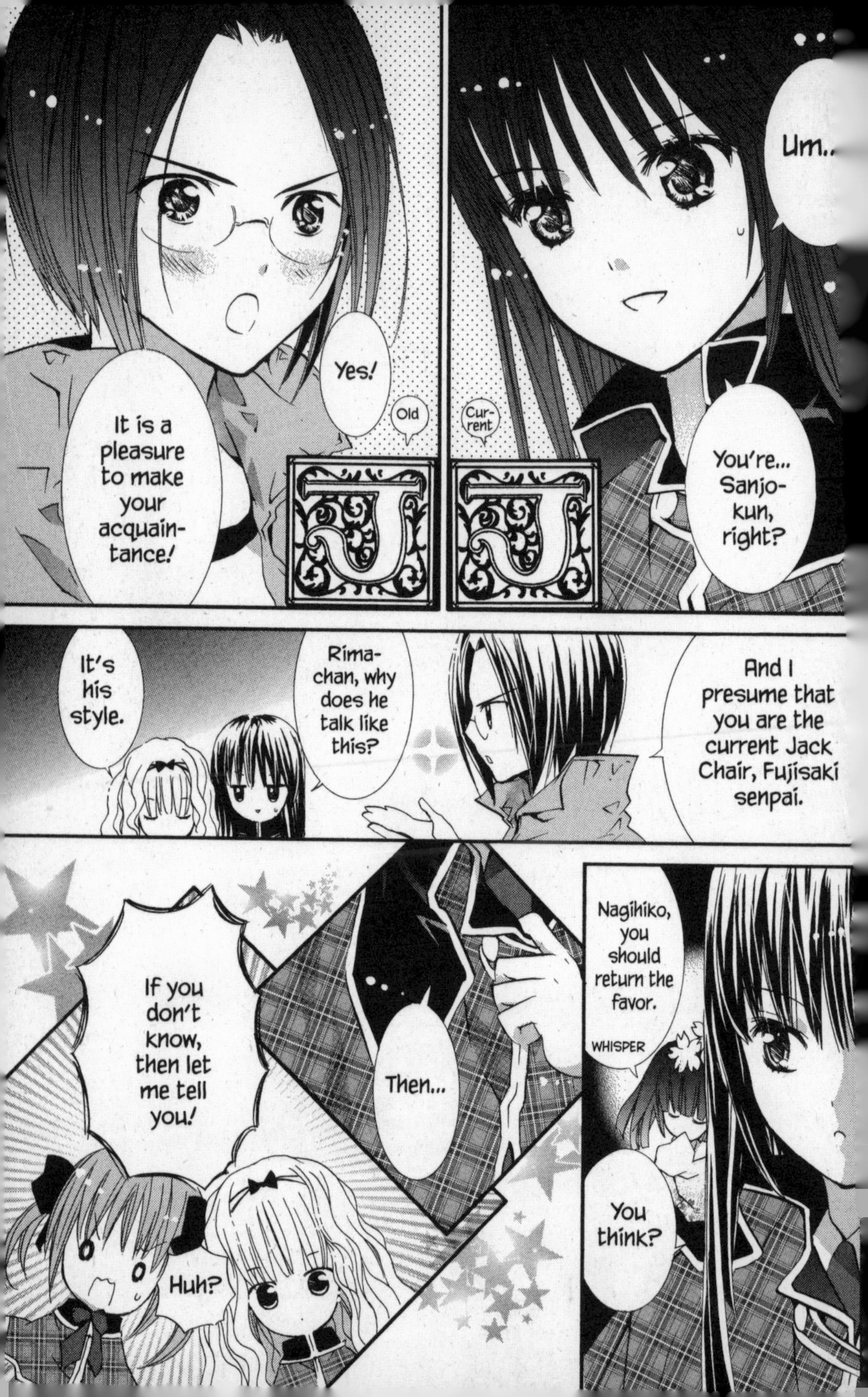
Um...
Cur-rent
You're... Sanjo-kun, right?
Yes!
Old
It is a pleasure to make your acquain-tance!
And I presume that you are the current Jack Chair, Fujisaki senpai.
Rima-chan, why does he talk like this?
It's his style.
Nagihiko, you should return the favor.
WHISPER
You think?
Then...
If you don't know, then let me tell you!
Huh?

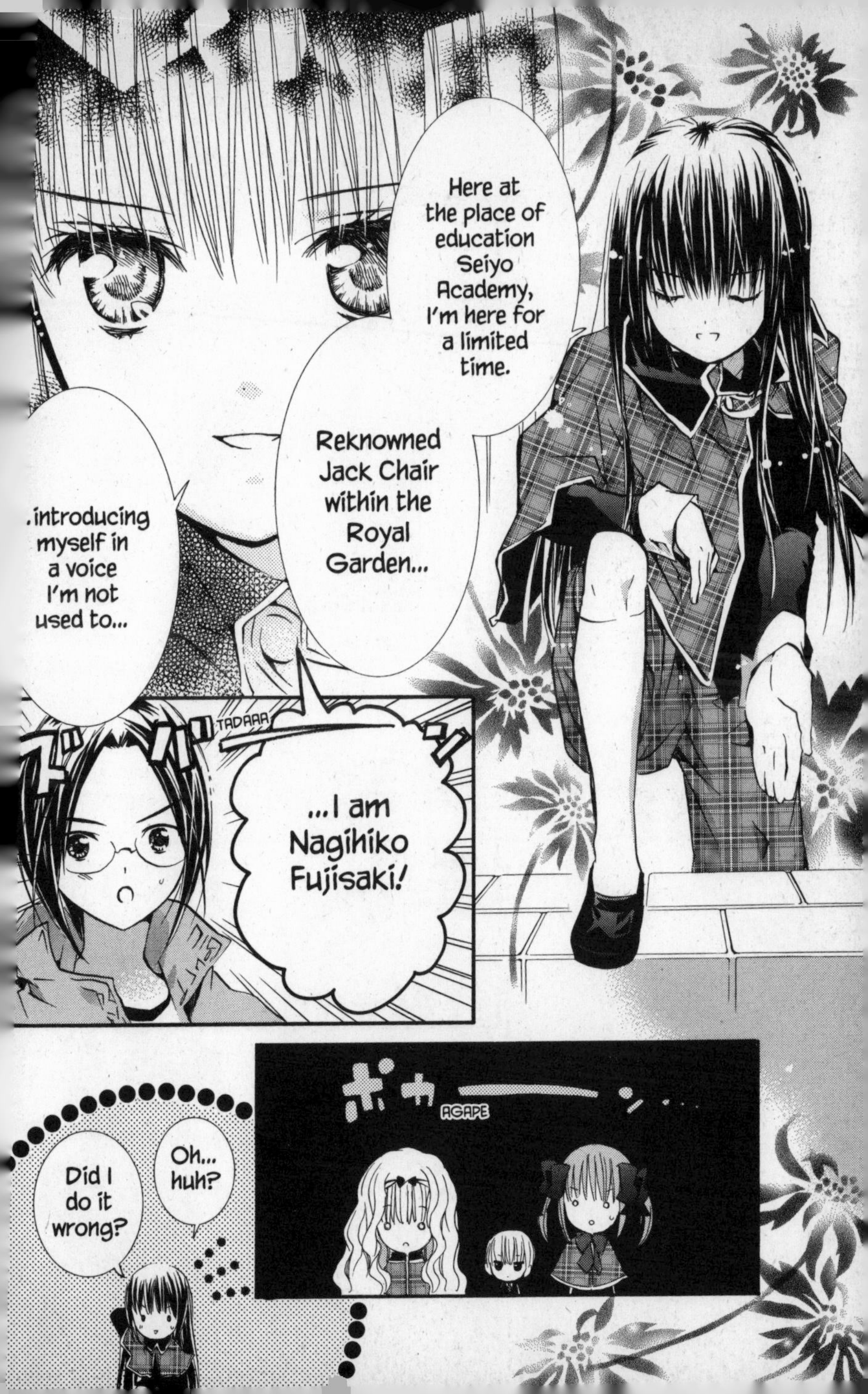
Here at the place of education Seiyo Academy, I'm here for a limited time.
Reknowned Jack Chair within the Royal Garden...
.introducing myself in a voice I'm not used to...
TADAAA
...I am Nagihiko Fujisaki!
AGAPE
Oh... huh?
Did I do it wrong?

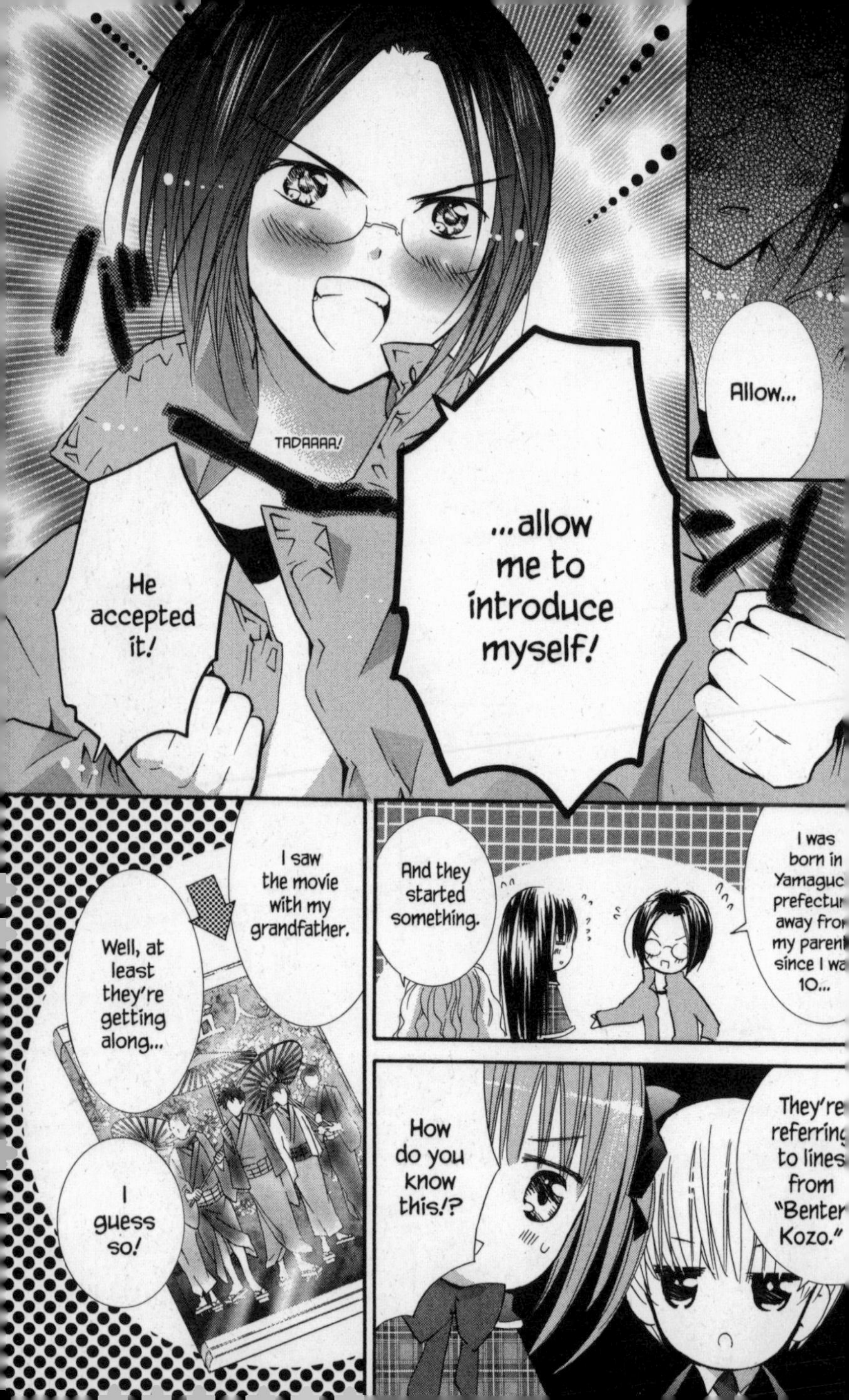
Allow...
...allow me to introduce myself!
TADAAAA!
He accepted it!
I was born in Yamaguc prefectur away fron my parent since I wa 10...
And they started something.
They're referring to lines from "Benter Kozo."
How do you know this!?
I saw the movie with my grandfather.
Well, at least they're getting along...
I guess so!

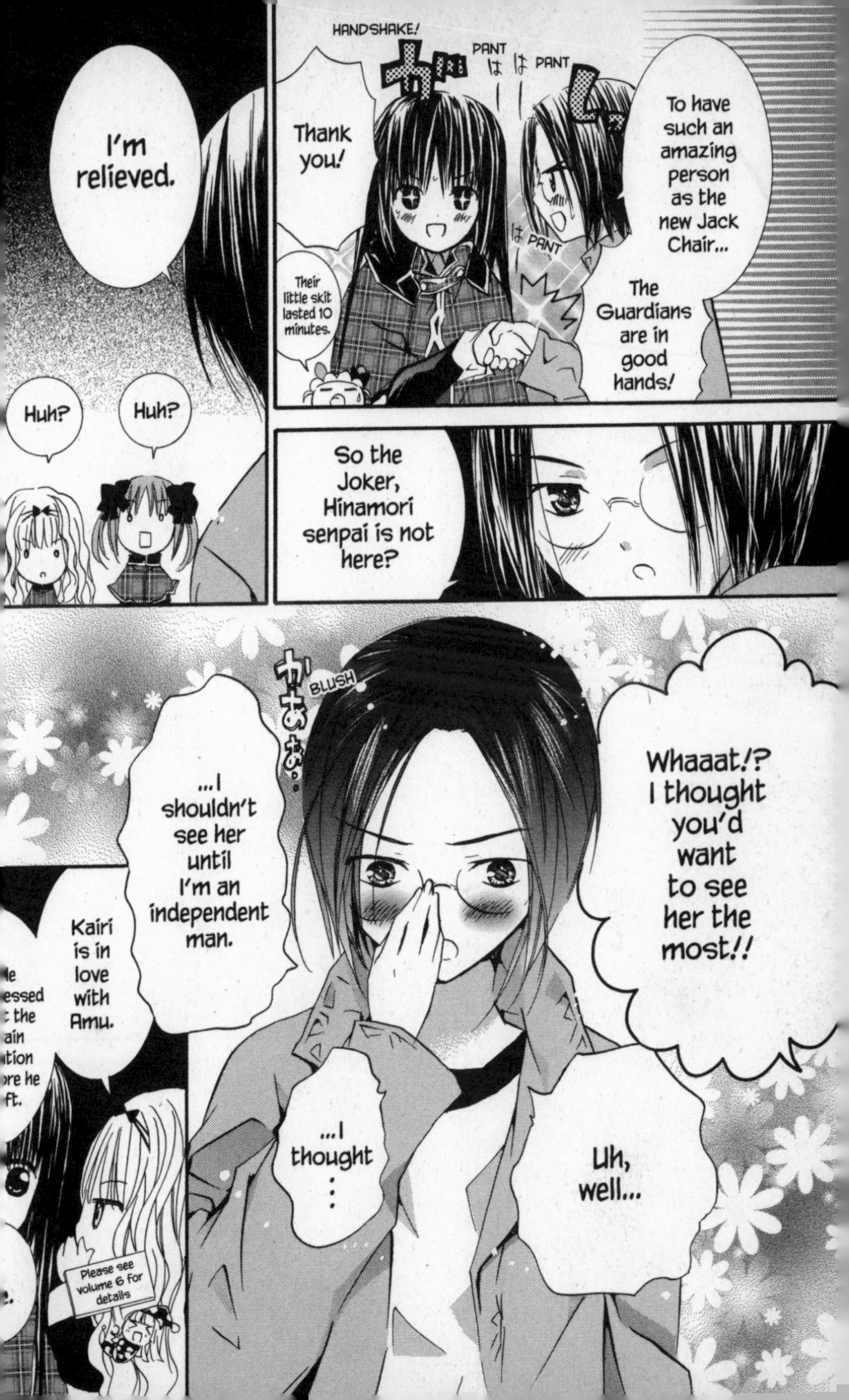

HANDSHAKE!
PANT PANT
To have such an amazing person as the new Jack Chair...
The Guardians are in good hands!
Thank you!
PANT
Their little skit lasted 10 minutes.
So the Joker, Hinamori senpai is not here?
I'm relieved.
Huh?
Huh?
Whaaat!? I thought you'd want to see her the most!!
BLUSH
...I shouldn't see her until I'm an independent man.
Kairi is in love with Amu.
Uh, well...
...I thought...
Please see volume 6 for details

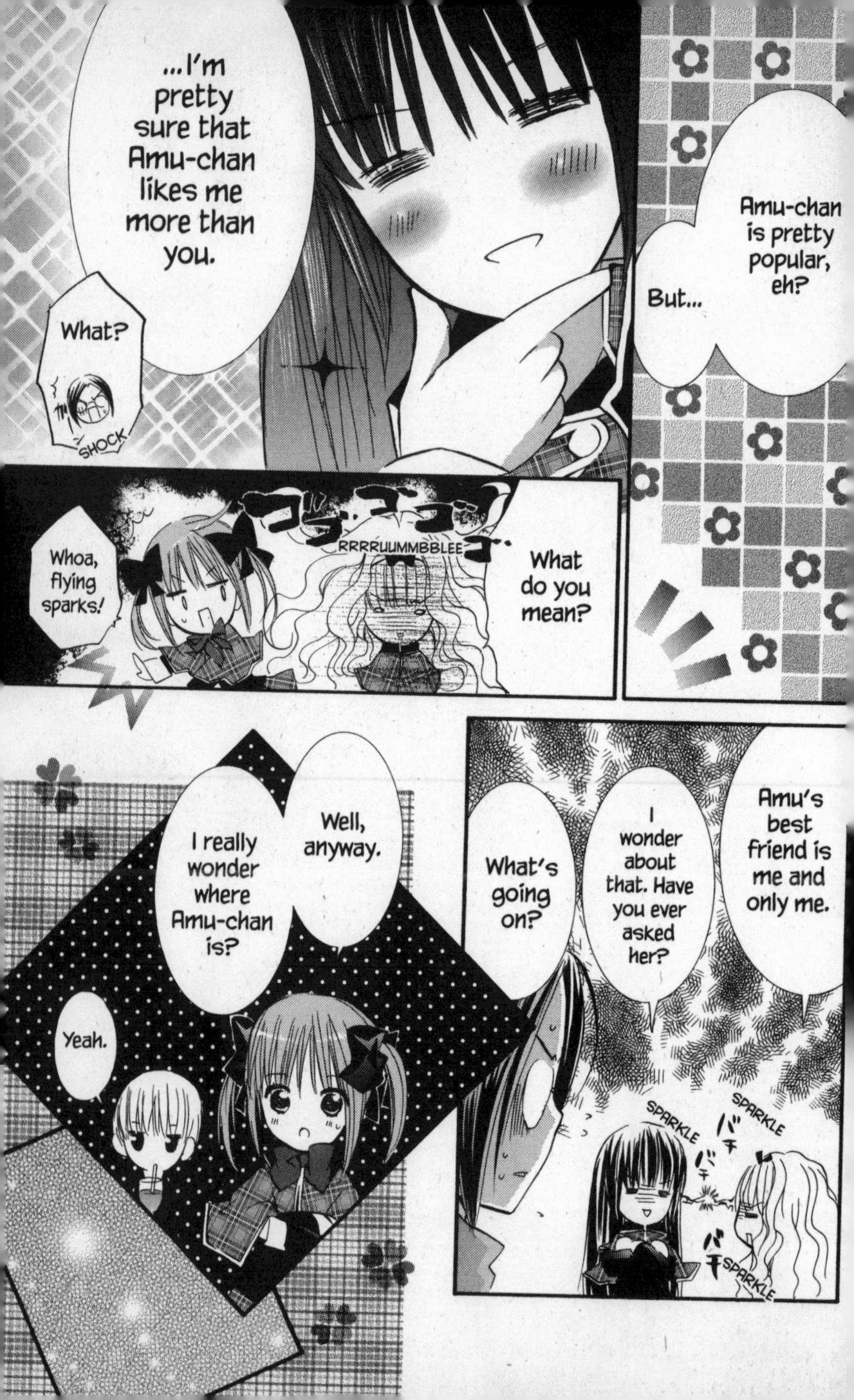
Amu-chan is pretty popular, eh?
But...
...I'm pretty sure that Amu-chan likes me more than you.
What?
SHOCK
What do you mean?
RRRRUUMMBBLEE
Whoa, flying sparks!
Amu's best friend is me and only me.
I wonder about that. Have you ever asked her?
What's going on?
SPARKLE
SPARKLE
SPARKLE
Well, anyway.
I really wonder where Amu-chan is?
Yeah.

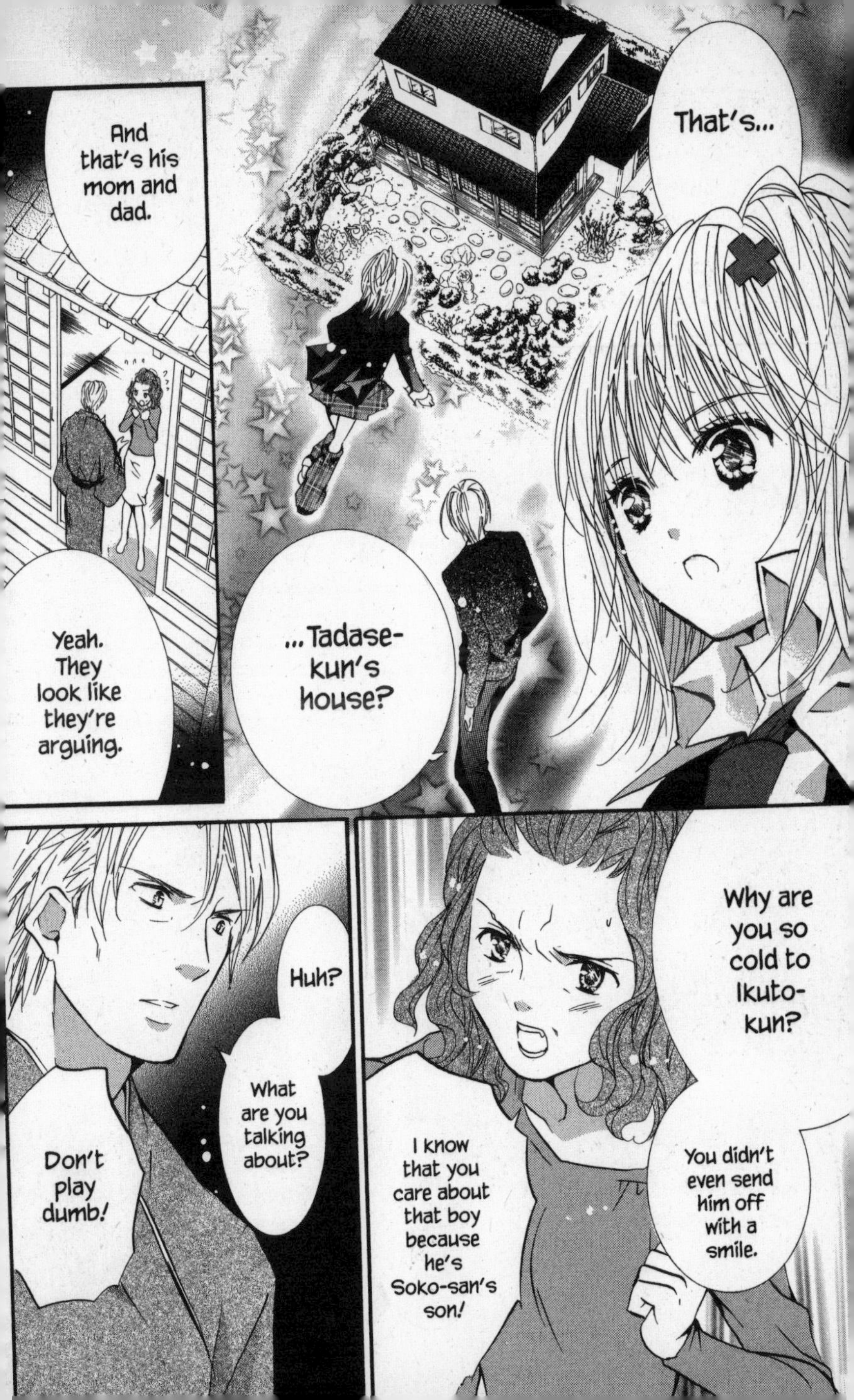
That's...
...Tadase-kun's house?
And that's his mom and dad.
Yeah. They look like they're arguing.
Why are you so cold to Ikuto-kun?
You didn't even send him off with a smile.
I know that you care about that boy because he's Soko-san's son!
Huh?
What are you talking about?
Don't play dumb!

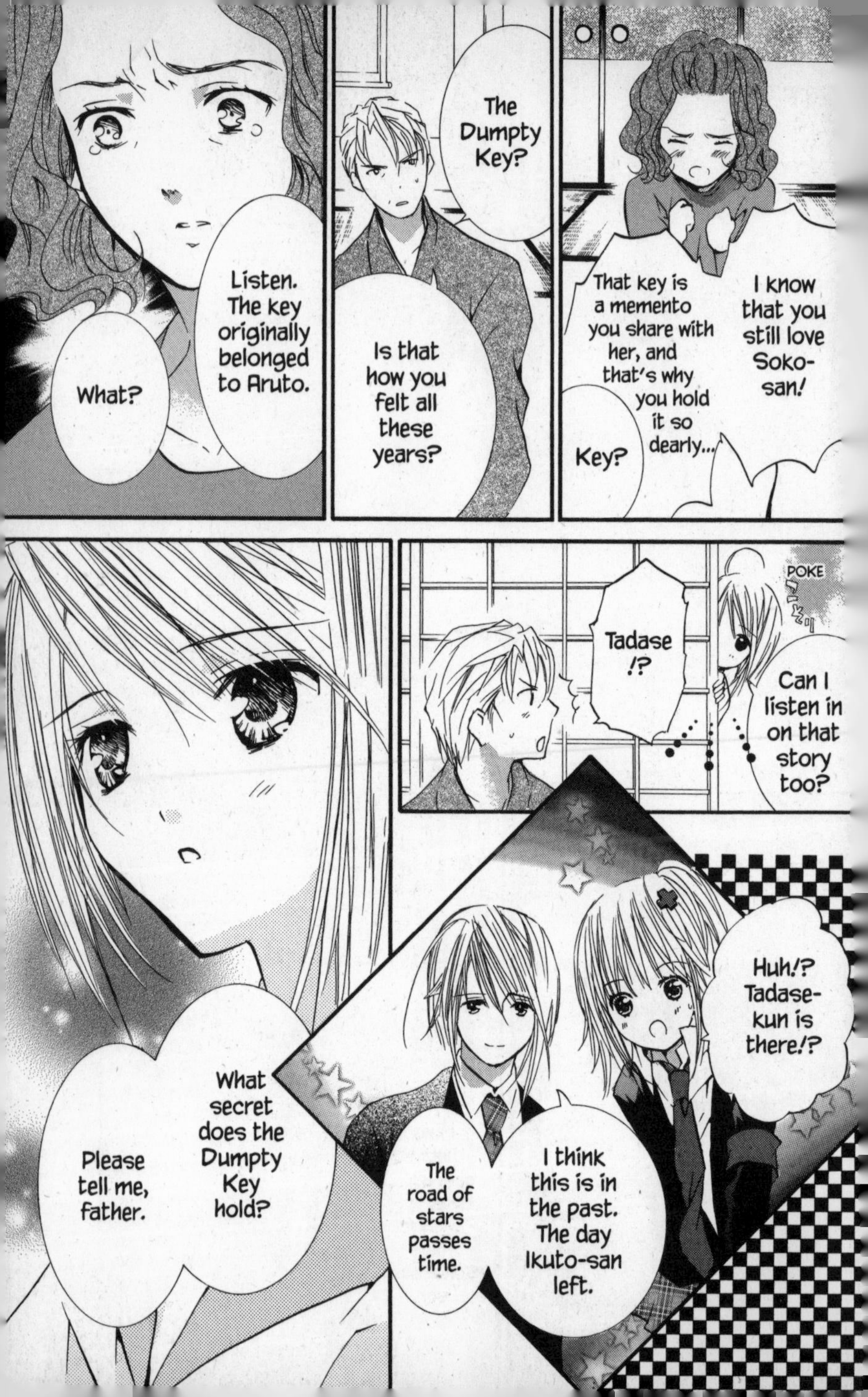
I know that you still love Soko-san!
That key is a memento you share with her, and that's why you hold it so dearly...
Key?
The Dumpty Key?
Is that how you felt all these years?
Listen. The key originally belonged to Aruto.
What?
POKE
Tadase !?
Can I listen in on that story too?
Huh!? Tadase-kun is there!?
I think this is in the past. The day Ikuto-san left.
The road of stars passes time.
What secret does the Dumpty Key hold?
Please tell me, father.

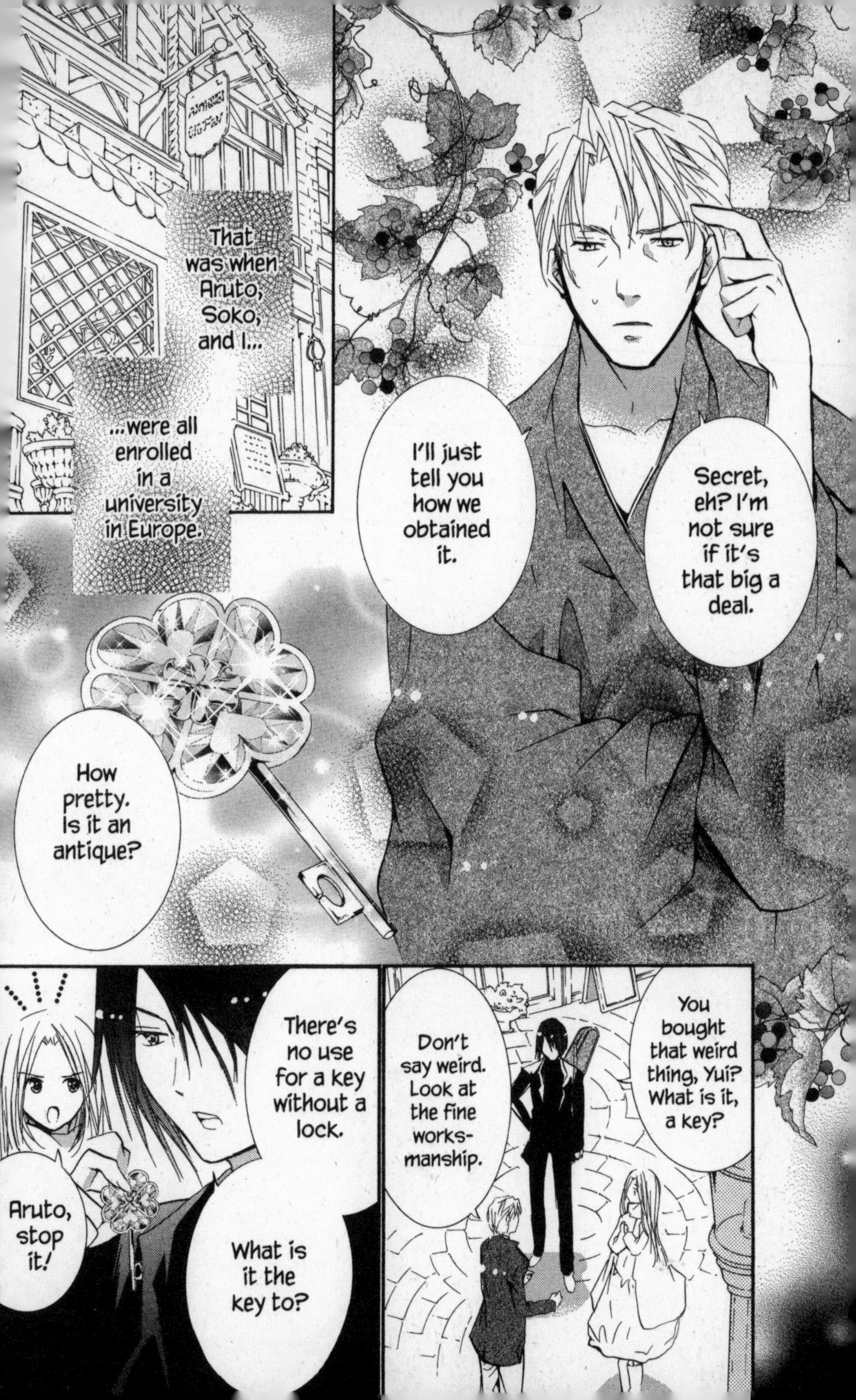
Secret, eh? I'm not sure if it's that big a deal.
I'll just tell you how we obtained it.
That was when Aruto, Soko, and I...
...were all enrolled in a university in Europe.
How pretty. Is it an antique?
You bought that weird thing, Yui? What is it, a key?
Don't say weird. Look at the fine works-manship.
There's no use for a key without a lock.
What is it the key to?
Aruto, stop it!

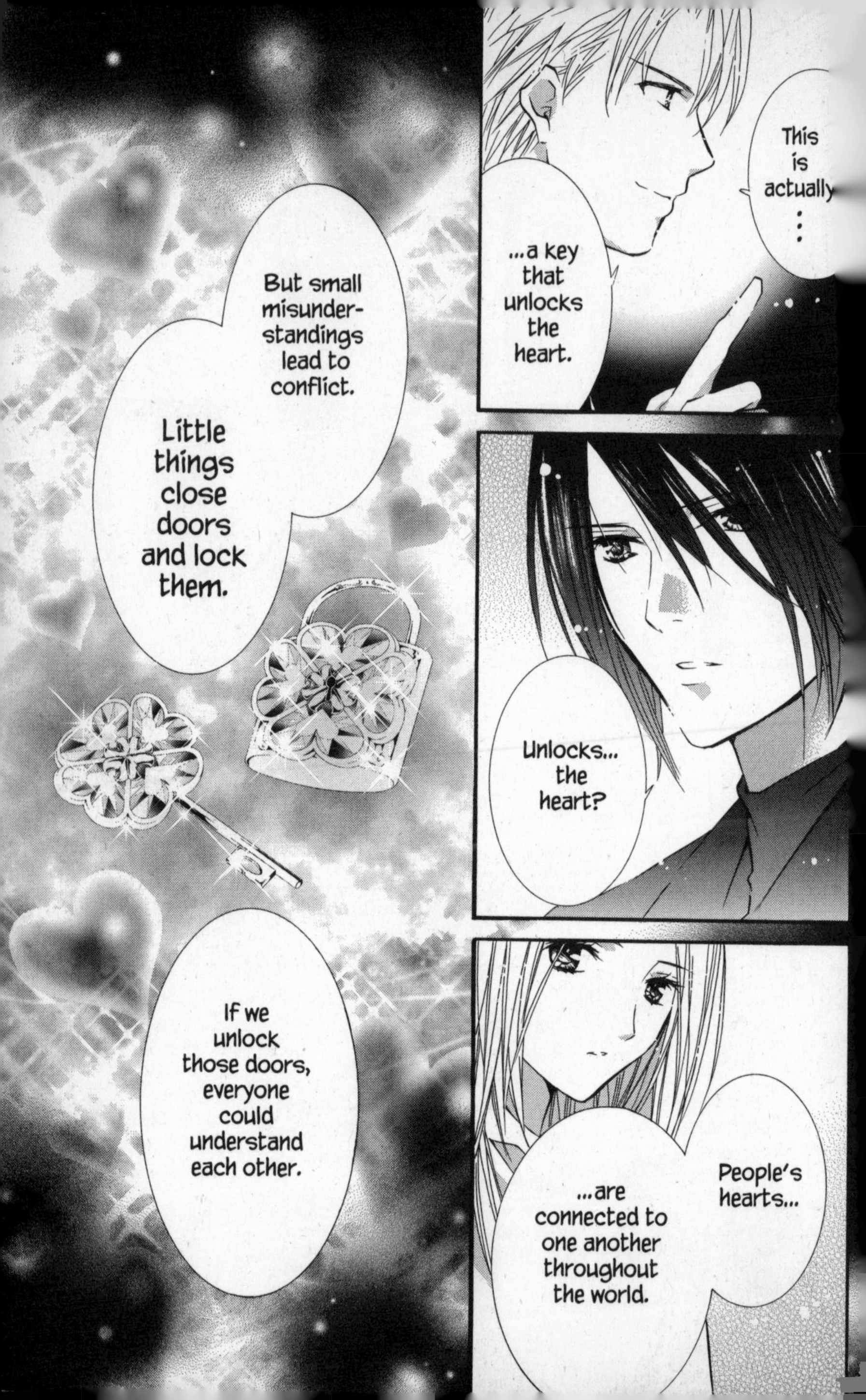
This is actually...
...a key that unlocks the heart.
Unlocks... the heart?
People's hearts...
...are connected to one another throughout the world.
But small misunder-standings lead to conflict.
Little things close doors and lock them.
If we unlock those doors, everyone could understand each other.

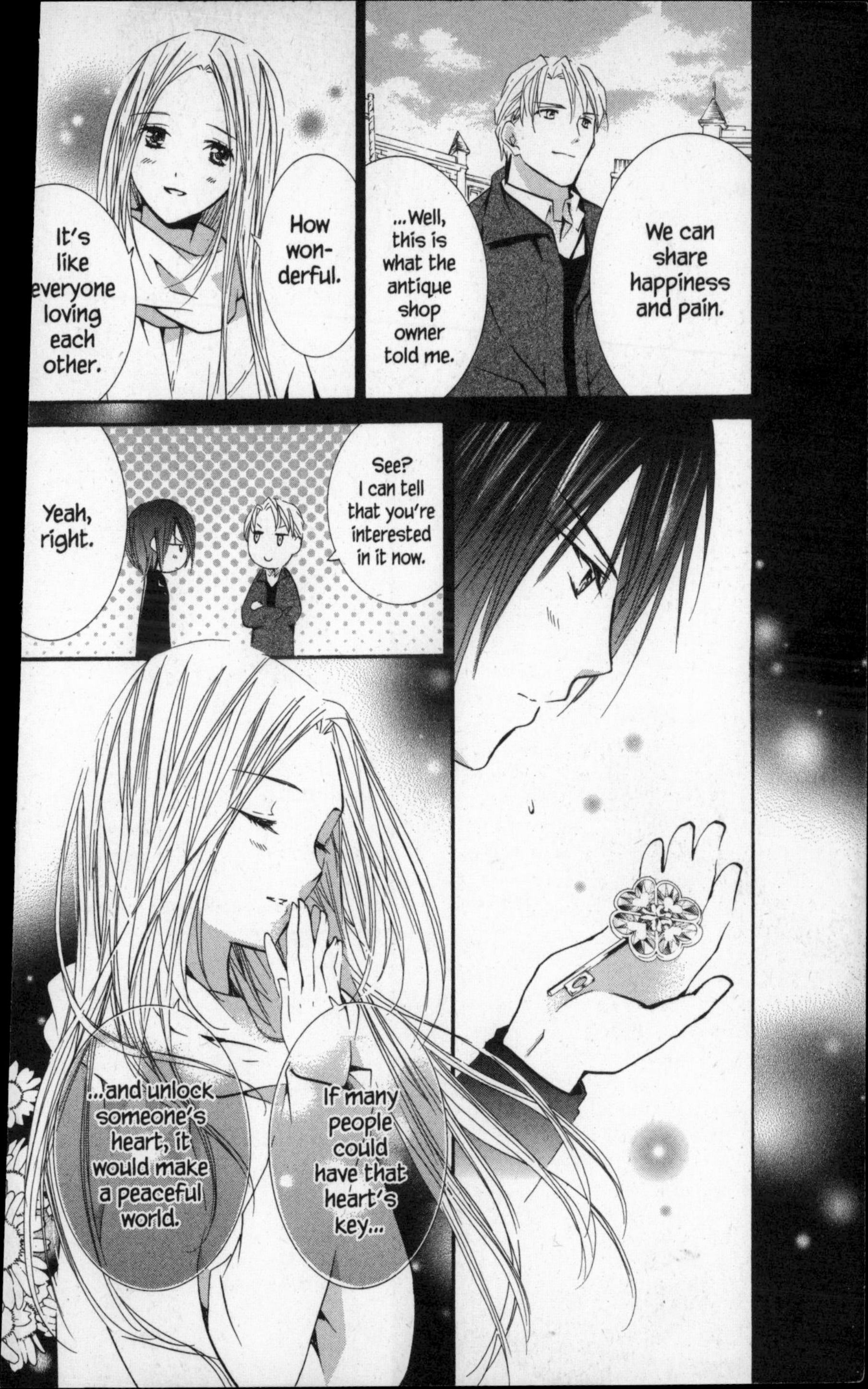
We can share happiness and pain.
...Well, this is what the antique shop owner told me.
How wonderful.
It's like everyone loving each other.
See? I can tell that you're interested in it now.
Yeah, right.
If many people could have that heart's key...
...and unlock someone's heart, it would make a peaceful world.

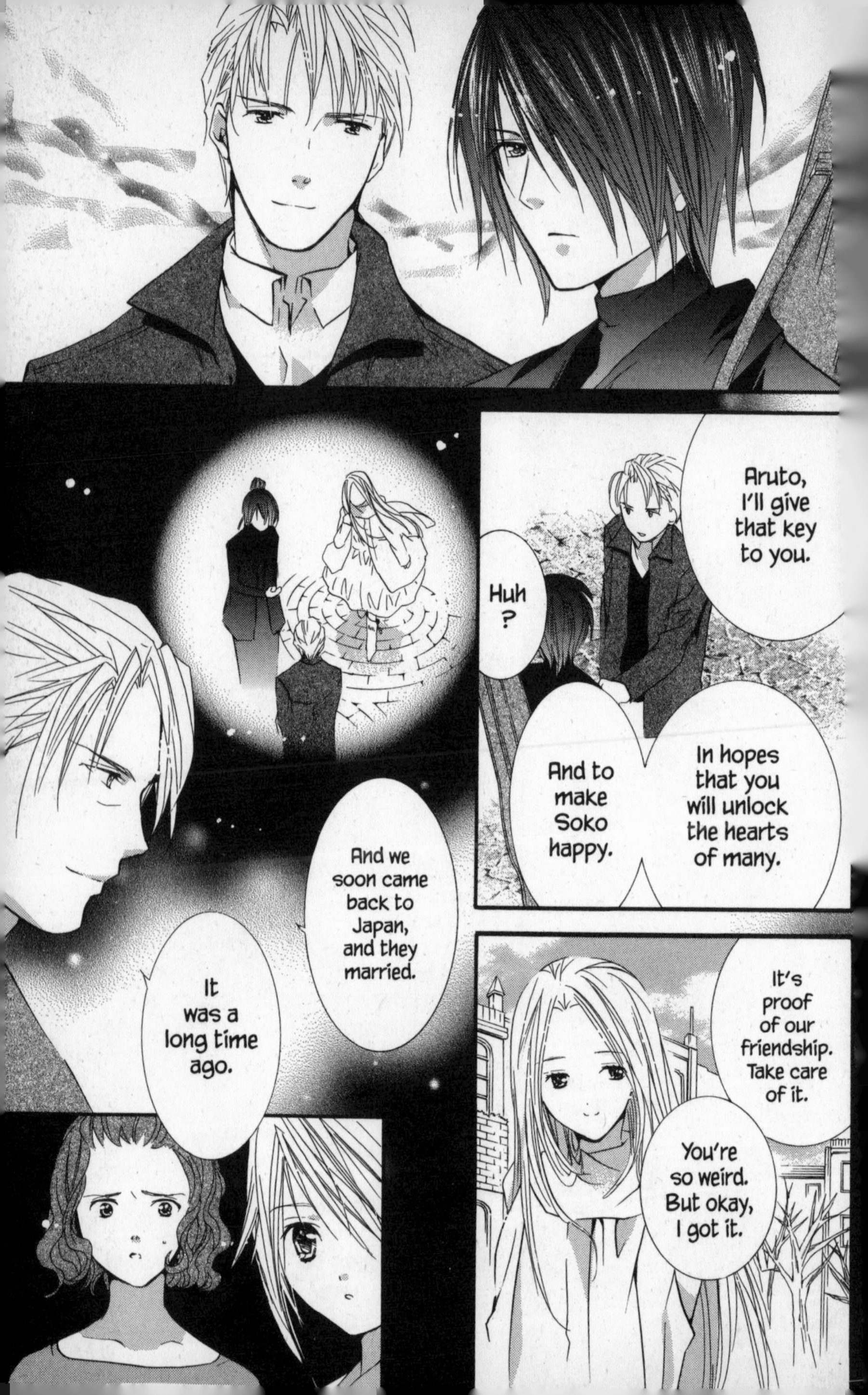
Aruto, I'll give that key to you.
Huh?
In hopes that you will unlock the hearts of many.
And to make Soko happy.
It's proof of our friendship. Take care of it.
You're so weird. But okay, I got it.
And we soon came back to Japan, and they married.
It was a long time ago.

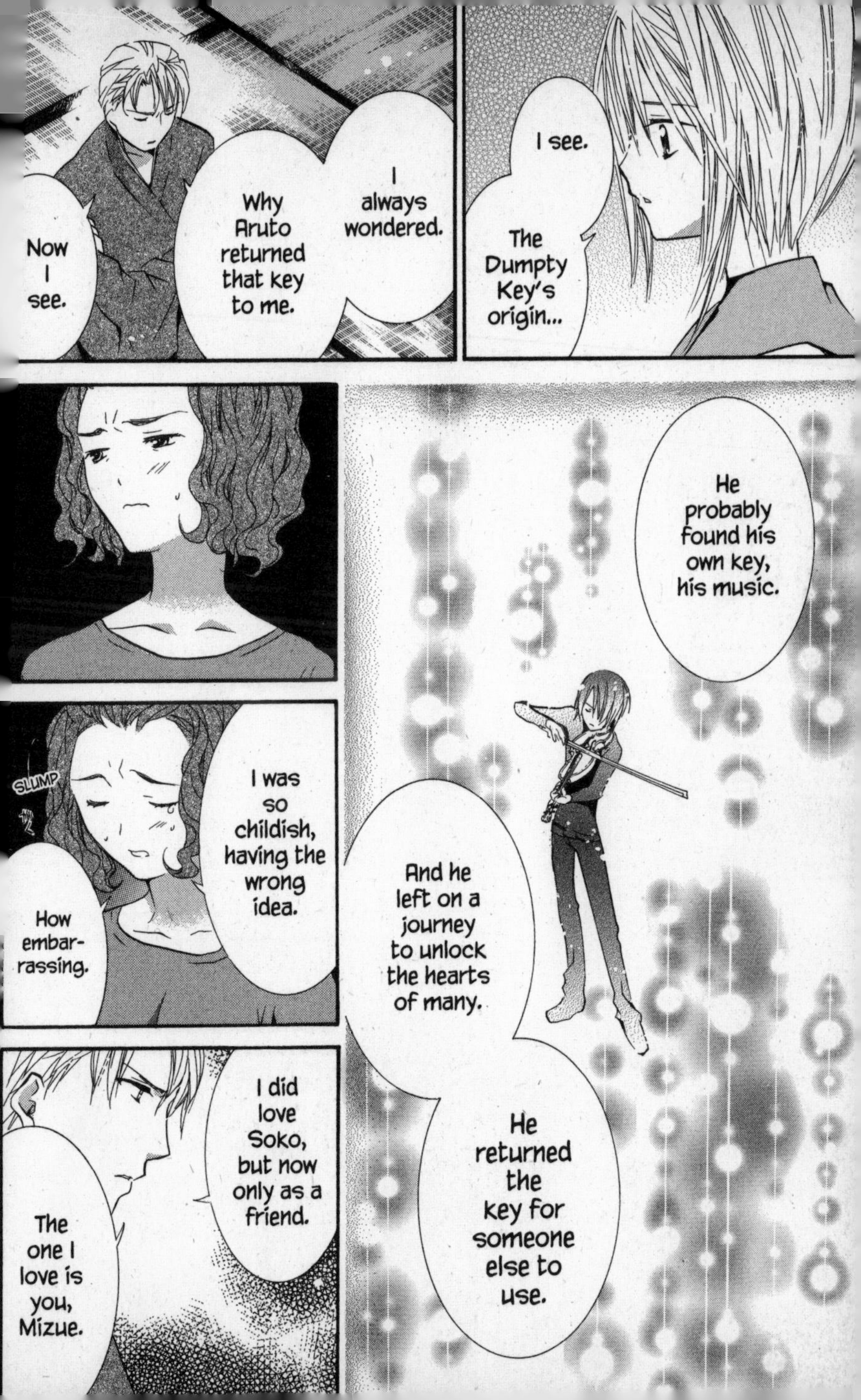
I see.
The Dumpty Key's origin...
I always wondered.
Why Aruto returned that key to me.
Now I see.
He probably found his own key, his music.
And he left on a journey to unlock the hearts of many.
He returned the key for someone else to use.
SLUMP
I was so childish, having the wrong idea.
How embarrassing.
I did love Soko, but now only as a friend.
The one I love is you, Mizue.

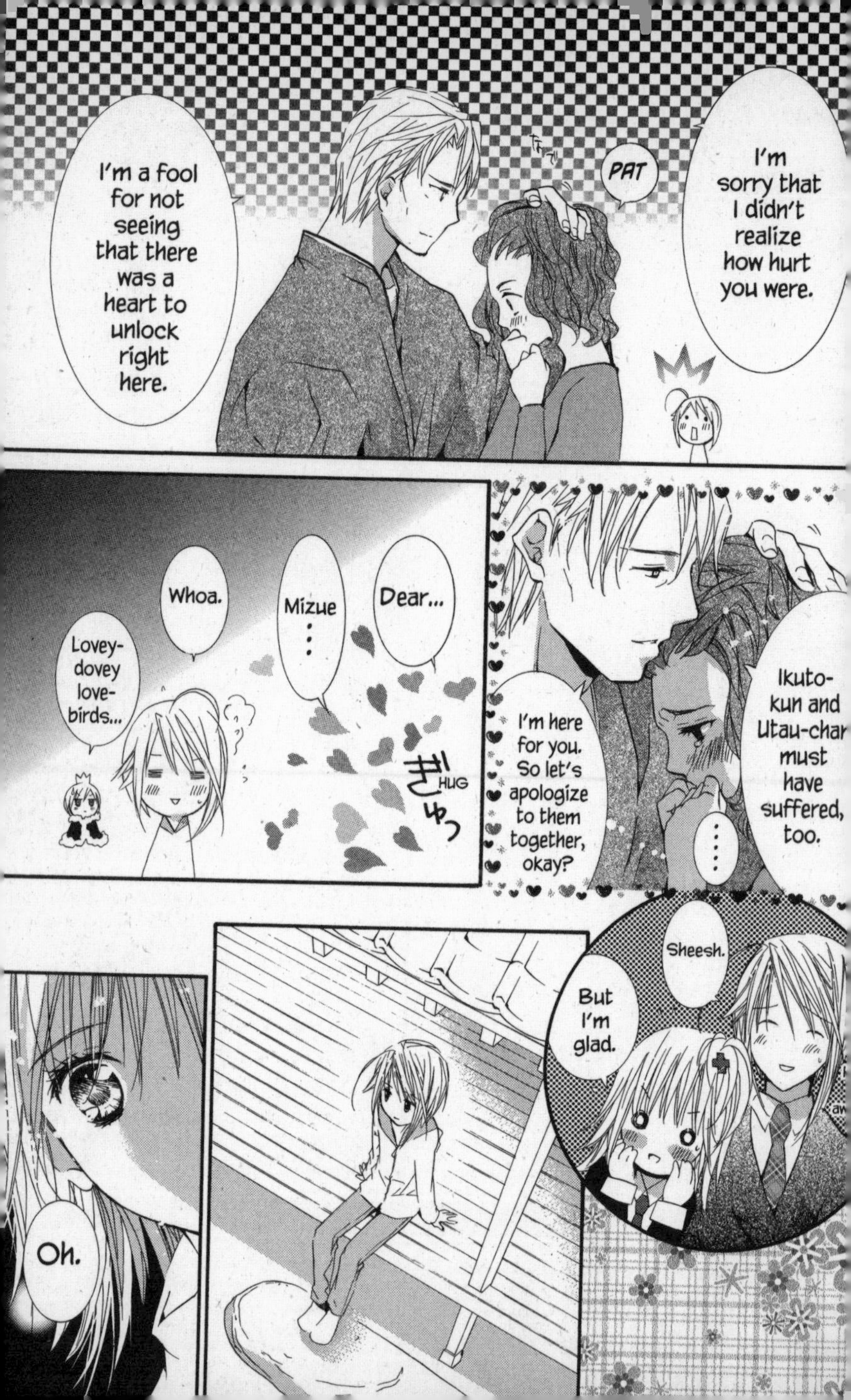
I'm sorry that I didn't realize how hurt you were.
PAT
I'm a fool for not seeing that there was a heart to unlock right here.
Ikuto-kun and Utau-chan must have suffered, too.
.....
I'm here for you. So let's apologize to them together, okay?
Dear...
Mizue ...
ぎゅっ HUG
Whoa.
Lovey-dovey love-birds...
Sheesh.
But I'm glad.
Oh.

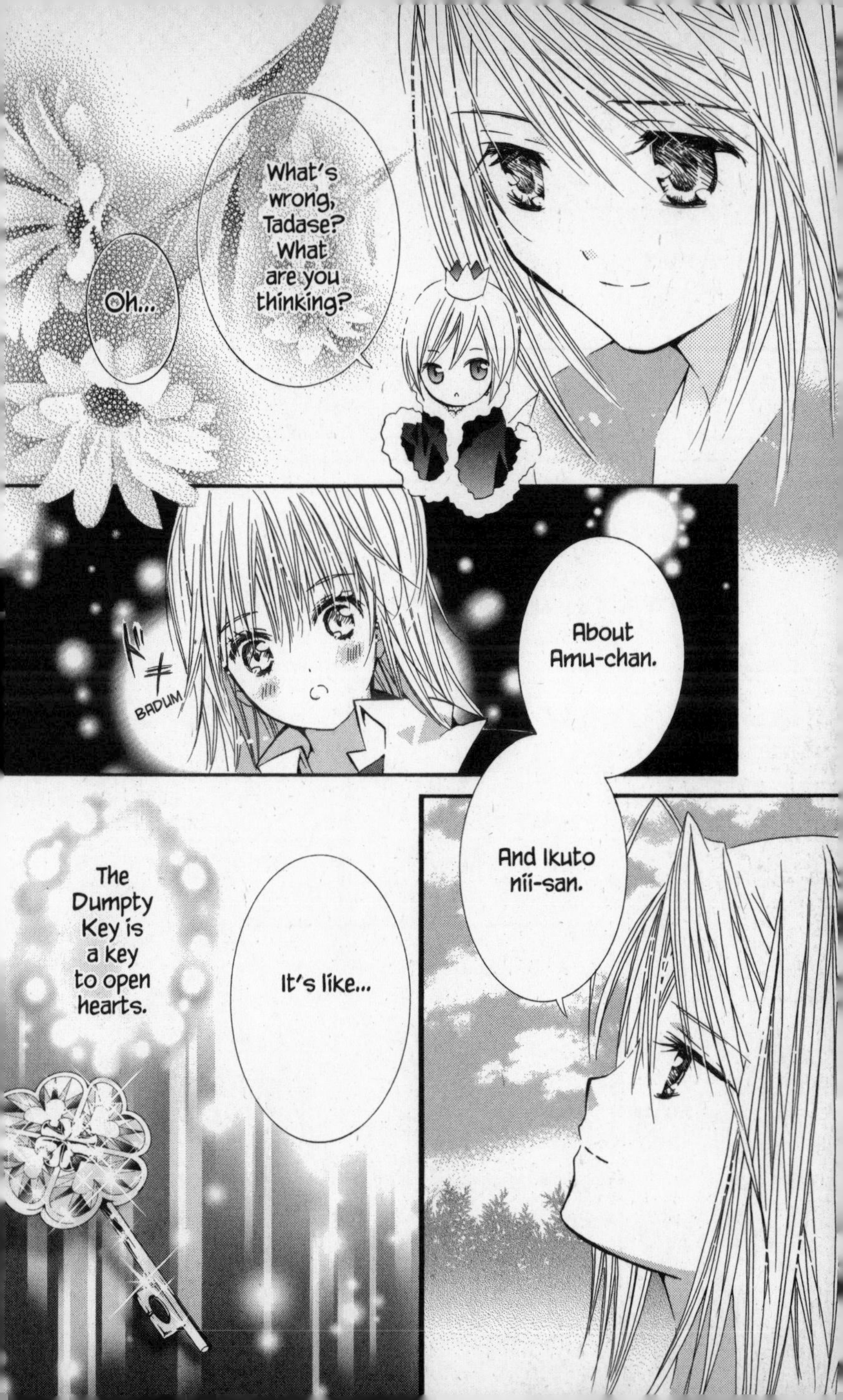

What's wrong, Tadase? What are you thinking?
Oh...
About Amu-chan.
BADUM
And Ikuto nii-san.
It's like...
The Dumpty Key is a key to open hearts.

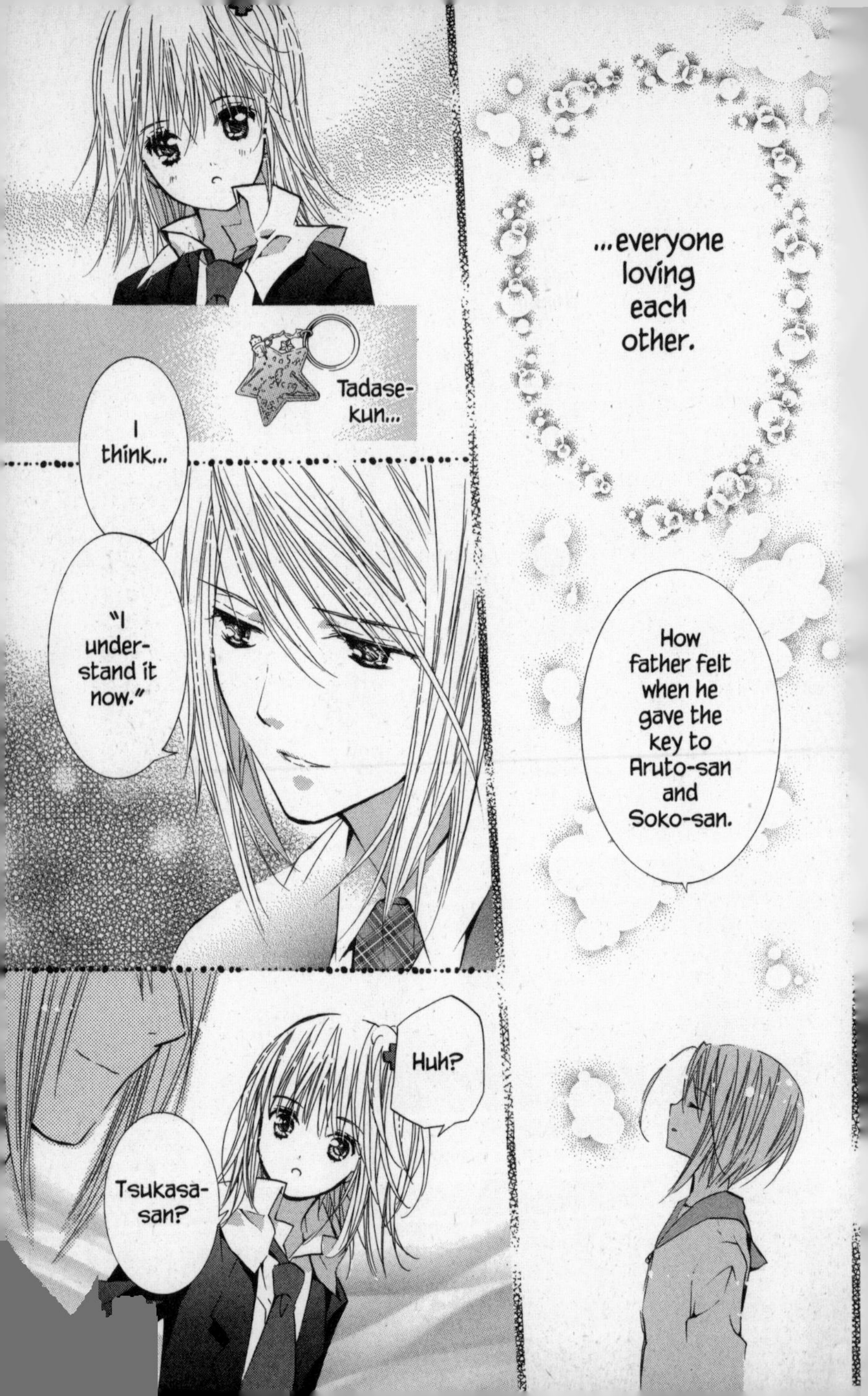
...everyone loving each other.
How father felt when he gave the key to Aruto-san and Soko-san.
Tadase-kun...
I think...
"I understand it now."
Huh?
Tsukasa-san?

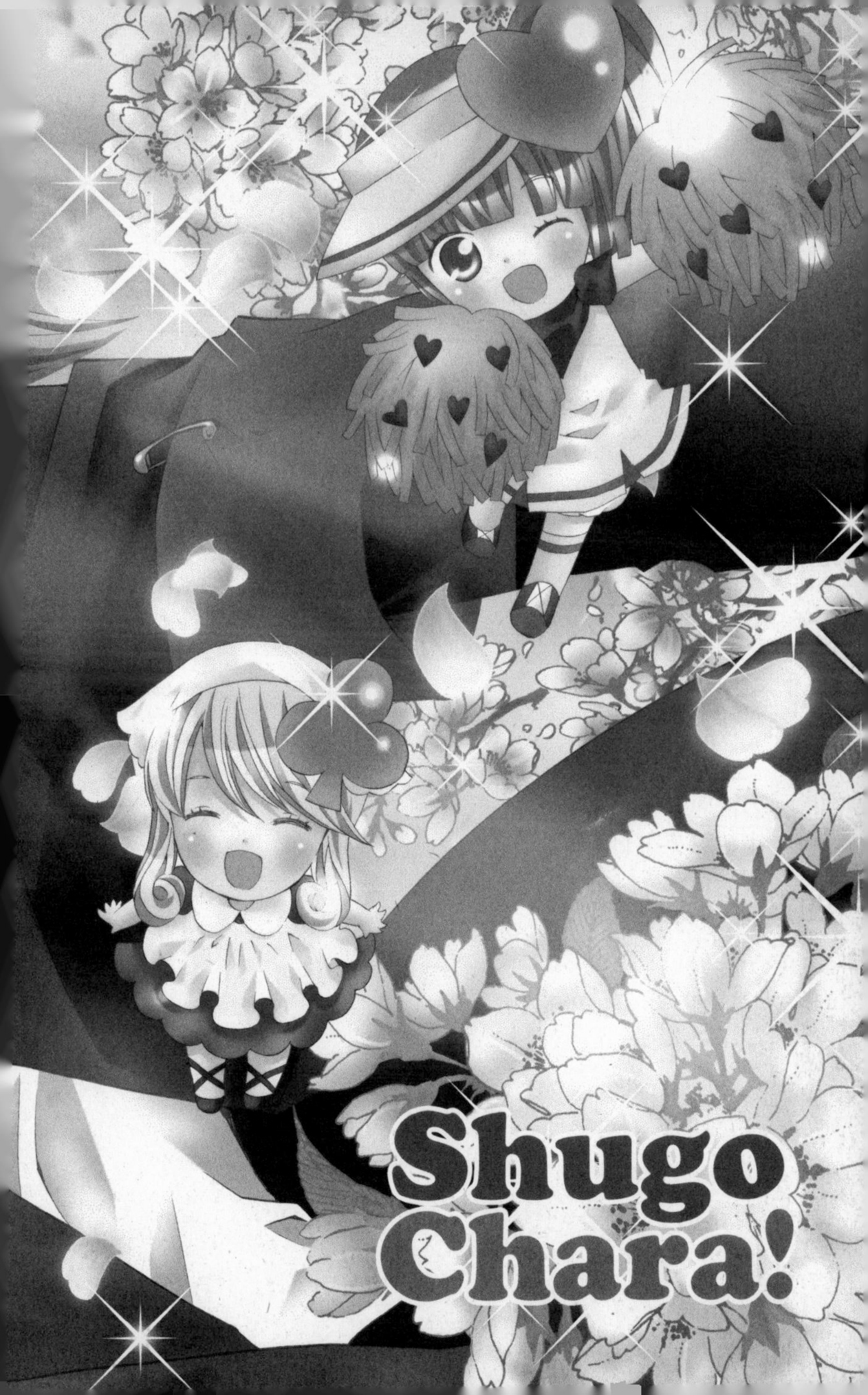
Shugo
Chara!

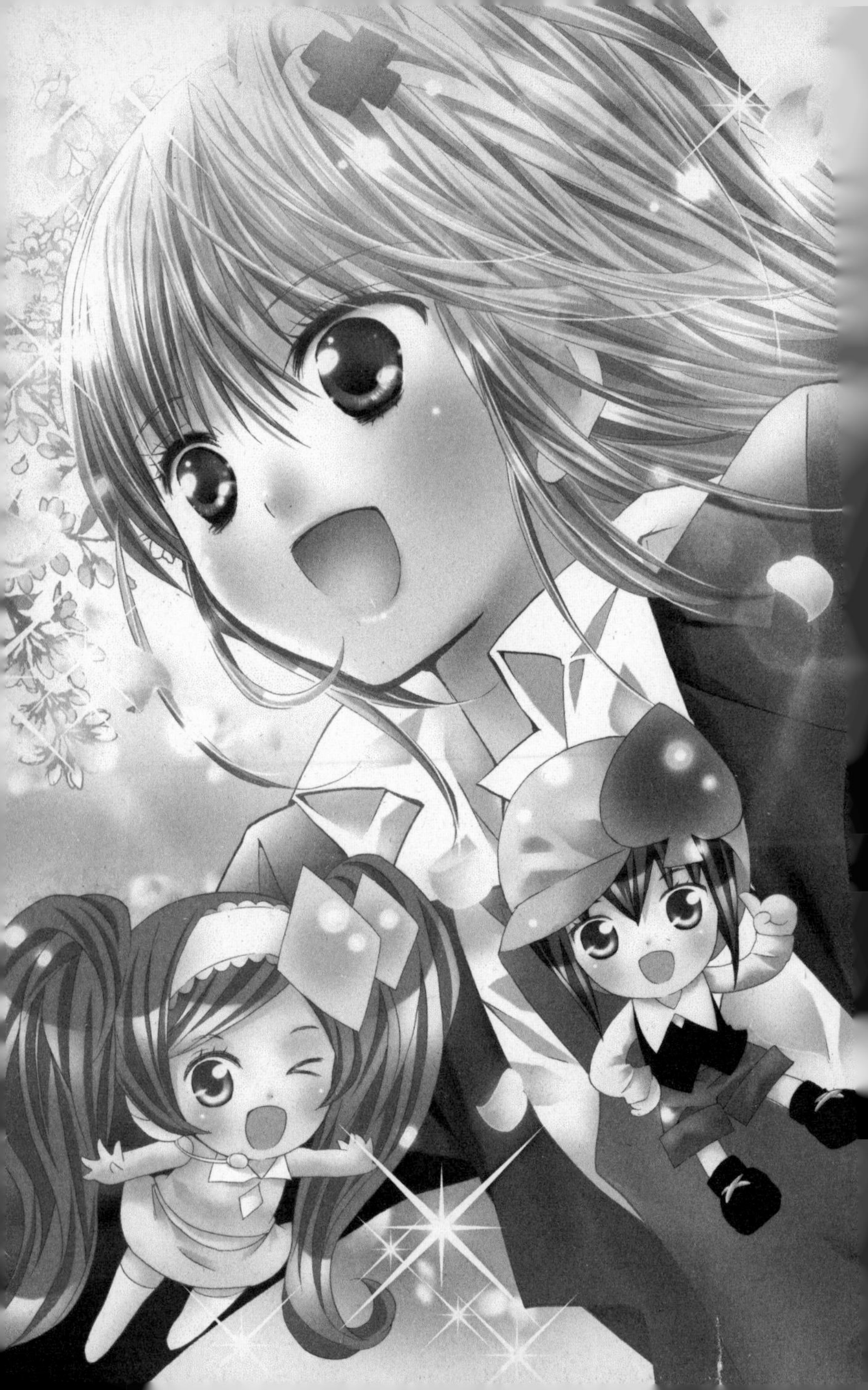

Shugo
Chara!

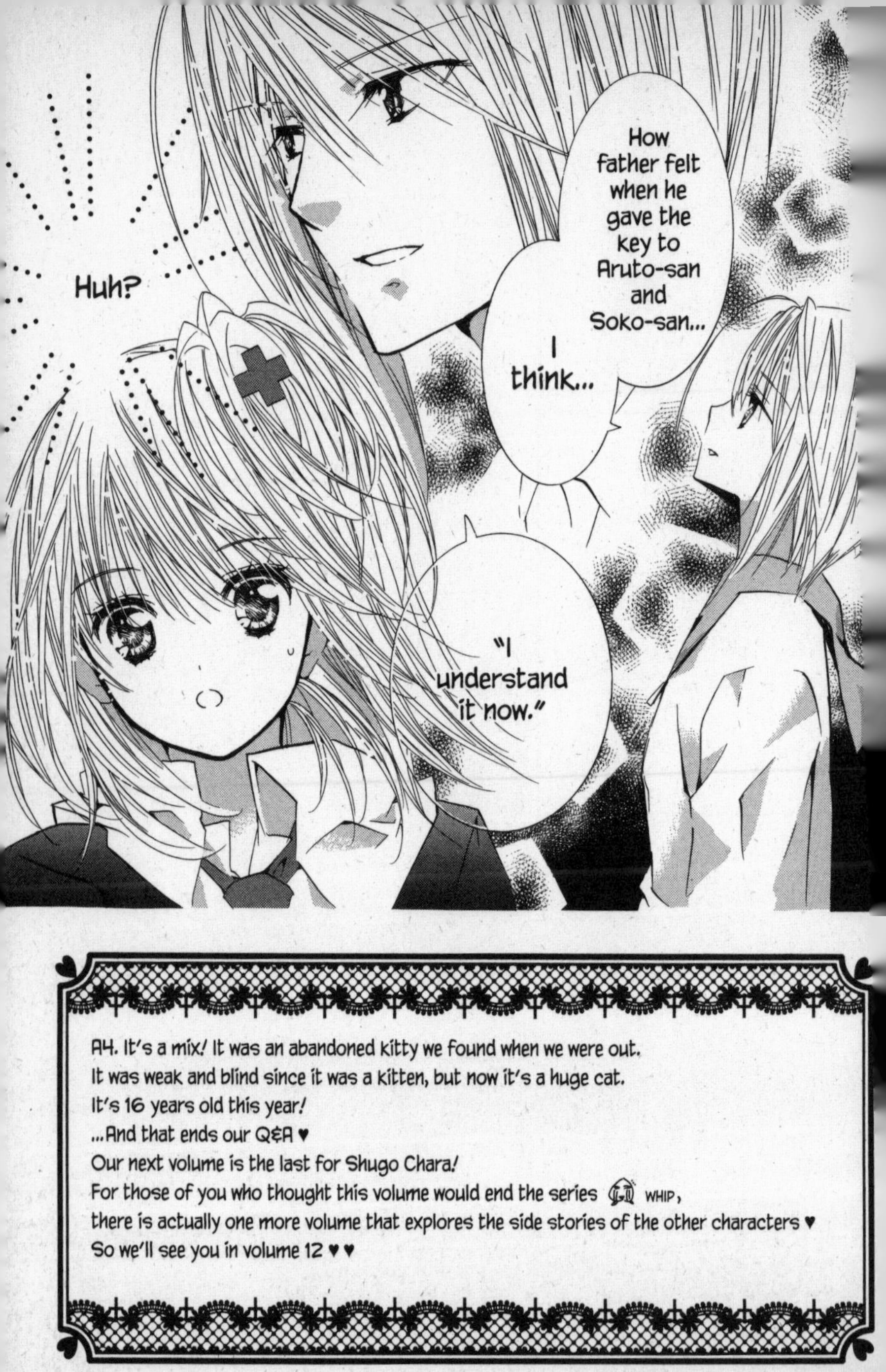
How father felt when he gave the key to Aruto-san and Soko-san...
I think...
"I understand it now."
Huh?

A4. It's a mix! It was an abandoned kitty we found when we were out.
It was weak and blind since it was a kitten, but now it's a huge cat.
It's 16 years old this year!
...And that ends our Q&A ♥
Our next volume is the last for Shugo Chara!
For those of you who thought this volume would end the series WHIP,
there is actually one more volume that explores the side stories of the other characters ♥
So we'll see you in volume 12 ♥ ♥

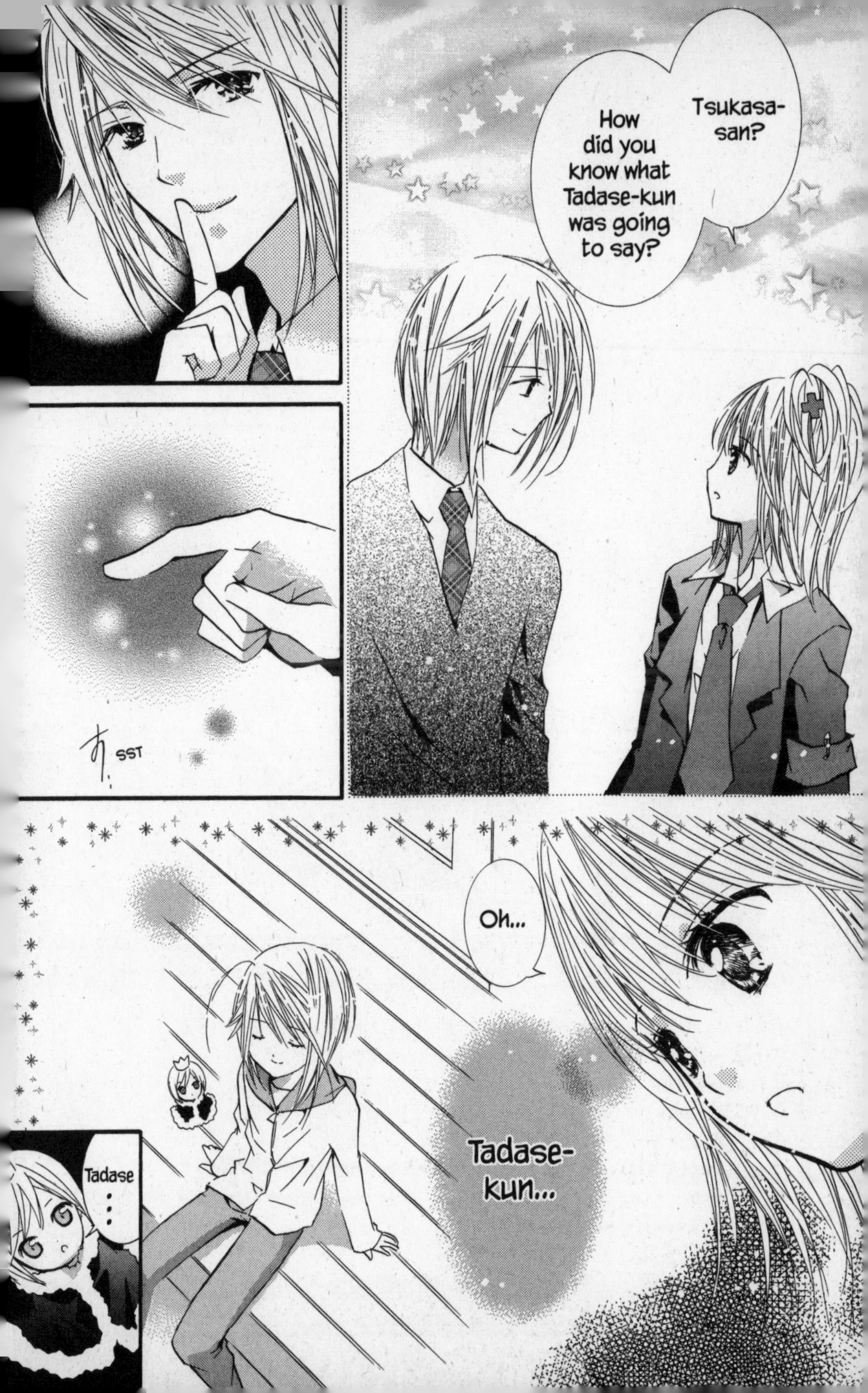
Tsukasa-san?
How did you know what Tadase-kun was going to say?
SST
Oh...
Tadase-kun...
Tadase
...

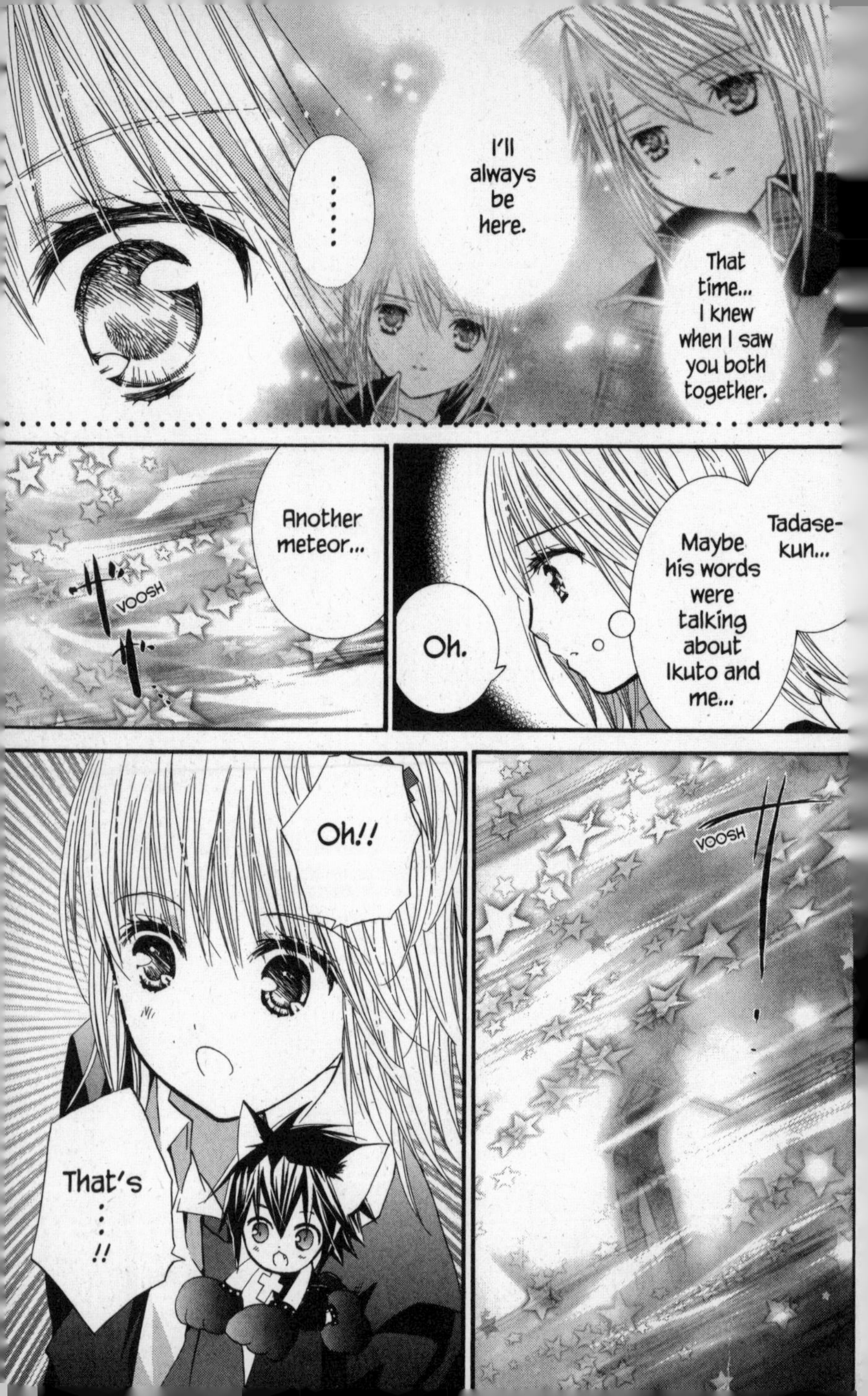
That time... I knew when I saw you both together.
I'll always be here.
......
Tadase-kun...
Maybe his words were talking about Ikuto and me...
Oh.
Another meteor...
VOOSH
VOOSH
Oh!!
That's ......!!

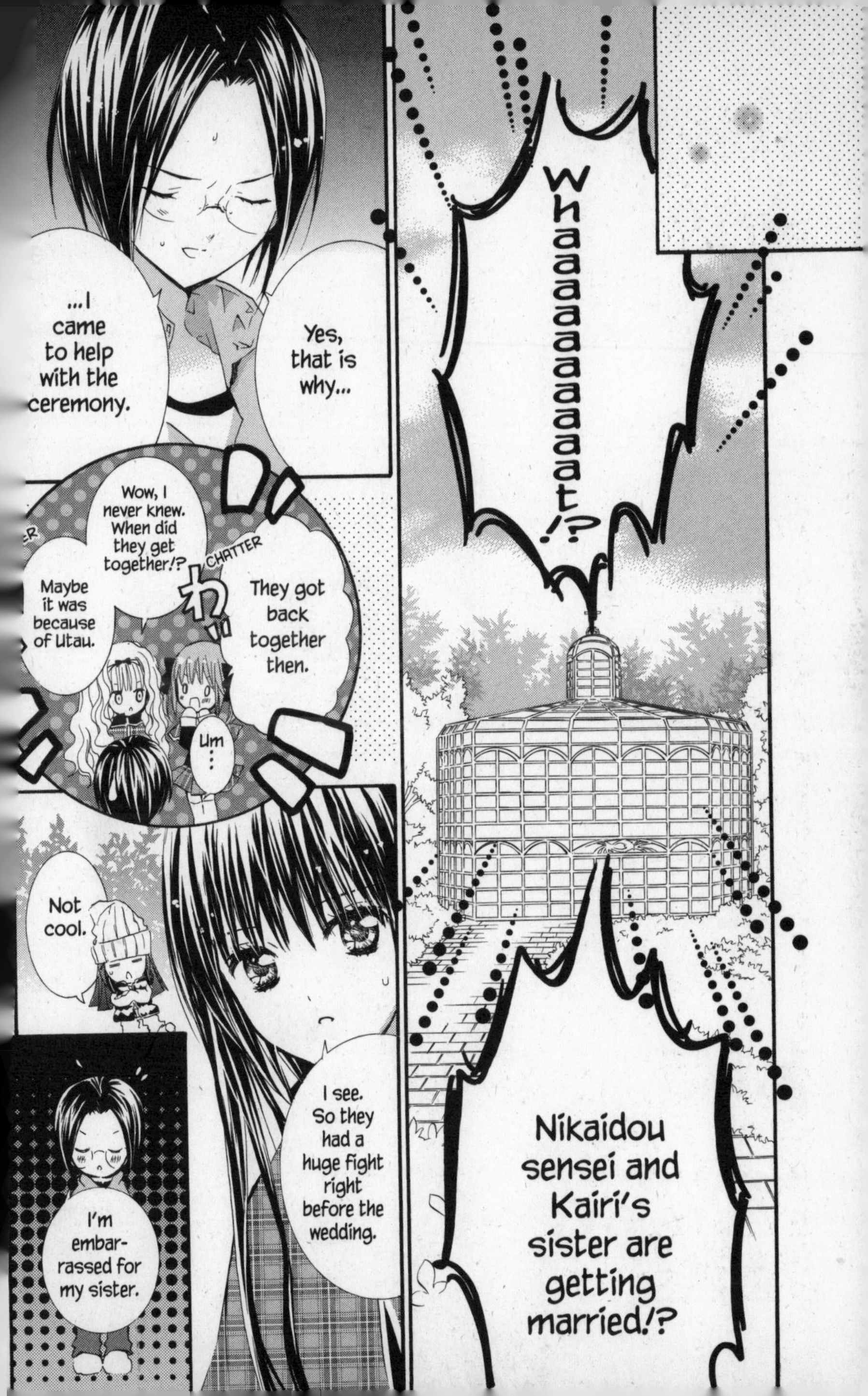
Whaaaaaaaaaat!?
Nikaidou sensei and Kairi's sister are getting married!?
Yes, that is why...
...I came to help with the ceremony.
They got back together then.
Wow, I never knew. When did they get together!?
CHATTER
Maybe it was because of Utau.
Um...
I see. So they had a huge fight right before the wedding.
Not cool.
I'm embarrassed for my sister.

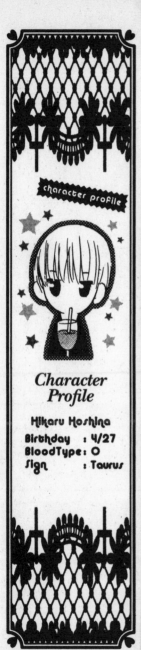

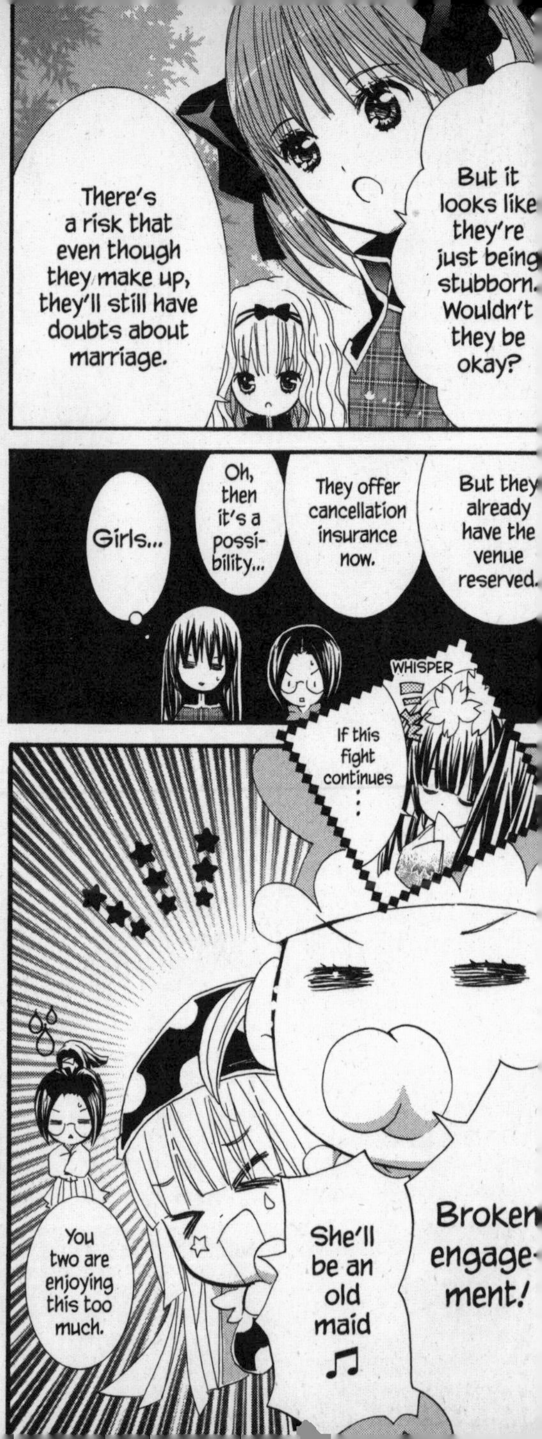
But it looks like they're just being stubborn. Wouldn't they be okay?
There's a risk that even though they make up, they'll still have doubts about marriage.
But they already have the venue reserved.
They offer cancellation insurance now.
Oh, then it's a possibility...
Girls...
WHISPER
If this fight continues...
Broken engagement!
She'll be an old maid ♪
You two are enjoying this too much.

character profile

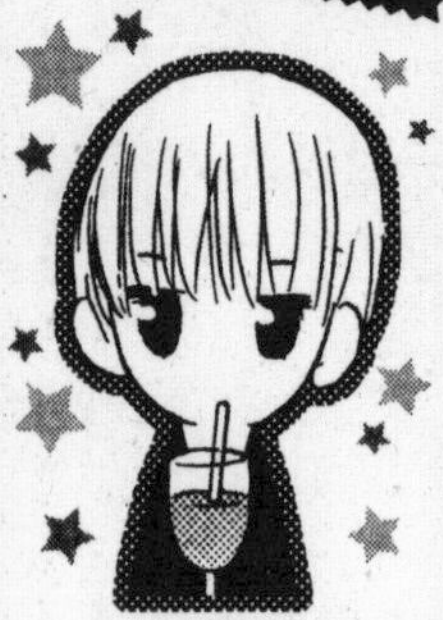

Character Profile

Hikaru Hoshina

Birthday : 4/27
BloodType : O
Sign : Taurus

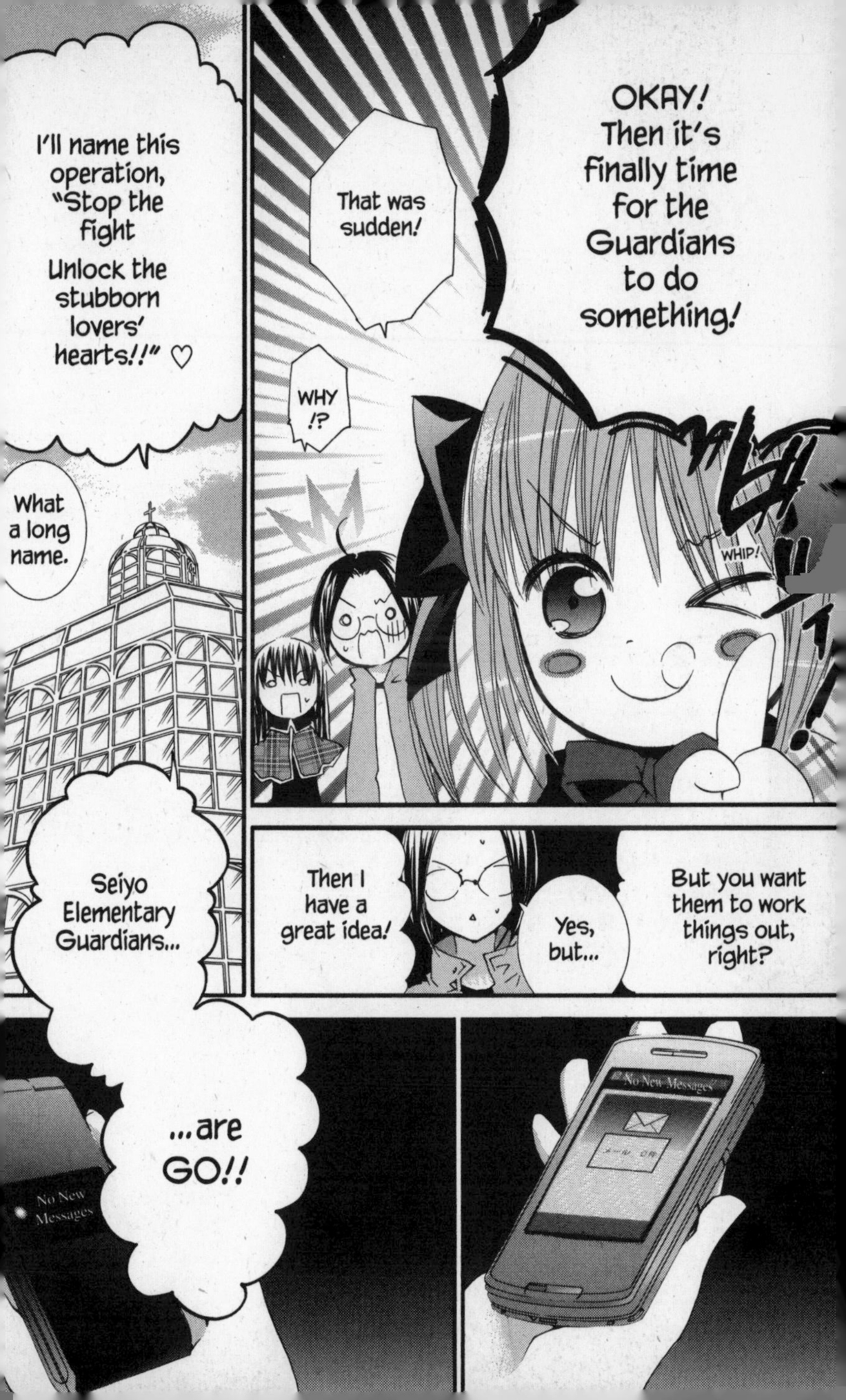

OKAY! Then it's finally time for the Guardians to do something!
WHIP!
That was sudden!
WHY!?
But you want them to work things out, right?
Yes, but...
Then I have a great idea!
I'll name this operation, "Stop the fight Unlock the stubborn lovers' hearts!!" ♡
What a long name.
Seiyo Elementary Guardians...
No New Messages
...are GO!!
No New Messages

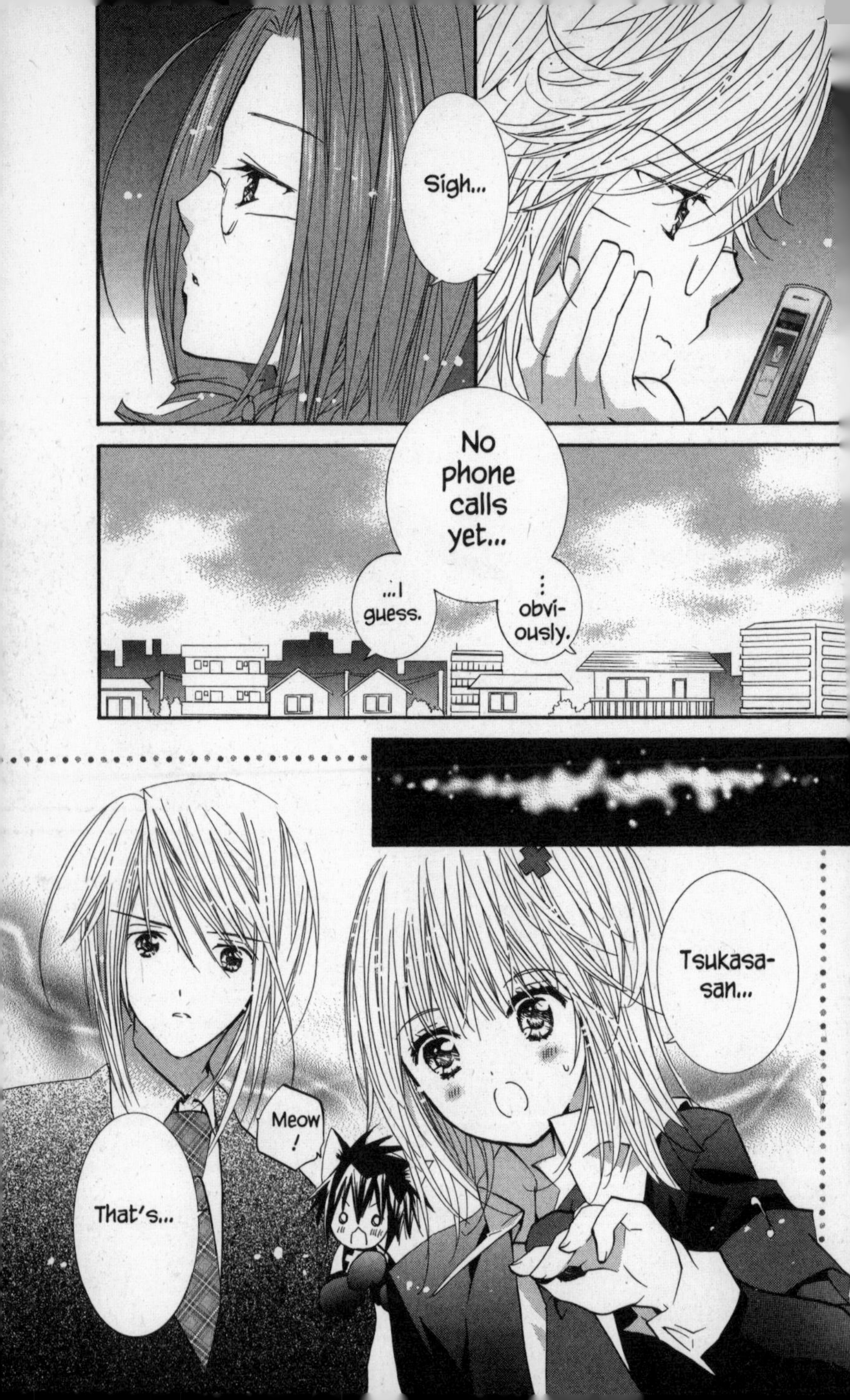
Sigh...
No phone calls yet...
...obviously.
...I guess.
Tsukasa-san...
Meow!
That's...

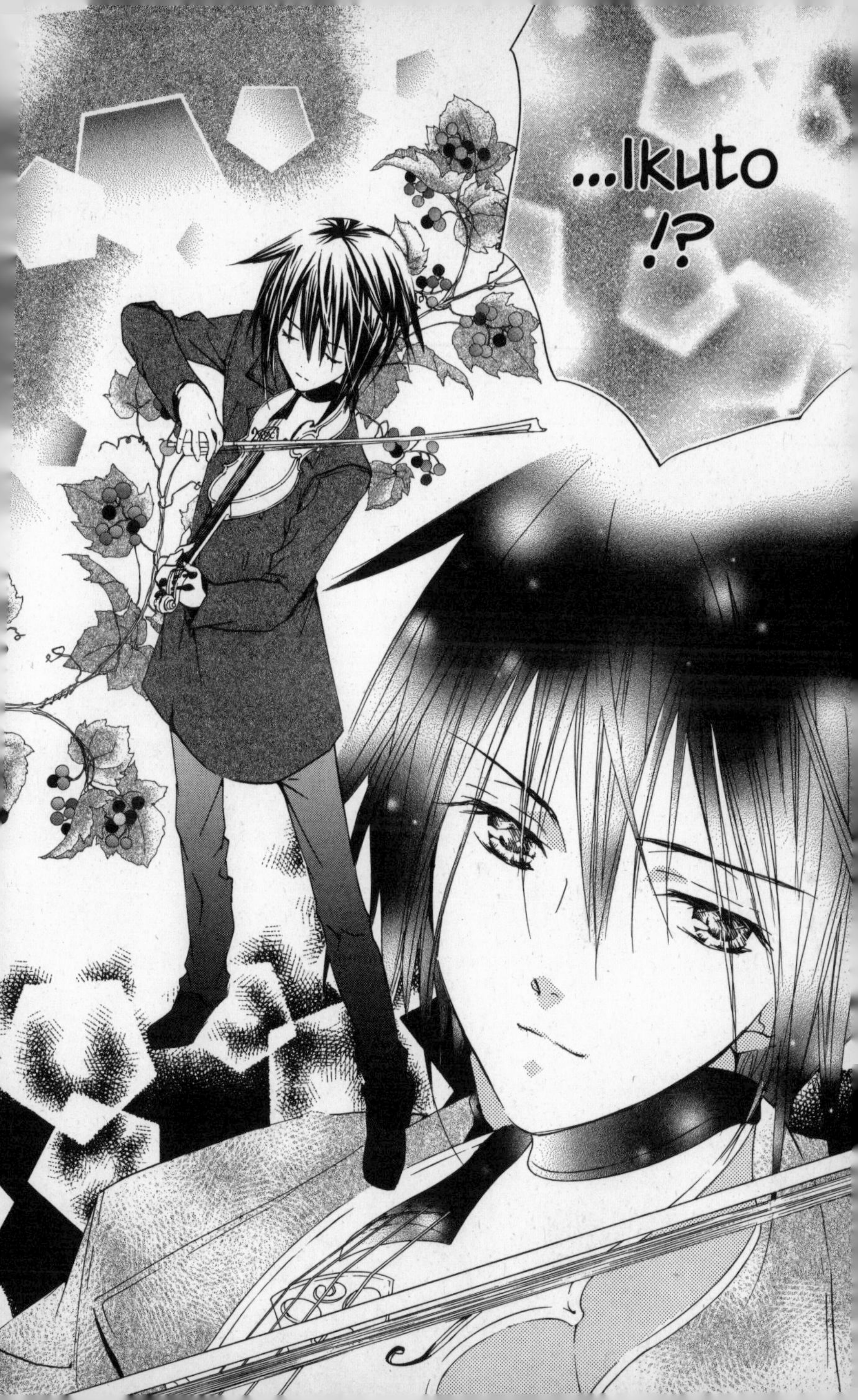
...Ikuto
!?

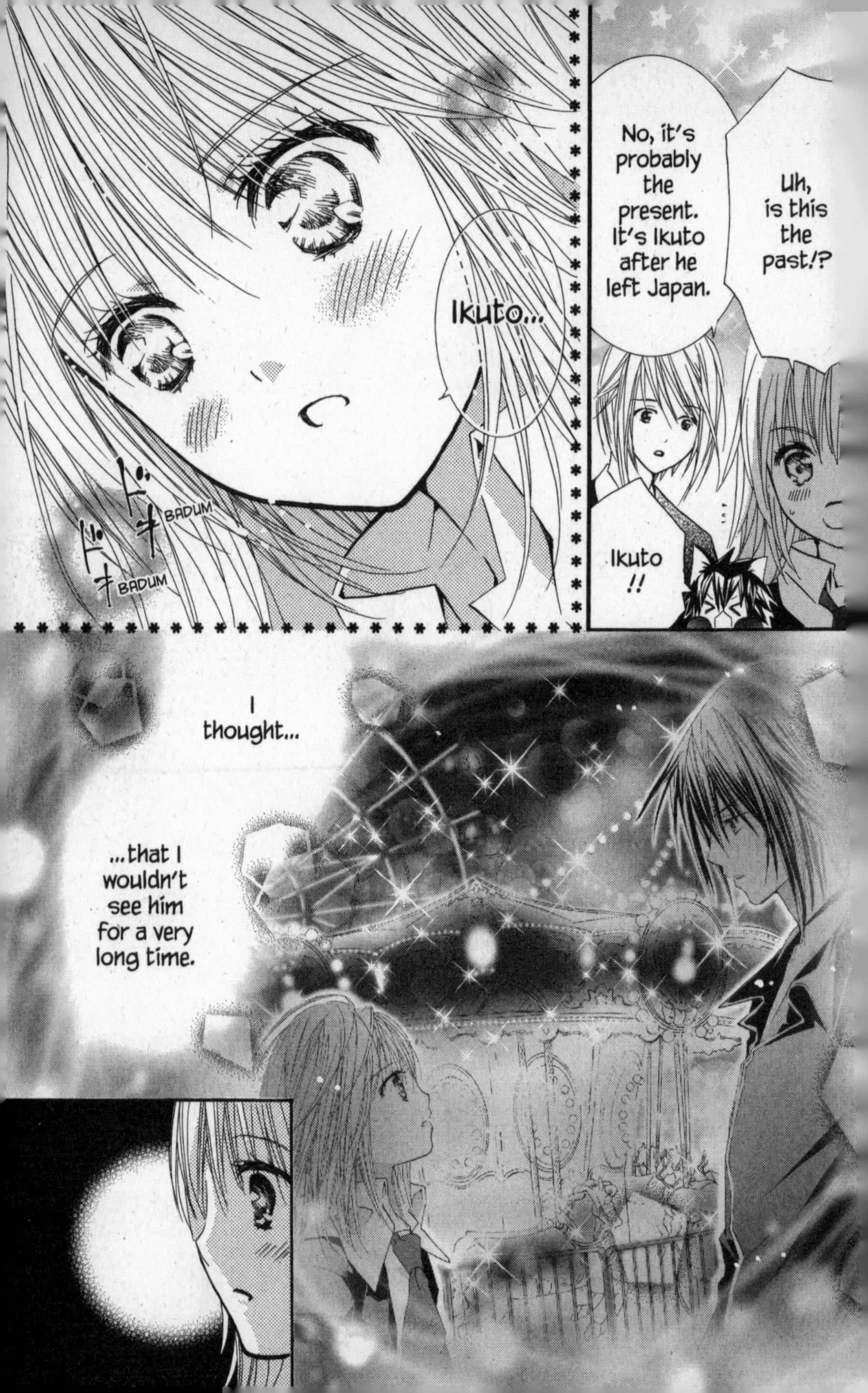
Uh, is this the past!?
No, it's probably the present. It's Ikuto after he left Japan.
Ikuto!!
Ikuto...
ドキ BADUM
ドキ BADUM
I thought...
...that I wouldn't see him for a very long time.

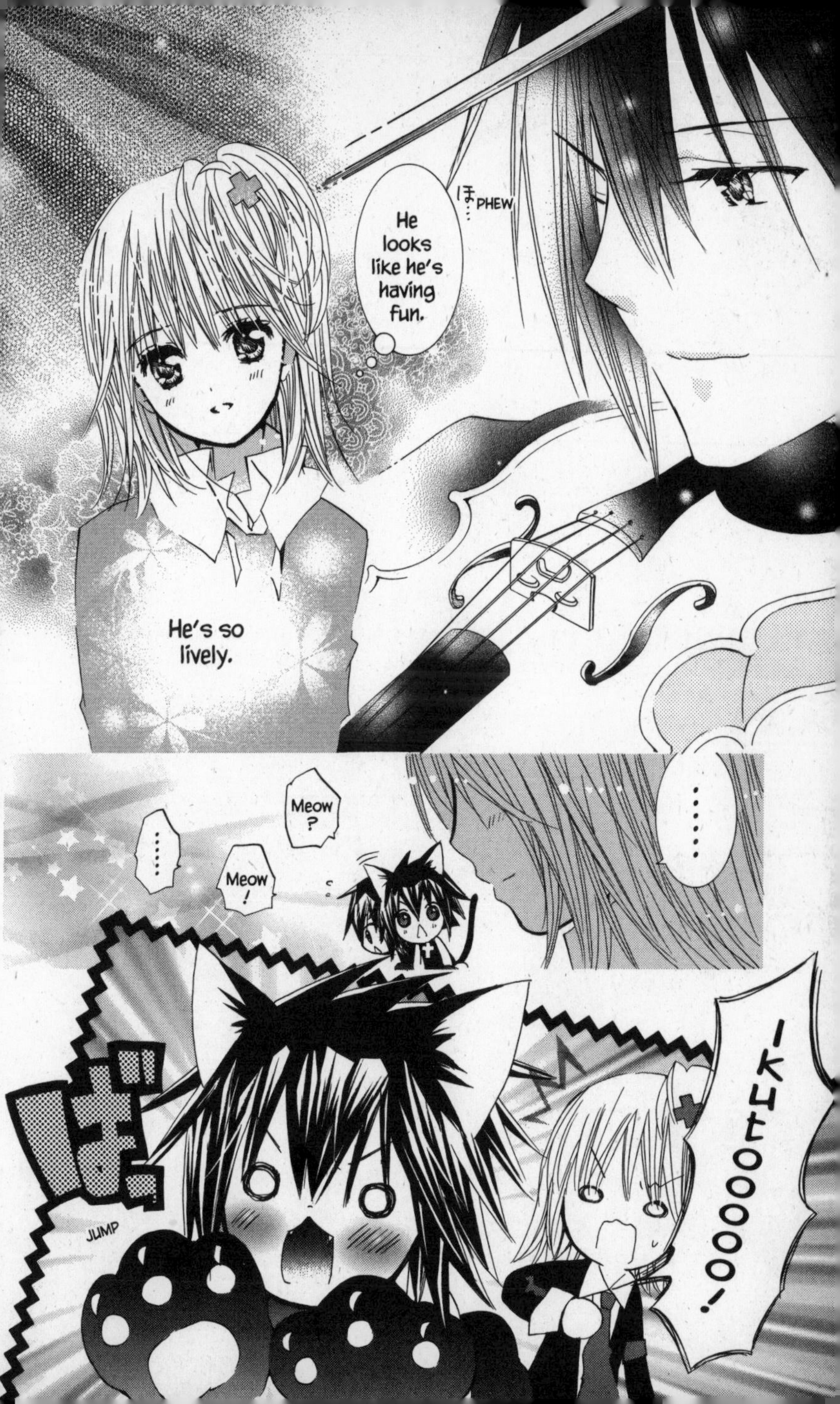

ほ… PHEW
He looks like he's having fun.
He's so lively.
......
Meow?
Meow!
......
IKUTOOOOOO!
JUMP

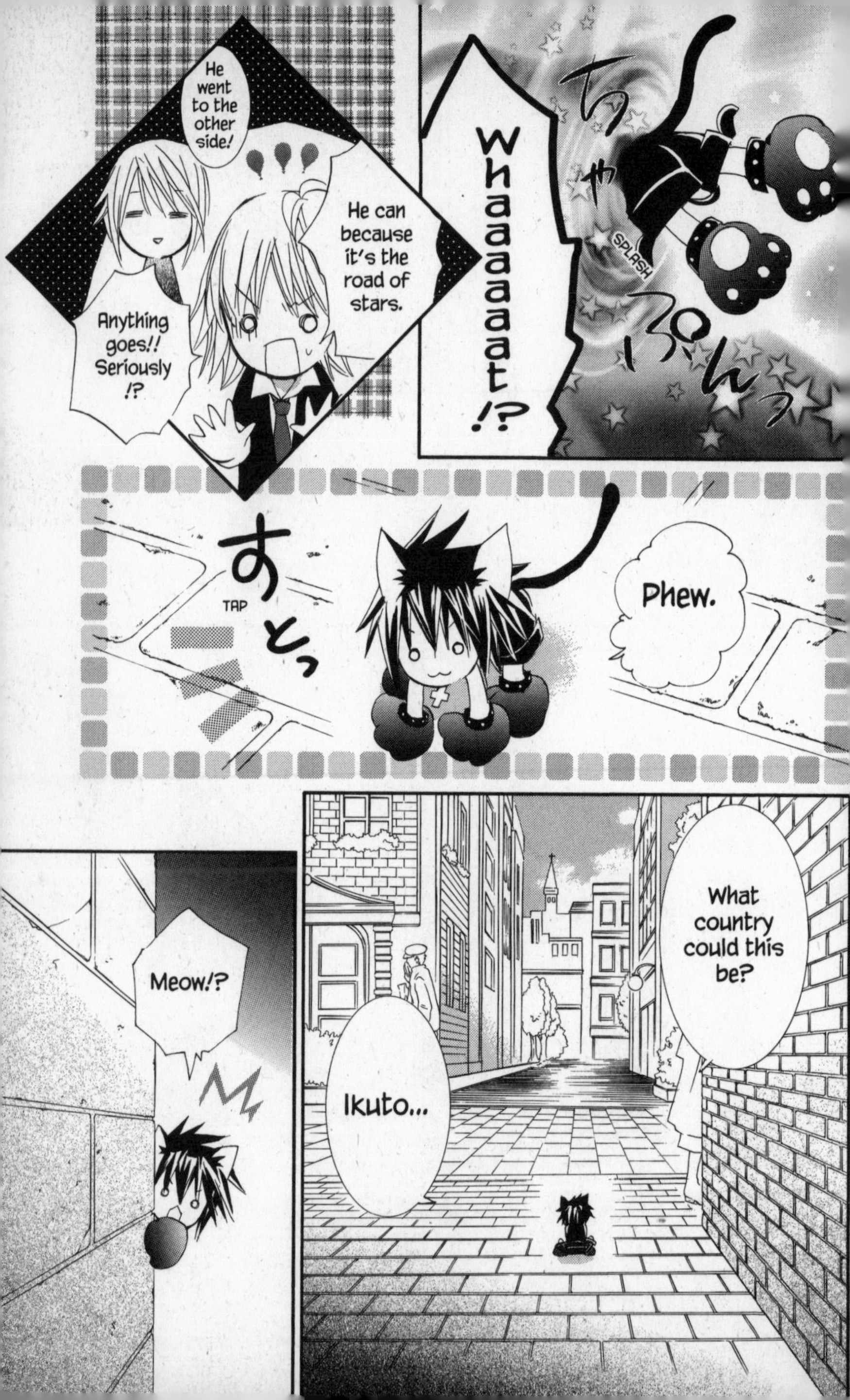
Whaaaaaat!?
SPLASH
He went to the other side!
He can because it's the road of stars.
Anything goes!! Seriously!?
Phew.
TAP
What country could this be?
Ikuto...
Meow!?

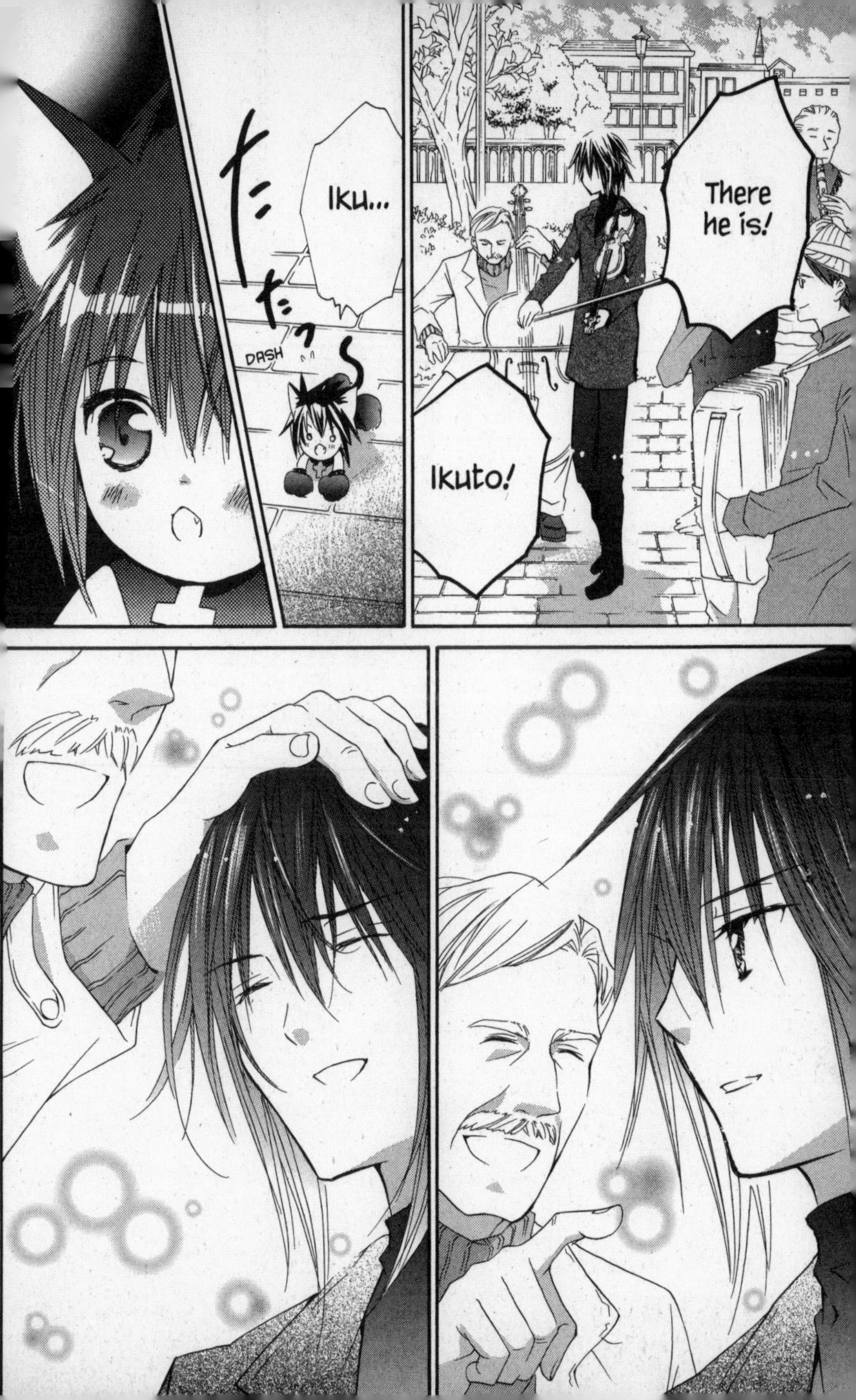
There he is!
Ikuto!
Iku...
DASH

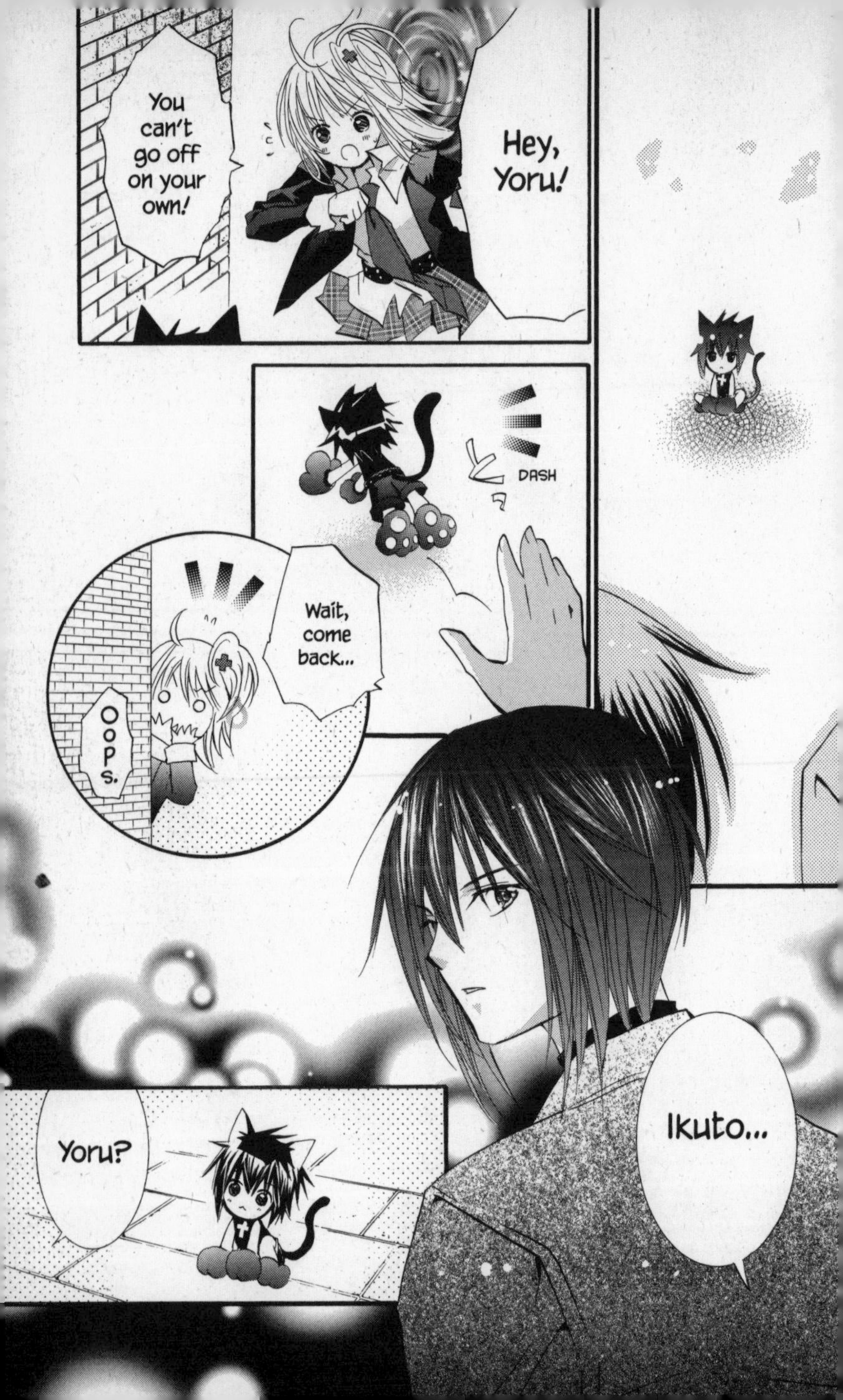
Hey, Yoru!
You can't go off on your own!
DASH
Wait, come back...
Oops.
Ikuto...
Yoru?

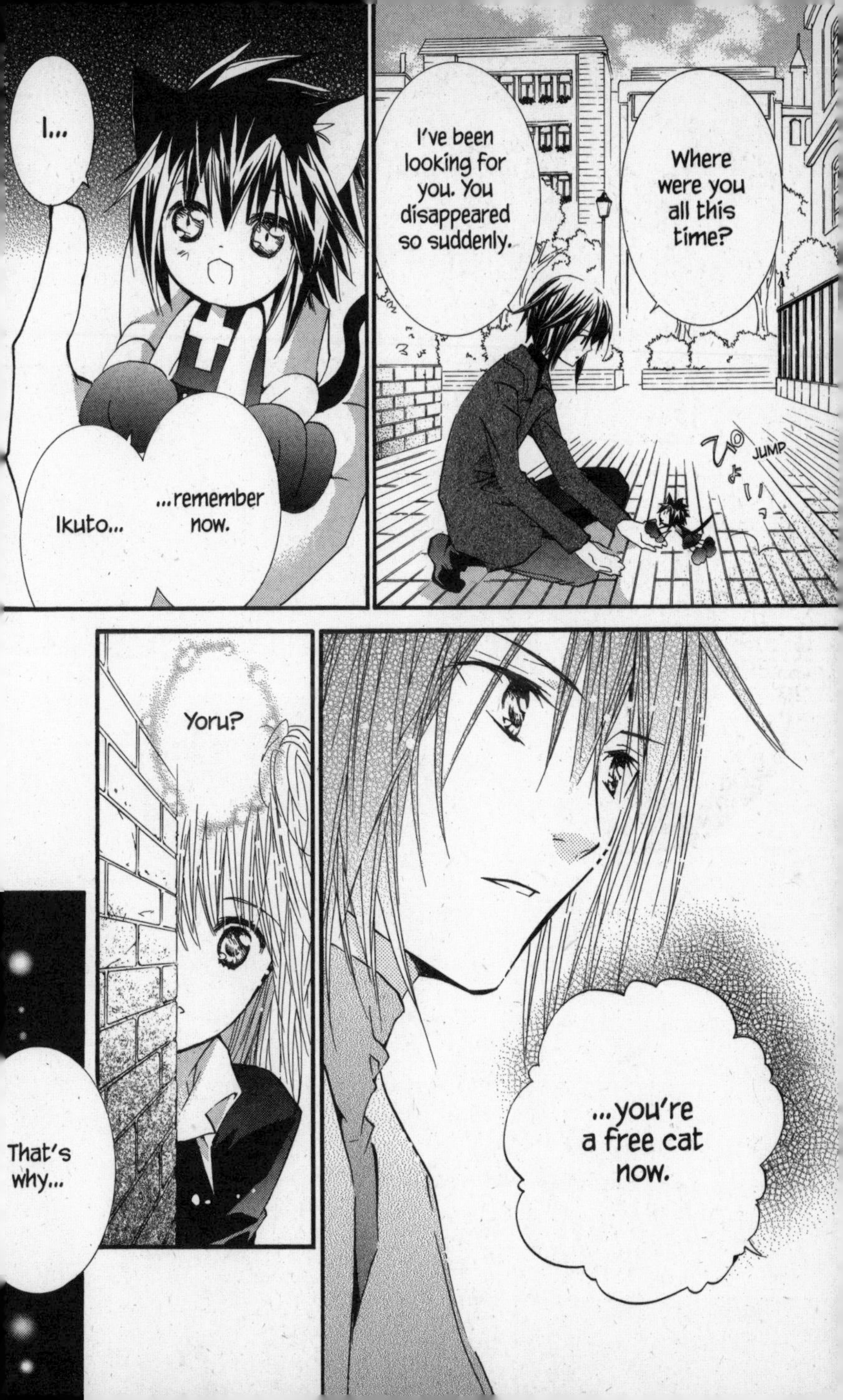
Where were you all this time?
I've been looking for you. You disappeared so suddenly.
JUMP
I...
Ikuto...
...remember now.
...you're a free cat now.
Yoru?
That's why...

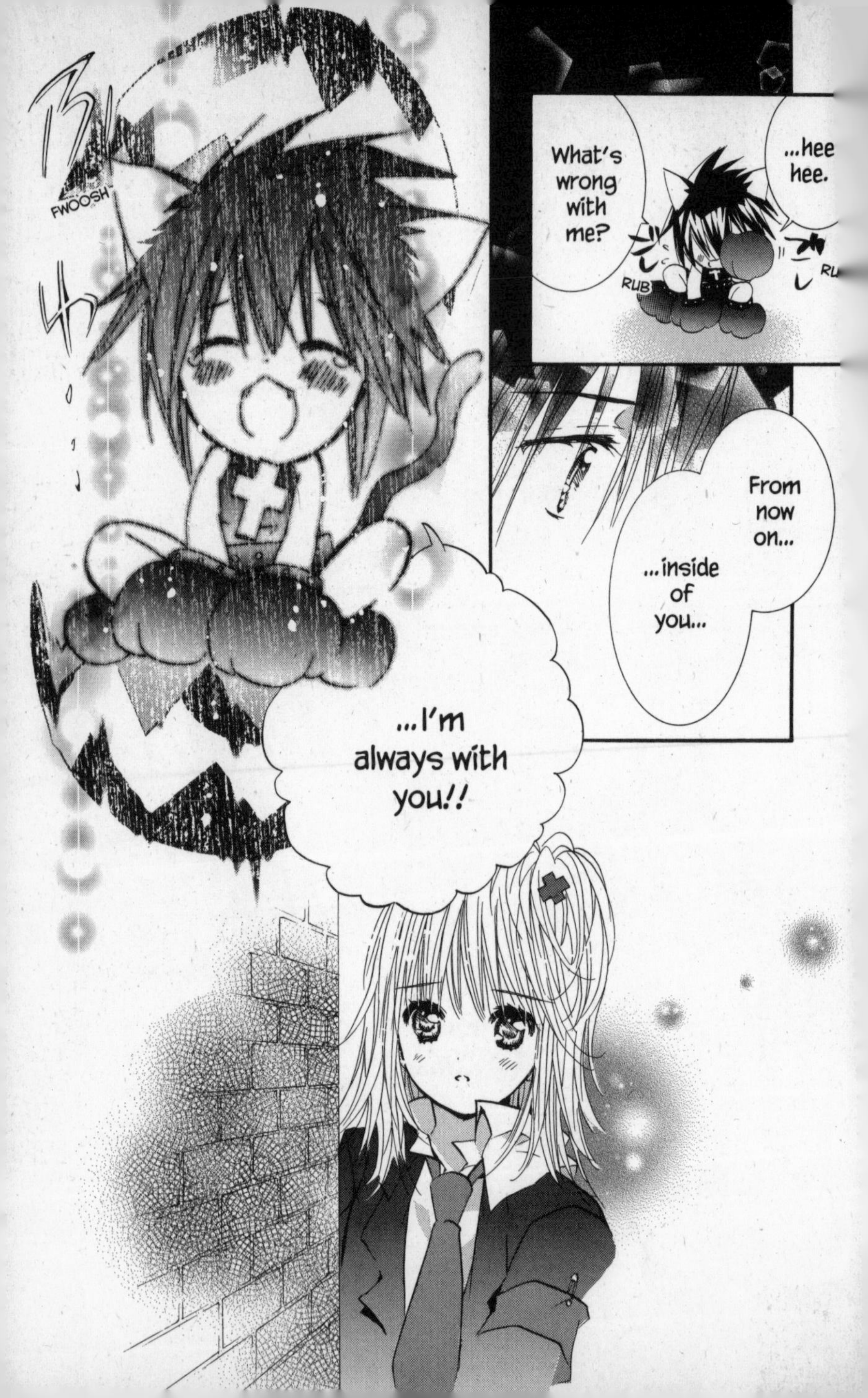
...hee hee.
What's wrong with me?
RUB
RUB
From now on...
...inside of you...
FWOOSH
...I'm always with you!!

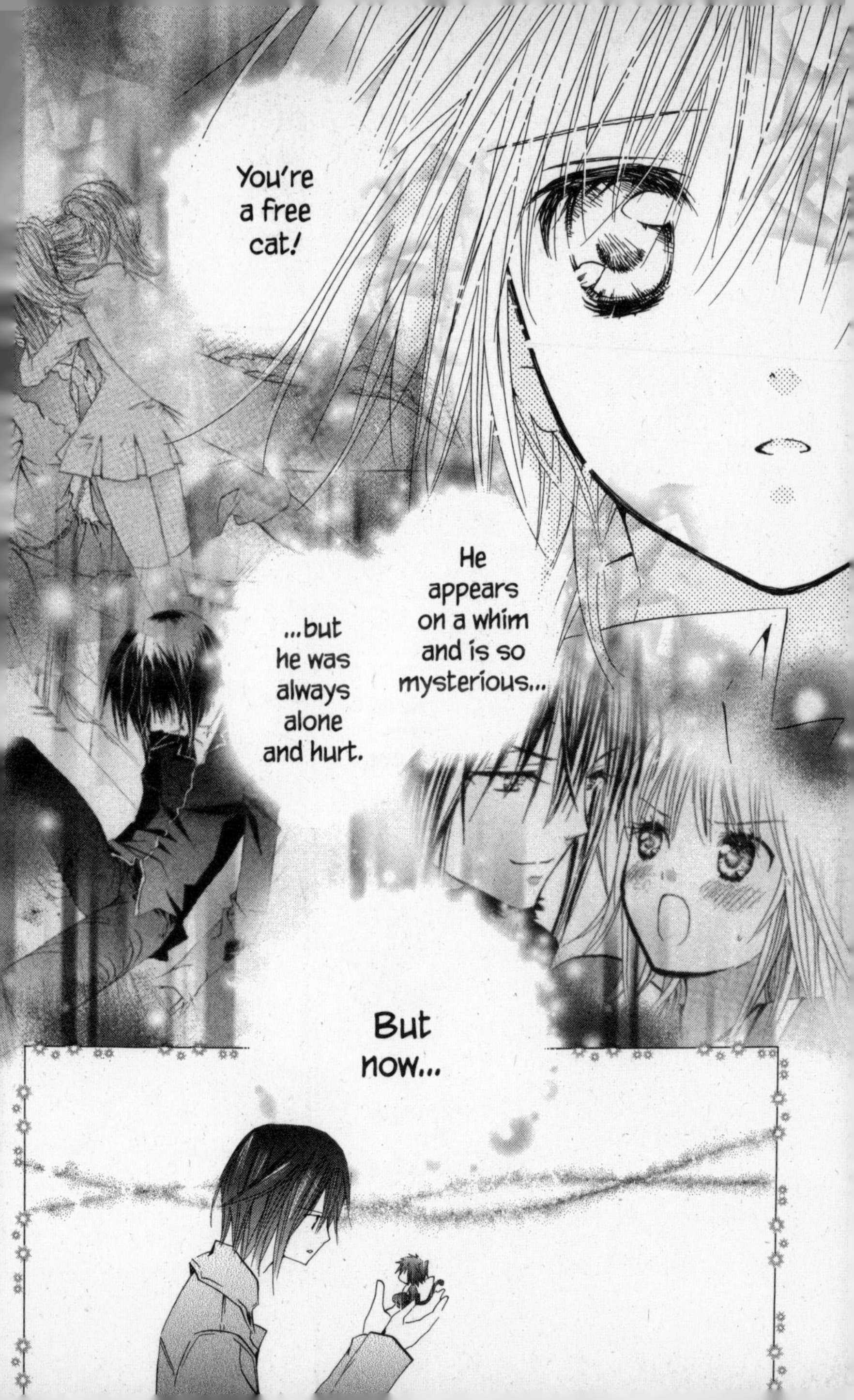
You're a free cat!
He appears on a whim and is so mysterious...
...but he was always alone and hurt.
But now...

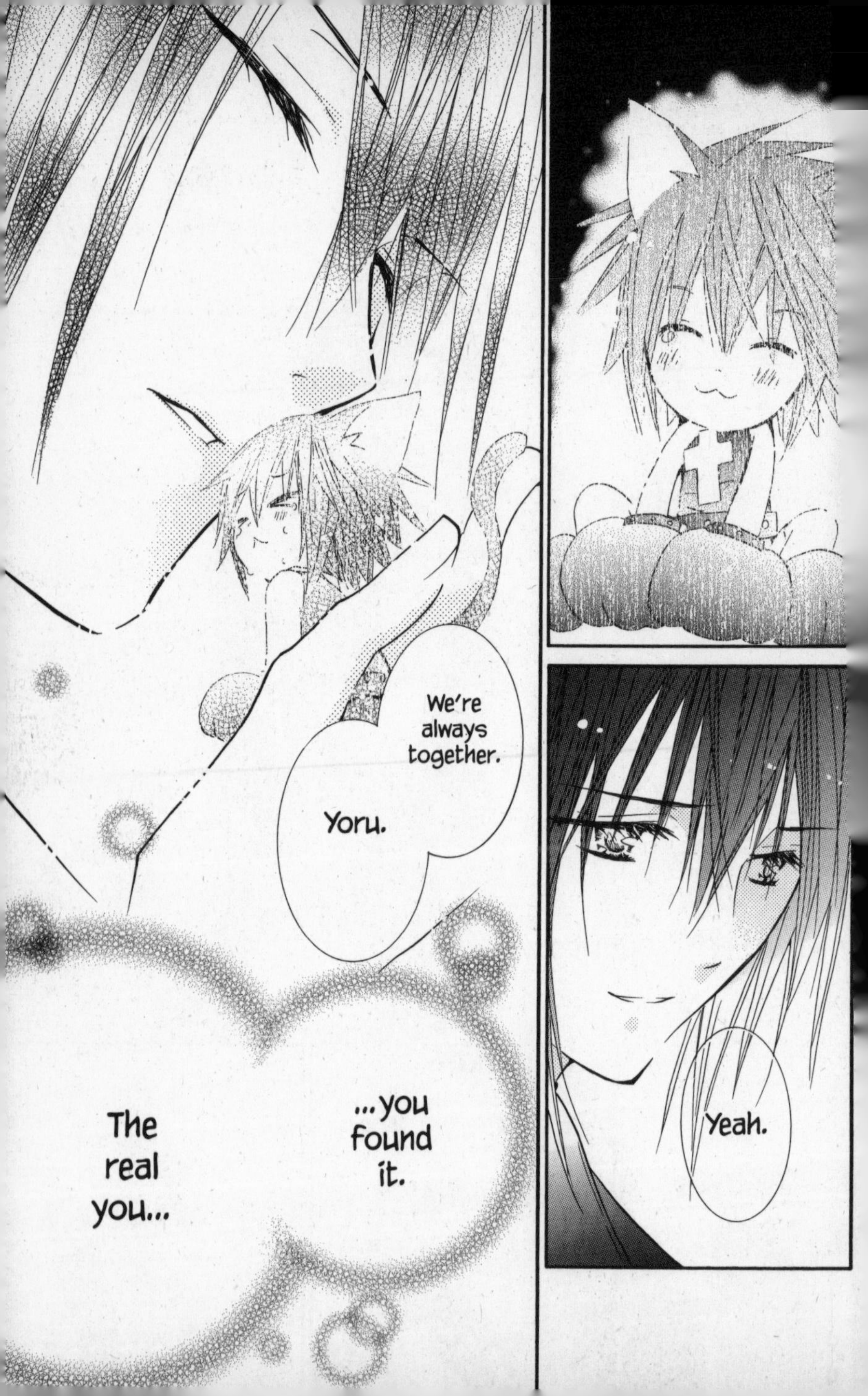
Yeah.
We're always together.
Yoru.
...you found it.
The real you...

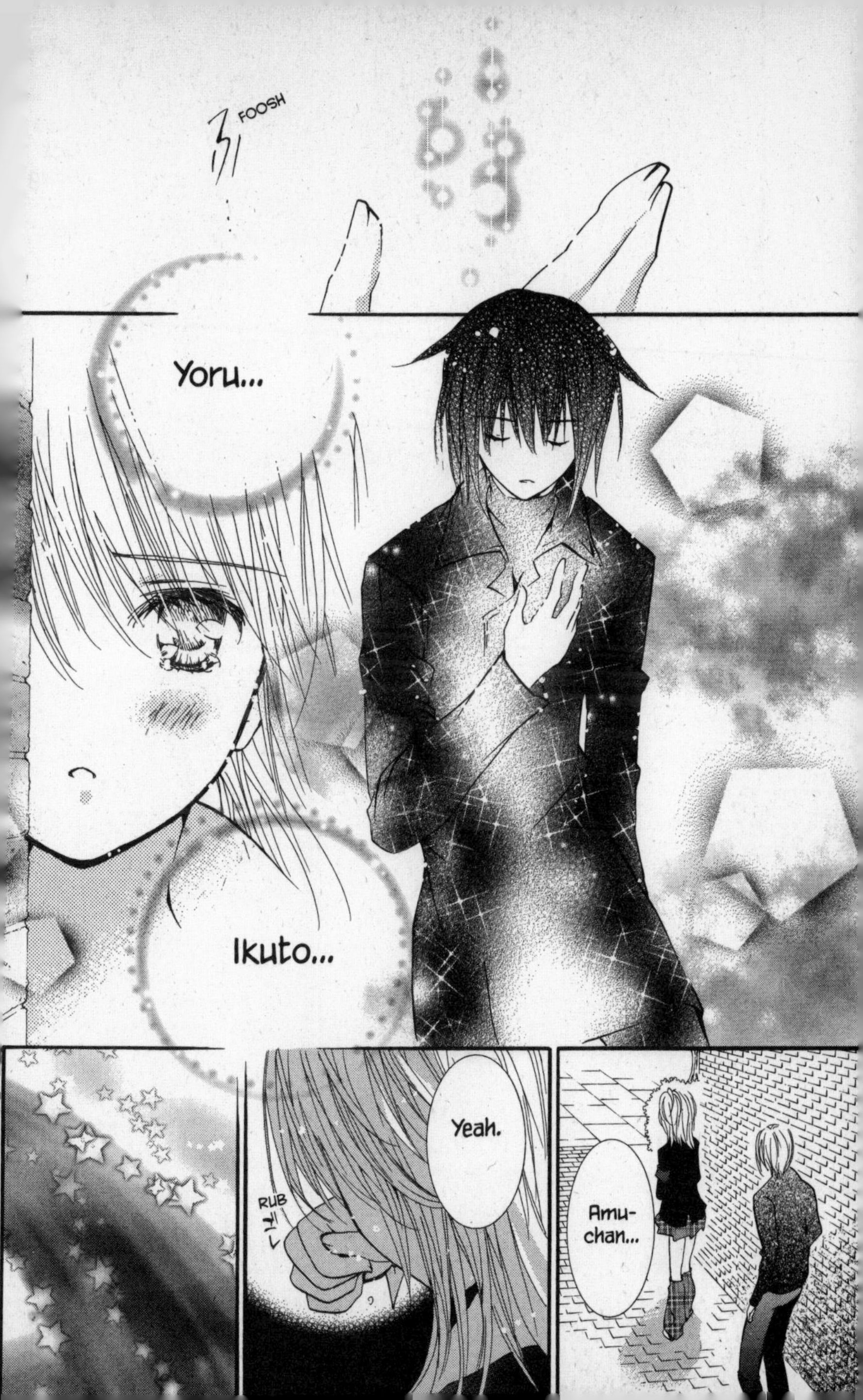
FOOSH
Yoru...
Ikuto...
Amu-chan...
Yeah.
RUB

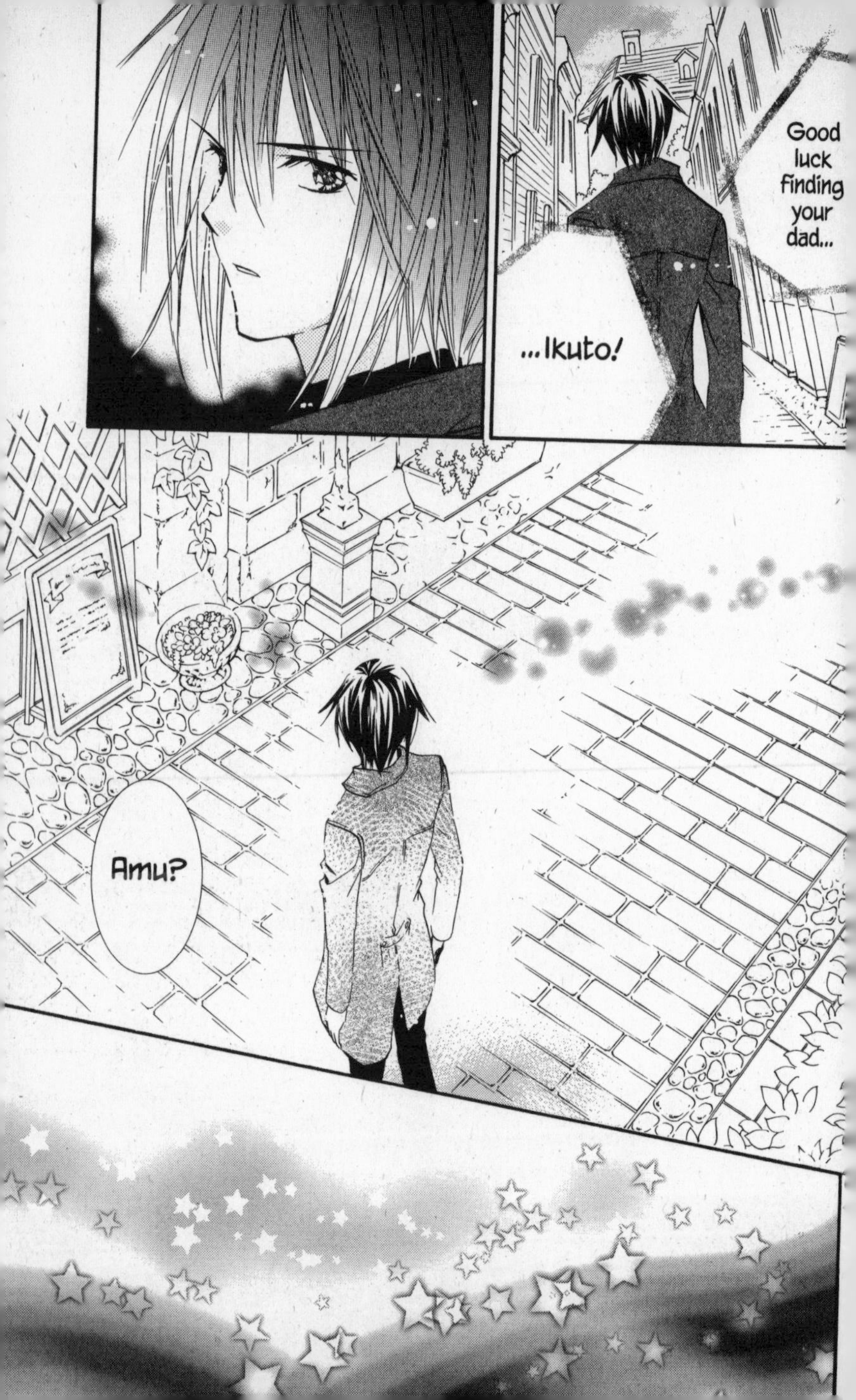
Good luck finding your dad...
...Ikuto!
Amu?

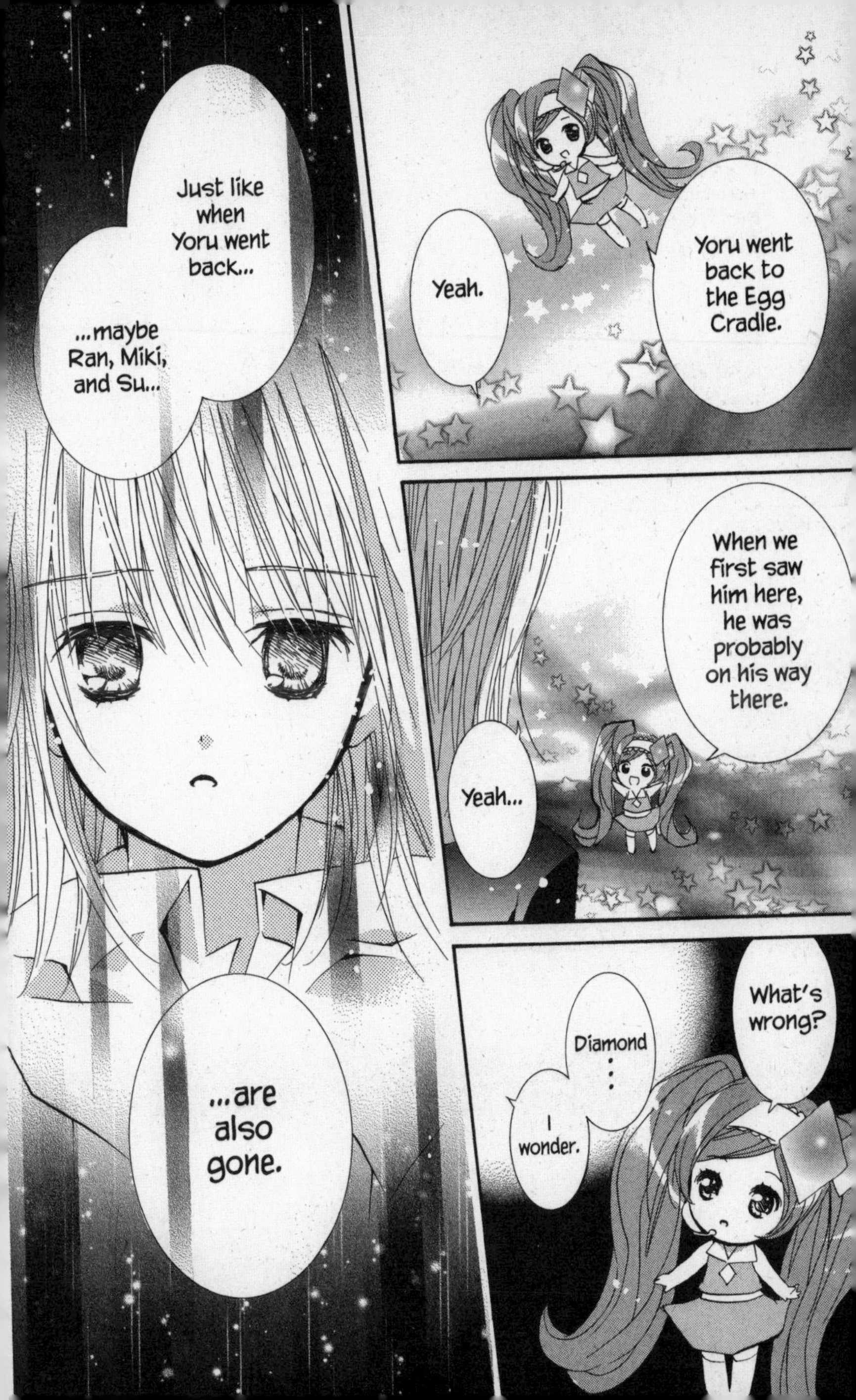
Yoru went back to the Egg Cradle.
Yeah.
When we first saw him here, he was probably on his way there.
Yeah...
What's wrong?
Diamond... I wonder.
Just like when Yoru went back...
...maybe Ran, Miki, and Su...
...are also gone.

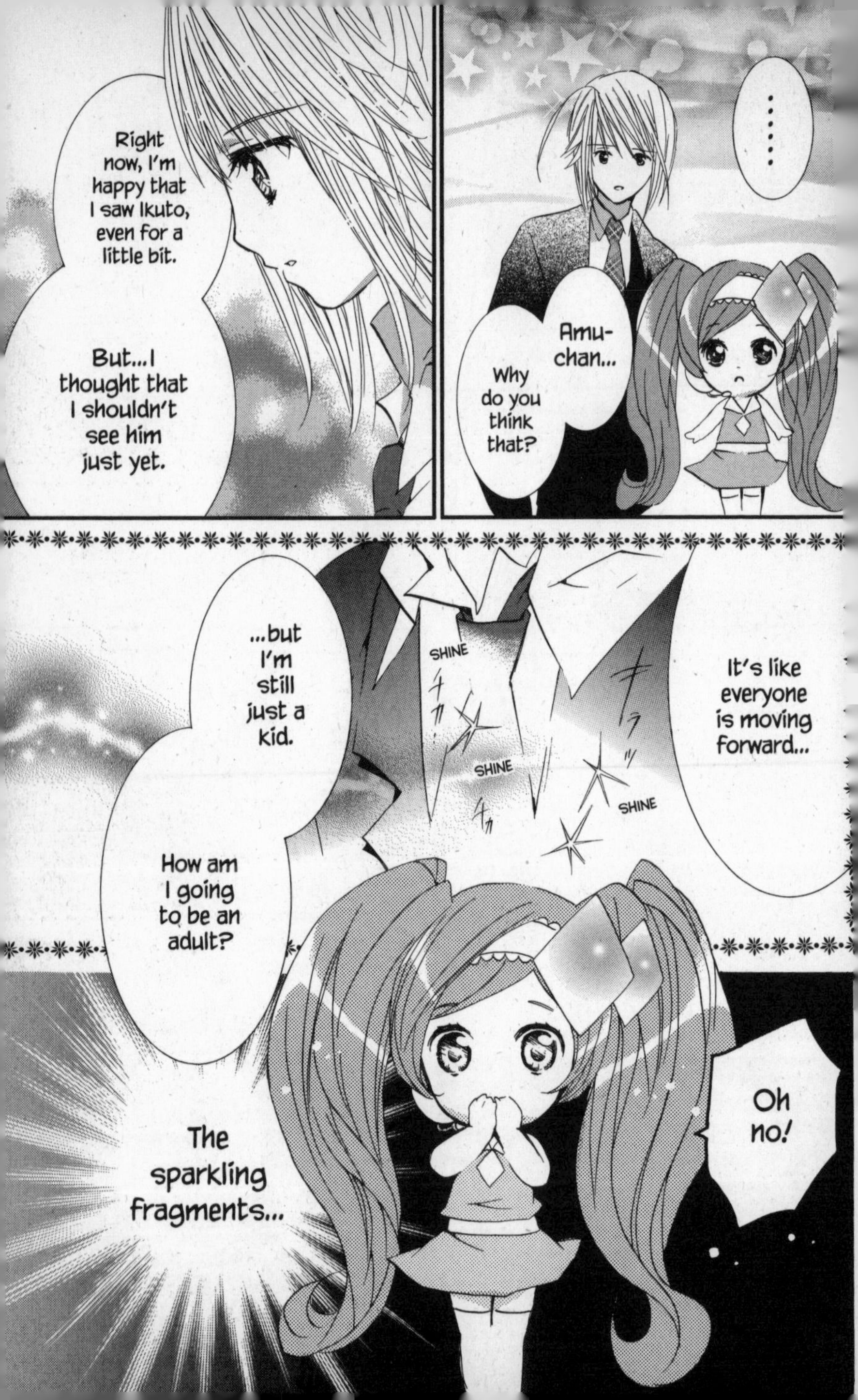
......
Amu-chan...
Why do you think that?
Right now, I'm happy that I saw Ikuto, even for a little bit.
But...I thought that I shouldn't see him just yet.
It's like everyone is moving forward...
SHINE
SHINE
SHINE
...but I'm still just a kid.
How am I going to be an adult?
Oh no!
The sparkling fragments...

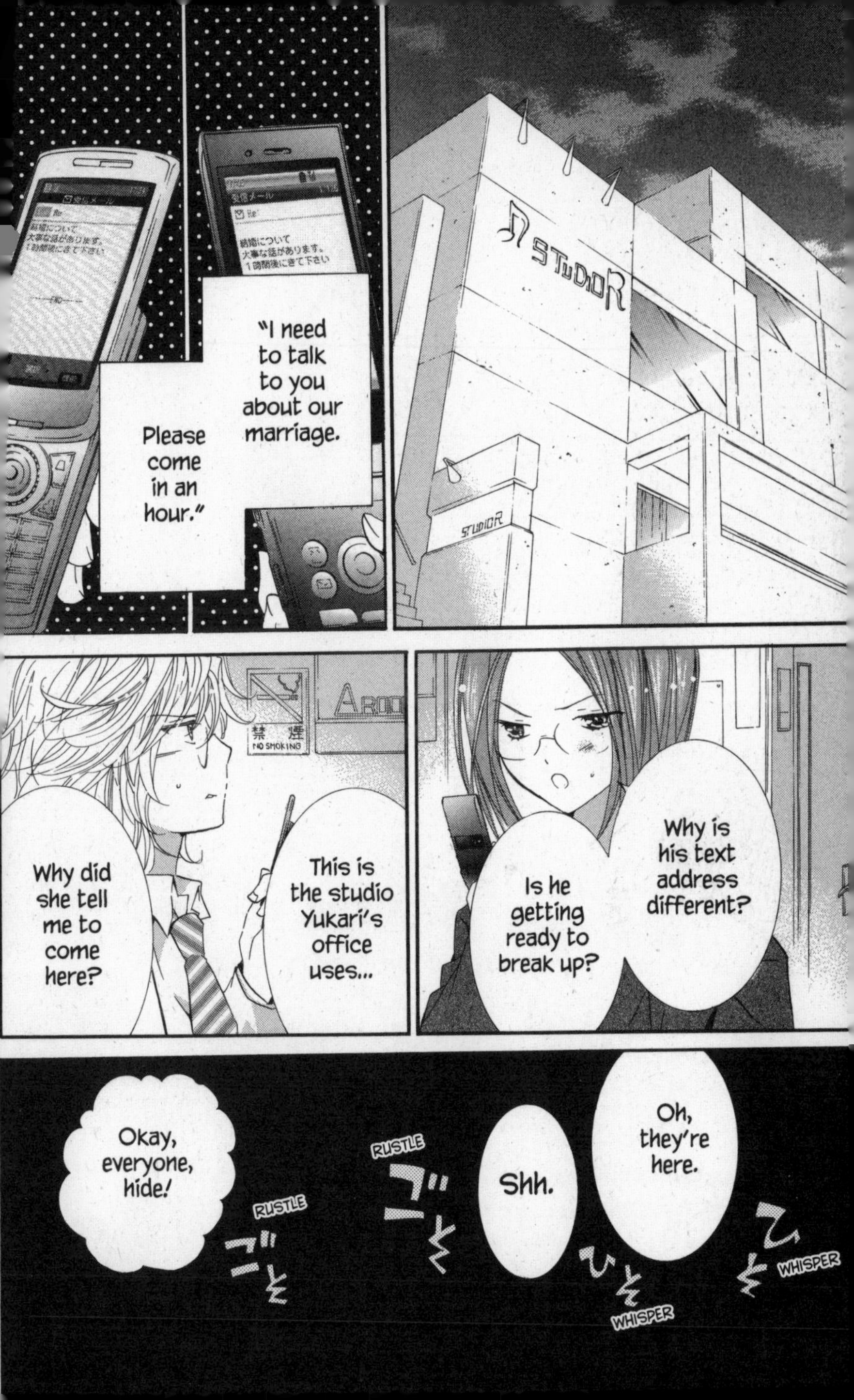
STUDIO R
結婚について 大事な話があります。 1時間後にきて下さい
"I need to talk to you about our marriage.
Please come in an hour."
Why is his text address different?
Is he getting ready to break up?
禁煙 NO SMOKING
This is the studio Yukari's office uses...
Why did she tell me to come here?
Oh, they're here.
WHISPER
WHISPER
Shh.
RUSTLE
Okay, everyone, hide!
RUSTLE

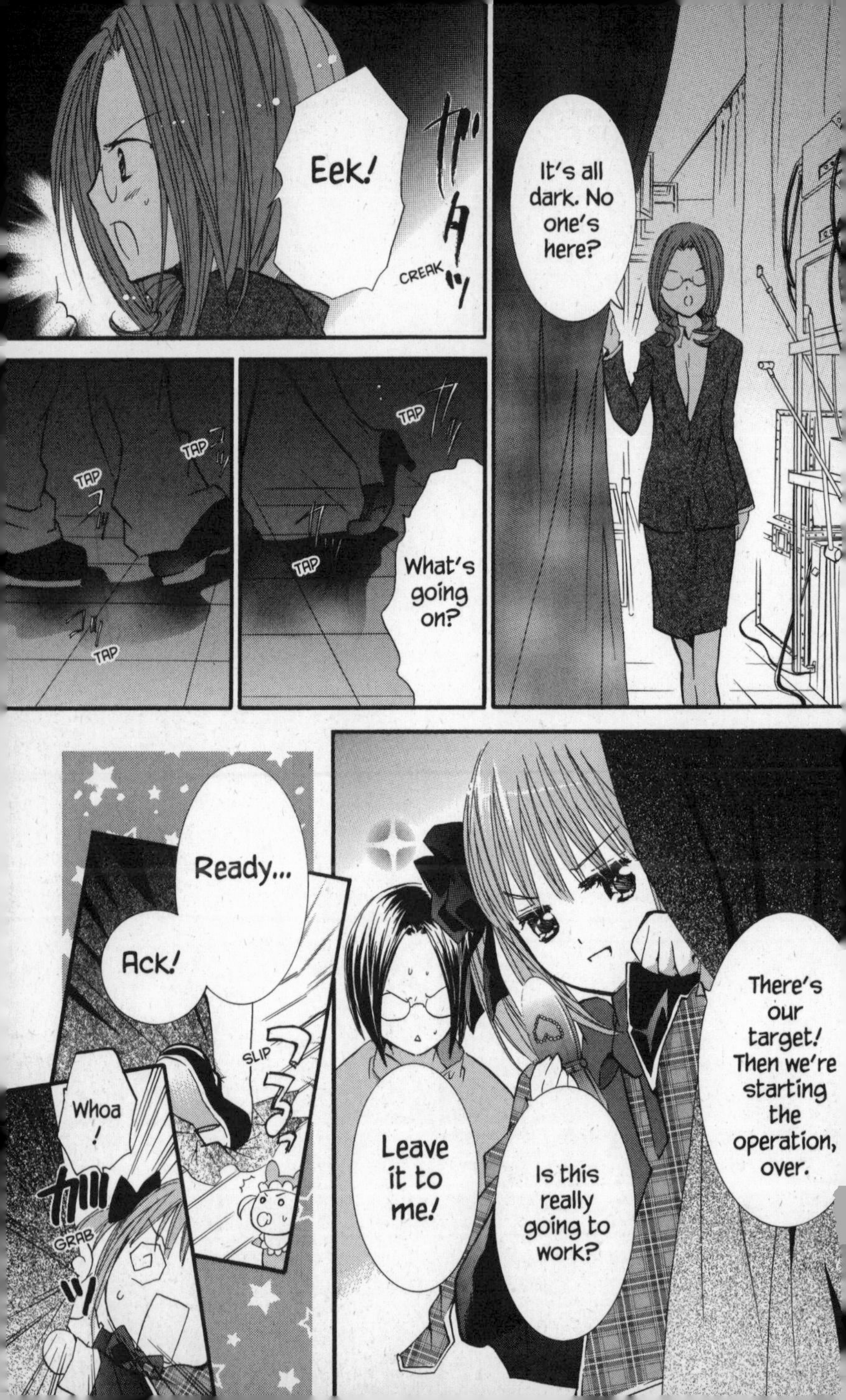
It's all dark. No one's here?
Eek!
CREAK
TAP
TAP
What's going on?
TAP
TAP
TAP
There's our target! Then we're starting the operation, over.
Is this really going to work?
Leave it to me!
Ready...
Ack!
SLIP
Whoa!
GRAB

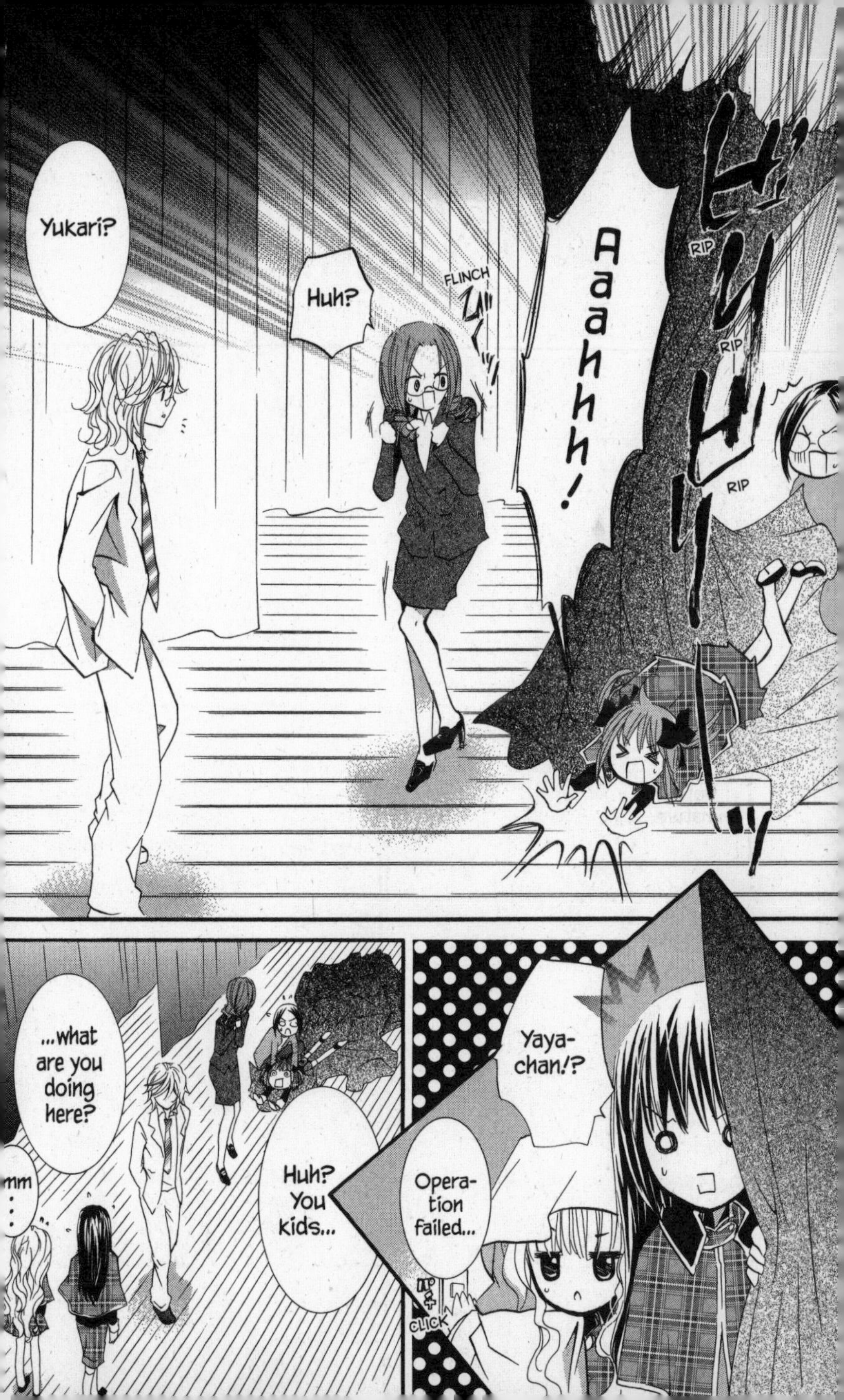
RIP
RIP
RIP
Aaaahhh!
FLINCH
Huh?
Yukari?
Yaya-chan!?
Operation failed...
CLICK
Huh? You kids...
...what are you doing here?
mm...

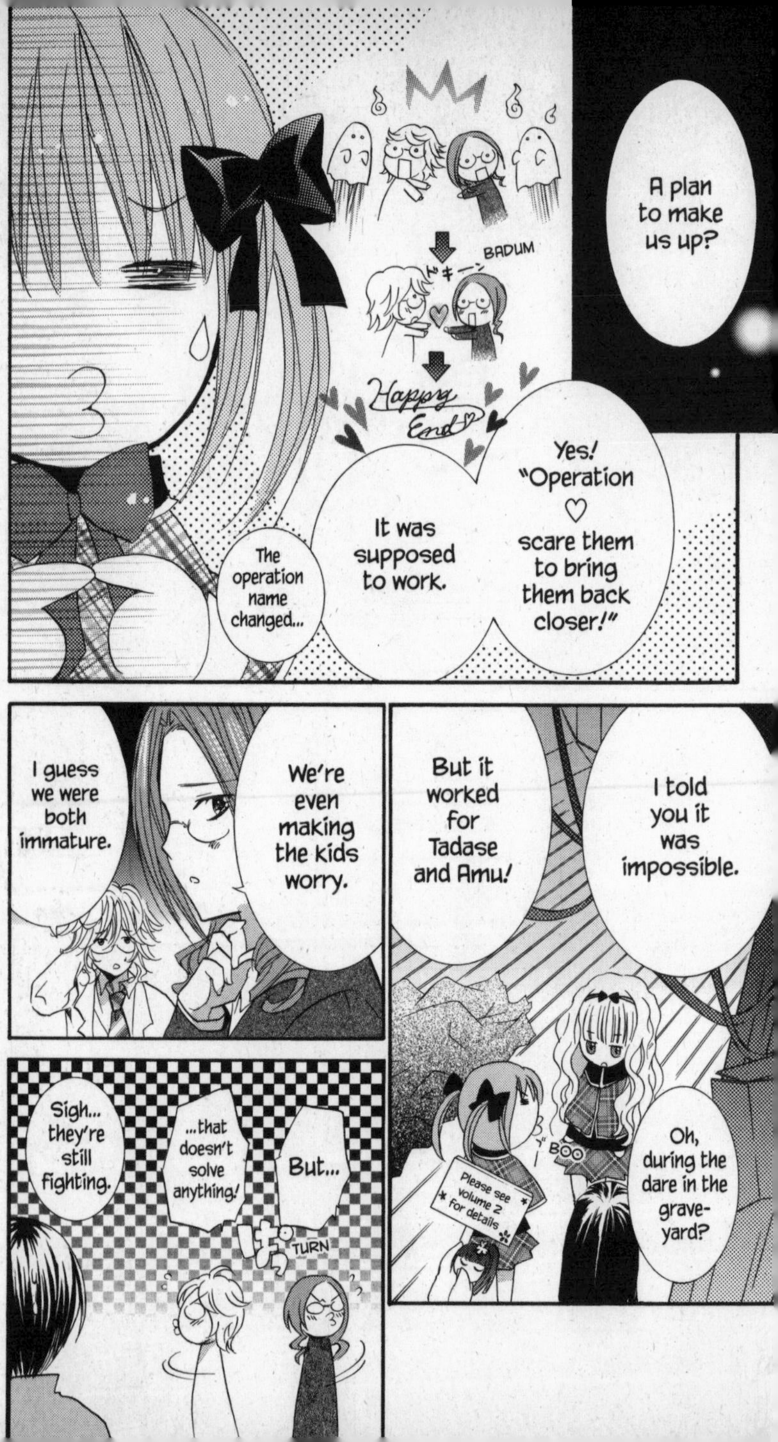

A plan to make us up?
BADUM
ドキーン
Happy End♡
Yes! "Operation ♡ scare them to bring them back closer!"
It was supposed to work.
The operation name changed...
I told you it was impossible.
But it worked for Tadase and Amu!
Oh, during the dare in the graveyard?
BOO
Please see volume 2 for details
We're even making the kids worry.
I guess we were both immature.
But...
...that doesn't solve anything!
Sigh... they're still fighting.
TURN

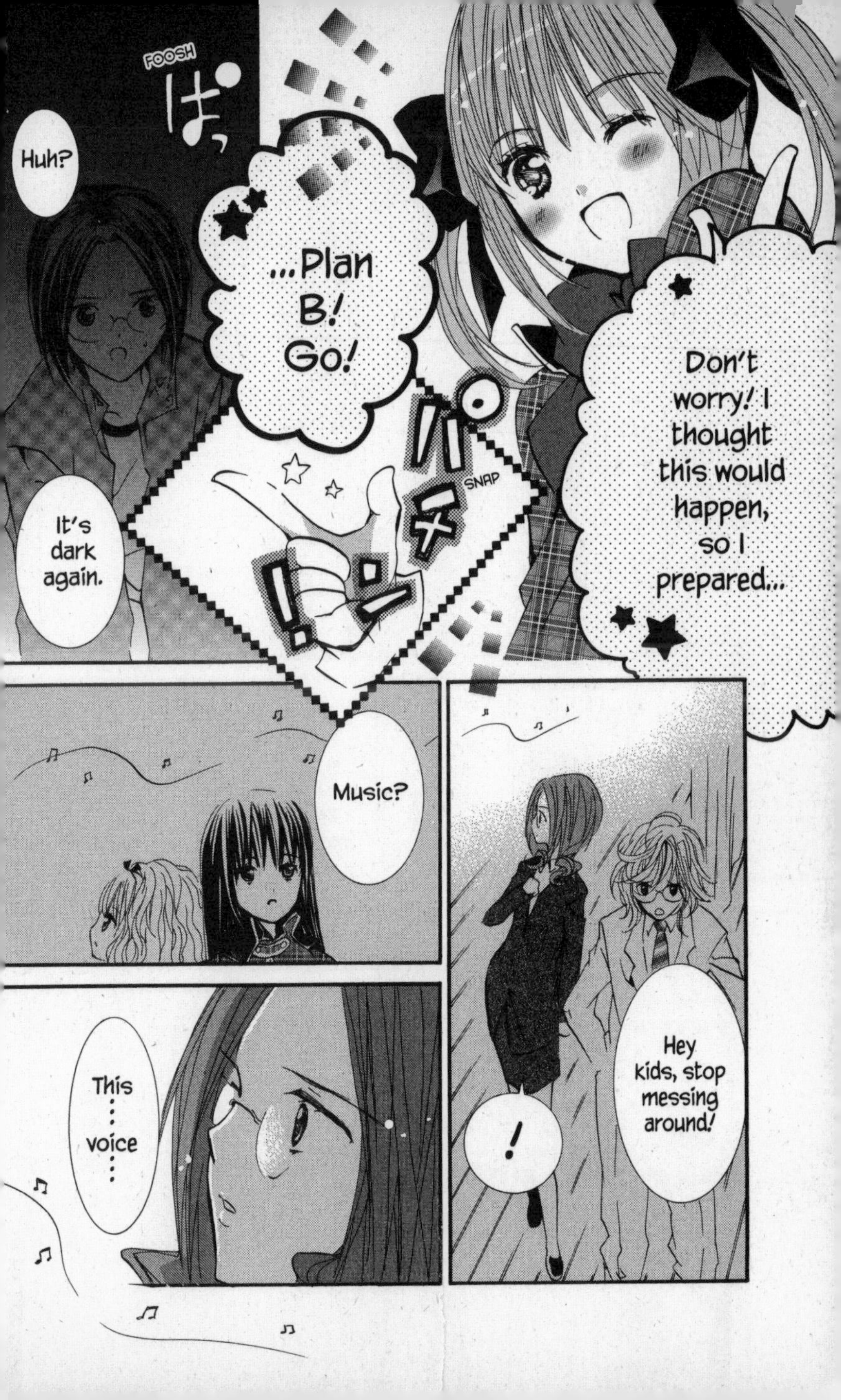
Don't worry! I thought this would happen, so I prepared...
...Plan B! Go!
パチン!
SNAP
ぱっ
FOOSH
Huh?
It's dark again.
Hey kids, stop messing around!
!
Music?
This... voice...

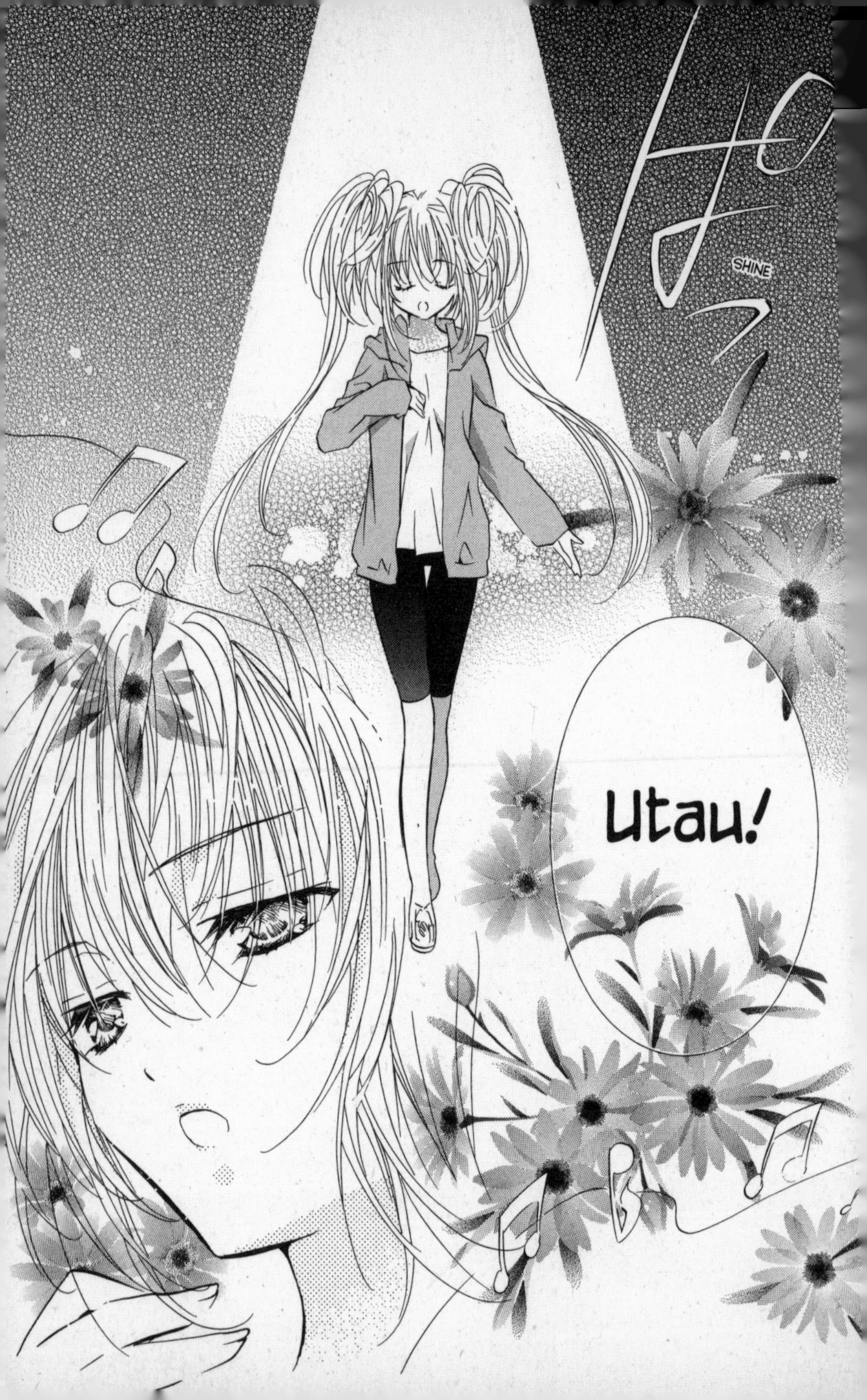
はっ
SHINE
Utau!

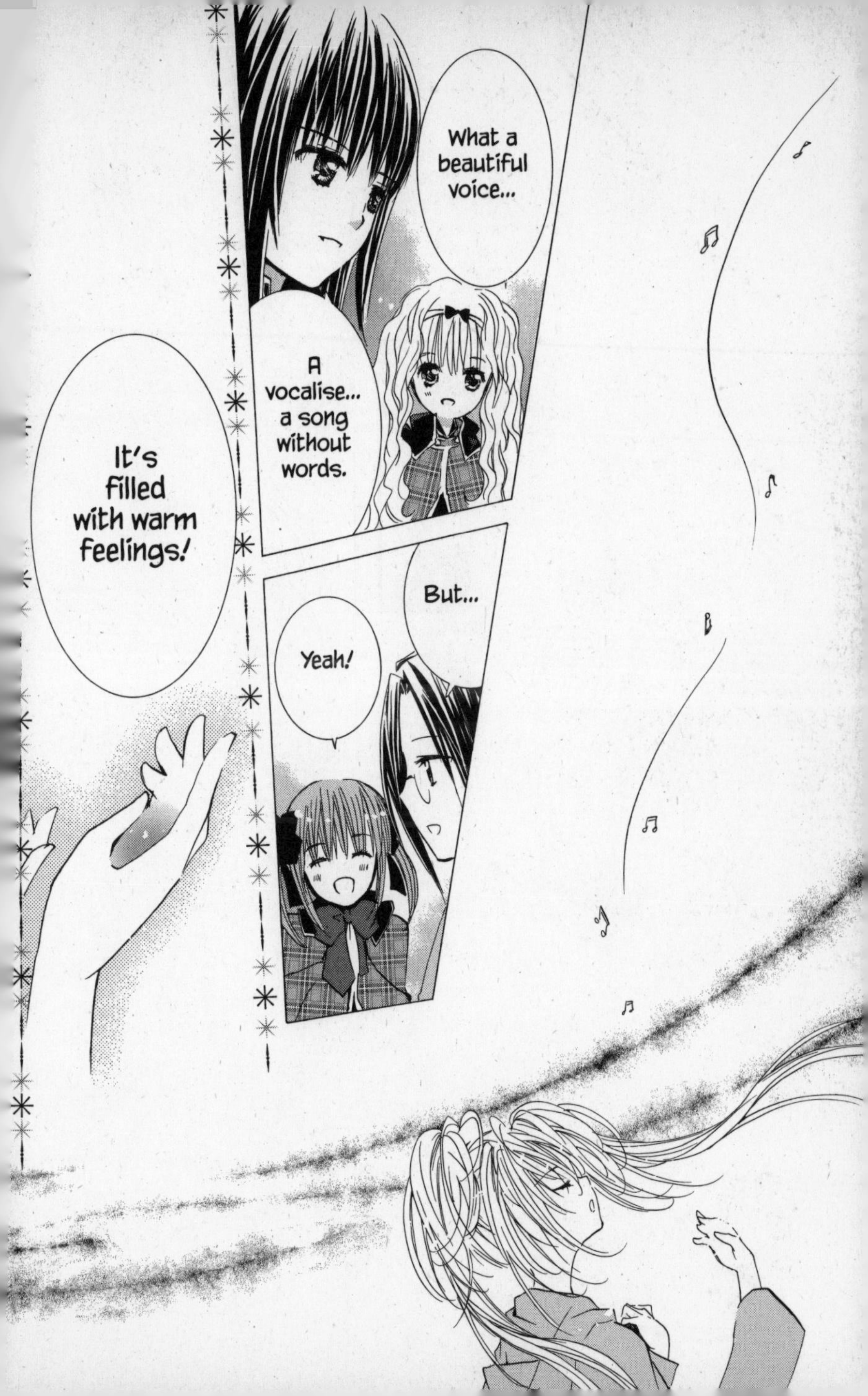
What a beautiful voice...
A vocalise... a song without words.
But...
Yeah!
It's filled with warm feelings!

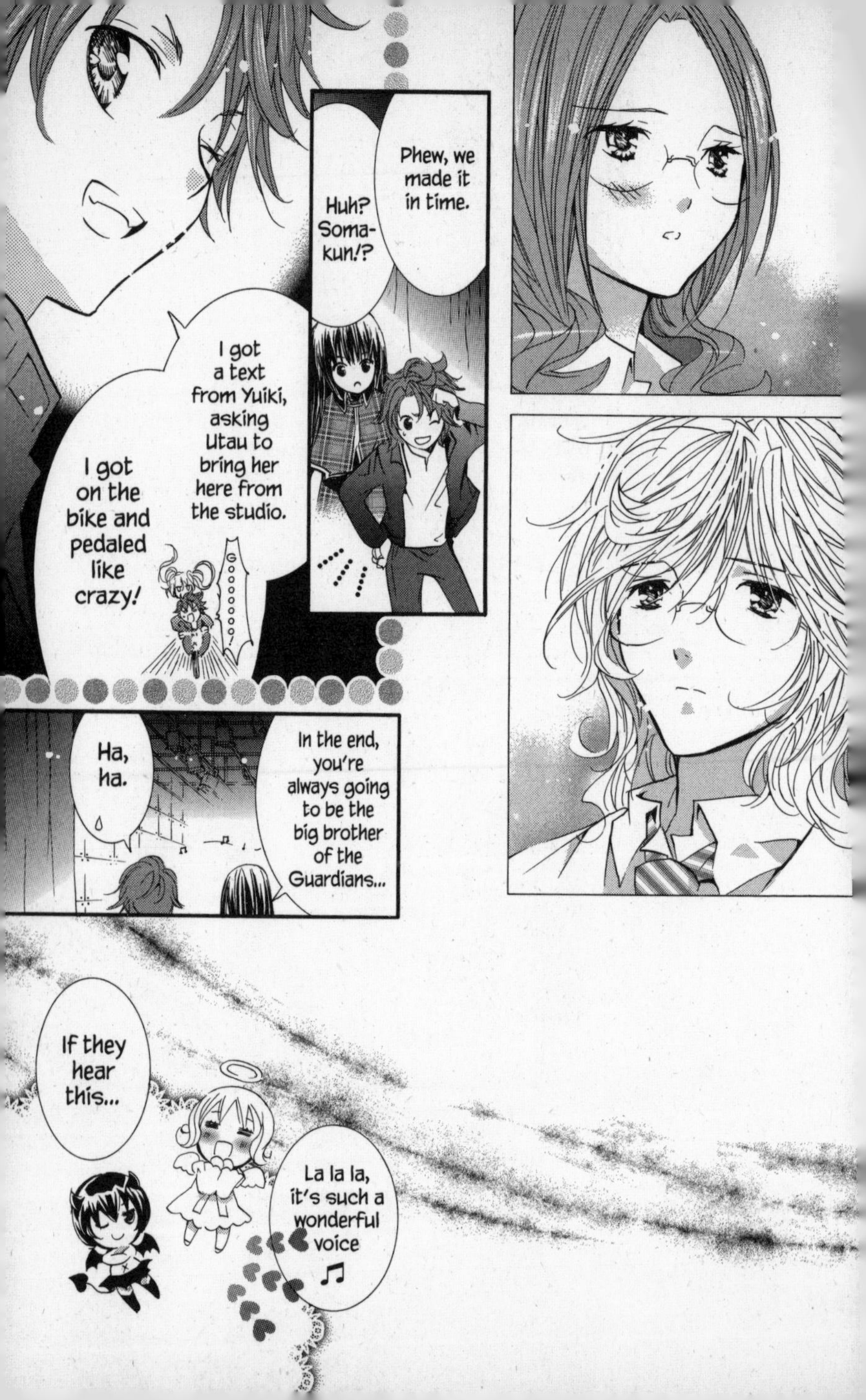

Phew, we made it in time.
Huh? Soma-kun!?
I got a text from Yuiki, asking Utau to bring her here from the studio.
I got on the bike and pedaled like crazy!
Goooooooo!
In the end, you're always going to be the big brother of the Guardians...
Ha, ha.
If they hear this...
La la la, it's such a wonderful voice ♫

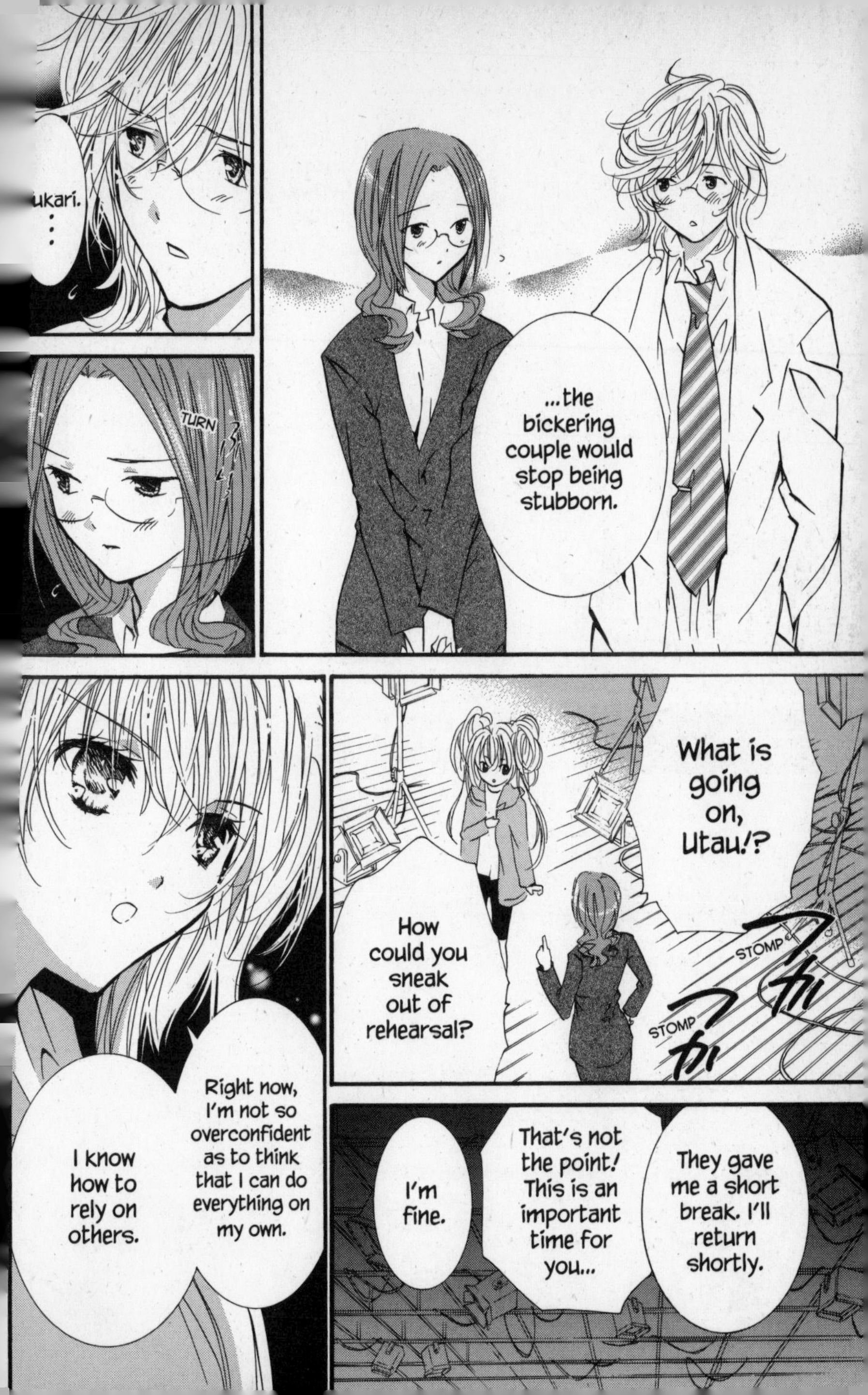
...the bickering couple would stop being stubborn.
ukari.
...
TURN
What is going on, Utau!?
How could you sneak out of rehearsal?
STOMP
STOMP
They gave me a short break. I'll return shortly.
That's not the point! This is an important time for you...
I'm fine.
Right now, I'm not so overconfident as to think that I can do everything on my own.
I know how to rely on others.

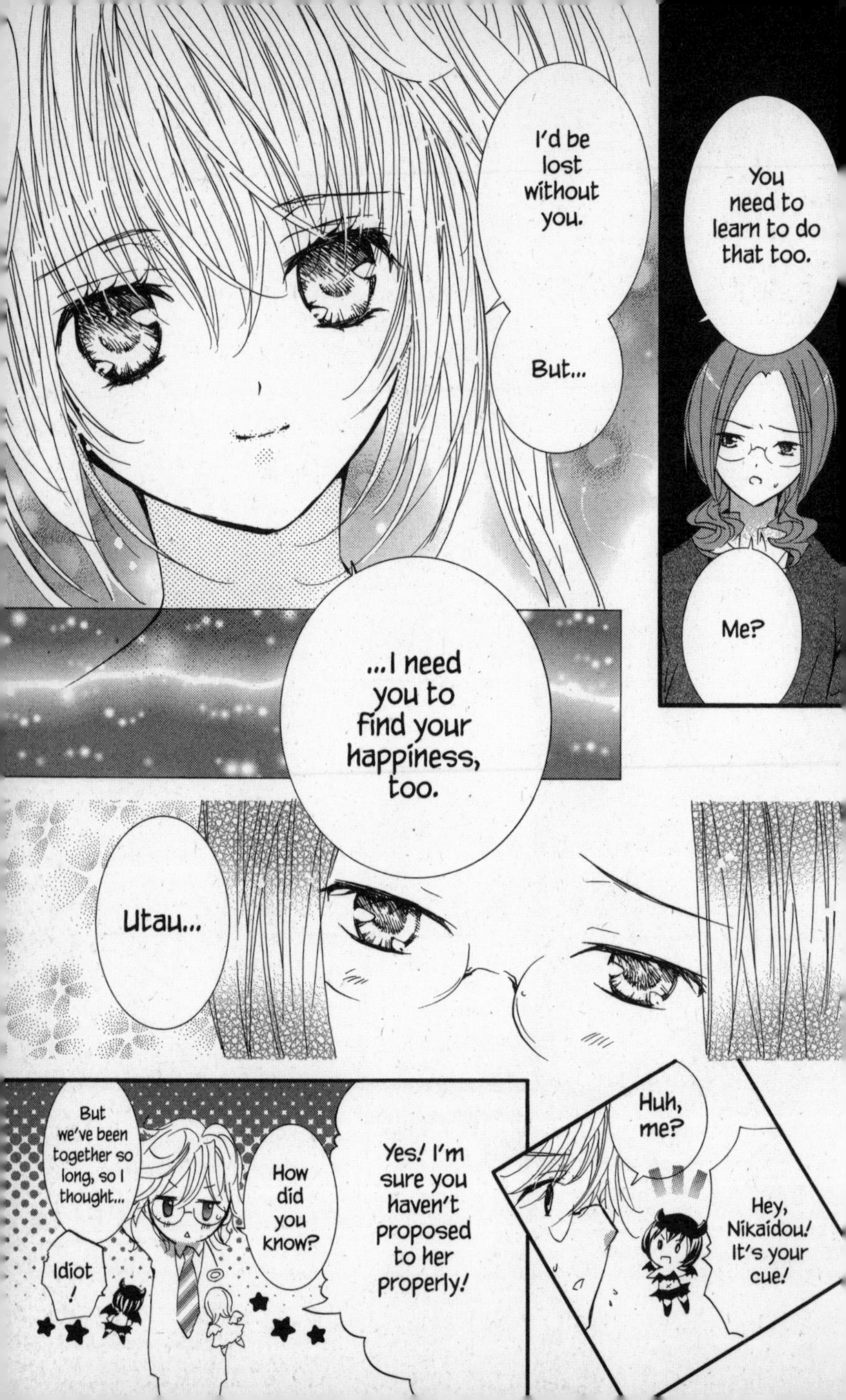
You need to learn to do that too.
Me?
I'd be lost without you.
But...
...I need you to find your happiness, too.
Utau...
Huh, me?
Hey, Nikaidou! It's your cue!
Yes! I'm sure you haven't proposed to her properly!
How did you know?
But we've been together so long, so I thought...
Idiot!

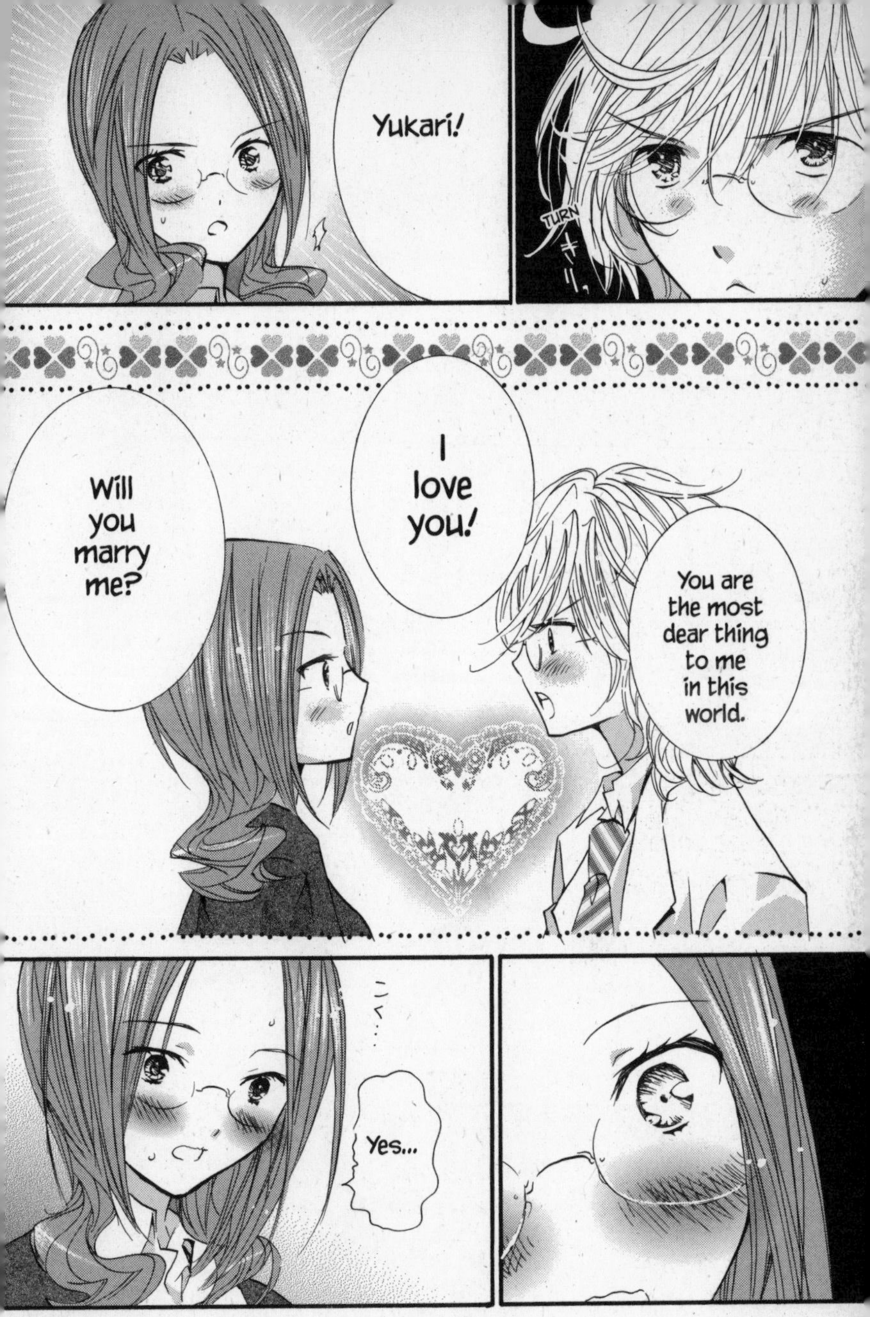
TURN
Yukari!
You are the most dear thing to me in this world.
I love you!
Will you marry me?
Yes...

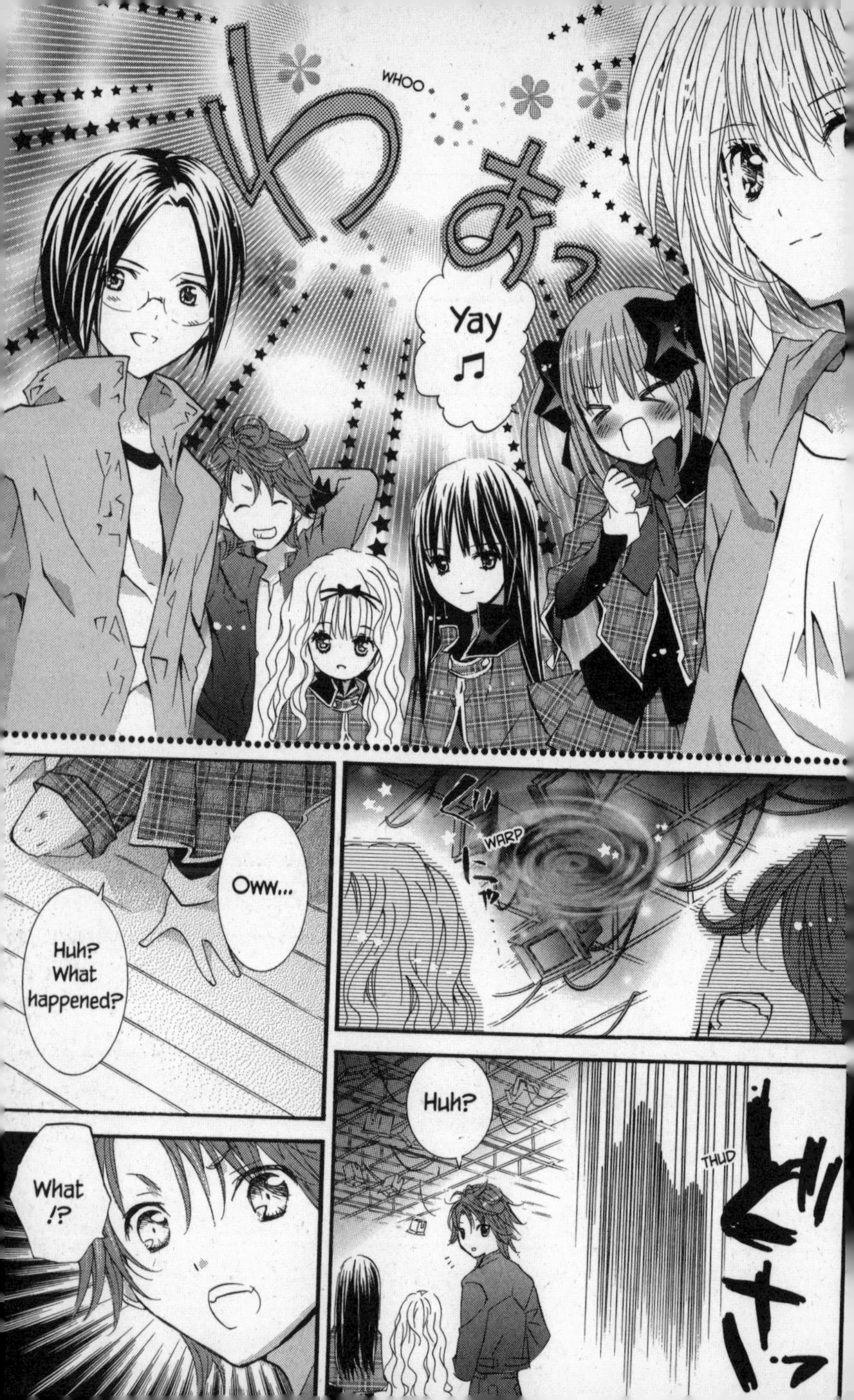
わあっ
WHOO
Yay ♫
WARP
Oww...
Huh? What happened?
Huh?
THUD
What !?

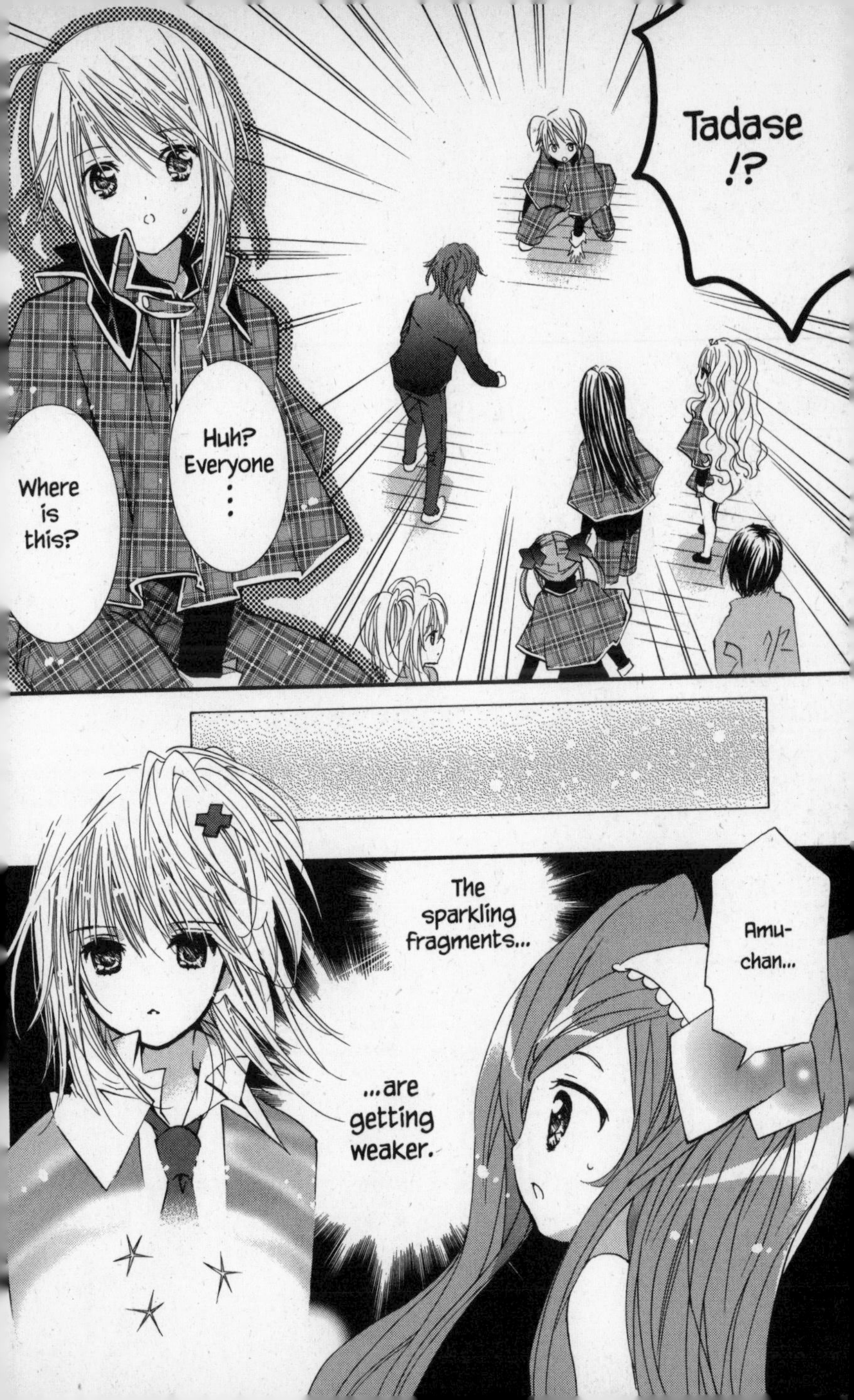
Tadase !?
Huh? Everyone ...
Where is this?
Amu-chan...
The sparkling fragments...
...are getting weaker.

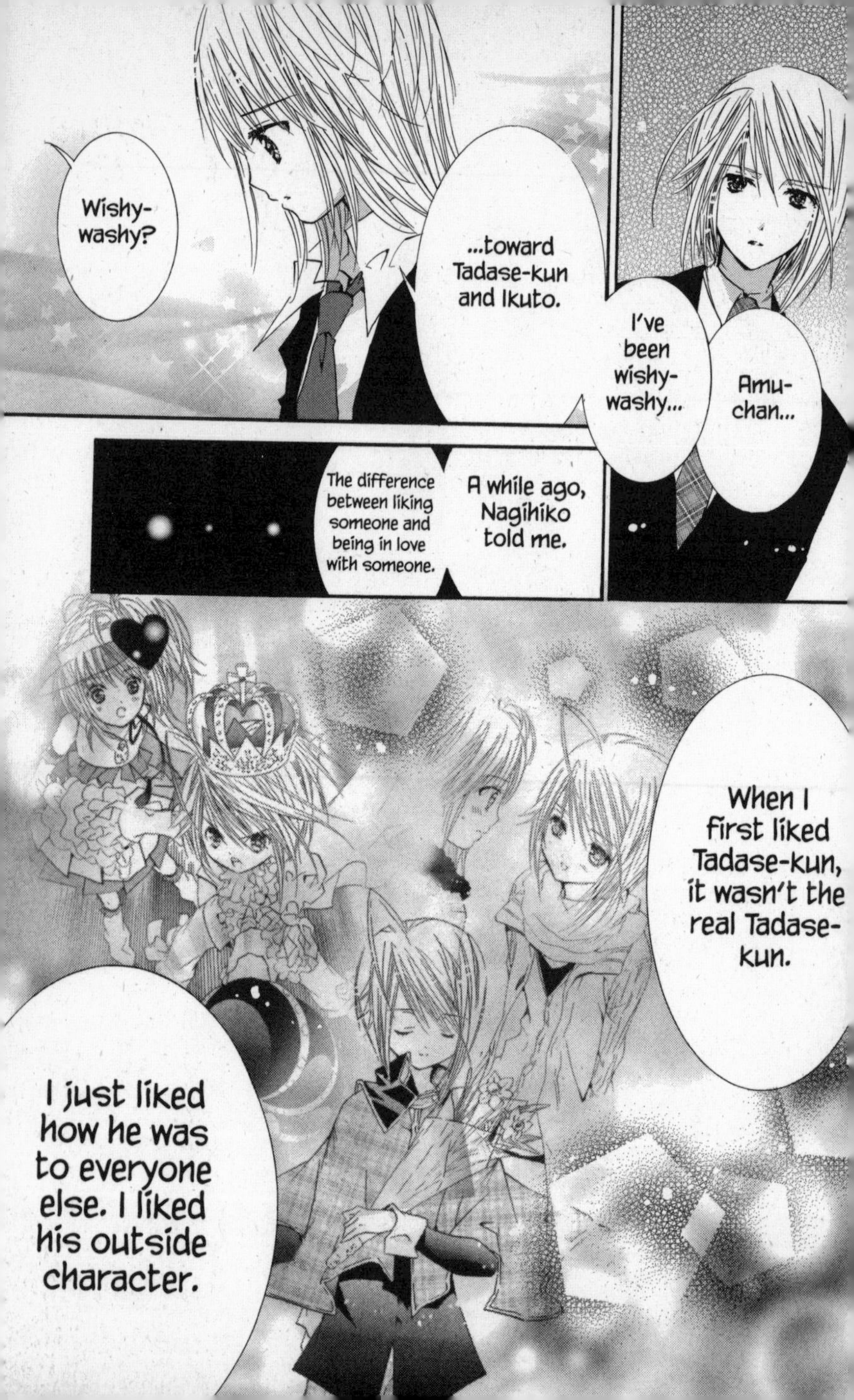
Amu-chan...
I've been wishy-washy...
...toward Tadase-kun and Ikuto.
Wishy-washy?
A while ago, Nagihiko told me.
The difference between liking someone and being in love with someone.
When I first liked Tadase-kun, it wasn't the real Tadase-kun.
I just liked how he was to everyone else. I liked his outside character.

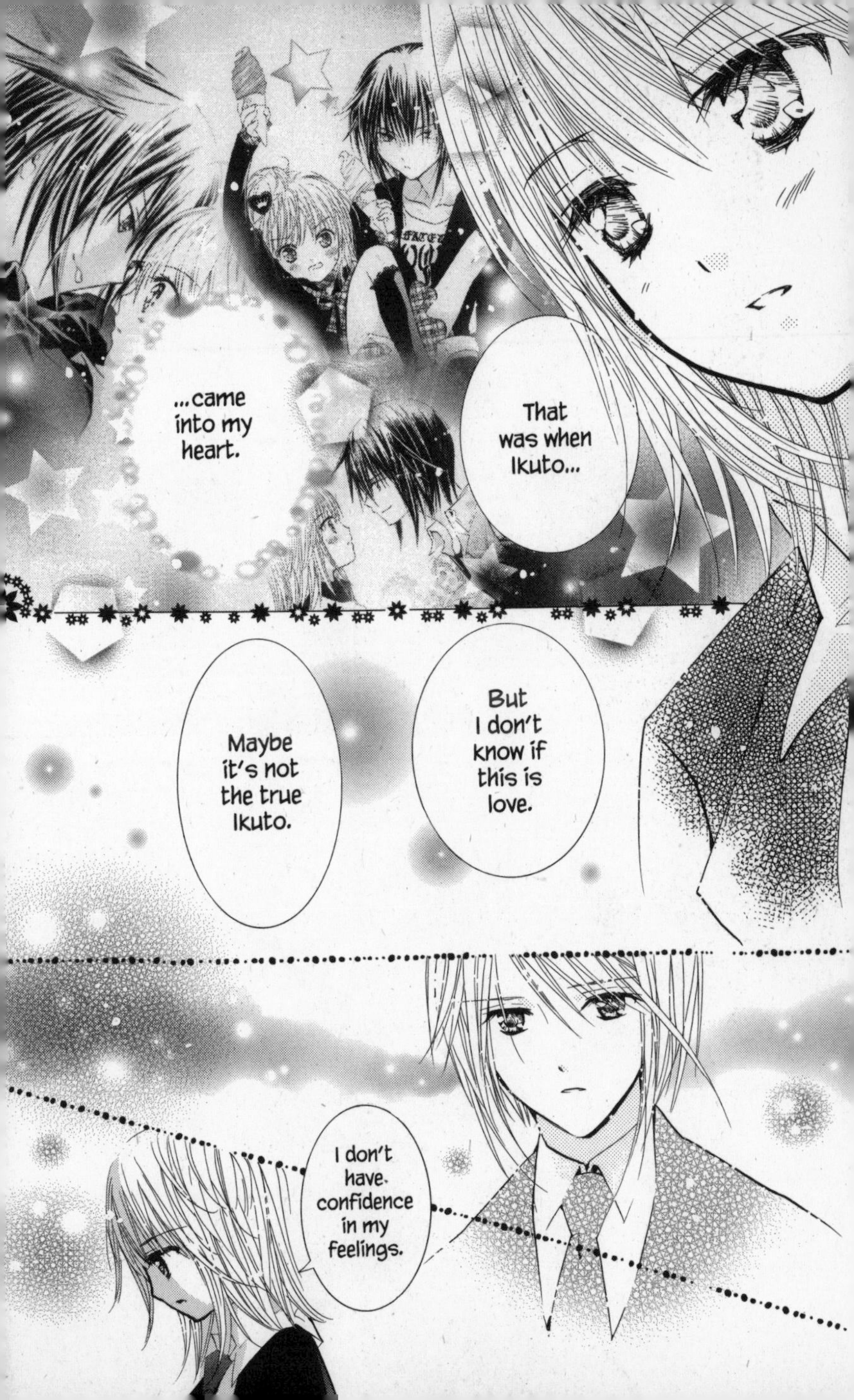
That was when Ikuto...
...came into my heart.
But I don't know if this is love.
Maybe it's not the true Ikuto.
I don't have confidence in my feelings.

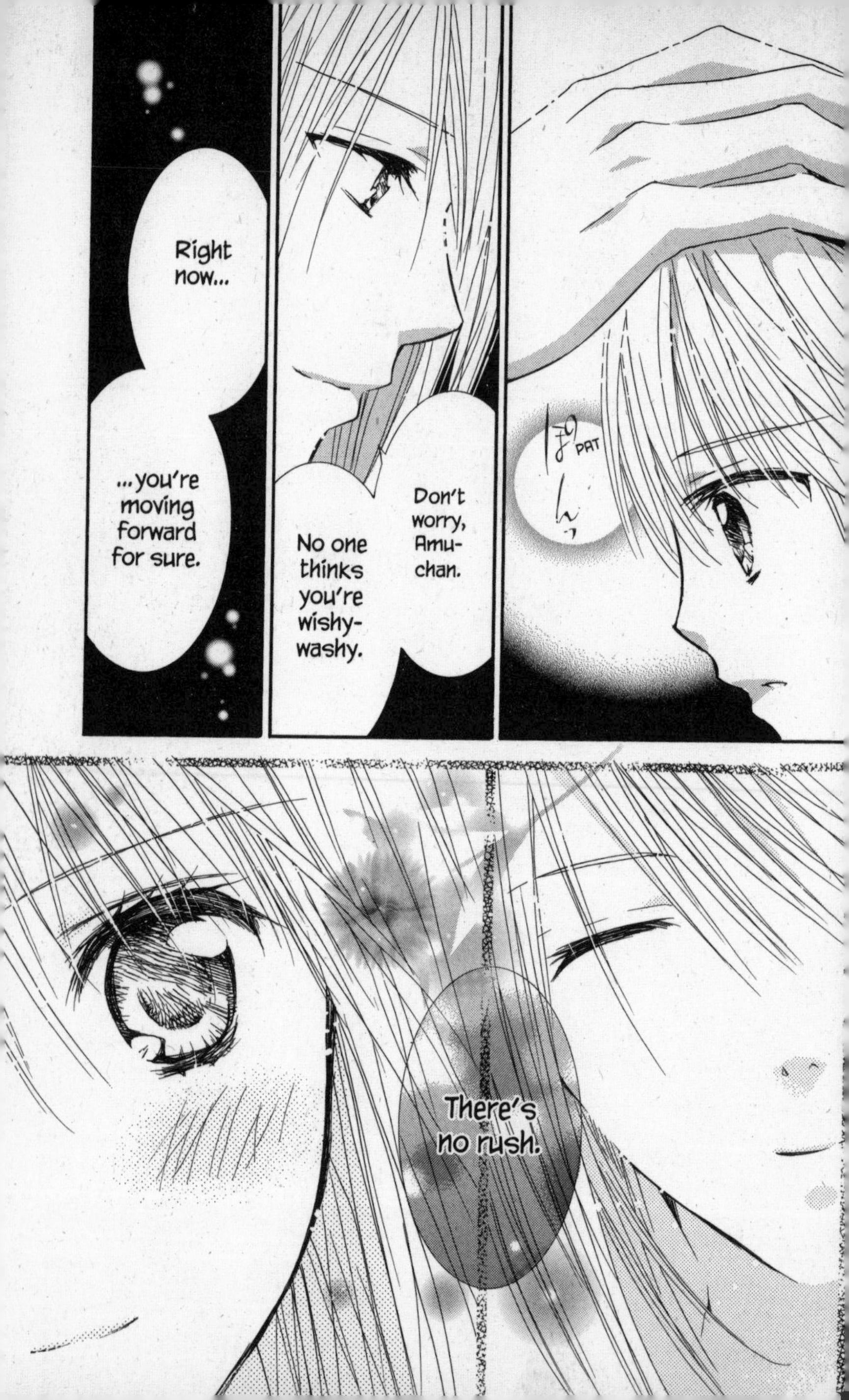
ぽん PAT
Don't worry, Amu-chan.
No one thinks you're wishy-washy.
Right now...
...you're moving forward for sure.
There's no rush.

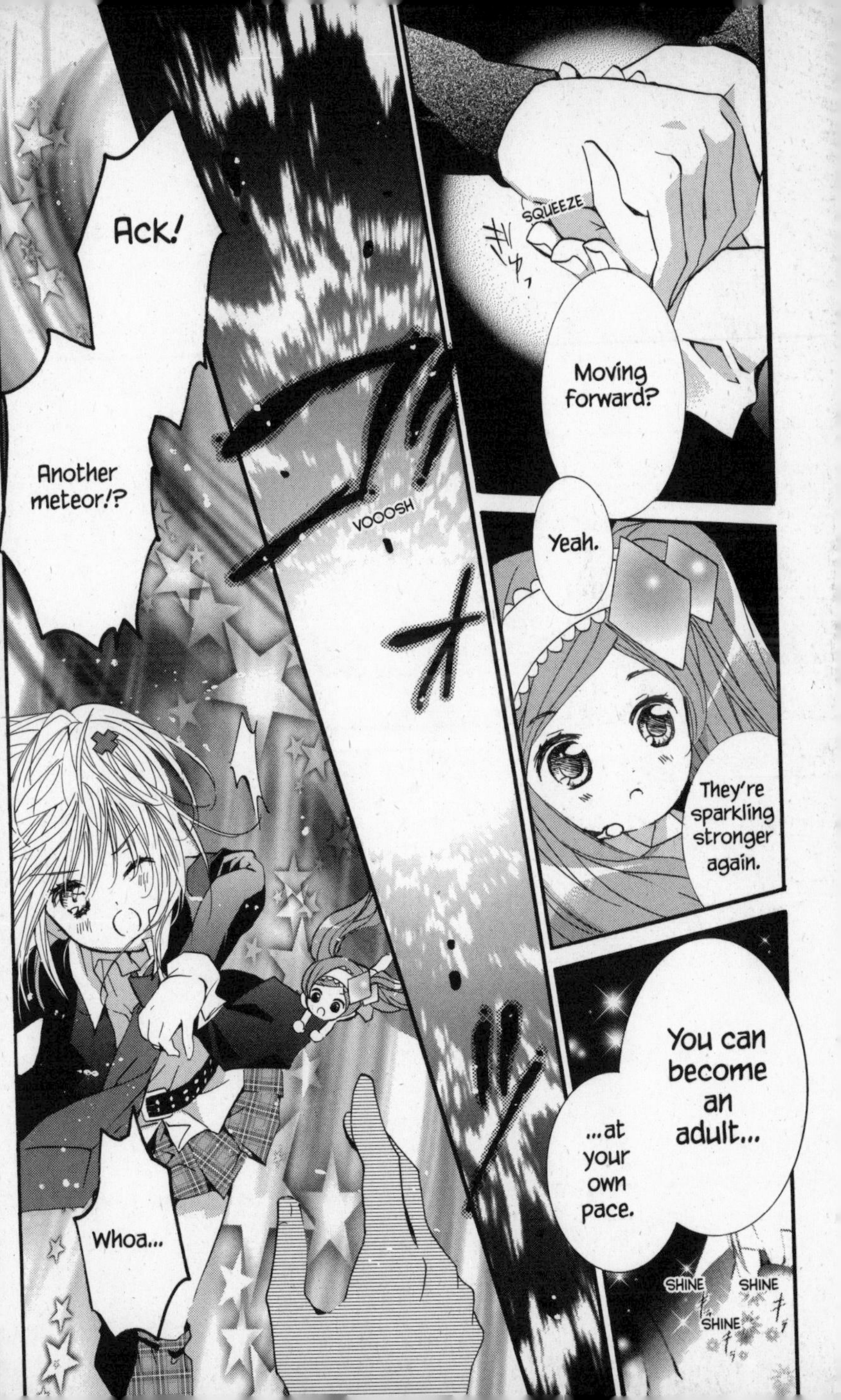
SQUEEZE
Moving forward?
Yeah.
They're sparkling stronger again.
You can become an adult...
...at your own pace.
SHINE
SHINE
SHINE
VOOOSH
Ack!
Another meteor!?
Whoa...

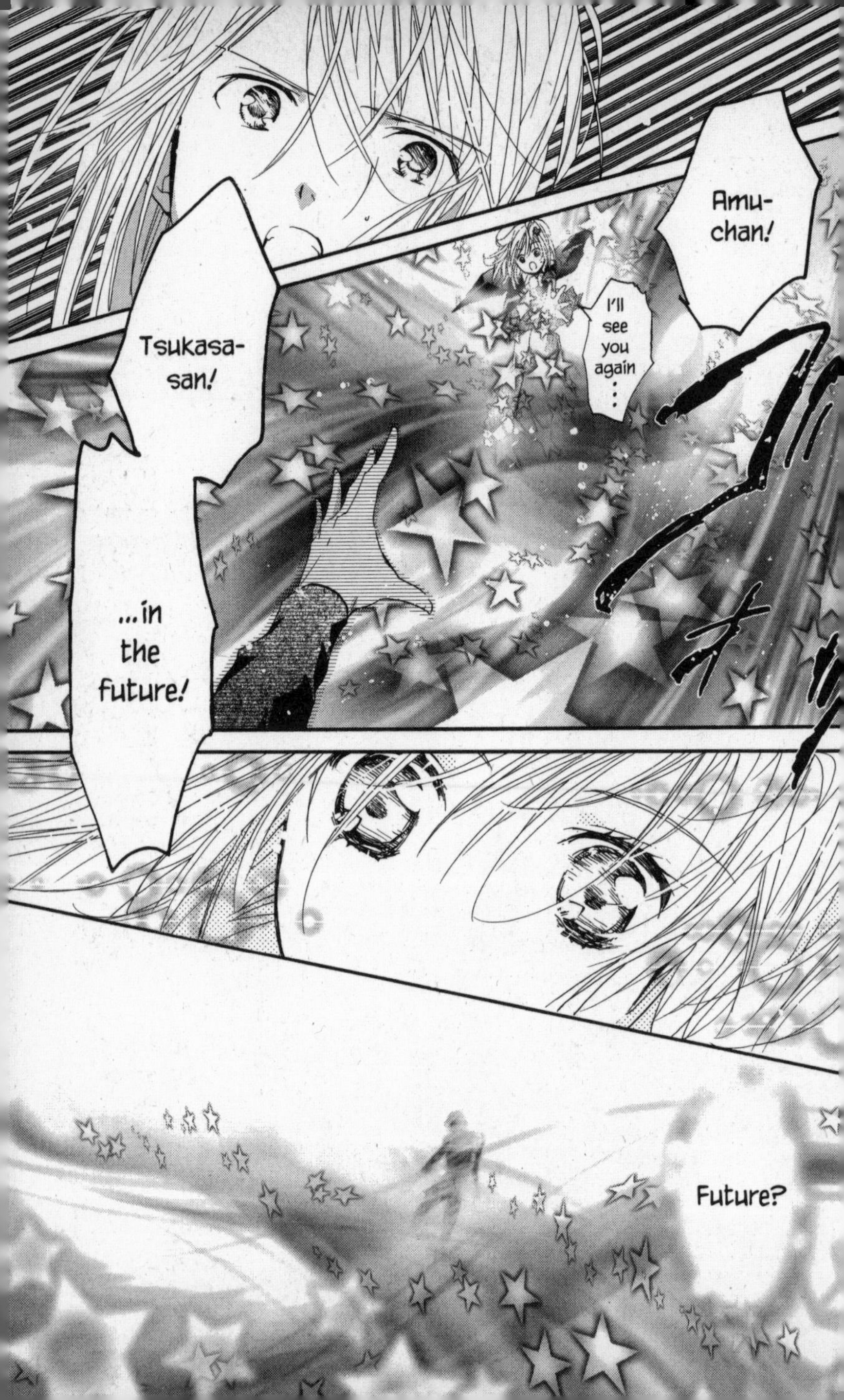
Amu-chan!
Tsukasa-san!
I'll see you again...
...in the future!
Future?

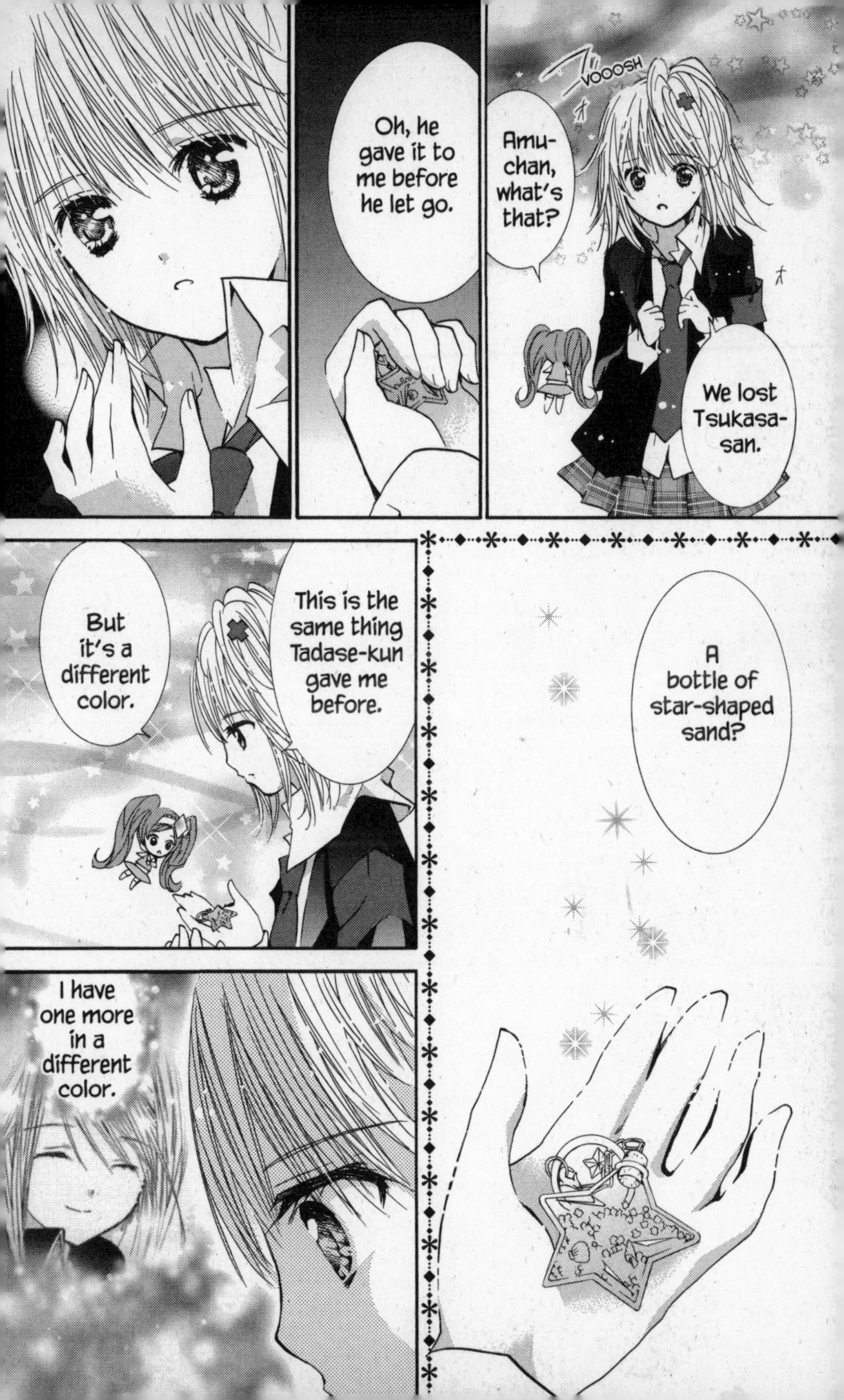

VOOOSH
Amu-chan, what's that?
We lost Tsukasa-san.
Oh, he gave it to me before he let go.
A bottle of star-shaped sand?
This is the same thing Tadase-kun gave me before.
But it's a different color.
I have one more in a different color.

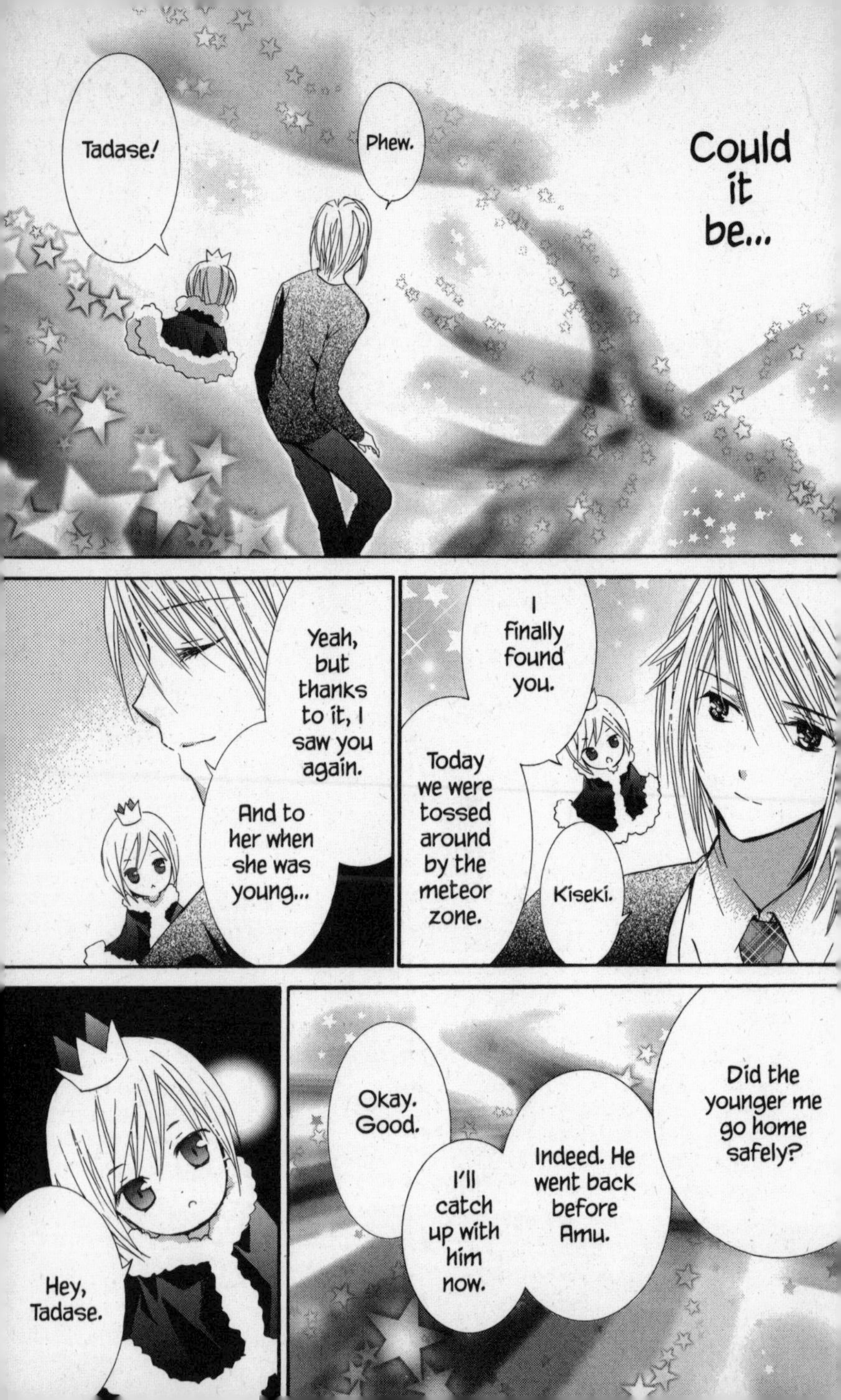
Could it be...
Phew.
Tadase!
I finally found you.
Kiseki.
Today we were tossed around by the meteor zone.
Yeah, but thanks to it, I saw you again.
And to her when she was young...
Did the younger me go home safely?
Indeed. He went back before Amu.
Okay. Good.
I'll catch up with him now.
Hey, Tadase.

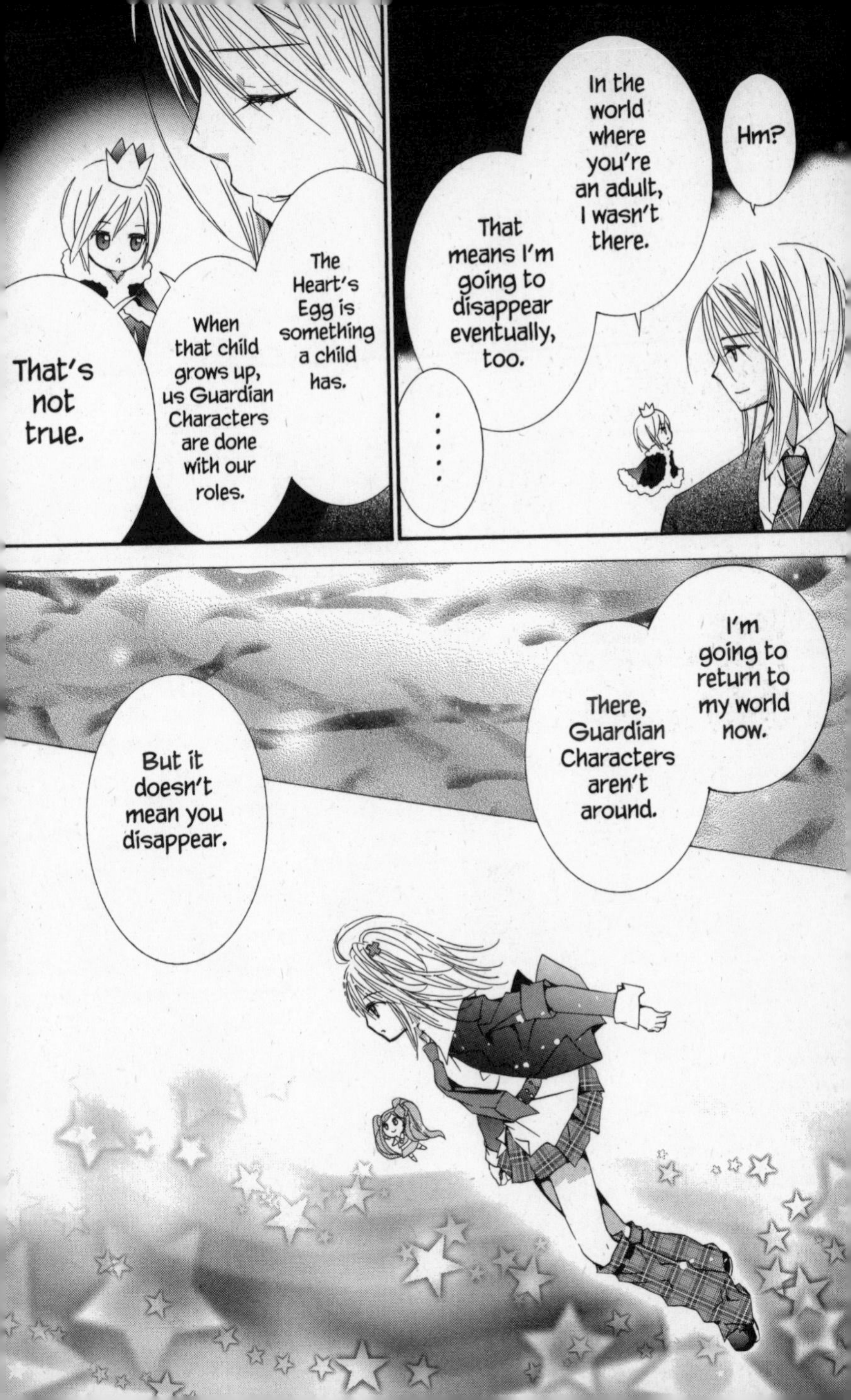
Hm?
In the world where you're an adult, I wasn't there.
That means I'm going to disappear eventually, too.
.....
The Heart's Egg is something a child has.
When that child grows up, us Guardian Characters are done with our roles.
That's not true.
I'm going to return to my world now.
There, Guardian Characters aren't around.
But it doesn't mean you disappear.

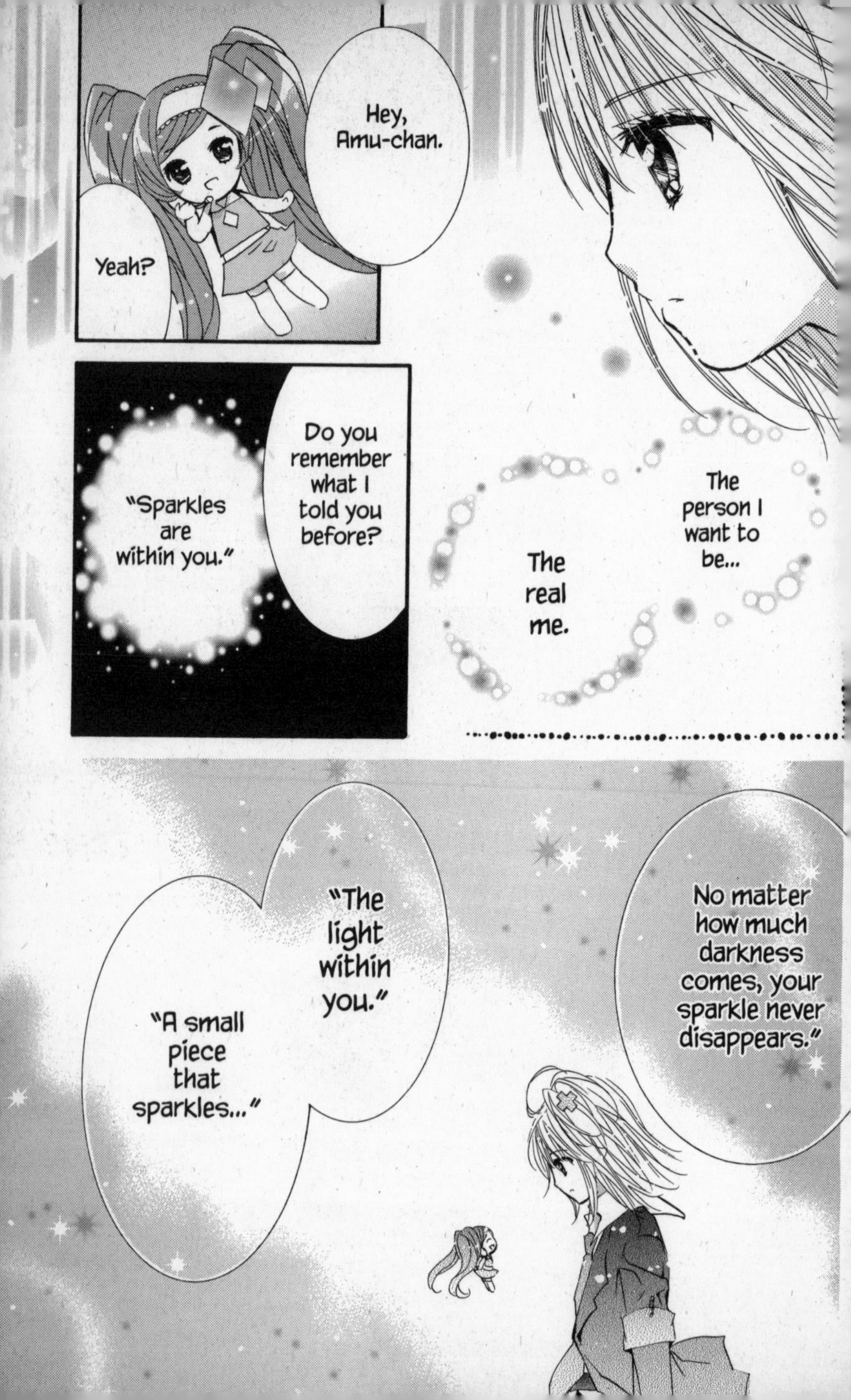
The person I want to be...
The real me.
Hey, Amu-chan.
Yeah?
Do you remember what I told you before?
"Sparkles are within you."
"No matter how much darkness comes, your sparkle never disappears."
"The light within you."
"A small piece that sparkles..."

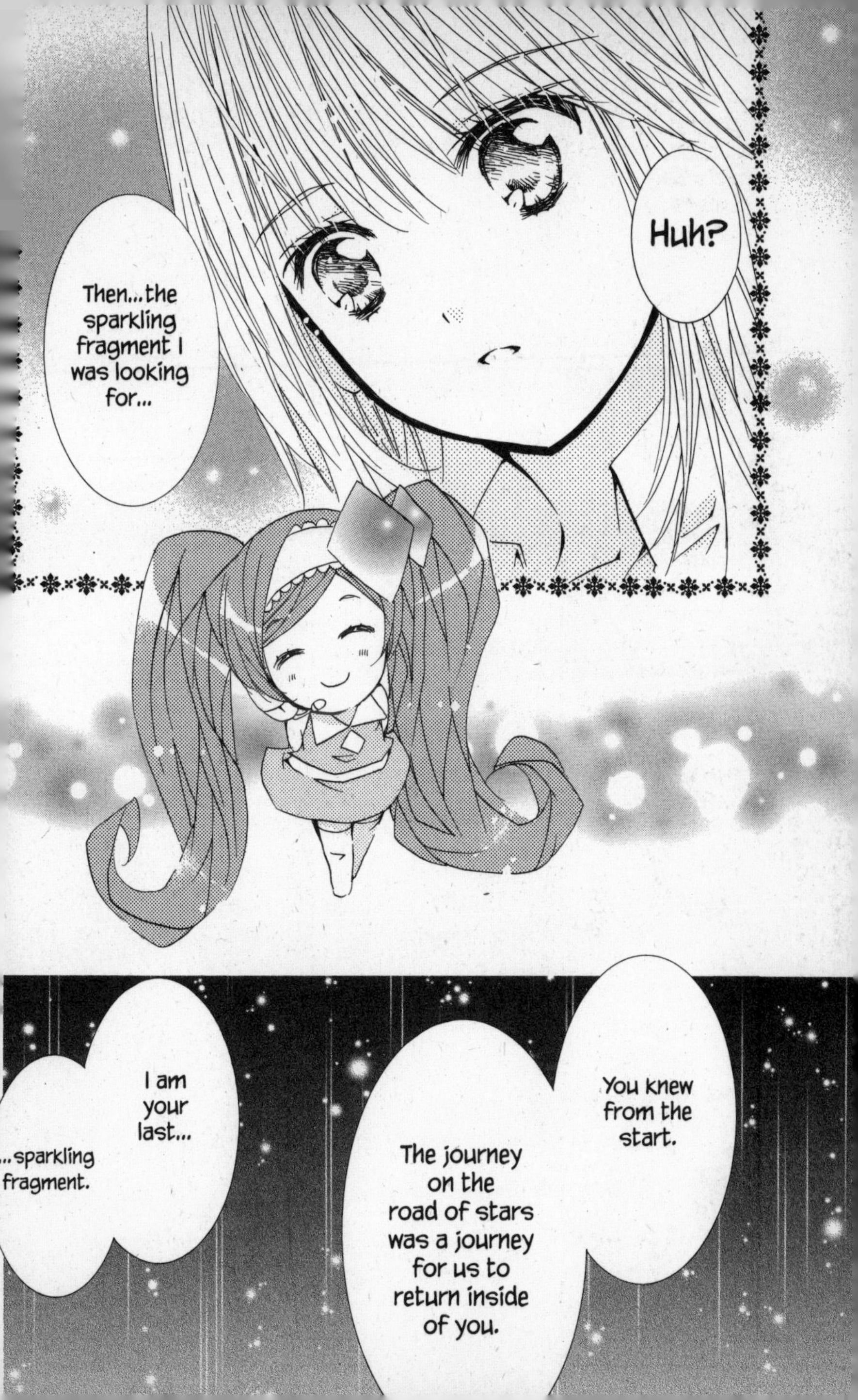
Huh?
Then...the sparkling fragment I was looking for...
You knew from the start.
The journey on the road of stars was a journey for us to return inside of you.
I am your last...
...sparkling fragment.

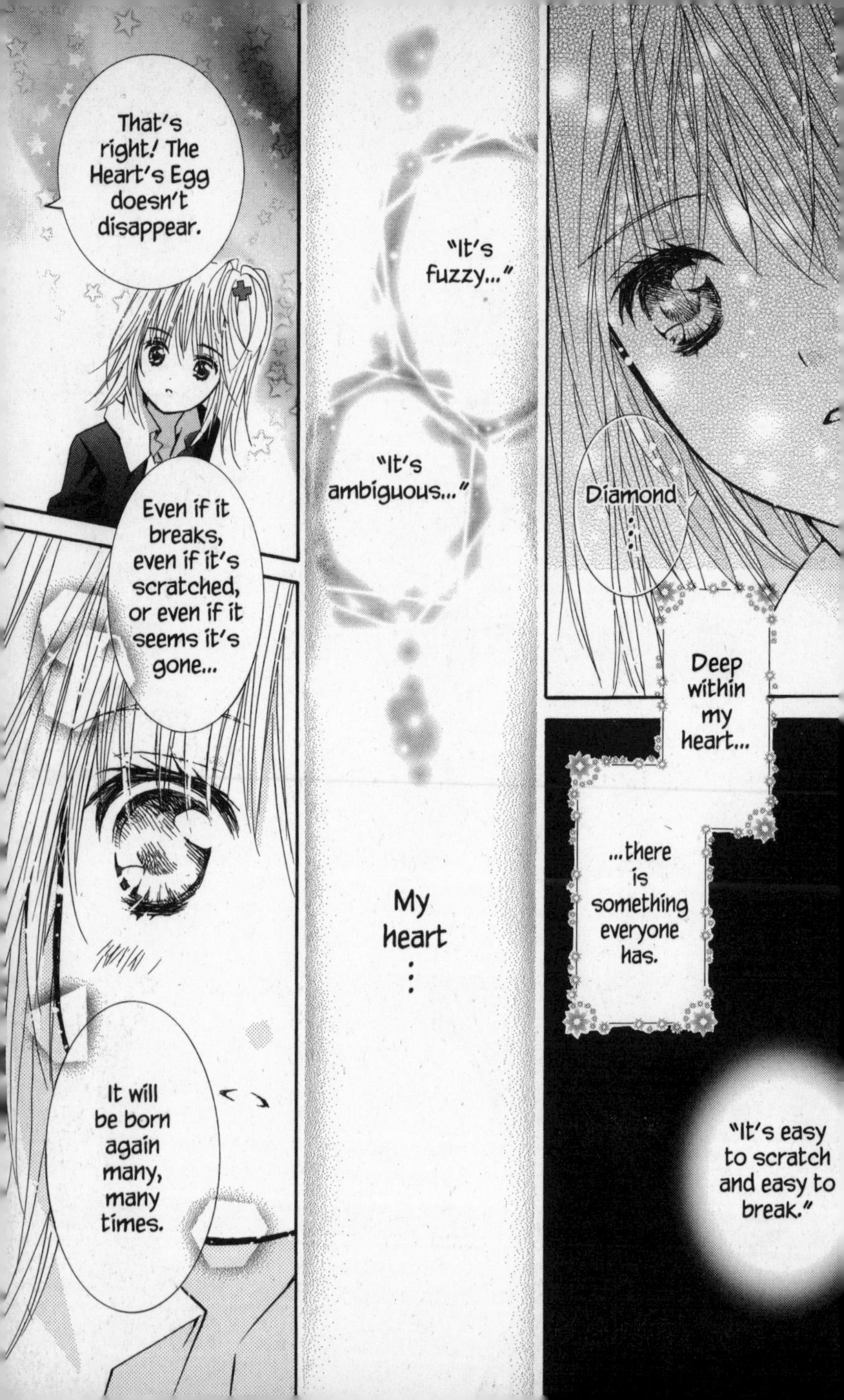
Diamond...
Deep within my heart...
...there is something everyone has.
"It's easy to scratch and easy to break."
"It's fuzzy..."
"It's ambiguous..."
My heart...
That's right! The Heart's Egg doesn't disappear.
Even if it breaks, even if it's scratched, or even if it seems it's gone...
It will be born again many, many times.

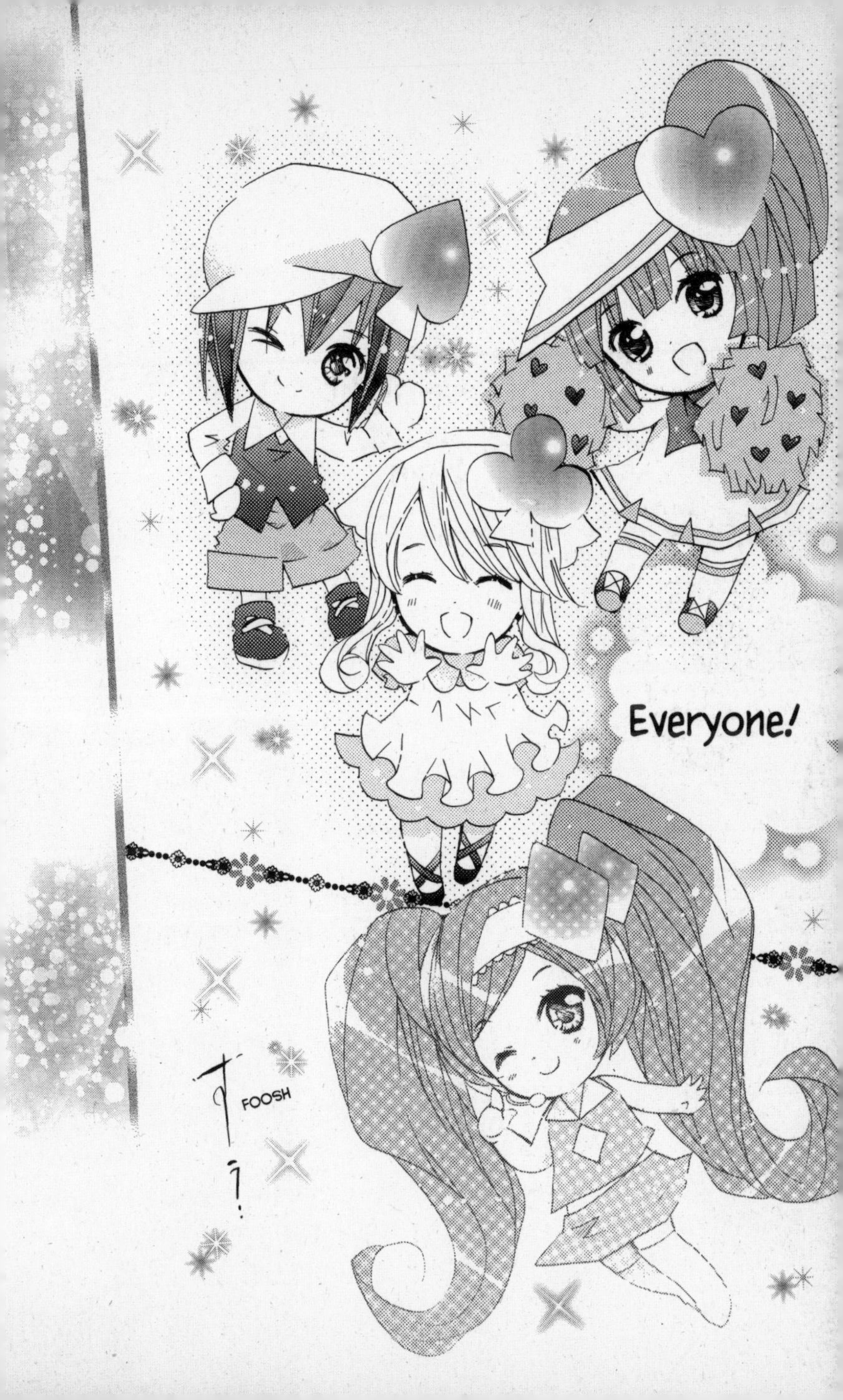

Everyone!
FOOSH

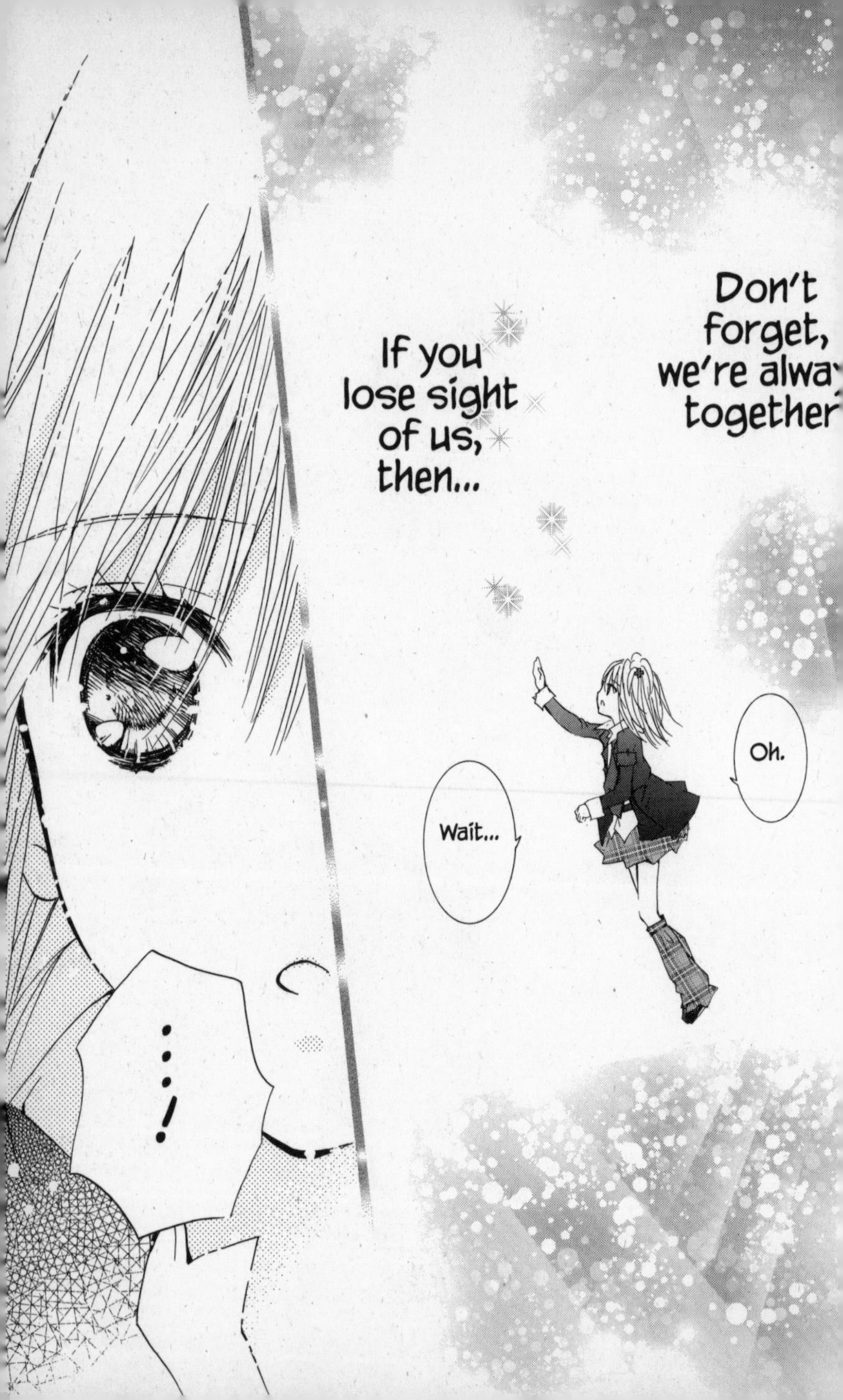
Don't forget, we're alwa together
If you lose sight of us, then...
Oh.
Wait...
...!

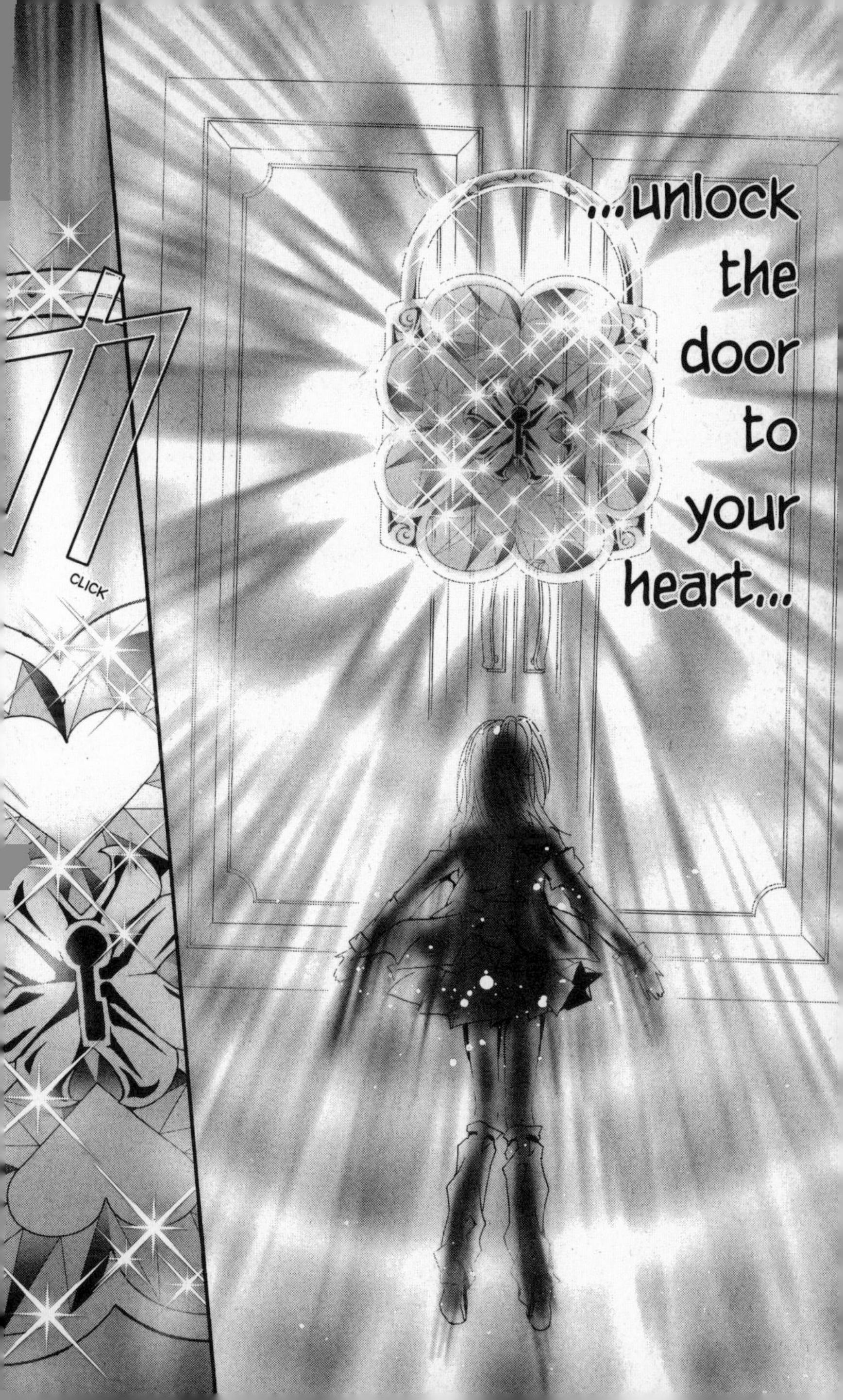
...unlock the door to your heart...
CLICK

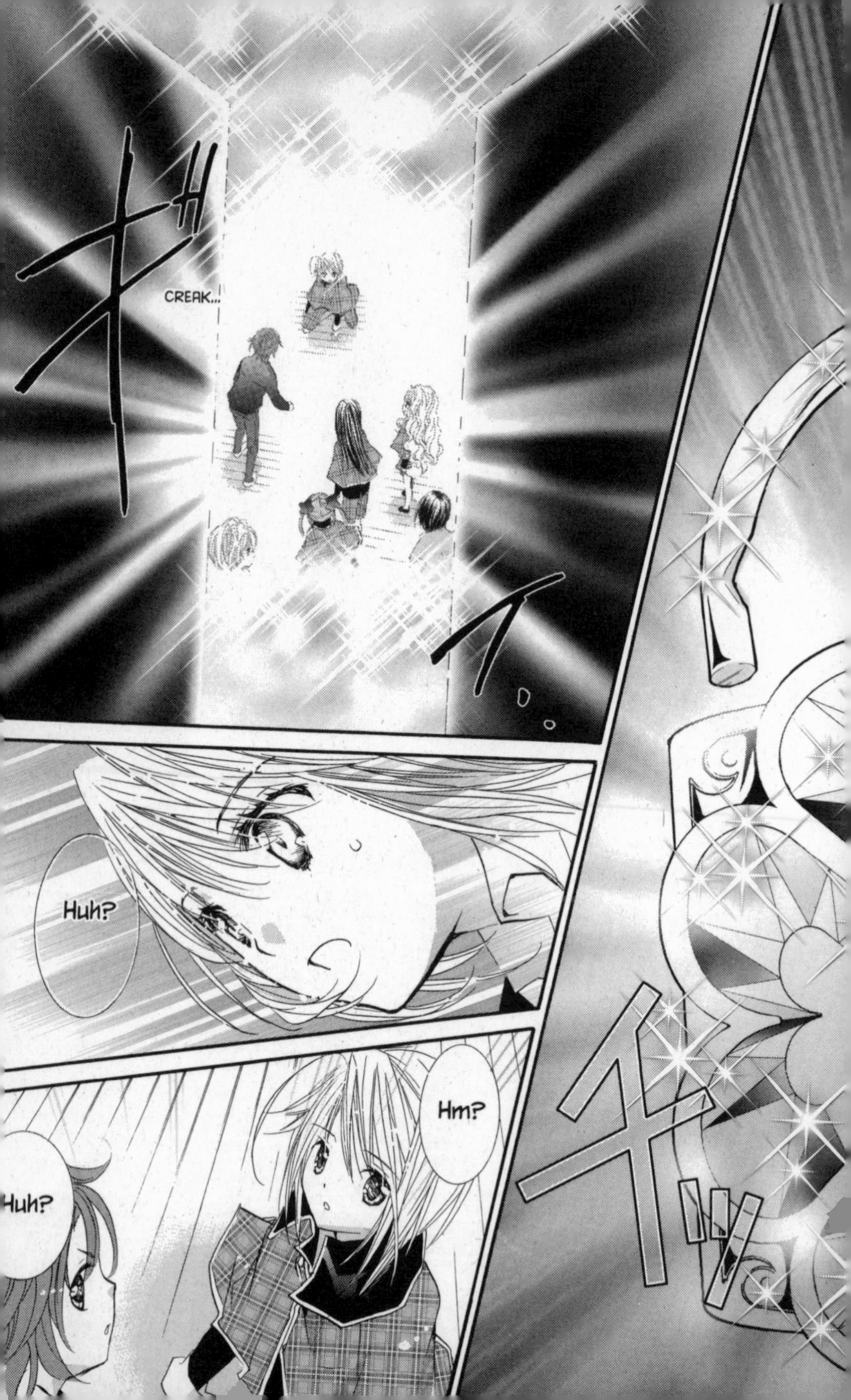
CREAK...
Huh?
Hm?
Huh?

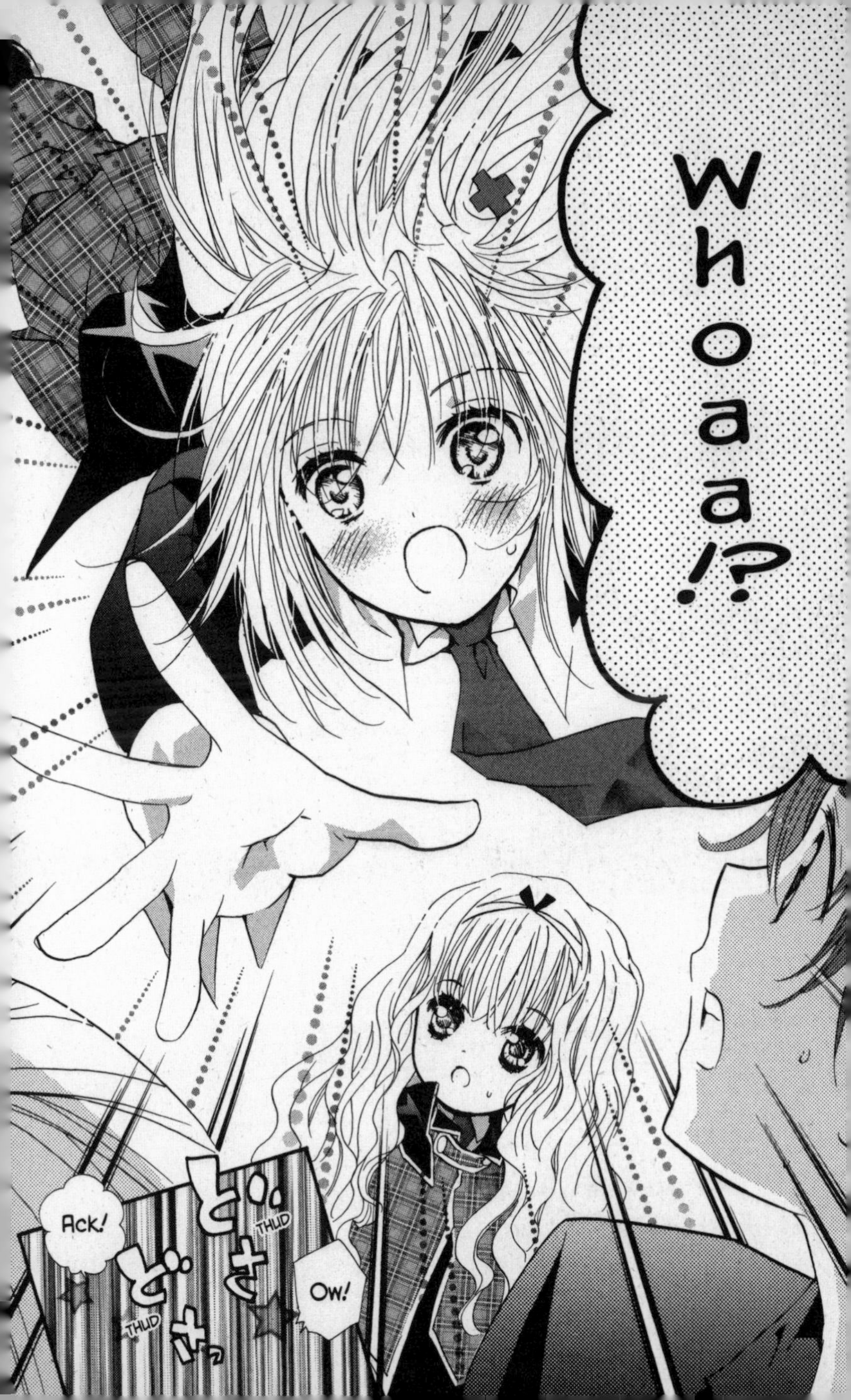
Whoaa!?
Ow!
どさ THUD
どさっ THUD
Ack!

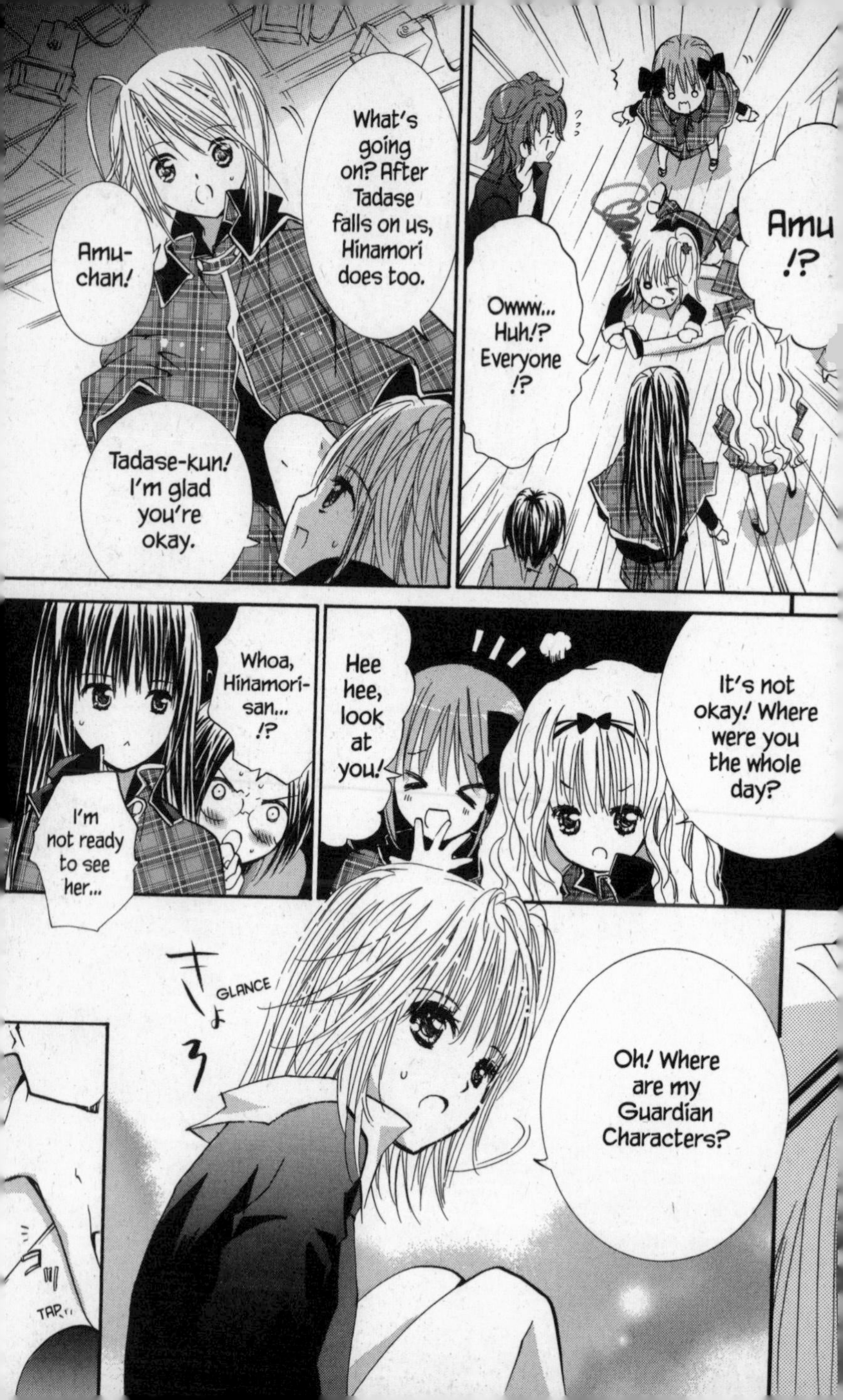
Amu !?
Owww... Huh!? Everyone !?
What's going on? After Tadase falls on us, Hinamori does too.
Amu-chan!
Tadase-kun! I'm glad you're okay.
It's not okay! Where were you the whole day?
Hee hee, look at you!
Whoa, Hinamori-san... !?
I'm not ready to see her...
Oh! Where are my Guardian Characters?
きょろ
GLANCE
TAP...

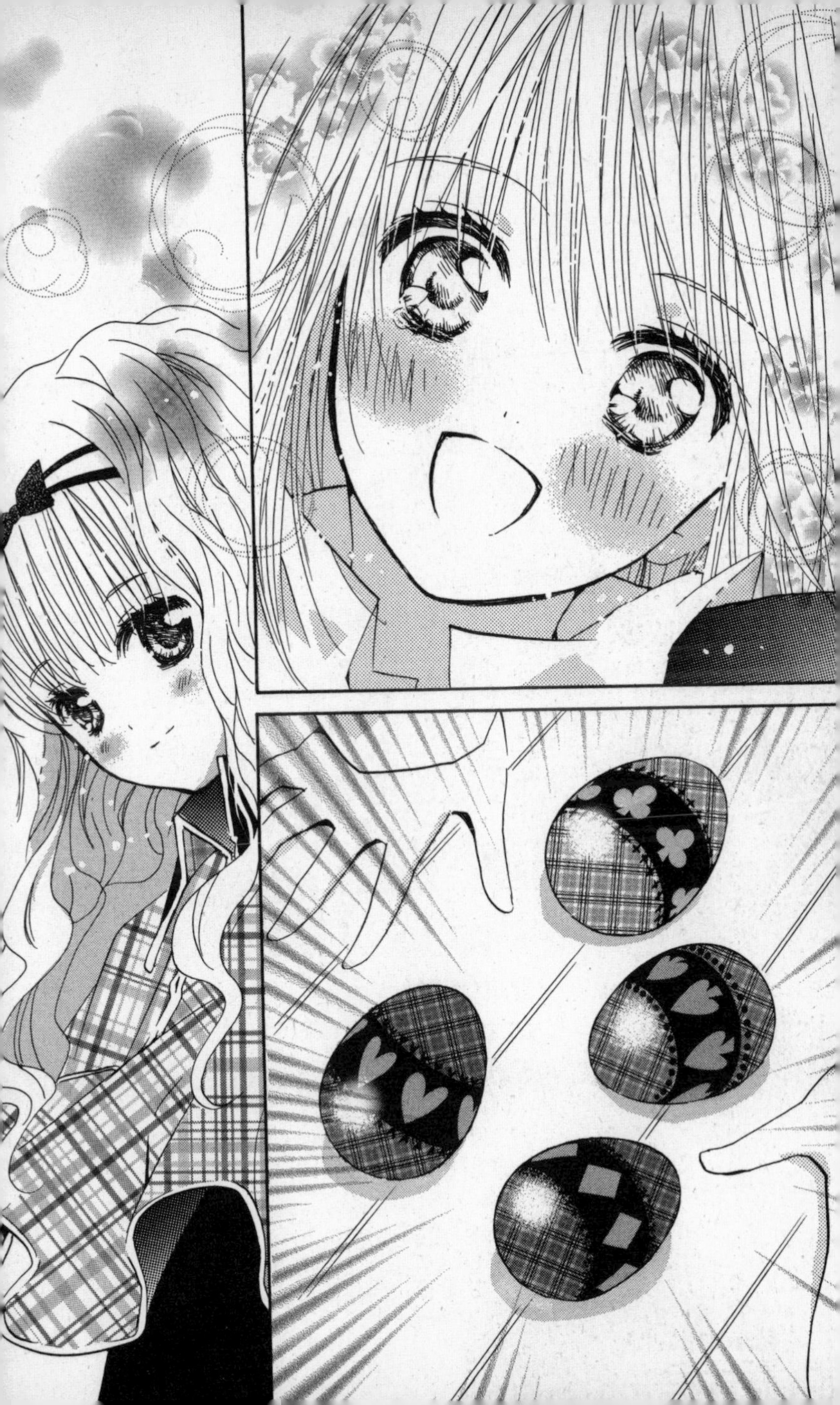

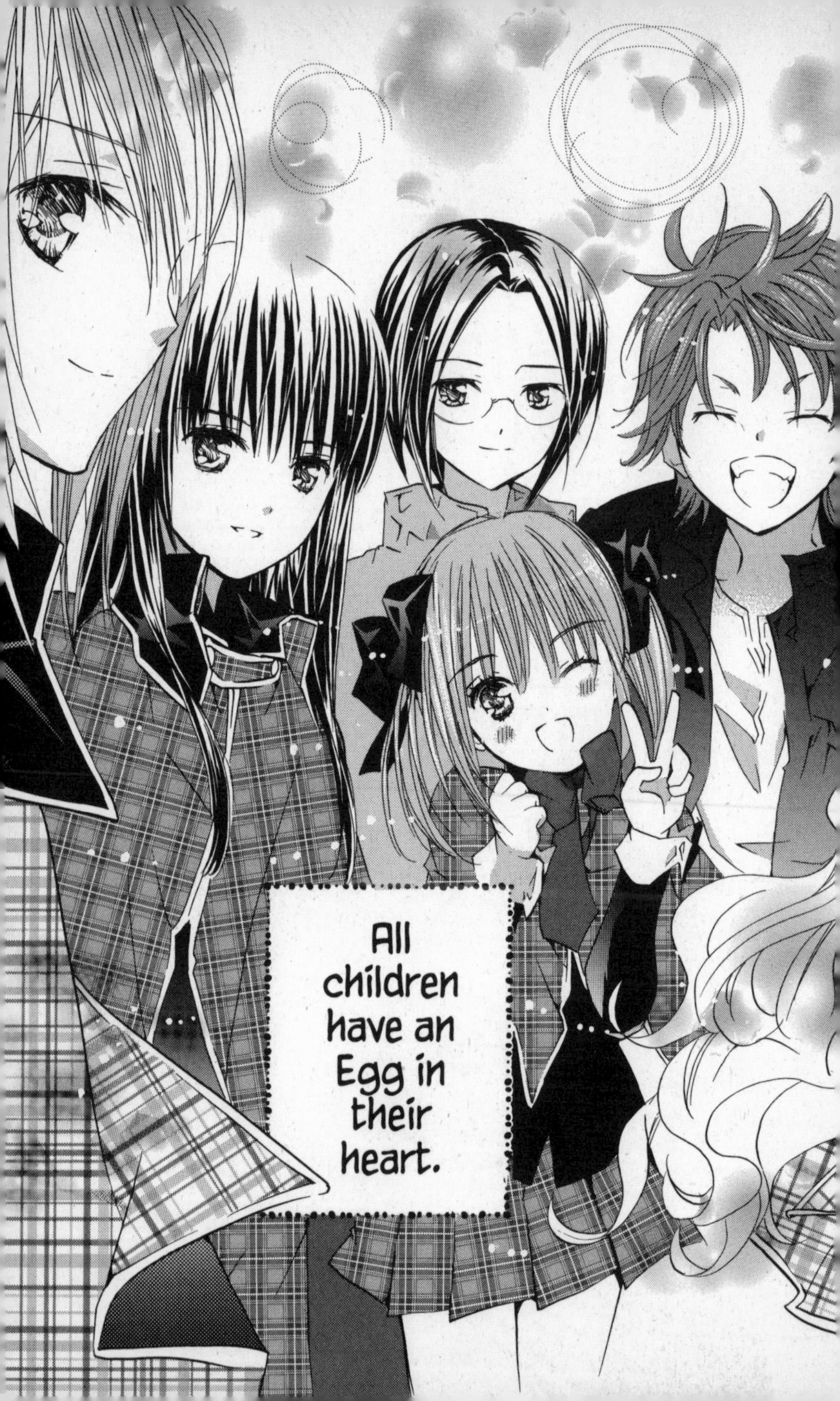
All children have an Egg in their heart.

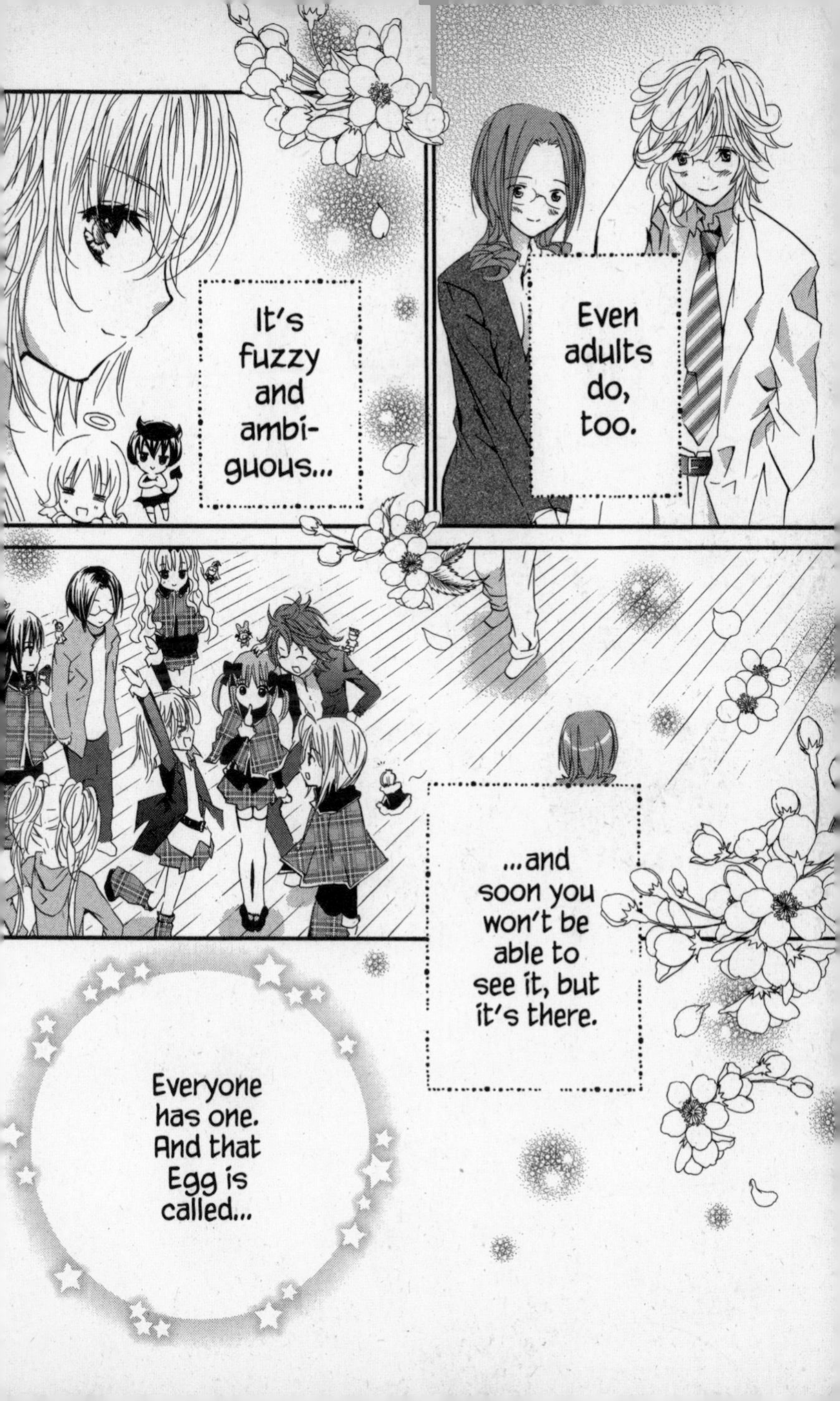
Even adults do, too.
It's fuzzy and ambiguous...
...and soon you won't be able to see it, but it's there.
Everyone has one. And that Egg is called...

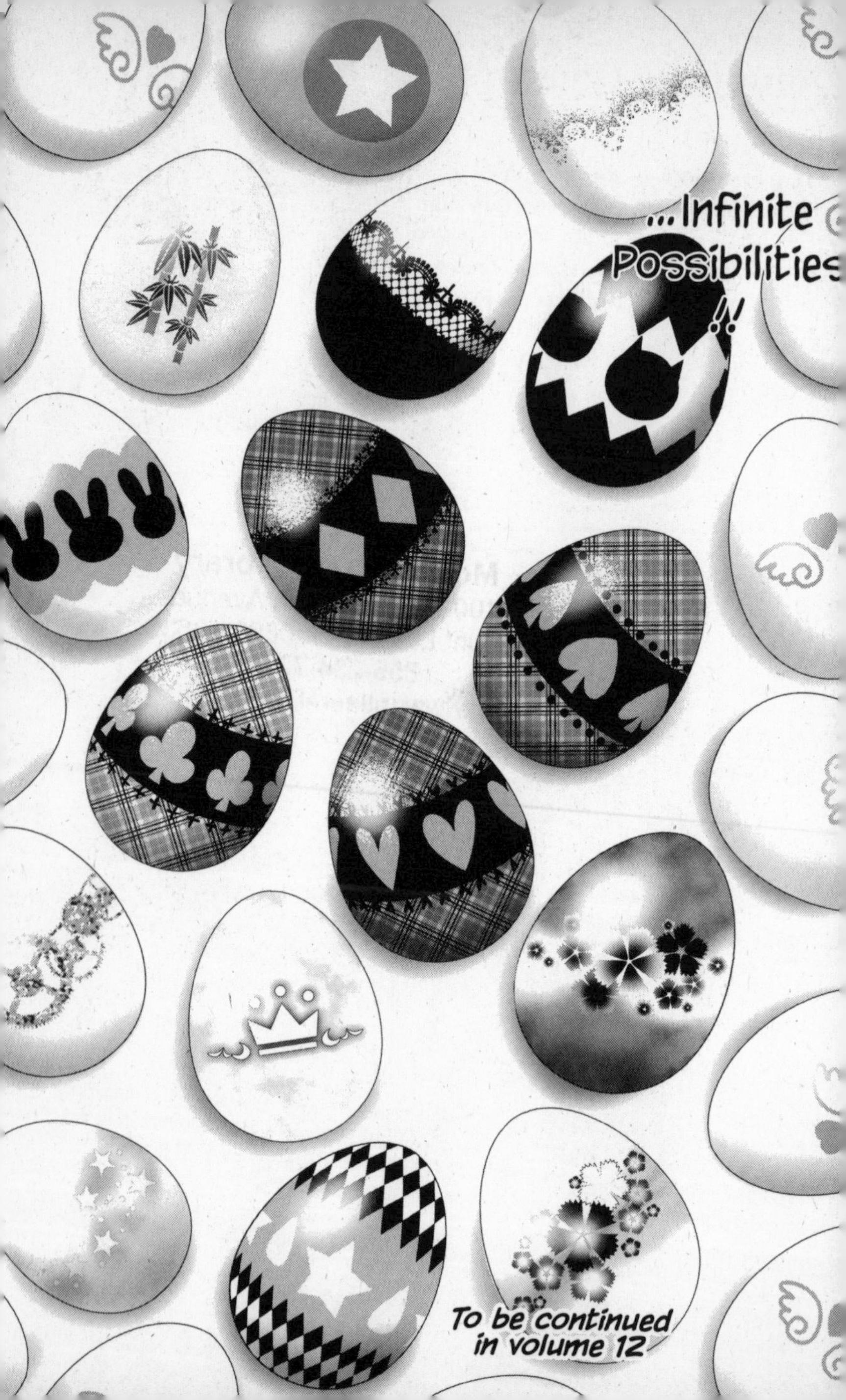
...Infinite Possibilities !!
To be continued in volume 12

About the Creators

PEACH-PIT:
Banri Sendo was born on June 7.
Shibuko Ebara was born on June 21st.
They are a pair of Gemini Manga artists
who work together. Sendo likes to eat
sweets, and Ebara likes to eat spicy stuff.

Translation Notes

Japanese is a tricky language for most Westerners, and translation is often more art than science. For your edification and reading pleasure, here are notes on some of the places where we could have gone in a different direction in our translation of the work, or where a Japanese cultural reference is used.

Urashima Taro, page 48

The story of Urashima Taro is a Japanese legend and fairy tale. It is about Taro, a fisherman, who saves a turtle from bullying children. In return, the turtle offers to take Taro to a palace under the sea. Taro meets a princess there named Otohime, and spends some time with her. When he decides to return to his village, the princess gives him a chest, with instructions never to open it. Taro returns home, but he doesn't recognize anyone. He realizes that a few days in the palace was many, many years on land and everyone has passed away. In grief, he opens up the chest and a white smoke comes out. Taro turns into an old man.

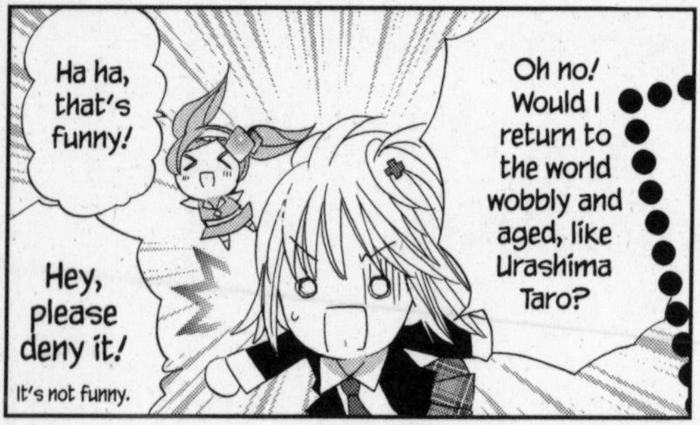
Oh no! Would I return to the world wobbly and aged, like Urashima Taro?
Ha ha, that's funny!
Hey, please deny it!
It's not funny.

Benten Kozo, page 97

Originally a kabuki (Japanese stylized theatre) play, Hikaru is mainly talking about the movie version. The story is about a group of five thieves. Nagihiko is arranging the most famous line from the play, when the character reveals himself out of a disguise.

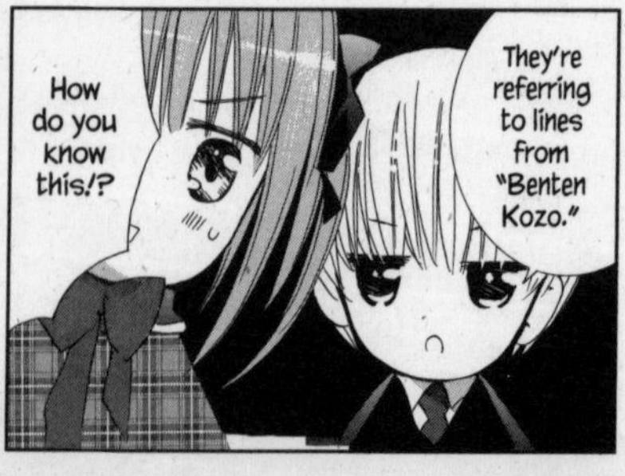
They're referring to lines from "Benten Kozo."
How do you know this!?

TOMARE!

[STOP!]

You're going the wrong way!

Manga is a completely different type of reading experience.

To start at the *beginning*, go to the *end*!

That's right! Authentic manga is read the traditional Japanese way—from right to left. Exactly the *opposite* of how American books are read. It's easy to follow: Just go to the other end of the book, and read each page—and each panel—from right side to left side, starting at the top right. Now you're experiencing manga as it was meant to be!